the
CUSTOMER MANAGEMENT
scorecard

MANAGING CRM FOR PROFIT

neil woodcock

merlin stone

bryan foss

KOGAN
PAGE

London and Sterling, VA

To Doreen (Mum) and Stan, Josie and Edgar
Bryan Foss

To my wife Ofra and my daughters Maya and Talya, my principal customers
Merlin Stone

To Mum, Dad, Julia, Callum and Aliya – thanks, as always, for your support
Neil Woodcock

First published in Great Britain and the United States in 2003 by Kogan Page Limited

Apart from any fair dealing for the purposes of research or private study, or criticism or review, as permitted under the Copyright, Designs and Patents Act 1988, this publication may only be reproduced, stored or transmitted, in any form or by any means, with the prior permission in writing of the publishers, or in the case of reprographic reproduction in accordance with the terms of licences issued by the Copyright Licensing Agency. Enquiries concerning reproduction outside those terms should be sent to the publishers at the undermentioned addresses:

120 Pentonville Road	22883 Quicksilver Drive
London N1 9JN	Sterling VA 20166-2012
UK	USA
www.kogan-page.co.uk	

© Bryan Foss, Merlin Stone and Neil Woodcock, 2003

The right of Bryan Foss, Merlin Stone and Neil Woodcock to be identified as the authors of this work has been asserted by them in accordance with the Copyright, Designs and Patents Act 1998.

ISBN 0 7494 3895 9

British Library Cataloguing-in-Publication Data

A CIP record for this book is available from the British Library

Library of Congress Cataloging-in-Publication Data

Foss, Bryan.
  Customer management scorecard / Bryan Foss, Merlin Stone and Neil
Woodcock.
     p. cm.
Includes bibliographical refrences and index.
  ISBN 0-7494-3895-9
  1. Customer relations–Management.   I. Stone, Merlin, 1948- II.
Woodcock, Neil. III. Title.
  HF5415.5 .F677 2003
  658.8'12–dc 21
                                           2002014807

CMAT™ is a registered trademark.

Typeset by Saxon Graphics Ltd, Derby
Printed and bound in Great Britain by Bell & Bain Limited, Glasgow

Contents

List of figures

List of tables

List of contributors

Julie Abbott, IBM
Alison Bond, ABA Associates
Sarah Boussofiane, Ogilvy One
Andy Brown, IBM
Roland Bushoff, formerly IBM Netherlands, now Twijnstra Gudde
Professor Clarke Caywood, Northwestern University
Mark Cerasale, IBM
Roger Clarkson, IBM
Dave Cox, Swallow Information Systems
Tony Dobbs, IBM
Vanessa Donnelly, IBM
Mike Faulkner, Customer Management Journal
Genevieve Findlay, IBM (at time of writing)
Peter Floyd, IBM (at time of writing)
Bryan Foss, IBM
Thorsten Gorchs, IBM
Lada Gorlenko, IBM
Peter Hayes, Quadrant
Iain Henderson, QCi
Matt Hobbs, IBM
Dave Irwin, Acxiom Corporation
Mahnaz Khaleeli, IBM
Peter Lavers, QCi
Colin Livingstone, IBM
Antoine Martinez , University of Newcastle upon Tyne

Rob Mattison, IBM
Jane McCarthy, Detica
Hans Neerken, IBM
Raymond Pettit, ERP Associates
Emma Reeves , IBM
James Richie, IBM
David Selby, IBM
Michael Starkey, De Montfort University and QCi
Professor Merlin Stone, IBM and QCi
Clare Traynor, Spelthorne Borough Council
Juergen Uhl, IBM
Divya Verma, IBM (at time of writing)
Teresa Waring, University of Newcastle upon Tyne
David Williams, QCi
Neil Woodcock, QCi
Professor Len Tiu Wright , De Montfort University

Foreword

This book is one of the many outcomes of the strong cooperation between IBM and QCi, an OgilvyOne company, in the area of customer management. For several years, Neil Woodcock, Chairman and founder of QCi, Bryan Foss of IBM, and Professor Merlin Stone, of both IBM and QCi, have led a diverse and relatively informal team drawn from both companies and from among clients, universities and other suppliers of customer management systems and services. This extended team, which shares a common interest in raising the standards of customer management worldwide, has developed a comprehensive knowledge base showing how well companies throughout the world manage their customers. QCi has led this work by developing CMAT (the Customer Management Assessment Tool), the only truly independent standard for measuring how well companies manage their customers.

IBM, one of the world's largest suppliers of systems and services relating to CRM implementation, has sponsored a number of studies using the research version of the tool – CMAT-R, and has carried out a number of client engagements in which its consultants used CMAT. Raising the standards of customer management is an important task. Successful companies have shown that CRM brings benefits to shareholders, customers and employees. However, the task is not easy – there are many aspects of customer management where companies are clearly having difficulties and performance seems to be in decline.

IBM and OgilvyOne (the world's largest relationship marketing agency) hope that through our commitment to the extensive publication of research, case studies and consulting reports, we will accelerate learning about customer management, thereby making progress easier for the many clients who rely on us for customer management systems and services.

Reimer Thedens
Chairman/CEO, OgilvyOne Worldwide

Ginni Rometty
General Manager, IBM Global Services

Acknowledgements

Bryan Foss

My IBM experience with clients and colleagues worldwide has provided an enormous opportunity to expand my own knowledge of customer management and successful business transformation. This book is the most recent analysis and summary of years of results and shared experience in customer management diagnosis, benchmarking and implementation. Support and encouragement for these efforts has come from my IBM colleagues Richard Lowrie, Mark Chetwood and Mark Greene, with too many others to name individually. Strong and valuable mutual links now exist between QCi, Ogilvy and IBM. David Hicks, Paul Weston, David Williams and the other QCi directors have all been ready to network, sharing their knowledge and gaining from experiences with our colleagues, clients and other partners. Above all I have benefited enormously from working with Merlin and Neil for some years, through the evolving alliances of various companies, each concerned with the development of exceptional customer management capabilities.

Merlin Stone

This book is the culmination of a lot of hard work, not just by Neil, Bryan and myself, but by the many colleagues from IBM and other companies and organizations who have contributed to the book. So thanks are due to all the contributors, many of whom I had to hound so that they produced their contributions on time. However, all the experience that enabled us to produce this book has come from working with our clients all over the world. Naming individual clients would be inappropriate, and in some cases it would breach confidentiality agreements, so I hope those clients who read this book feel properly appreciated by us! My manager at IBM, Paul Clutterbuck, has given me the time to produce this book, but has unfortunately not benefited from the long periods of e-mail silence from me that he might have expected as a result – the book probably added to the volume of correspondence. My thanks are also due to the rest of our small business research team at IBM – Fola Komolafe, Abigail Tierney and Marina Parshikova. Strong support for our efforts has also come from IBM senior management. Finally, no acknowledgement would be complete with reference to Mike Wallbridge, who brought me into what was called 'database marketing' in the 1980s, and who has remained a staunch supporter – as client and friend – ever since.

Neil Woodcock

My 22 years of working life have provided a few challenges, but none so big as trying to understand how to make money from a seemingly obvious set of techniques such as CRM! It seems that in the stampede for efficiencies in companies, customer management has been downgraded to a drab and dreary set of processes, or even degraded to ugliness in some cases – we all have irresistible stories of appalling customer service! I have worked with a few people who strive for something different, who truly believe that the customer is at the heart of all successful companies. I'd like to thank the people I have worked with who have provided me with inspiration over the last few years: my colleagues at QCi, Paul Weston, Paul Rayfield, David Williams, David Hicks and Robin Mitchell to name five; Reimer Thedens and Nigel Howlett from Ogilvy One; Michael Starkey from De Montfort University; numerous clients and friends such as Dave Crawshaw from Britannia Building Society, David Bearman from Boots, Jon Furmston of BT, Anne Gowan from the Telegraph Group, Peter Georgeu from Direct Response SA, Richard Johnston from Schlumberger-Sema, Andrew Hartley from Kleinwort Capital, Derek Holder from the IDM and Richard Lees from The Database Group; my wife Julia, for her stunningly sensible reflections on consumer behaviour and insights into what works for consumers; and finally, Bryan and Merlin, always an inspiration, and great to work with too. I look forward to continued discussion and debate with you all!

Introduction

Neil Woodcock, Merlin Stone and Bryan Foss

This book has two main aims:

1. To stimulate further debate on the subject of customer management (CM).
2. To provide practical guidance about how companies can create more value from CM.

CM is a critical subject for many businesses. Many companies, especially large ones, have spent big budgets on new systems, strategies and channels for managing customers. However, this book shows that large businesses are performing poorly in this area and that businesses generally may not be adding value through their customer management activities. However, some businesses have obtained significant benefits from improving their CM. This book also shows that companies that are performing poorly in CM are forgoing the significant benefits that arise from managing customers well.

The authors, together with colleagues from our own companies and the many partners who use QCi's Customer Management Assessment Tool (CMAT) diagnostic process, have carried out over 300 global assessments of blue chip companies. We have worked on many CRM projects in all sectors, across the world. We have learnt much about what works and does not work. Our research into the relationship between customer management and business performance is leading edge and practical. It is carried out by trained consultants and follows a well-defined and rigorous methodology.

We would welcome your feedback (positive or negative) on this book. Please use it to discuss with us or tell us what you think of the findings. You can do this through the contact area on QCi's Web site (www.qci.co.uk).

This book is in five parts. Part 1 documents the findings of QCi's global research into the state of customer management. Parts 2–5 consist of papers exploring various aspects of customer (relationship) management. In the first half of this book, the term 'customer management' is used more commonly, rather than CRM, because CMAT does not assume that customers of the companies assessed are necessarily being managed in a relationship. In Parts 2–5, the term 'customer relationship management' is used more commonly, as these chapters focus on situations in which customers are being managed within relationships.

PART 1: THE SCORECARD RESULTS AND CONCLUSIONS

The problem

Part 1 documents the results of our new research on customer management (CM). The figures from our CMAT assessments across the world show that companies are not improving how they manage customers. In fact, it seems they are getting worse. CMAT results correlate strongly with business performance, so we can be fairly certain that this means business performance is declining and economic value is not just being wasted, as before, but may actually be destroyed. Our work also shows that despite this, many companies do get positive returns from CRM, but that payback and risk depend on a company's CM competencies, in other words, where it is starting from. Companies that perform poorly in CM must construct and manage their CM projects much better if they are to get the returns they desire.

There are many reasons why CM is not working in many businesses today. The two key reasons are a lack of authoritative leadership, and a lack of education about how CM can deliver value.

Most senior managers do not see CM as supporting the working of their company's value chain, so that value can be created at each stage of CM and built on in the next stage. Most companies still work in silos. Different departments do things that affect customers in different ways, and coordination is often weak. Senior managers must demonstrate more practical CM leadership. They must show their organizations how to build on strengths and fix what is broken. However, senior managers often do not know what their company's strengths and weaknesses actually are, in terms of how they are managing customers today. Our CMAT assessments show a wide gap between perception and reality. When they determine strategies and investment priorities, senior managers could do much more to access the experience of front-line staff. This should lead to more practical plans for development and use of their CM capabilities, resulting in a much lower failure rate.

Improving performance to emulate best practice

For companies that are prepared to re-examine their approach to CM, the prize is large. Although CM performance does differ between sectors and between geographies, the characteristics of companies that perform best in CM differ little. From our work we have identified characteristics that define best performing companies. This list of characteristics should be a key focus for senior managers and stimulate debate about the situation in their own companies.

Scope of the research

Our research base is already one of the largest of its type and is developing fast. This research covers most key countries. We show that customer management performance differs remarkably between countries. The research appears to confirm what many have observed: that larger companies find it more difficult to manage customers competently than smaller companies.

QCi and its partners have conducted over 300 CMAT assessments in many sectors in the following countries: Australia, Austria, Belgium, Canada, China, France, Germany, Hong Kong, Ireland, Israel, Korea, Japan, Luxembourg, Malaysia, Netherlands, Singapore, South Africa, Spain, Switzerland, Taiwan, UK and USA.

Industry sectors covered include:

- automobile;
- dot.com;
- energy (oil, utilities);
- financial services, including general retail banking, mortgage banks, credit cards, insurance of all kinds, private banking, investment management and wealth management;
- industrial charities;
- distribution;
- logistics;
- manufacturing;
- marketing services;
- petrochemical;
- public sector;
- publishing and media;
- retail;
- retailing;
- telecommunications;

▌ travel;
▌ utilities.

The primary findings in this book, apart from the detailed geographic analysis in Chapter 3 and the Acxiom-sponsored US study focusing on the management and use of customer data and the new IBM-sponsored Netherlands insurance study (included at the end of the empirical research section as Chapters 13 and 14, as their results have not been included in the preceding analysis), are analysed from full CMAT benchmarks we have on the database.

This book was produced just a little too early for us to show the results of a new South East Asian CMAT study, sponsored by Ogilvy One and carried out with the help of IBM's clients. Preliminary analysis of these studies is confirming what our CMAT work in Korea, Malaysia, Singapore and Taiwan had already shown, that all the issues encountered elsewhere in the world are just as relevant in this region. However, we seem to be encountering much greater variability in results, so we shall explore this aspect in detail in the special report to be issued on these studies. The variability may be in line with the maturity of each market, in terms of for how long companies in different countries have been working to improve customer management. We would expect Singapore to be more advanced than Malaysia, which in turn would be slightly more advanced than Thailand, and so on. However, within-country variability is likely to be large, with best practice companies showing the way for others, irrespective of the general level of performance in that country.

In field at the time this book went to press were two major IBM-sponsored studies in North America, one focusing on banking and one on insurance. The early results of a Japanese study sponsored by Ogilvy One have been included as a section in Chapter 3. Although its results do not form part of the general analysis of that chapter, they are placed in that chapter so that comparisons can be made easily. The extensive CM experience of the authors and their colleagues supplements these findings with comment.

A full CMAT assessment takes two to four weeks to complete. It typically involves interviewing around 30 individuals within a business unit of a company from senior management to front-line customer-facing people, to seek 'hard evidence' for the answers to 260 best practice questions that form the full CMAT assessment. We stress the word 'evidence', because time and again we witness the difference between what top management honestly believes happens within the organization and the reality. We call this the great 'customer management illusion'. A full CMAT assessment involves a significant commitment from the company in providing executive time and in paying for it. The sponsor always signs off the assessment results.

The geographic and sector analysis (Chapter 3) was carried out via research studies in various countries and sectors. A CMAT-R research project involves interviewing 30 to 75 organizations, across a number of industry sectors, or around 25 organizations within a single industry sector. A CMAT-R assessment involves a two to three hour in-depth interview with one to three senior executives and covers approximately 50 of the key questions within the CMAT model. Although a two to three hour interview cannot gather the extensive evidence that a CMAT provides, assessors probe interviewees to justify the answers given. Because research assessments are not evidence based, intention versus reality cannot be verified. This results in scores being in the order of 15–20 per cent higher than a full assessment, but adjustment is possible for consistency of analysis. A CMAT-R project is usually sponsored by QCi or one of its partners and can involve an investment of up to US $400,000. Another essential element is the involvement of academics from a university business school. The process involves academic partners to ensure academic validation of the results and so that the publication of research results is disseminated to a wide audience, including trade magazines and academic journals.

The time series analysis of the CMAT data used the CMAT question-set covering the following periods:

- Period 1: 27 full CMAT assessments carried out in July 1998 to December 1999.
- Period 2: 33 full CMAT assessments carried out in January 2000 to June 2001.

We can only draw comparisons over time if the sample dataset for each period is similar. The companies assessed in each period were very similar. They were all large (more than 500 employees), blue chip (all instantly recognizable company names) companies from different sectors. The periods had a similar sector composition. In each period more than two-thirds of the companies were from Europe. The companies in each period were similar in terms of how long they had been involved in CRM and the value they obtain from it.

All chapters in Part 1 except 13 and 14 are written by Neil Woodcock of QCi, Michael Starkey of De Montfort University and QCi and Professor Merlin Stone of IBM and QCi. Sarah Boussofiane of Ogilvy One contributed the Japanese section to Chapter 3.

The sequence of chapters more or less follows the CMAT model. It is as follows:

Chapter 1 explains how the CMAT model works.

Chapter 2 summarizes the overall results.

Chapter 3 explores comparisons of results between countries and regions.

Chapter 4 introduces the idea of the customer management value chain and identifies the main areas of customer management in which companies seem to be creating and/or destroying value.

Chapters 5–12 consider the results by area of CMAT model: analysis and planning (5), proposition (6), customer management activity (7), people and organization (8), IT (9), process management (10), measurement (11) and customer experience (12). Each chapter follows the same format, analysing the scores, extract and analysis of some key facts and figures from the research, followed by examples of good practice.

Chapter 13 describes the recent Acxiom-sponsored US study, focusing on data management. Chapter 14 describes the recent IBM-sponsored study of the Dutch insurance industry. This work was carried out with the active co-operation of BSn, a Dutch business school that has as one of its main foci the education of insurance industry managers. Chapter 15 identifies some key trends in the development of customer management, Chapter 16 explores the issue of developing a business case for improving customer management, and Chapter 17 proposes guidelines to ensure successful implementation of improvements to customer management.

PARTS 2–5

Parts 2 to 5 document some of the latest thinking from IBM, Qci and their business partners concerning the management of CRM.

Part 2: Measurement, systems and data

This continues the strong measurement theme established in Part 1. It explores some approaches to measurement and the infrastructure needed for measurement (including systems selection and integration and data warehousing and advanced analytic techniques.

Chapter 18 explores the idea of e-CRM (where the e may be enterprise or electronic) and the return on investment that can be achieved. Chapter 19 describes some recent IBM-sponsored research on the use of business intelligence and then presents a case study of the use of business intelligence in managing retail CRM. Chapter 20 describes the use of advanced business intelligence analytics to improve the returns from CRM.

Chapter 21 ranges widely over systems aspects, not just measurement, but provides an overview of many of the issues faced by companies in choosing and integrating systems to support CRM, as well as a quick guide to the process of selecting CRM systems, and an overview of future technologies that will be used to manage customers. Chapter 22 focuses on the difficult issue of how data about the customer experience (usually one of the weakest areas in CMAT assessments) can be brought into the systems and processes for managing customers.

Part 3: The sectoral view

This focuses on new sector material, with chapters on public sector CRM, telecommunications, and business to business.

Chapter 23 is a composite chapter, in which we have tried to put together the knowledge of many different parties regarding CRM in the public sector. It covers everything from an overview of the main issues involved in CRM strategy and implementation in the public sector, to three case studies of the use of measurement and segmentation in the public sector. Chapter 24 is also a composite chapter, discussing aspects of CRM in telecommunications, starting with an analysis of the main CRM issues facing telecommunications companies, and concluding with several case studies of CRM implementations, focusing mainly on the business intelligence aspects.

Chapter 25 provides an overview of business-to-business CRM. It explores how CRM is increasingly seen as an integral part of supply chain management, and some of the systems and measurement implications of this.

Part 4: Channels and media

This focuses on channel and media issues, with a chapter on multi-channel customer management followed by two chapters on the use of e-mail in customer management, and one on ensuring customer usability of new media.

Chapter 26 explores the new area of multi-channel customer management. It defines the topic, explores the reasons for taking a multi-channel approach, looks at the benefits and problems, and concludes with a checklist of questions companies should pose before rushing into large projects in this area.

Chapter 27 describes new research on the extent to which companies are in control of their CRM practices in the e-mail channel. The international research shows significant variability in performance. Chapter 28 focuses on some of the issues discussed in Chapter 27: how companies can manage the escalating volumes of e-mail contacts with customers and associated data volumes. Chapter 29 examines the issue of usability of new media, why it is important – with a case study of the public sector – and how it can be measured.

Part 5: Implementation and the future

This focuses on implementation and the future, with chapters on customer and staff loyalty, customer service standards, and programme sponsorship and governance, followed by a review of the major CRM issues likely to be the focus of much CRM work in the future.

Chapter 30 gives an overview of the main issues involved in managing customer and staff loyalty and gives the results of a survey exploring the relationship between the two.

Chapter 31 gives the result of a recent study assessing the quality of customer service in the UK. It highlights the problem of declining service standards.

Chapter 32 covers sponsorship and governance of CRM and related programmes. It focuses particularly on the role of senior managers and on organizational issues. Chapter 33 identifies some of the main CRM issues that companies will be focusing on in the future.

Part 1

The scorecard results and conclusions

1

What is CMAT?

Neil Woodcock, Michael Starkey and Merlin Stone

CMAT is the leading customer relationship management (CRM) assessment approach for organizations that want to understand how well they are managing their customers and to compare this performance to a global benchmark. Trained and accredited assessors, who are experienced CRM practitioners within QCi or one of its alliance partners, carry out the CMAT Assessment. Based on 260 questions covering the whole QCi model of customer management, the assessment has been carried out in many organizations globally. Each assessment question is based on known and demonstrable good practices from QCi clients and from accepted industry leaders. A 'scoring based on evidence' approach is taken to answering each question, and a broad range of people, from senior directors to operational level practitioners, is interviewed. The approach is designed specifically to identify clear plans, real delivery and an identifiable effect of each of the practices questioned. In this way the all too common gap between senior management perception and the 'sharp end' reality is often identified.

The output of the assessment is a report and board-level presentation that positions the organization against a relevant benchmark of other organizations. It also provides a quartile positioning for each of 31 CRM areas into which the sections of the customer management model are divided. Typically between 50 and 100 prioritized recommendations are made by the assessor based on observations made during the interviews.

THE SCOPE OF A CMAT ASSESSMENT

The CMAT model is shown diagrammatically in Figure 1.1.

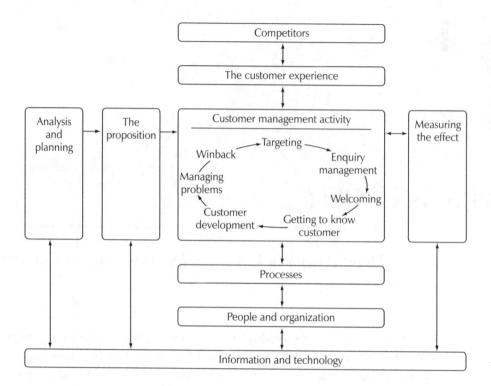

Figure 1.1 The QCi customer management model

Analysis and planning

Everything starts with understanding the value and behaviour of different customers and different customer groups. This understanding, derived mainly from internal information and knowledge sources, drives more questions, which will in turn help define research, competitor assessment and external analysis activity. Once a clear and comprehensive understanding has been developed, customers and prospects need to be segmented so that planning activity can be as effective as possible. This planning will be focused on enabling the organization to REAP the value of its customer base, focusing on retention, efficiency, acquisition and penetration (REAP).

Analysis and planning includes:

▮ strategic input to customer management planning;
▮ customer transaction analysis;
▮ lifecycle understanding;
▮ profiling and external analysis;
▮ lifetime value monitoring;
▮ customer and prospect segmentation;

- competitor analysis;
- tacit knowledge management;
- contact and management planning.

Proposition

Once the customers to be managed (or explicitly not managed) have been defined, propositions need to be developed that will match the needs of these customers and that will be attractive to new customers. There will often be different propositions for different groups. These propositions need to be defined at a detailed level that drives the experience the customer can expect in dealing with the organization, its products, and its partners or channels. It is therefore critical that the propositions are communicated effectively to both customers and the people who deliver them.

Proposition includes:

- customer needs research;
- overall proposition development;
- segment proposition matching;
- service standards;
- proposition external communication;
- proposition internal communication.

Information and technology

Technology exists to help organizations acquire, manage and use the vast amount of information involved in managing customers. It is an enabler[1] rather than a deliverable in its own right, but managed badly it can also be a stopper. An organization needs to understand what information it has available, what it is missing and how to manage the information. The technology then needs to deliver the current information to relevant people at the right time in order for them to fulfil their role in managing customers. Of course, technology must be reviewed constantly against changing needs and development in the technology itself.

Information and technology includes:

- sourcing and understanding customer information;
- information planning and quality management;
- functions of existing systems;
- review of current systems;
- development of new systems.

People and organization

Customer management people need to be recruited, managed, developed and motivated within a supporting structure. The term 'customer management people' also needs to be considered in its widest context, extending to suppliers and channels as well.

People and organization includes:

▌ organizational structure;
▌ role identification;
▌ competencies definition and gap analysis;
▌ training requirements and resources;
▌ objective setting and monitoring;
▌ supplier selection and management.

Process management

Processes are often difficult to implement and manage formally in an environment with so many sales and marketing people. But clear, consistent processes are essential to all areas of customer management and to achieving constant and step-change improvements. Also, processes need to be reviewed constantly for acceptability from both the customers' point of view and the organization's point of view.

Process management includes:

▌ process identification and documentation;
▌ process communication;
▌ monitoring of process acceptability;
▌ process benchmarking;
▌ process improvement.

Customer management activity

Customer management activity is about implementing the plans to deliver the proposition across the customer lifecycle.

Targeting

Targeting is about delivering the defined propositions accurately to the customer and prospect groups identified in the planning activity. It is not enough to simply run campaigns at regular intervals aimed at different groups. Targeted activity also needs to be based on triggers from individual customers and prospects, even to the point of allowing individuals to target the organization when they are ready, rather than the other way around.

Targeting includes:

▌ campaign planning;
▌ buying trigger identification;
▌ personalization;
▌ integration with channels;
▌ over-targeting prevention.

Enquiry management

The management of enquiries is the vital, and often missing, link between campaign or trigger-based promotional activity and a successful sale. Enquiries start as soon as an individual expresses an interest and continue through qualification, lead handling and result reporting. The processes and measures that enable the value of enquiries to be maximized need to cover the same areas.

Enquiry management includes:

▌ enquiry collection;
▌ enquiry processes and quality standards;
▌ qualification methods;
▌ lead distribution;
▌ result feedback and research.

Welcoming

New customers, and those upgrading their relationship, need to be welcomed. This activity ranges from the often forgotten simple 'thank you' through to sophisticated contact strategies. Welcoming activity needs to ensure that new customers are comfortable dealing with the organization and that they know how to get the most out of their relationship. It ensures that the high-risk 'post purchase' phase of any new customer relationship has the maximum chance of success.

Welcoming includes:

▌ identification of new customers;
▌ understanding why they were won;
▌ initial welcoming activity;
▌ monitoring of early dealings;
▌ getting customers' views.

Getting to know

Although a lot might have been known about new customers when they were still prospects, it is unlikely this will be enough information on which to build a long and valuable relationship. But new customers need to be convinced that there is something in it for them if they are to give more information about themselves. When the information is collected it needs to be used and maintained.

Getting to know includes:

- information collection priorities;
- attitude and satisfaction information;
- understanding customers' moments of truth;
- recognizing key customers;
- ongoing relationship 'health checks'.

Customer development

By really getting to know customers it becomes possible to understand which ones warrant (and need) higher levels of management activity. Just as importantly, it can be decided which ones do not warrant significant further relationship investment. This means that maximum investment can be made in the relationships that are likely to be of the highest mutual value. Specifically, customer development includes:

- customer ownership;
- segment development strategies;
- key account management;
- cross-selling and up-selling;
- proposition tailoring.

Managing problems

All relationships will go through difficult phases. The best organizations are able to predict and identify problem areas before major complaints and relationship break-downs occur. But even when these do happen they often offer the opportunity for a relationship-enhancing set of remedial measures. A well-handled complaint is often communicated to more 'referrals' than a well-handled sales cycle.

Managing problems includes:

- dissatisfaction and risk-of-loss triggers;
- intensive care activity;
- complaint reception;

- complaint handling and follow-up;
- root cause analysis;
- satisfaction checking.

Winback

Winning back recently lost customers is one of the least exploited 'acquisition' methods. If a new competitor's welcoming activity is poor then customers lost to them are likely to be the most receptive to 'come back' messages. However, it is important to be sure that it is only good customers that are targeted for winback activity and that when they are won back they are treated as returning customers and not as brand new customers.

Winback includes:

- identifying reasons for loss;
- managing customers out;
- deciding which customers to win back;
- winback programmes;
- welcoming winback customers.

Measuring the effect

Measurement of all elements of customer management activity forms feedback into the planning process ensuring continual improvement and thus building sustainable competitive advantage. It also enables individuals and channels to understand how well they are performing their roles and how much they are contributing towards the overall customer management success of the organization.

Measuring the effect includes:

- strategic measures;
- key performance indicators;
- corporate measures cascading down to individuals;
- campaign measurement;
- channel management.

Customer experience

Measurement activity needs to be supplemented with an understanding of the customer experience of dealing with the organization. The links between what customers say they feel, what they actually feel and what they 'do' need to be understood clearly if loyalty is to be maximized. Every opportunity also needs to be taken to ensure that people at all levels within the organization are very clear about how their activity appears to customers. Customer experience includes:

- satisfaction monitoring;
- event driven research;
- loyalty analysis;
- mystery shopping;
- benchmarking.

HOW A CMAT ASSESSMENT IS CARRIED OUT

Planning

This starts with a half-day briefing session for the assessor from a senior team within the organization. During this session the attendees establish the current 'perceived' stage of development in CRM, key business issues at the time and any initiatives that are under way. They will also agree the list of individuals to be interviewed, the appropriate benchmarks, and identify the material to be covered in the review phase.

Review

The assessor will review all of the background material provided. This typically includes marketing plans, research material, satisfaction surveys, literature, and Web sites.

Interviewee preparation

A briefing pack is distributed to all the people within the organization who are to be interviewed. This will explain the objectives and approach for the assessment and what they need to bring to their interview session. The briefing pack is followed up with a phone call to book the interview.

Interviews

Typically, five to six days of interviews are carried out at relevant locations. Each interview is structured by the assessor to cover the topics relevant to the individual, but is more engaging than a simple question and answer session. The assessor will be looking for clear evidence to support the answers given. Interviews last between 60 and 90 minutes.

Report preparation

The assessor prepares a detailed report based on the information and evidence collected in the interviews. The report will cover:

- An overall score against best practice and a management summary.
- Scores and a summary report against each element of the customer management model.
- Comparisons at a detailed sub-section level of company performance against a relevant benchmark.
- A quartile positioning for each area based on all the assessments on the CMAT database.
- Recommendations, ranging from tactical quick wins to highly strategic, identified by the assessor during the interviews.

Feedback workshop

This is a half-day feedback workshop with the management team to facilitate discussion of results and obtain outline 'buy-in' to the need for further action.

Strategic prioritization module

Recommendations are developed into a prioritized action plan agreed by all. This is achieved at a half-day workshop following individual input of key stakeholders. Prioritization is usually based on ROI opportunity from improvements, with consideration of how difficult it is to achieve each change or new capability. The prioritization module is a major input to the CM programme management governance system, the importance and structure of which is explained more fully later in this book.

THE BENEFITS OF CMAT ASSESSMENT

They are these:

- It provides an objective, quantified assessment of how well the organization currently manages its customers.
- The resulting scorecard correlates with business performance.
- It benchmarks the organization against a relevant set of other organizations, industries and geographies.
- It aligns the senior management team behind a common understanding of what is really happening in CRM in the organization.
- It identifies both quick-win and deeper, more strategic actions that can and should be carried out.
- It forms a clear 'baseline' against which improvements delivered by a CRM programme can be measured.
- It requires very little time from client staff.
- Interviews and questioning result in skills transfer from the assessment team to client people.
- It provides a broad-based check that an organization has its CRM foundations in place before it invests in specific programmes or technology.
- It provides high value input to business cases, IT development, organizational change and business planning for CRM investment.
- It provides input to merger and acquisition strategies.
- It can provide input to analysts and influencers on company assets and corporate competence.

NOTE

[1] Woodcock, N (2000) Does CRM performance correlate with business performance? *Journal of Interactive Marketing* (UK), April.

2

Overall analysis

Neil Woodcock, Michael Starkey and Merlin Stone

CUSTOMER MANAGEMENT PERFORMANCE IS DISAPPOINTING

The average CMAT score is 33 per cent, which means, in CMAT scoring terms, 'some commitment, some progress'. In most cases, this means that progress is patchy, uncertain and unconvincing and therefore unlikely to have a solid and permanent effect on business performance. So the overall standard is not great, and we explain in this book why this is so. But is customer management improving?

CMAT benchmarking results are now available over more than a three-year period. This means that we can identify whether performance is improving over time. The results are surprising. They present a disturbing picture of CM in most countries and sectors.

Companies appear to be experiencing real problems in implementing CM. Spend on CRM is estimated to have trebled over the last three years, but the overall level of competence in customer management seems to be falling. At best, companies are wasting the opportunity that is well within their own hands to grasp. At worst, they are destroying value and/or investing in failure. The 'destroying value' comment (see Table 2.1) does not refer to all companies. We know (from our business case studies) that some companies investing in customer management have increased value in the period. However, in comparing the performance of two sample sets of similar companies over time, we can see that the general competency in the area of customer management has not improved, and has even decreased. Generally, companies are, despite the hype and investment, more likely to be destroying economic value from their customer management effort.

Table 2.1 Creating and destroying customer value

% Scores	Period 1	Period 2	Comment on whether value is being created or destroyed
Analysis and Planning	30	27	Some destroying of value
Overall customer management planning	28	25	Some destroying of value
Planning for customer acquisition	27	18	Value being destroyed
Planning for customer retention	30	35	Created
Planning for customer development	24	25	No real change
Understanding competition	49	41	Value being destroyed
Knowledge management	23	16	Value being destroyed
The Proposition	30	27	Some destroying of value
Developing the proposition	33	30	Some destroying of value
Communicating the proposition	33	29	Value being destroyed
People and Organization	40	39	No real change
Creating the organization	43	38	Value being destroyed
Managing your people	40	38	Some destroying of value
Managing suppliers	38	40	Some creation of value
Information and Technology	40	35	Value being destroyed
Acquiring customer information	49	43	Value being destroyed
Managing customer information	32	28	Value being destroyed
Current system functions	32	36	Created
Developing new systems	52	38	Value being destroyed
Process Management	30	31	No real change
Ongoing process management	32	29	Some destroying of value
Process improvement	32	35	Some creation of value
Customer Management Activity	33	32	No real change
Targeting	30	30	No real change
Enquiry management	40	40	No real change
Welcoming	29	30	No real change
Getting to know/healthcheck	25	21	Value being destroyed
Ongoing management	28	30	Some creation of value
Managing dissatisfaction	42	40	Some destroying of value
Winback	21	9	Value being destroyed
Measuring the Effect	35	36	No real change
Measuring customer management overall	31	30	No real change
Measuring the effect of campaigns	37	35	Some destroying of value
Measuring the effect of channels	37	39	Some creation of value
Measuring the effect of individuals	37	39	Some creation of value
The Customer Experience			
Understanding satisfaction and loyalty	34	25	Value being destroyed
Experiencing what customers experience	27	26	No real change
Using benchmarks	33	34	No real change
Comment index and criteria	*Occurs when...*		
Some destroying of value	when >1% and <4% less in current period than last		
Some creation of value	when >1% and <4% more in current period than last		
Value being destroyed	when performance is 4% or more worse than last year		
Value being created	when performance is 4% or more better than last year		
No real change	When two periods are within 1% of each other either way		

WHY THE SCORES HAVE DECLINED

Although we cannot infer that individual companies' scores are declining, as few companies have been assessed twice in three years, the overall fall in scores is worrying. Could it be because the companies assessed initially were those most interested in CRM, while those who were assessed later were actually later entrants into CRM? No, because many of the companies assessed later had been involved in CRM and similar approaches for 10 or more years; some were indeed household names for the quality of at least some of their CM activities. Table 2.1 illustrates the areas where customer management competence has increased and reduced. Because of the clear correlation between each area of the CMAT model with business performance[1], the table also shows where customer management value is being created and destroyed.

WHY COMPANIES ARE PERFORMING SO POORLY, DESPITE THE INVESTMENT

The findings in this book have led us to the following conclusions.

Senior executive ownership and leadership is required

This appears to be less of an issue now than it was, although still only one in five companies have executives on the board with responsibility for CRM (that is, constituting more than 50 per cent of their role). But our results show that, as yet, these executives are not increasing their companies' CM effectiveness. Why is this? Our explanation is as follows:

▌ Managers have a short-term focus; financial objectives are often set quarterly or at best annually. CM approaches often take longer to pay back, unless activities are carefully planned. Also, managers are often in a role as a stepping stone 'career development' move, and their performance in a function is only judged over a short period of time.

▌ Managers do not see change through. For example, investment in CM systems is clearly taking place, but not enough is invested in changing the behaviour and attitudes of employees, so little actually changes.

▌ Senior managers ignore the basics of what defines good CM and business performance. Some consultants and senior managers are obsessed with 'dramatic change' and new concepts. Plans that take a company's current business model, tighten it up in places and adapt it slightly in others, do not seem to appeal to managers obsessed with dramatic change. Unfortunately, there are just too many of these managers, and some consultancy firms encourage this attitude and even feed on it. Our research shows that significant benefits can be achieved more quickly and easily, and certainly more cheaply, through incremental change, often fixing areas that senior management do not know are broken!

▊ Senior managers do not recognize their companies' CM strengths and weaknesses. Our research shows those senior managers' views on their company's strengths and weaknesses are often different before and after a CMAT. So, project priorities and implementation programmes developed without a thorough review of the current position are likely to be founded on myths.

▊ Senior managers appear to rarely have the real authority or appetite to challenge the status quo and work across the enterprise.

Too much thinking, too little doing

Analysis[2] shows the cerebral nature of enterprises. Companies over-complicate CM. Too much time is spent defining strategy and programmes, and too little time in implementing them. It is easy to postulate and theorize, much harder to deliver. Complication occurs in part because typically *committees* design CM approaches, often removed from the reality of customers. Processes become over-engineered to cope with the most complex situation, and become difficult to use.

Functional and departmental silos

Customer management is still implemented by functions and departments, even though there is an increasing use of enterprise-wide systems. This silo approach does not support building value through the various stages of CM, from analysis and planning through to people. This approach is also dysfunctional from the perspective of customers, who expect to be managed consistently across departments.

Great is small!

Larger companies find it harder to manage customers than smaller companies. Our research seems to confirm this. Though this book does not examine why (more research is needed), many reasons come to mind. However, larger companies could themselves examine why smaller companies do better.

CM is 'champion' based

CM behaviours (for example, customer profitability analysis and managing customers based on their value) are often not embedded in the culture of an organization. Hence, people change roles and their thinking is either lost or moves with them. We have seen examples of this in companies that have repeated a CMAT after a year or so. Scores often fall in a previously high-scoring area because the relevant senior manager or a key player in the particular area has moved on.

More education is required

Knowledge of good customer management techniques and practices is not widespread. Education in customer management is lacking, despite the efforts of many institutes, associations and forums. Key concepts (for example, simpler ones such as decile analysis, or more complex ones such as customer value forecasting or measuring the success of retention management against control groups) are still not widely used. Outbound contact strategies are surprisingly rare. Customer service competencies are under-valued. Lifetime value consideration is used patchily. Enquiry follow up is random and ad hoc. The list goes on. Good training does exist in some companies. Direct or database marketing principles (particularly in relation to analysis, campaign management, lead management, customer retention and measurement) underpin good CM. But in many companies direct marketing has a poor image, and this can lead to rejection of its experiences and contributions.

There remains a belief that IT is a panacea

IT is not the panacea it is often thought to be. 'Global CRM in 90 days' was a widely advertised claim by a large software company; how attractive but misleading! IT can enable and even drive the business model, but a company must define its CM model first. This then defines the role of IT as a key enabler. The rest of the organization must be aligned and usually must change, at least a little but often very substantially over time. All this takes time. Data is the building block of many companies' CM management efforts. Our research[3] shows that data management remains one of the stumbling blocks to creating value in this area.

Poor implementation of customer management projects

We discuss this fully in Chapter 15. CMAT assessments regularly reveal unrealistic roadmaps, irrelevant business cases, poor (often absent) programme management, and many failed projects.

IT'S NOT ALL DOOM AND GLOOM

Despite all the above, there are many examples of very effective practices in companies we have assessed. Some are included in this book. Analysis of CMAT scores shows that the characteristics, activities and foci shown in Table 2.2 are most closely associated with high (top quartile) scores, and hence overall business performance.

Each area of CM identified by the CMAT model correlates significantly with business performance.[4] There is some difference between CM performance between countries and sectors, but there is a marked similarity in the characteristics of successful CM across sectors and geographies.

NOTES

[1]   Woodcock, N (2000) Does CRM performance correlate with business performance? *Journal of Interactive Marketing* (UK) April.
[2]   Woodcock, N *Companies Think in Boxes* (unpublished working paper).
[3]   Stone, M, Findlay, G, Evans, M and Leonard, M (2001) Data chaos – a court case waiting to happen, *International Journal of Customer Relationship Management*, **4** (2), pp 169–84.
[4]   Woodcock, N (2000) Does CRM performance correlate with business performance, *Journal of Interactive Marketing* (UK) (April).

Table 2.2 Characteristics most closely associated with high scores

Analysis and Planning	
Determine your competitive arena and the competitive challenge facing your company. Determine which companies are trying to win your best present and future customers, or increase their share of business from these customers.	
Ensure that the company's strategic objectives are communicated through the organization in a way that links them to the retention, efficiency, acquisition, penetration in CM (we refer to these as the REAP measures).	
Be clear about profit and where it comes from; in particular, from which customers.	
Determine how much you can afford to spend on acquisition, development and retention of different customer groups, and align resources to value (and maybe needs) segments.	
Be greedy for knowledge from customers, staff and partners.	
Proposition	
Develop clear and differentiated propositions aimed at those customers you want to manage.	
Determine how you can build loyalty among key value groups.	
Cascade the proposition from high-level brand values to influence the organization's behaviours.	
Communicate your customer propositions well to employees, partners and customers, and measure the resulting behaviour and attitude change.	
Customer Management Activity	
Overall	Develop practical and efficient acquisition, development, retention and efficiency plans.
Acquisition ▌ Targeting ▌ Enquiry management ▌ Winback	▌ Develop and measure effective enquiry management processes that identify future customers and business that will be good for your company (convertible, profitable, retainable etc). ▌ Develop winback programmes for selected former customers.
Early retention ▌ Welcoming ▌ Getting to know	▌ Provide thanks – as a courtesy and reinforcement of purchasing decision. ▌ Ensure early relationship service-management works. ▌ Monitor early transactions for indications of usage, higher future potential or risk of early attrition. ▌ Build an understanding of customers: how they want to be managed and what their potential might be.
Repeat purchase ▌ Ongoing management ▌ Managing dissatisfaction	▌ Let customers service (manage) themselves and their data. ▌ Try to predict defections through customer feedback and contact analysis. ▌ Proactively contact high value groups regularly. ▌ Manage key accounts in ways that are mutually beneficial. ▌ Identify dissatisfaction and manage it timely and well. ▌ Encourage a no-blame and learning culture in the whole organization. ▌ Don't underestimate the value of good customer service. In these days of choice and when customers have the confidence to change, their service experience is key .
People and Organization	
Provide customer management leadership with cross functional/departmental authority.	
Ensure the organization is flexible enough to support customer-oriented decision making.	
Align objectives throughout the organization to focus on profitable customer management.	
Recruit and develop people with the right skills and orientation.	
Ensure that incentives and rewards encourage desired CM behaviours.	
Understand employee satisfaction and commitment and its relationship with CM.	
Actively manage those partnerships and alliances that affect your customers.	
Measurement	
Measure customer behaviours, attitudes and activities and their impact on ROI.	
Measure how different media (touch points and types) affect CM results.	
Measure and learn from campaigns.	
Measure the effectiveness and efficiency of individuals.	
Customer Experience	
Understand how customer commitment (buying, responding) and customer satisfaction are related.	
Understand performance in individual and combined (relationship) moments of truth at all customer contact points, absolutely and relative to competition.	
Benchmark against others, in the company's competitive arena and outside it.	
Information and Technology	
▌ Understand priorities and dependencies that support ROI from CM. ▌ Understand customer data application, acquisition and maintenance. ▌ Increase visibility of appropriate customer data (to employees and partners). ▌ Increase visibility of customer data (to customers). ▌ Understand and implement support for the business integration requirements driven by CM.	
Process	
▌ Define and integrate processes based around the proposition. ▌ Replicate or grow successful processes for improved ROI.	

3

Customer management around the world

Michael Starkey, Neil Woodcock, Merlin Stone and
Sarah Boussofiane

This chapter gives the result of our studies using our research tool, CMAT-R, in a number of countries. Table 3.1 shows the inter-country comparison of approximately 250 CMAT-R studies carried out in Europe (including Switzerland, Austria, UK, Germany), North America and Asia Pacific. Additional studies are already under way which will continue to supplement and maintain the currency of this data. These are summarized in the Introduction to the book. Two of them (US and Netherlands) are covered in Chapters 13 and 14, while the early results of the Japanese study are discussed at the end of this chapter.

In this table, each cell has three entries. The first entry is the rank order of the factor within country. For example, in the top left cell the figure is 1. This means that in the Swiss study, companies on average scored better on people factors than on other factors. In the last row, this number takes a different meaning. It is the ranking of the country overall average versus those of other countries. In this case, the 1 in the left hand cell means that Switzerland scores highest. The second figure (per cent) is the actual average score achieved. The third figure is the score relative to the European average. Where the score is the same, there is an = sign. It is of course = for all European scores.

Table 3.1 shows that Switzerland is the clear leader with an overall score of 63 per cent, followed by Austria, the UK and Germany. North America and Asia Pacific both trail with a score of 44 per cent.

People and Organization (which our earlier studies[1] show a high correlation with business performance) is ranked first everywhere except North America and Asia Pacific. This is encouraging, as it shows that companies are generally not making the mistake of over-investing in technology before dealing with the people issues. North

Table 3.1 CMAT-R model section scores by country, all industry sectors. Ranking, actual % performance and relative performance against European average

	Switzerland	Austria	UK	Germany	Euro-Avg.	N. America	AsiaPacific
People & Organization	1= 71% +4%	1 67% =	1 62% −5%	1= 63% −4%	1 67% =	3 46% −21%	5 38% −29%
Proposition	1= 71% +6%	2 65% =	3 57% −8%	1= 63% −2%	2 65% =	7 37% −28%	7 35% −30%
Measurement	3 67% +8%	3 62% +3%	4 55% −4%	3 54% −5%	3 59% =	1 50% −9%	4 45% −14%
Customer Management Activity	4 65% +10%	5= 56% +1%	5 53% −2%	5= 49% −6%	5 55% =	5 41% −14%	6 42% −13%
Information & Technology	5 63% +8%	5= 56% 1%	2 63%+8%	7 47% −8%	4 55% =	4 43% −12%	1 59% +4%
Analysis & Planning	6 61% +7%	4 59% +5%	7 50% −4%	5= 49% −5%	6 54% =	2 48% −6%	3 48% −6%
Process	7 59% +6%	7 55% +2%	8 45% −8%	4 51% −2%	7 53% =	6 39% -14%	2 51% −2%
Customer Experience	8 43% -2%	8 51% +6%	6 51%+6%	8 42% −3%	8 45% =	8 36% −9%	8 25% −20%
Overall	1 63% +6%	2 59% +2%	4 54% −3%	5 52% −5%	3 57% =	=6 44% −13%	=6 44% −13%

America, by contrast, seems to be very data driven, with a relatively strong performance in the areas of Analysis and Planning and Measurement. However, in the home of marketing we would have expected a much stronger score for the proposition. Perhaps in North America companies are taking for granted that a strong product proposition necessarily translates into a strong customer proposition. Not so!

NORTH AMERICA

The overall score for North American financial service corporations (NAFS) is 44 per cent, which is 13 per cent below the European average. Canadian banks lead the North American results with 50 per cent, with USA banks (41 per cent) and other USA financial (credit card and e-broking) organizations (42 per cent) trailing behind. This result is not surprising. Canadian banks are well known for their concerted and consistent attempts to improve their customer management. There are a number of well-known public case studies, and banks in other parts of the world tend to look to the Canadians for examples of good customer management practice.

So how do NAFS companies perform in the top three areas associated with business performance? The best North American score is in Measurement, but this is 10 per cent below the European average and 17 per cent below the best performing country in Europe.

North America is weak in People and Organization (46 per cent, 21 per cent below European average, and 28 per cent below the best the best performing country in Europe) and Customer Management Activity (41 per cent, 15 per cent below European average, and 24 per cent below the best the best performing country in Europe).

The area where performance is most similar to Europe is in Analysis and Planning: determining customer worth, behaviour, attitudes and segmentation. We believe this similarity indicates a standard global approach to this area, typical of a 'first-pass' approach. In other words companies appear to carry out certain types of analysis, sometimes with the help of companies that supply services or software for customer analysis. These companies thereby gain insights into customer behaviour, but because of their lack of investment in data, analytics and deployment, these analyses do not really add strategic value to the company. Typically, this first-pass analysis makes use of a partial customer dataset available within the company. This normally includes basic customer geo-demographics, product sales volume, and revenue. Sometimes gross profit is included, but the data used for this is often incomplete and error-ridden. This analysis may involve some data cleaning and enhancement (although the company rarely carries out enough of this) and may include a first set of customer behaviour analysis. This may range from simple counts and rankings to the use of regression models, propensity modelling, CHAID and clustering techniques. This analysis tends to throw up some interesting observations around customer value groups and basic retention/acquisition issues. It may begin to offer insight into what *'best customers'* look like. These analyses may be strongly orientated towards optimising the results of individual campaigns, rather than longer-term optimisation of customer management.

Identification and analysis of best customers is rarely combined (where appropriate) with attitudinal (for example, satisfaction/commitment), activity (for example, marketing, service, complaint, credit) or prediction of future customer value, to develop real insights. The first-pass analysis often focuses on definitions (for instance, how do you define a lost customer? What is margin? What is a customer?) and data integration (Why haven't we got this data? Why can't we pull customer data together more easily? How do these data sources relate?) and may lead to the definition of data enhancement projects. However, data enhancement projects rarely use the most effective and automated data profiling techniques, and are often not built upon over time. Instead, first-pass analysis is carried out again the following year, or in the next project stage, with the same incomplete observations.

Companies that progress beyond this first pass will obtain a more realistic view of the customer profitability of different segments: They are characterized by:

▌ better understanding of the impact of cost to serve on customer profitability;
▌ additional insights into the role of different channels;
▌ identification of potential high value segments in their base (amongst lower deciles);
▌ understanding and management of retention of different types of customers (different needs groups), including prediction of defection, subtler acquisition and targeting approaches;
▌ quantification, understanding and prediction of switching behaviour, and understanding of its impact on the quality of the customer base;
▌ the existence of programmes to manage customers over time, often using behavioural feedback;
▌ an understanding of the relationship between behaviour and attitudes;
▌ understanding how their customer management processes affect customer attitudes and behaviour (for example, the impact of sub-standard delivery of 'moment of truth' areas) and hence acquisition, retention and penetration.

A small number of financial institutions have shown that doing all the above provides an excellent return on investment.

The Proposition score for NAFS overall is low (although this is misleading because for Canadian companies it is much higher). This indicates that propositions (a set of brand values transformed into an intended customer experience and specification of how the company must behave to deliver the experience) are undefined and no doubt similar, with mainstream organizations offering much the same undifferentiated product and service. Customers no doubt have little loyalty to this approach, with any apparent loyalty probably being apathy or inertia-based.

The score for Information and Technology is also low, but this is acceptable considering that the other scores indicate a relatively undefined CRM business model and poorly defined processes. A key learning outcome relating to CRM systems is that they will not add value unless the business model and processes they need to support are well defined.

Although the picture of customer management in North America is a disappointing one, our research work offers hope for those enterprises that are prepared to invest in practical customer management. Substantial change and investment is required to improve scores to European levels, but the rewards will be great in terms of increased business performance. Most companies were quite consistent in their scores, so if they take a balanced approach to the development of their customer management capability, our evidence is that they will be able to get significant gains in the areas of competitive advantage, growth and profit.

Our recommendation is therefore that these companies should aim to develop competence across the CMAT model, improving the relatively good performance in Analysis and Planning and Measurement, and investing heavily in people and organizational development and implementation of customer management activities, supported by using appropriate information and technology enablers.

CANADA

A different picture (Table 3.2) emerges for Canadian companies, although the sample size is small (n = 6), so we should treat these results with care.

Table 3.2　CMAT-R scores of Canadian and US retail banks

	Canadian banks %	Rank	USA retail banks %	Rank
Analysis & Planning	51	5	47	2
Proposition	59	1	31	=7
People & Organization	55	=2	44	3
Information & Technology	55	=2	42	4
Process Management	43	7	38	6
Customer Management Activity	41	8	40	5
Measurement	55	=2	49	1
Customer Experience	45	6	31	=7
Overall	**50**		**42**	

The ranking analysis shows that Canadian companies have genuinely worked to differentiate themselves through their propositions. They have invested more in the people and organizational side of CRM and place more emphasis on information and technology. In common with those of their European counterparts who have done this, they are likely to be struggling to achieve acceptable returns from the IT investment. This is because the day-to-day customer management activities (how IT can support the organization in enabling excellence in customer management) and processes are not as well defined (low scores). In Europe, the failure rate of CRM projects is very high. According to the Hewson Consulting Group over 30 to 40 per cent fail to deliver the anticipated benefits (see Chapter 17, Guidelines for successful CRM implementation).

In fact, the day-to-day implementation of customer management is a key area for improvement in most Canadian companies. They appear to have developed the ideas (relatively good scores for analysis and planning and proposition) but are struggling to put them into operation. They appear to have looked to IT to help do this, but have perhaps underestimated the need to develop a more detailed clarity about the role of IT in their organizations and transformation programmes.

According to a recent Forrester[2] research study, Canada's consumer banking industry had supported a history of contrived competition until the mid-1990s. However, the past five years have been characterized by the following factors:

▌ Waning customer loyalty: largely in light of online development.
▌ Failed mergers: based on the federal government's denial of two proposed bank mergers in early 1998.
▌ New competitors: particularly those offering online full service banking as well as specialized services.
▌ Recent legislation: making it easier for foreign entrants and increasing direct access to the Canadian payments system.

As a result, banks have taken, or are projected to take, very different strategies for sales and customer service and for internal processing and technology.

GERMANY

Although German companies score quite well in the critical area of People and Organization, significantly, they score poorly against other European countries in the two other critical elements of customer management. Specifically:

▌ They score poorly in Customer Management Activity (49 per cent). This is the day-to-day acquisition of prospects, and subsequent retention and cross selling activity. This needs to be improved. CMA is where thinking is put into practice and actually leads to revenue generation.
▌ They are relatively weak on Measurement in CRM (54 per cent), this means measuring retention, acquisition, penetration and cost to serve, and linking this to achievement of business objectives. It has a high impact on business performance: what gets measured gets done!

German companies score poorly in Analysis and Planning. They need to do more to determine which customers they want to acquire, manage and develop. German companies certainly do not have a strong focus on Information and Technology in CRM. (A low CMAT IT score has a low correlation with business performance so a low score here is not normally critical to business success). However, the very low relative score for IT in German companies is a cause for concern. For instance, it may be one of the reasons why Analysis and Planning, Customer Management Activity and Measurement scores are relatively low, as IT supports these activities. IT competence is critical to business performance in high cost/low margin markets where operationally excellent business models are required. Here, a lack of focus on IT will lead to gross inefficiencies and will be a severe inhibitor to competitiveness and growth.

German companies are also relatively weak on process development. The detailed scores suggest they are likely to have processes defined (indeed, they focus on process development), but find it hard to improve processes quickly or to ensure that these processes are employee and customer friendly. As with Swiss companies, German companies make only basic attempts to understand the experience, loyalty and commitment of customers. This is a key area where improvement is required in highly competitive markets.

Overall, these results present a somewhat troubled picture for customer management in Germany, with below-par performance in critical areas of customer management (18 points behind the European average in the top three critical areas). Looking at the process scores suggests an inability to change things quickly. German companies score similarly to the UK in the way they manage customers overall, but the make-up of the scores is different, with the UK scoring better in the areas most closely linked with business performance (+5 points difference).

SWITZERLAND

The scores for Switzerland are on average 6 per cent higher than the European average across the model, and about 20 per cent higher than in Asia Pacific. In any analysis we have carried out, in any country, the scores recorded in the Swiss research are impressively high.

Results like this, of course, cause an observer to look closely at the research methodology. The research questions and CMAT methodology applied were consistent, the researchers, although different individuals, were fully trained and accredited by QCi. Quality assurance processes on the initial interviews were also carried out by QCi, and by the same quality assurance person for all of the research exercises. The timing of the research is not a contributory factor, because our work shows that customer management scores are not generally improving over time[3]. The audience for the research was very similar in terms of company type and level of person interviewed. There could be a difference in the openness and understanding of the people interviewed: perhaps people in Switzerland were blindly confident about what they thought their companies did? This possibility can only be proven if the same companies carry out a full CMAT, which is evidence-based. Our interviewers, who were experienced Swiss management consultants and therefore understand the nature of business dialogue in their country, have dismissed this, and there is no reason why we should suspect this to be the case. Hence, our research conclusion is that the results are significant and that Swiss companies do indeed manage customers better than the other sampled regions.

Another factor adds weight to the strong Swiss position in customer management. Three of the four highest scoring elements for Swiss companies (People, Measurement, Customer Management Activity) were the top three areas that our research has shown correlate most strongly with business performance[4]. Given the relationship between overall CMAT score and business performance[5], the implications for Swiss companies entering new geographies are interesting. If they can transfer expertise from Switzerland to other countries, they are very likely to be able to gain market share quickly from local incumbent companies struggling to develop customer-focused operations. However, the 'if' is a big 'if'. The difficulty in transferring expertise[6] in the customer management area and ensuring the success of new CRM projects[7] is well documented. If Swiss companies develop a successful approach to replicating their CM abilities in foreign markets, the world should watch out! However, they need to listen to, and act upon, customer feedback, and understand better what factors in the overall proposition lead to customer loyalty and commitment. With this vital element missing, Swiss companies may lose out in an increasingly competitive world, with increasingly fickle consumers. A deep under-standing of customers and how this may translate into development of a strongly customer-focused proposition (particularly product design and the development of 'emotional' loyalty through customer transactions) may well be the key differentiator between companies.

AUSTRIA

Austrian companies score well and are above the European average in all areas. They know which customers they want to manage and how these customers behave. They have developed solid propositions and have well-developed infrastructures, in terms of people and IT, which can support the proposition. Customer Management Activity, the day-to-day management of customers, is also solid. Measurement performance is good. They score particularly well in the Customer Experience, listening to customers, and understanding what they have to do to improve customer management.

The profile of scores against the areas of the CMAT model which correlate most strongly with business performance (People, Customer Management Activity and Measurement) while creditably high, is not nearly as strong as in Switzerland, with the top three areas, People, Customer Management Activity and Measurement totalling +5 points above average, compared with Switzerland's stunning 23 points. The results therefore show a solid rather than an exceptional performance. Although the overall scores are good, Austrian companies should focus on improving their customer management activity and on developing clearer propositions. Also, in the critical people area, Austrian companies score only 1 point above average, so they should continue their work on people and organizational development in CRM.

UNITED KINGDOM

The UK ranking of sections is similar to the others (this shows a similar focus, although the actual scores are generally below the European average), apart from IT, Process and the Customer Experience. The UK focuses heavily on IT, and has the highest ranking for IT, but has the worst score for defining Processes. It has poor scores for both Analysis and Planning (which customers do we want to manage and how?) and Customer Management Activity, and the worst score for Proposition (how should we manage customers?)! Perhaps this is one of the reasons why IT CRM systems have such a poor success record in the UK. It is almost as though UK companies want to buy success through IT, without going through the pain of developing the business model or addressing critical success factors. The Customer Experience score is excellent, and shows that although UK companies may not be strong yet in managing customers, they are learning quickly about what customers want and how they want to be managed. The question is, will UK companies be able to facilitate the step-change required to catch up with some of their global competitors?

The poor score in Analysis and Planning is important. Understanding which customers you want to manage, and what aspects of acquisition, retention and development need improving, is fundamental to good customer management practice. Why are UK companies lagging behind other European countries here? We believe it might be an educational or cultural issue, with too few professional marketers with 'direct' or 'database' marketing experience in place in senior roles in UK companies compared with their European peers, despite there being many such people at more junior levels. Poor scores in Proposition and Process are revealing. Although these factors correlate less strongly with business performance, low scores here do tend to show that a company is unclear about how to manage customers and is probably busy cutting costs, or blindly following (equally poor) competitors with 'me-too' type offers. Measurement also is rather weak, and this is an important area linked closely with business performance.

The UK picture, therefore, is not particularly healthy, with too strong a focus on IT and too weak a focus on Measurement, Proposition, Customer Management Activity, and Analysis and Planning. UK companies appear to want IT to solve their CRM issues, without being prepared to invest in the understanding of customer behaviour, the proposition required or in the processes necessary to support the business model to manage these customers. Before investing so much in IT, UK companies need to be clearer about the customer management business models they need to deploy and the processes they want IT to support.

DEVELOPING ASIA PACIFIC

The results for 'developing Asia Pacific' (Korea, Taiwan, Malaysia) companies are very different. The ranking is quite different and the actual scores are much lower than their European counterparts in most areas. The exceptions to this are the areas of Process, IT and, at a push, Analysis and Planning. It is interesting that developing Asia Pacific companies had their strongest focus in these areas, perhaps showing the strong cerebral and process-oriented nature of their business mentality. In fact, the overall balance of research results for this region (strong focus on Analysis and Planning, Process and Proposition; low focus on Customer Management Activity, Measurement and Customer Experience) suggests that Asia Pacific companies are prone to too much intellectualizing in Customer Management and not enough doing. However, it could also be argued that many companies are at a very early stage in the evolution of CRM, so what they are doing is thinking about what to do, and building their infrastructure.

The People ranking was low and the actual per cent score was very low in this area. An analysis of the research response indicates that the reasons for this clearly lie in the cultural roots in the region. The main issues for companies are:

▮ The ability of the organization to react quickly to market changes (for example, decision making is a hierarchical process, with most ideas being originated or at least very heavily filtered at senior levels).
▮ The need for senior leadership in customer management (for example, the customer experience cuts across different departments and functions and senior leadership is required to ensure cross-enterprise cooperation).
▮ Empowerment (a command and control culture is very evident here).
▮ Identification of competency gaps in customer management.
▮ Incentives and rewards for achievement of targets.

The people area is a key issue for many companies in this region, but change is likely to be slow because organizational behaviour appears to be strongly embedded in the behavioural norms, or culture, of this region. We are already seeing evidence that western companies owning companies in this region will be the quickest to improve here. Local employees in this region increasingly want their local management to adopt western employment practices and motivational techniques. We did see one local credit card company that had taken steps to go against the norm of a blame culture and had specifically embedded within its marketing plan that there should be a no-blame culture.

Not surprisingly, it was one of the better performers. Hiding behind traditional accepted cultural norms should not be accepted as a valid reason not to employ best customer management practices.

Day-to-day customer management activity needs significant improvement in almost all areas. As a small example, in terms of managing dissatisfaction, a blame culture still exists in this region. This affects the ability of an enterprise to learn where it is going wrong, where the service pressure points are and so on. Openness of enterprises, a no-blame culture and a willingness to learn are important facets of successful organizations. (Our analysis of high performing questions shows these factors to have a very high correlation with business performance[8].)

The Proposition score was also very low in this region. There is less of an obvious definition of what it means to be a customer of one company rather than that of another. This is reflected in much 'me too' marketing, an array of very similar products and similar customer service approaches. It is expected that society as a whole will begin to embrace change very quickly in this region, and companies that can be set up to react quickly to this will be able to gain a significant competitive advantage.

JAPAN

As mentioned in the Introduction to this book, the results of the Japanese study sponsored by Ogilvy One were coming in as this book went to press. In this section, we summarize the results that arrived literally the day before this book went to press, and draw some early conclusions. A more comprehensive report will be issued later. Meanwhile, the reader will have more time than the authors did and may wish to make further comparisons.

Interviews were carried out with 20 leading companies, the majority being in the top 10 for their sector. Sectors were as follows:

▓ six financial services;
▓ six services;
▓ six manufacturers;
▓ two communication services.

Interviews were with senior managers: the board-level director responsible for CRM, marketing/sales/strategic planning heads or CRM operations heads.

The average score for the Japanese study was 35 out of 100. This score was lower than the global average score (at time of completion of the study) for CMAT-R studies of 51. Among the three industry sectors, financial services had the highest score while manufacturing scored the lowest: more or less consistent with global studies, reflecting heavy intermediation and/or product focus in manufacturing and tough competition for customers in financial services.

Table 3.3 Japanese results

	Average	Max	Min	Financial services	Services	Manufacturing	Global
Analysis & Planning	33	61	12	45	35	17	51
Proposition	33	56	19	41	34	24	58
People/Organization	40	70	7	48	38	36	57
Data and IT	21	42	2	25	27	9	51
Process	41	75	11	45	46	30	50
CM Activity	35	69	16	45	37	22	51
Measurement	42	72	8	55	42	29	54
Customer Experience	30	57	7	38	26	26	39
Total	35	61	13	44	36	24	51

The range of results for individual companies was large, from over 61 per cent to as low as 13 per cent. The results are given in Table 3.3. The highlights are as follows:

█ The research found companies that have good CM practices in many areas, and companies that have hardly started to implement customer management. Typically the best companies are those that have been doing CM for many years and have imported international learning.

█ The definition and standardization of processes is reasonably good in many organizations; however these are designed around efficiency and internal structures, rather than customers.

█ Seventy per cent of organizations have standard processes and measurement for inquiry and complaint handling, but only 15 per cent check customer acceptability of their customer management processes.

█ Most of the companies surveyed collected individual customer data, but no organizations were using it fully to plan and drive their CM activity. Most organizations had never undertaken any real depth analysis of their data, and few use it to target valued customers differentially, or to develop and retain customers.

█ Most CM activity was in response to customers' actions, rather than approaching customers proactively. Eighty per cent do not have specific development programmes for valuable customers.

█ Ownership at board level is relatively high in Japan compared to the global picture. However, typically the vision amounts to broad customer focus, rather than a specific CM mission. Also there is low alignment further down the organization and at the front line.

▌ The top seven performing areas were customer management ownership, understanding of volume/margin managed by channels, organization support for implementing strategies, identification of processes, lead distribution agreements, channel cost to serve, and timescales for complaint resolution. These all averaged above 50.

▌ The worst seven performing areas were getting to know/health check, planning for customer acquisition, using benchmarks, segmented targeting, winback, acquiring customer information, and information planning. These all averaged below 25.

In summary, Japan is at a relatively early stage in the evolution of customer management. However, the early signs are that senior management are involved, and the door to importing ideas – from other companies and other countries – is firmly open.

IMPORTANCE OF THESE FINDINGS

These are important findings. We are not aware of any research, anywhere, that compares in detail customer management capability across the world. The correlation of customer management capability with business performance is clear. Companies should use the results of this research to learn from, adapt and improve on the capabilities of competitors (or partners) from other regions.

NOTES

[1] Woodcock, N, Starkey, M and Stone, M (2000) *The Customer Management Scorecard: The state of the nation*, Business Intelligence.

[2] Forrester Research Inc. (2001) *Canada's Big Banks Unravel*, May, Forrester Research, Cambridge, Mass.

[3] See chapters 4–12 of this book.

[4] Woodcock, N, Starkey, M and Stone, M (2000) *The Customer Management Scorecard*, Ch 3, Business Intelligence.

[5] Woodcock, N (2000) Does CRM performance correlate with business performance, *Journal of Interactive Marketing* (UK), April.

[6] Woodcock, N, Starkey, M and Stone, M, Ibid, Ch 6.

[7] Stone, M, Foss, B, Harvey, R, Scheld, B and Whitaker, R (2001) Global customer management, Ch 12 in *Successful Customer Relationship Marketing*, ed B Foss and M Stone, Kogan Page, London.

[8] QCi [accessed 9 August 2002] *QCi Model Results Analysis* [Online] www.qci.co.uk.

4

Where companies can create and destroy value

Neil Woodcock, Michael Starkey and Merlin Stone

INTRODUCING THE CUSTOMER MANAGEMENT VALUE CHAIN

The CMAT model can be used to analyse the contribution of customer management (CM) to corporate value (Figure 4.1). Value is defined here in its broadest sense of stakeholder or owner value. For companies owned by stockholders, value is represented by share value. For companies owned by customers (customer mutuals), value is usually represented by customer dividends or bonuses (or more recently potential privatization value, or risk of failure). For companies owned by employees (cooperatives), value is usually represented by bonuses paid on earnings. For publicly owned organizations, a mixture of cost of provision and quality of service usually represents value. For charities, a similar mixture represents value, with the services received by beneficiaries of charities being important. Recent business news challenges whether some quoted companies, through management compensation and option schemes, are being run for their executives' personal benefit!

Behind some of these forms of value lies value to customers. Value to customers is usually measured in terms of the appropriateness of what they receive (benefits) relative to what they have to pay, either directly or indirectly (for example, user costs, taxation). In most cases, stakeholder value and customer value are closely related, though the relationship between the two can diverge in the short run for all sorts of reasons: for example, government intervention, lack of competition and customer inertia. However, in the long run the two rarely go in different directions. It is not the role of this book to prove this assertion, but if true it means that enhancing customer value is critical for most organizations. Enhancing customer value is not done solely by CM: simply producing excellent products and at low cost is another feasible route. In our earlier work, we have investigated many different models of customer management, and investigated the contribution made by the types of good CM practices that are the focus of CMAT.[1]

Before analysing how good CM practices improve customer value, let us examine the value to the different groups of people in the value chain:

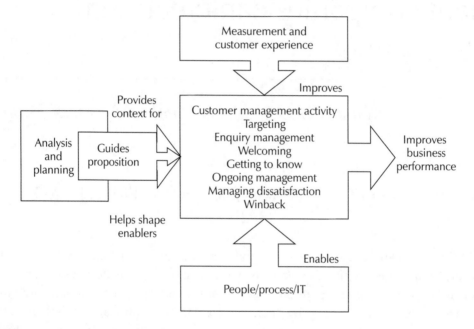

Figure 4.1 The customer management value chain

▌ Value for customers is implicit in the CMAT model and covered throughout this book. It is the fundamental driver of shareholder value. Customer value is created through the development and effective delivery of the right proposition to the right customers.

▌ Value for employees and partners, and how to create it, is an important focus of the People and Organization section of the CMAT model. Our business performance research shows that people and organization are the most important contributors to business performance.

▌ Value for shareholders is based not just on profit but is determined by the stock market, based on a number of factors. If a company is perceived to be managing customers and opportunity well, the share price may go up. CRM is now one of the main foci of large companies' presentations to analysts. In one case, a company made such a presentation, claiming that it managed its customers well. When the analysts challenged it and asked how it knew this, the answer was that IBM was using CMAT to find out! The company turned out to have a top-decile performance, overall and for its sector, so the company was right, but now knows and can prove it! Share value can also be influenced by the way decisions on improvements to customer management capabilities are announced and subsequently managed.

FOCUSING ON CUSTOMER VALUE

The next few chapters focus on how value to customers can be created or destroyed. Value can be created, destroyed or ignored at any customer management stage, but most value is created by organizations that compound value creation at each CM stage by using and building on the gains created in other stages. Table 4.1 explains in more detail how using the CMAT model value can be created.

It can be seen how value is influenced at each stage of the model. Maximum value occurs when all elements of the model are managed together rather than independent parts: joined-up management creates maximum value (this point is reinforced in Chapter 16, The business case for customer management). Thus, knowing which customers to manage enables you to develop a more appropriate proposition. A good proposition will help you to shape your organization and align your people, processes and IT infrastructure. Good measurement will improve customer management activities and so on.

This chapter has given a brief overview of the relationship between good customer management and value. The next few chapters investigate the relationship between customer management and customer value in each of the sections of the CMAT model. They give our research results, examples of best (and some poor) practices and war stories.

NOTE

[1]   Stone, M, Machtynger, L and Woodcock, N (2000) *Customer Relationship Marketing*, Kogan Page, London.

Table 4.1 How value can be created

Analysis and planning: creating value through insight, knowledge and effective planning	
Value is initially created by: █ understanding which customers you want to manage; █ understanding how much you can afford to spend in acquiring and retaining them; █ putting the appropriate plans in place to acquire the customers that will add value over time; █ retaining those who are worth retaining; █ developing those with potential, efficiently. Planning is also used to match resources to gross value, so that time spent on attracting, retaining or trying to develop customers is relative to likely value.	Value is often destroyed through █ a lack of customer knowledge and insight; █ absent (or poor) data quality and / or data analysis; █ a mismatch of costs to revenues; █ missing or ineffective planning.
Proposition: creating value through a proposition that helps you find, keep and develop those customers you want to manage	
Value is created: █ when you are in a position to develop a proposition to attract similar customers, retain them and develop their value; █ when your proposition development involves all your supply chain providers (to ensure that your proposition can actually be delivered); █ when you communicate your proposition to staff who actually manage customers and to their immediate managers, so that they manage customers in a way that is consistent with the proposition; █ when you support the delivery of the proposition with incentives, rewards, competency development, process standards, measures, IT content and accessibility.	Value is often destroyed through: █ poor targeting or disparate incentive measures that encourage poor quality lead generation; █ propositions that are poorly defined or articulated or go no further than a set of brand values; █ propositions aimed at low value customer groups (a problem compounded from poor analysis and planning); █ poor communication of the proposition to the people delivering the proposition (employees and partners) and the people experiencing it (customers).

Table 4.1 (cont)

People and organization: creating value through effective people and partners	
Value is created when:	Value is destroyed:
▌ you have clear visible leadership for CM; ▌ internal communication works smoothly, especially between customer-facing staff and between them and the rest of the organization; ▌ you have slick decision-making structures and the right competencies; ▌ motivation and supplier management are employed as key enablers of good customer management; ▌ ability to execute is made practical through an appropriate strategy and governance system for business transformation.	▌ when there is no clear board level leadership and commitment to CM; ▌ when the organization stifles quick decision making relating to CM; ▌ where objectives are misaligned with the goals of the organization; ▌ when incompetent people or ineffective systems influence the customer experience; ▌ when employees are not motivated and rewarded or when suppliers are badly managed; ▌ when ability to execute is undermined by inappropriate culture or poor governance of business transformation programmes.
Processes: creating value by being customer centric	
Value is created when all customer management processes are: ▌ defined with the customer proposition in mind; ▌ based on an in-depth understanding of how they will affect customers.	Value is destroyed when processes: ▌ confront or conflict with good customer management; ▌ are set in stone and cannot be changed.
Information and technology (including data): creating value through efficiency, service and intelligence	
Value is created when: ▌ IT applications support or enable new processes; ▌ customer and transactional data is acquired and managed professionally; ▌ customer and transactional data is made available to customers, partners and employees where and when it is required; ▌ integration of systems reflects or enables appropriate integration of the business.	Value is destroyed where: ▌ data of poor quality is acquired; ▌ data is stored with no specific purpose; ▌ data is poorly maintained; ▌ contact permissions are not stored; ▌ systems are not available at key customer contact points; ▌ fragmentation of systems limits CM capabilities; ▌ customer access is not provided.

Table 4.1 (cont)

Measurement: creating value through understanding of performance	
Value is created when:	Value is destroyed if:
▌ what gets measured gets done! ▌ the relationship between resource, activities and performance is understood, which enables CM resources to be managed effectively.	▌ effectiveness and efficiency are not measured and then action taken; ▌ the organization does not learn from its activities, successes and failures.

Customer experience: creating value through understanding the customer experience	
Value is created when there is an understanding of how:	Value is destroyed when:
▌ satisfied and committed the customer is; ▌ the customer experiences the different aspects of the proposition, which is essential for monitoring whether your proposition is being received as it has been designed to be; ▌ you recognize that the customer experience is dependent on being able to understand and respond in a timely and appropriate manner when customer needs change.	▌ poor customer experiences or your proposition are not known about or are ignored; ▌ you focus on customer satisfaction and not on customer commitment; ▌ you do not benchmark the experience of your customers against that provided by competitors and best of breed suppliers in other markets.

Customer management activities: creating value through excellent acquisition, retention, development and recovery activities	
Value is created when:	Value is destroyed:
▌ the plans are put into action, targeting the right customers efficiently; ▌ you make the most of all enquiries received and responses to outbound contacts; ▌ you ensure new customers understand, use and enjoy your product; ▌ new customers are retained and developed; ▌ you service customers well; ▌ you manage well customers who are dissatisfied; ▌ customers can easily configure what your company offers to meet their needs. All of this can be done through a variety of channels, which are appropriate both to the customer and your business.	▌ simply through inactivity; ▌ when your CM activities are not aligned with your CM plan (maybe because the plan did not exist or was poorly communicated); ▌ when your CM processes leak value through poor control and inefficiency (eg enquiries wasted); ▌ if your customers leave without being asked why; ▌ if your customers become inactive and are not stimulated back into action; ▌ when you stop focusing on customer service excellence; ▌ when customer dissatisfaction is handled badly.

5

Analysis and planning

Neil Woodcock, Michael Starkey and Merlin Stone

Table 5.1 shows where customer management (CM) value is being created and destroyed in analysis and planning of the model. Companies appear to be focusing increasingly on customer retention, probably because of the wider awareness that customer acquisition is more expensive than retention. However, the table indicates that this increased focus appears to be carried out at the expense of overall planning and of acquisition planning. Understanding competition still performs well, although deep analysis of competitive positioning is usually absent. Knowledge management scores have fallen, largely because bigger organizations find it hard, in practice, to gain benefits from the capture and use of tacit (for example, soft, intangible) knowledge, without the process becoming too resource-intensive.

Table 5.1 Analysis and planning

% scores	Period 1	Period 2	Whether value is being created or destroyed
Analysis and planning	30	27	Some destroying of value
Overall customer management planning	28	25	Some destroying of value
Planning for customer acquisition	27	18	Value being destroyed
Planning for customer retention	30	35	Created
Planning for customer development	24	25	No real change
Understanding competition	49	41	Value being destroyed
Knowledge management	23	16	Value being destroyed

CHARACTERISTICS OF THE HIGHEST-PERFORMING COMPANIES

The following recommendations are derived from analysis of how high-scoring companies analyse and plan.

▌ Determine your competitive arena and the competitive challenge facing your company. This will help you, first, understand your competitors; second, determine which customer groups you can manage now; and third, determine what you need to change, and how much you need to spend, to attract different customer groups.

▌ Communicate your strategic CM objectives throughout your organization.

▌ Ensure that these objectives link to and influence retention, efficiency, acquisition and penetration (REAP measures). Develop practical REAP plans, which lead to identifiable required actions for the whole organization.

▌ Be clear about profit and where it comes from. To do this well, companies have to understand the acquisition, retention and development behaviours of their customers and the cost of acquiring and managing customers. You can then develop a picture of current and future customer profitability and its determinants. You need to be very careful not to assume that your brand strength will always allow you to cross-sell. Many companies have justified mergers or acquisitions, and investments in organizational and technical infrastructure, on over-optimistic business cases.

▌ From the list above, determine how much you can afford to spend on acquisition and retention of different customer groups, and align resources to market segments (for example, by value or needs groupings). One way of doing this is to determine the net present value (NPV) of different customer segments; apply a per cent probability to this (that is, we are 80 per cent sure of achieving US $300 NPV) and determine what per cent you can afford to spend on acquisition and retention.

▌ Be greedy for knowledge from customers, staff and partners. Knowledge from the 'front line' can help you develop insights and actions which can make a material difference to how you manage your customers.

EXAMPLES OF BEST PRACTICES

High technology intermediary: market portfolio direction and competitive positioning

The business unit of this intermediary (business to business, computer equipment and peripherals) used a very effective method of determining its competitive position and

Table 5.2   Selected facts and figures from research

Overall customer management planning	
28% of companies hold three years or more of sales purchase information Only 19% HAVE carried out basic decile value analysis	Transaction data from over at least three years is being collected and analysed, at least in part, by almost one in three companies (28% of those that can, do), but often this data is not being analysed at a customer level in a way that affects practical plans. For instance, only 19% have carried out basic customer value analysis. Often companies carry out detailed, product-based analysis but have not built a basic understanding of the value differences of different types of customer.
54% DO NOT recognize customer behaviours in planning.	Marketing planning processes are not yet focused on customer behaviour, attitude and CM efficiency. Generally, plans produced are long-winded, too general and largely *irrelevant* to actual operational staff. (Often the people producing these plans will readily admit this.) Many companies use marketing planning models from the pre-database era. Although they may have been updated and refreshed, they are fundamentally flawed because they do not encourage understanding of customer behaviour and attitudes, or planning to influence it in order to improve long-term customer value and profitability. Most organizations do not recognize how their performance varies in the areas of retention, efficiency, acquisition and penetration. Nor do they recognize these topics in their marketing planning. **War story: depreciating customer database value** An organization's directors simply did not believe it was losing 15% of customers a year. They had always been told that attrition was around 2% but this was net attrition: they were losing 15% and gaining 13%. The customers acquired were of much lower potential value than the customers lost, so the value of their customer base was falling fast.
56% do not match segmentation in planning with the actual way the organization works	Segmentation is still a relatively cerebral activity for most companies. It is often used to help define acquisition programmes, but rarely to help guide customer retention. **War story: impractical segmentation** A company had carried out an excellent segmentation project and built a really good understanding of its customers. It decided to put customer segments on the front screen of the call centre system. The problem was the segment names: names like 4A/01B (low empathy) and 5D/01B (high propensity) gave no clue to their meaning, so staff did not know what to do with customers from different segments.
11% DO use some form of customer lifecycle model	11% of companies find it useful to follow the customer's lifecycle from suspect to prospect through to advocate, measuring the input/output of each stage and developing different treatments (marketing programmes) at different stages to improve performance.

Table 5.2 (cont)

Acquisition	
62% DO NOT have any formal prospect contact strategies 62% DO NOT use target acquisition costs 2% of companies have near-miss monitoring	Acquisition planning is often no more sophisticated than a sales plan based on 'acquisition at any cost'. Many of the research facts on the left support the 'acquisition at any cost' conclusion. Target acquisition cost (allowable cost of sale) is rarely used. Few companies employ contact strategies aimed even at high-value prospects. Very few companies ask new customers *why* they came to them and from *where*. This can be useful input in proposition development and in both acquisition and retention programmes (customers may leave you for the same reasons!). It will help you identify competitors' weaknesses.
Retention	
63% of companies still DO NOT measure retention rates	Although there is an increased focus on retention, this occurs in the absence of *detailed analysis* of retention (eg by value group). Looking at retention by value group (eg by decile) can be revealing. Examining it by value/needs group can contribute significantly to reducing value loss in any organization.
19% understand lifetime value 4% understand their customers' position in lifecycles	There is not a wide *application* of lifetime value (LTV), although this has improved from 1 in 8 to 1 in 5 over the period. Most experienced practitioners agree that LTV has validity in most markets, but only if applied sensibly. The longer the lifetime estimated, the lower the probability of the value being achieved in practice. Five years is commonly used (depending on the purchase cycle of course), and acquisition, retention and development plans are often based on this sort of timeframe. The application of LTV principles is one of the characteristics of best-performing companies.
7% of companies have game plans for high-value groups	A simpler application of LTV is simply to identify the highest value groups among your customers and manage them differently. Surprisingly, less than 1 company in 14 actually applies this learning in practice. Companies may do the analysis, but it does not get applied. It is critical, though. A company might find that it earns 80% of its profit from 20% of its customers. If it examined the top 10%, it might find that they were responsible for more than 50% of profit. If the company carried out a decile analysis on this top 10%, it might find that 2% of its customers were responsible for 30–40% of profit. A stunning thought – and the company had better not lose any of these 2%! Yet only a few companies *actually* manage these key accounts any differently.
Development	
39% DO NOT consider propensity to buy in their cross-selling activity	Although most companies (61%) consider propensity to buy in their cross-selling activity, only 1 in 10 utilizes some form of propensity model to help it determine which customers to cross-sell to. Blanket cross-selling, or the use of simple profiles, still exists in most companies and is usually very wasteful of resources.
45% DO NOT use cross-sell triggers	Almost half of the companies researched do not recognize and use triggers (during an inbound service call for instance) to identify cross-sell opportunities.
4% can identify product portfolio sequences	Few companies bother to look at the typical purchase sequence of products, and their impact on customer development. 4% of companies have priced and positioned products as lead (maybe loss-making) products in order to improve the take-up of other products.
6% have segment development plans	Only 6% of companies have specific plans to move a customer, or segment, from a *current* value to a *projected* value. Again, this suggests that at best companies carry out campaign-based activities (with short-term objectives) rather than customer-based activities (combining short and long-term objectives).

Table 5.2 (cont)

Competitor understanding	
58% of companies track competitive promotions	*Understanding of the competition* is one of the highest-scoring sections in the assessment. Most companies track competitive market share and promotional activities. Not all do anything with it, but nevertheless the learning obtained from tracking is valuable for adjustments to product, promotional and pricing approaches. **War story: competitor information store** An organization was very proud of its competitor information 'cupboard', but to save it getting messed up and things taken they kept it locked. They claimed that people knew how to get the key and used it frequently. On examination most of the material was in totally pristine condition and had clearly never been touched.
19% position their customer offer against competitors	However, there is a lack of understanding of the more strategic aspects of competitive positioning. For instance: ▊ What is the relative profit situation? ▊ What is the competitive position in key customer groups? ▊ How should the company be positioned against the competition to attract high value customer segments?
Knowledge management	
8% capture, distribute and analyse tacit knowledge effectively (so that it influences what the company actually does)	The knowledge management area of the research assesses the collection, distribution and use of TACIT (soft, intangible, difficult to code) and CODED (hard, tangible, easy to code) customer knowledge.
14% of companies DO NOT capture and share TACIT knowledge (eg between channels and head office)	The facts show that very few companies have discovered how to capture and use tacit customer knowledge, although our work shows most are trying.

defining its strategic direction and detailed proposition. The company first identified broad segments of potential customers. It used a third-party data provider to do this, defining companies by industry type, size, and a derived field to define purchasing policy (centralized or devolved). It came up with five segments.

It then defined the relative attractiveness of each segment. The weighted criteria for attractiveness included annual spend, size of segment, growth of segment, propensity to be loyal, price sensitivity, channel choice and risk. This was done in a workshop with experienced company people, who knew the market well. It was relative attractiveness they were interested in, not absolute values. This gave the 'y' co-ordinate for the market portfolio matrix (see Figure 5.1). For each segment, the workshop members ranked the top six or so requirements of each segment from a supplier in this area (they carried out research to help them do this). The requirements included price, product innovation, reliability, technical support, sales relationship, brand image, product design and appeal,

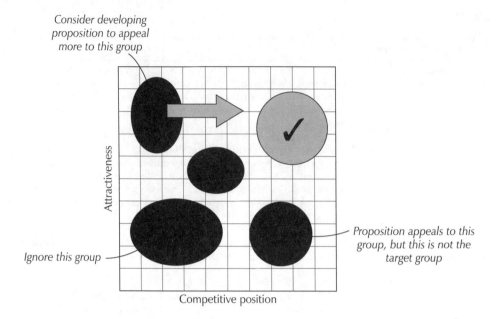

Figure 5.1 Directional policy matrix

product specification, invoicing accuracy and flexibility, complaint handling and key account management. The weightings varied by segment.

The next step was to determine the relative 'competitive position' of the company's proposition versus the competition. First, it defined the competition, and in so doing realized that the competitive arena was actually larger than it had thought! Second, in workshops, staff compared each competitor's offering against the ranked segment requirements. This provided the 'x' co-ordinate for the matrix.

This analysis enabled the company to examine its current positioning, that is, whether it had a proposition that attracted the segments it required. It also enabled it to determine future direction, that is:

- What it needed to do to attract other highly attractive segments, and how much this would be likely to cost.
- Whether it should primarily target apparently lower value segments, because no one else was.
- Who were the main competitors it needed to investigate.
- What it needed to do to differentiate itself better in key markets, if a particular market segment was crowded with competitors.
- Whether and how it should refine its acquisition and retention strategies based on the above analyses.

Financial services company: using profitability analysis

A European financial service provider (bank accounts, loans, mortgages, insurance, investments) carried out some relatively simple analysis to look at customer profitability. To do this, the company calculated the current value (CV) and net present value (NPV) from predictable income (for example, from committed revenue streams such as loan and mortgage payments planned) and NPV of less predictable income from cross-selling. It attempted to build in a contribution from the 'recommended' business from that customer, but for this company it proved too unreliable.

It then carried out a decile analysis combining CV and NPV of current customers, using actual and committed income. This showed that 77 per cent of the profit came from 20 per cent of the base. It used the results of some carefully constructed cross-selling tests to develop propensity models. These models were tested and adjusted to be, at worst, 68 per cent predictive. Then, based on these CV and NPV deciles, it plotted where the future value lay. The analysis chart showed that although the top decile had probably achieved its peak (older customers in this case), deciles 2 and 3 had a great deal of potential, with deciles 7 and 8 also containing some potential high-value segments (younger customers, still early on their value curve for this company). This was useful in that it helped it value the customer base, determine retention, development and 'exit encouragement' programmes to create more value, and develop segment profiles usable for acquisition, retention and development planning.

An analysis of retention behaviour of the investment value/needs segments (see Figure 5.2) showed that the company had a problem with its proposition to specific value/needs cells. The attrition of customers in high-value deciles within the 'facilities management' speculator group (a group that likes to speculate in financial markets, but wants a company to do all the work) appeared high. Research of these value/needs groups implied that the company's direct sales force needed specific competency development, and that laptop PCs, giving up-to-date portfolio information, should be used face to face with clients.

	Active sophisticated	FM'ed speculator	Liquid but cautious
	5%	10%	4%
	7%	15%	6%
	10%	12%	8%
	15%	19%	11%

Figure 5.2   Attrition (illustrated)/satisfaction by value/needs segment

Application of this knowledge has clearly created value for the company, as can be measured via the database. Possibly more importantly, this work led to a step-change in the understanding this company has of how to manage customers.

Consumer durables company: REAP planning framework

The company had carried out a CMAT assessment and wanted a framework for developing its required objectives and measures. It focused on the REAP concept and developed the framework shown here.

The mission and strategic levels were developed at board level, but each business function and then each individual was responsible for developing their own REAP objectives and measures (see Figure 5.3).

Financial institution: customer-centred (REAP) planning

A European financial institution applies REAP measures for developing plans for HR, sales, marketing and IT. Some extracts from its 1999/2000 plan (for retention and acquisition) may help show how this type of planning works. Its process for this type of planning is illustrated in Table 5.3 and Table 5.4.

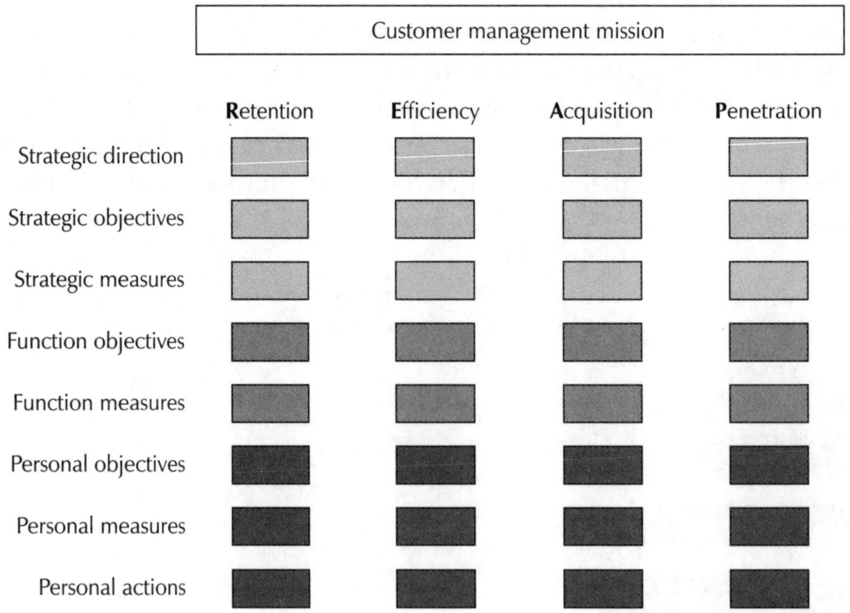

Figure 5.3 REAP planning framework

Table 5.3   REAP planning measures

Customer management mission	We will win and retain our chosen customers through the unbeatable value of the products we sell and the intimate ownership experience we provide.
Strategic direction (retention)	We will seek to understand the repurchase behaviour and motivations of our customers in great detail and use this to build effective programmes to retain all but the lowest value customers. We will be clear on what information we are going to collect and how we are going to use it to deliver an intimate relationship with those customers who want it. All our communication with customers will seek to build on previous contacts and demonstrate our 'one view' of all customers irrespective of where they choose to engage with us.
Strategic objective	Differentiate the level of intimacy applied to customers based on their current and future value.
Strategic measure	Different perceptions of the level of intimacy provided by the organization from customers of different values.
Functional objective (IT function)	Deliver automated cross-selling and prompts that relate to stored customer segment.
Functional measure	Percentage of calls where cross-sell offered is relevant to individual customer calling.
Personal objective (call centre agent)	Improve the caller's perception of yourself and the organization by using the most relevant information available to enhance the contact experience.
Personal measure	Percentage of calls where the system-prompted cross-sell message was delivered to the customer.
Personal action	Put large note on PC screen to remind me about mentioning the last contact that we had with each caller early in each call.

The real plan had five similar entries for retention, three for acquisition and penetration, and six for efficiency. This method of planning can lead to a very customer-centric approach to the work of all departments. Careful choice of KPIs provides clear improvement benchmarks.

BP Amoco Chemicals: sharing customer knowledge

BP Amoco Chemicals account managers were justifiably proud of how closely they got to know their customers and the depth of information they acquired. However, much of this information was in the form of high-value but unstructured 'nuggets'. These knowledge nuggets often related to accounts other than their own and there was a sense of frustration at not being able to 'log' this knowledge and share it with the other account teams who might find it useful. The solution was to extend their customer database system to enable unstructured pieces of information to be entered quickly and easily into

Table 5.4   Customer-centred (REAP) planning measures

People/HR	Data/IT	Policy/process	Communication	KPIs	Retention
Define competencies & knowledge required. Carry out competency gap analysis of inbound agents and improve training of inbound employees.	Ensure the customer product and claim data, and technical advice guides, are available to inbound online. Introduce 'case management' of enquiries, with performance reporting and escalation procedures.	Define process for handling this type of enquiry. Define process standards and KPIs with customer group. Monitor early performance thoroughly, and then case samples.	Carry out internal procedure through IMPROVE process. Add article to newsletter informing customers of our investment and improvement in this area.	Loss %. Satisfaction (process) %. Service standards to be defined.	Customer loss analysis shows that frustrations build because of lack of good and speedy advice during technical enquiries.
					Acquisition
Improve agents knowledge of: independent industry ranking of our products; relative strengths and weaknesses of competitor offerings.	Ensure data (propensity score and LTV field) and functionality (models) can be recorded.	Introduce simple propensity and LTV models to enable pre-scoring. Improve enquiry management process to identify high LTV enquirers. Improve process for high LTV follow-up. Introduce allowable cost of sale as a technique in acquisition.		Acquisition value. Acquisition quality %. Cost per sale. Conversion of top 20% enquirers.	Analysis shows current activity is converting a high % of low LTV (even loss making) prospects. Low conversion for higher LTV enquiries (reasons for non-conversion identified).

a central knowledge store. Each nugget had an entry in the central knowledge store but could also be 'pushed' to individual users or account teams as business highlights.

As well as being populated by the account teams, a central resource was established to scan various industry sources and publications and populate the knowledge base from these. This increased the value to the account teams still further. Account team members who knew they were going to have contact with customers used the knowledge or intelligence. It was also used centrally to look for new or interesting trends in the information being collected.

The research shows that many basic analysis and planning activities are not being done, and without this companies cannot know which customers they should be focusing on and develop appropriate propositions for each customer segment.

6

Proposition

Neil Woodcock, Michael Starkey and Merlin Stone

Disney's theme parks have a great proposition. The whole experience is compelling. Apparently, Disney insisted that each area of the park should have at its centre a magnetic attraction: the 'come to me', because its role was to beckon to customers. For most companies, the 'come to me' or proposition is weak. Just as with CM as a whole, intention and reality differ greatly. Indeed, articulation of the underlying values of the business, like so many mission statements, tends to get no further than the entrance hall or elevator wall, usually nicely framed. Rarely is there a lasting impact on how a business is run or on how it delivers service to its customers.

Buyers experience the lack of clear proposition every day. They are asked to buy too many poorly differentiated, me-too products. The proposition presented by the same company may vary across different channels. Companies' brand promises (for example, 'we value all our customers') are often not delivered through service in the retail outlet or on the Web. A regular, high-value customer of a credit card company who forgets to pay once may be treated in a rude manner. All these examples are due to poorly developed and/or delivered propositions. The scores in Table 6.1 reflect this.

CHARACTERISTICS OF THE HIGHEST-PERFORMING COMPANIES

The following recommendations are derived from analysis of how high-scoring companies manage their propositions:

- Develop clear differentiated propositions aimed at those customers you want to manage.

Table 6.1 The proposition

% scores	Period 1	Period 2	Whether value being created or destroyed
The proposition	30	27	Some destroying of value
Developing the proposition	33	30	Some destroying of value
Communicating the proposition	33	29	Value being destroyed

▊ Determine how you can build loyalty amongst key value groups.
▊ Translate the proposition from high-level brand values to simple statements that can be used to influence the behaviour of people who manage customers. A proposition is meaningless unless it can be delivered. In fact, an undelivered promise is worse than no promise at all: customers will feel let down.
▊ Communicate the proposition well to employees, partners and customers.
▊ Measure the behaviour and attitude change resulting from improved communication of the proposition.

EXAMPLES OF BEST PRACTICES

Financial services company: proposition development

Figure 6.1 shows the approach adopted by this financial services company in developing its customer propositions. All product managers have to adhere to this approach when launching a new product. There are milestone deliverables to demonstrate that each step has been completed. In all cases a clear set of prerequisites for the process must be determined.

A market strategy is required. This needs to define the market or markets being addressed and take into account other products the organization has that also address the markets. A product strategy is required, including the product lifecycle and the financial expectations for the product. A brand 'check' is also required to ensure consistency with overall brand messages and personality.

The 'what's important' phase requires qualitative research to be carried out to facilitate understanding of the wants and needs of the potential customers for the new product, including questions about every potential element of the proposition, from price and service standards to market channels. These findings are then formally mapped against a set of strengths and weaknesses for the new product, which has been independently developed by the product manager.

Table 6.2 Selected facts and figures from research

Developing the proposition	
9% DO involve all proposition stakeholders in its development	Fewer than 1 in 10 companies involve all the providers of the proposition (eg sales channels, service, technical support, product development, administration) in defining their proposition. No wonder so many propositions are undelivered – they are probably undeliverable because functions involved in delivery have never been consulted!
54% DO NOT have a clearly defined proposition	Less than half of companies researched actually define any proposition with *standards* that can be used to measure that the proposition is being delivered. The challenge is to translate the proposition into something that is REALLY understood by everyone (to help guide values, beliefs and behaviour) and then to ensure that these become embedded in the norms of the organization.
24% DO carry out needs research on customers and prospects	Only a quarter of organizations carry out true NEEDS research among either customers or prospects. Many more carry out other types of research but this does not reveal customers' underlying needs. It often focuses on views about the current or future product range.
9% DO carry out needs research by segment	Many propositions are developed which are simply irrelevant to high-value customers. Only about 1 in 10 carry out needs-based research by segment. **War story: irrelevant proposition** Rail companies often report their performance in stations using posters. A regional UK railway did this, but the elements that they chose to focus on, illustrated with large wall posters in the station, included factors such as 'temperature of carriage' and 'comfort of seats'. They did cover punctuality but ignored the other factors that were most important to customers, such as reliability, availability of seats, keeping customers informed, and cleanliness of trains. It will come as no surprise that they scored highly on most of the things they reported on! These last few points suggest that many companies do not recognize the determinants of customer repeat purchase (ie not just 'the brand' or television or marketing messages, or the loyalty scheme, but each and every experience with the brand). Some companies are simply confused about this whole area. Apart from consumer goods companies, there is limited recognition of the role of emotional loyalty as a input to proposition development.
Communicating the proposition	
36% DO NOT formally check that customers and prospects understand their proposition	The most successful companies focus on keeping the proposition in the minds of their customers and staff. Just over a third of organizations do not check that either their customers or their own staff fully understand their proposition. This usually means identifying measures that are easily understood and monitored, but that also reflect the key dimensions of the proposition. It also means always tying reward and recognition (not necessarily financial) mechanics to proposition measures.
17% DO NOT check that customer-facing staff understand their proposition	It is no wonder that various studies have shown that a high proportion of complaints are caused by a mismatch between what customers think they are entitled to and what the organization thinks it is providing. Actual service or product failures account for far fewer complaints. **War story: separate propositions within same company** One utility organization that was assessed had four separate market channels: sales force, call centre, direct mail and a Web site. Each channel had a source of support information on the proposition, and although managers tried to keep these synchronized, there were invariably differences. It was possible for prospects to get different versions of service entitlement and price from the four different channels, even though this was NOT the company policy.

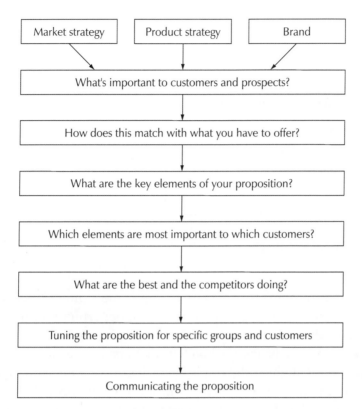

Figure 6.1 Developing the customer proposition

The main elements of the proposition are then identified. A decision is then made on whether to go for a segmented or 'vanilla' (appeals to everyone) proposition, and investigation takes place into competitors' propositions in the target segments or the whole market. The segment or market propositions are finalized and translated into briefs for internal and external communication activity, as well as being fed into the final stages of the development of the product itself.

Foods company: using emotional loyalty drivers to improve proposition and ROI efficiencies

A North American company identified the impact of building emotional loyalty on business performance via an approach that analysed category usage (high-value focus) against levels of emotional loyalty (see classifications in Figure 6.2). This analysis exploited a worldwide consumer equity study[1] and yielded new insights into the importance of focusing on emotional and not just behavioural loyalty.

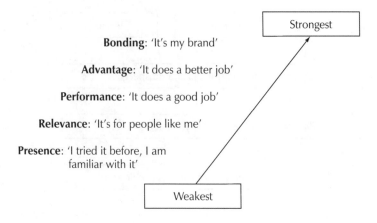

Figure 6.2 Emotional loyalty classifications

The analysis assessed a number of sectors in which the manufacturer was a leading player. The results shown here clearly illustrate the opportunity in the confectionery sector: that a high-value customer who is emotionally bonded is worth 11 times more than an average customer who has not bonded emotionally (see Figure 6.3).

The analysis also highlighted the challenge facing the manufacturer's brand. Sixty-three per cent of its market advantage over its major competitor could be attributed to its high-value emotionally bonded customers (see Figure 6.4), so it needed to identify those customers and focus investment on them.

As a result of this analysis the company revisited its segmentation strategy, focusing on emotional loyalty as opposed to value and behavioural loyalty. It began to consider the emotional drivers and added a new dimension to its segmentation approach. This new approach not only yielded significant efficiencies in targeting (analysis and planning), but also ensured that propositions are now developed to appeal to

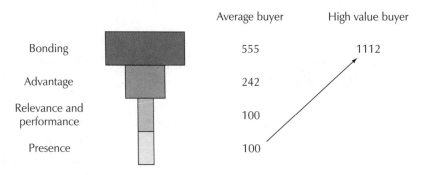

Figure 6.3 Indexed value of an emotionally bonded consumer: candy bars, North America

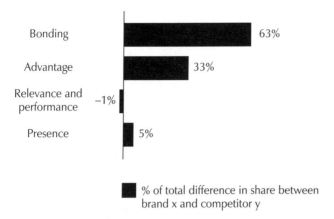

Figure 6.4 Impact of emotional loyalty on the difference in market share between Brand X and its major competitor: confectionery, North America

emotionally loyal customers. The company also identified the important impact of 'moments of truth' on emotional loyalty and plans to go on to qualify and quantify that impact over time.

Retail fast food outlet: proposition: a case study of living and measuring business values

The McDonald's fast food chain has translated its proposition into a set of business values, which are used to drive the entire global business. The founding fathers of the company set out four key values of the business and communicated them to all staff: quality, service, cleanliness and value. These described the basic company proposition. Objective descriptions of these dimensions were developed and these were tracked and monitored by area/regional managers who regularly measured each outlet against these dimensions. Performance against these measures formed a key component of staff remuneration, so these dimensions were not only in the front of their employees' minds as operational measures, but the impact on personal remuneration meant that they were considered to be really important by individual staff.

What was so simple, but effective, was that each dimension constituted an important part of the basic proposition.

▓ *Quality* measures compliance against core operating and product standards (particularly helpful in a franchised business). All staff in 'meal assembly' at the back of house have in front of them a picture and a detailed description of how each product should be presented. This is often shown in terms of 'too little pickle, too much pickle, just right' so all staff are clear about what needs to be done to achieve compliance. In staff briefings to launch new products, it is explained to staff why these dimensions are important and how these make the product different from competitors'. In marketing parlance, this means that product differentiation is understood and regularly maintained and measured at the customer interface. Product consistency is key to the company's basic proposition, 'Wherever you buy your fast food you know you'll get a consistent product'.

▌ *Service* measures delivery of detailed operational standards. Again, the company specified the service to be delivered in detailed operational manuals. Each franchise operator has to undergo detailed training in how to handle and motivate staff, queue length, how staff should greet and offer cross-sell/up-sell to customers and so on.

▌ *Cleanliness* measures how effectively product and service standards are being met. Observational standards cover staff cleanliness (hands, hair and clothing), how often table surfaces and floors are cleaned, and other aspects of front of house presentation. All these can be monitored and the company can track how well the outlet is delivering this part of the proposition. A benefit of the company's offer is, 'No matter where the outlet is, you can rely on knowing what food to expect and on getting it in clean surroundings'.

▌ *Value* measures how competitive the products are in their local markets. Many regional and area managers are trained to use a range of local interventions such as promotional and pricing offers to respond to competitors' offers and keep the McDonald's offer perceived as 'good value' in each of its markets. This has the added benefit of directing the corporate marketing budget to support local pricing incentives where they will have greatest impact. It also allows the company to maintain a higher price premium, discounting only where necessary.

Outlet managers expect to be monitored against these dimensions. and the area/region manager completes a checklist of them against a graduated scale. (A characteristic of good measurement systems is that they enable monitoring of movements in delivery, rather than simplistic yes/no responses.) The location manager must sign off this checklist before it is filed in the regional office. Improvement activities are focused on where performance is deteriorating. Here again, area managers may suggest interventions as they are trained in intervention diagnostics.

Another benefit from such a widespread and consistent measurement system is that it enables good practice to be identified. The service and product specification manuals are now built upon good practice in delivering high performance. It also means that all locations are measured against best practice next time they are inspected, so continually stretching business performance.

The measures work at several levels, with performance aggregated and reported at area, region and country level. Improvements form the basis of regular performance reviews between each manager and his or her superior. These measures work at every level of the business, and are aggregated into an overall performance measure presented at each Executive Board meeting.

This case study highlights what a company needs to do to translate its proposition into values that drive the business, and to ensure that these values are supported by measures that are understood and tracked at each level of the business. It is not enough just to articulate values. They must be translated into pervasive measures and staff incentives which work at all levels of the business, to ensure that they drive values, beliefs and behaviours. The company says that it knew this approach was working when the 'war stories' shared when their people met socially related to these values.

Gas company: proposition target helps plan communication messages

This gas company was developing a formal proposition framework for all its European businesses. It faced two challenges. First, the proposition needed to be tailored for different markets in different countries. Second, it needed to be communicated simply but effectively to the staff who would deliver it. The approach was to develop a central set of elements to the proposition and to define the basic European offer and quality standards for these elements. They included pricing, ordering, delivery, product quality and invoicing. Each separate European business could then tailor the core elements based on a 'shopping list' of tailored elements, again with Europe-wide quality standards. Each business was then encouraged to develop market-specific, value-added additions to the centrally defined proposition elements. The businesses then built communication messages around these value-added elements to form the basis of communication plans. The device used in each country to communicate all the elements of the proposition was a target (see Figure 6.5). This fitted well with the highly targeted nature of the business culture and with a very successful safety campaign called 'Target zero accidents'.

NOTE

[1] The Ogilvy Loyalty Index is Ogilvy One's proprietary analysis tool which analyses the value of building emotional loyalty for all markets (28), categories (70) and Brands (10,000) in the BRANDZ™ database. BRANDZ™ is a global Millward Brown Brand equity study, sponsored by the WPP group.

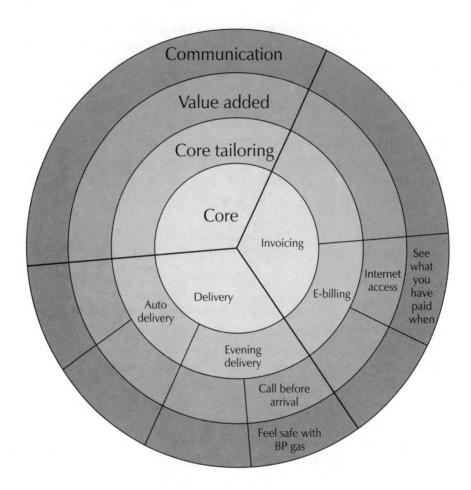

Figure 6.5 Gas company: proposition target helps plan communication messages

7

Customer management activity

Neil Woodcock, Michael Starkey and Merlin Stone

As Table 7.1 shows, there is little change in this section. However this section is one of the most important of all as it measures how customers are actually being managed on a day-to-day basis. 'Getting to know' and 'Winback' are the two areas where value is being destroyed. Getting to know is an area where a clear strategy has to be defined to collect defined data and capture it on systems, over time and across channels. The value of this data will not usually be apparent until a year or two after collection. Is the short-term focus of businesses one of the reasons why performance in this area is worsening? Best performing companies are stronger in this area.

We are not sure why Winback performance has decreased from an already low level. All companies assessed that running Winback campaigns (including those that only started after we assessed them!) get excellent paybacks on these campaigns, and some receive their best campaign return on investment (ROI) with this activity! Are companies embarrassed about going back to former customers?

Table 7.1 Customer management activity

% Score	**Period 1**	**Period 2**	**Whether value is being created or destroyed**
Customer Management Activity	33	32	No real change
Targeting	30	30	No real change
Enquiry management	40	40	No real change
Welcoming	29	30	No real change
Getting to know / healthcheck	25	21	Value being destroyed
Ongoing management	28	30	Some creation of value
Managing dissatisfaction	42	40	Some destroying of value
Winback	21	9	Value being destroyed

Table 7.2 Where value is being created

Overall	A critical characteristic of best-performing companies is the practicality of their plans, and how they apply the principles of customer acquisition, retention and development.
Acquisition: ▌ targeting ▌ enquiry ▌ winback	Develop and measure effective enquiry management processes through every channel (welcome, capture, qualify, fulfil, follow-up and close). Develop winback programmes for selected former customers.
Early retention: ▌ welcoming ▌ getting to know	Provide thanks, as courtesy and reinforcement of purchasing decision. Ensure early relationship service management works. This can be done by providing a *priority* service for early dialogue. Monitor early transactions. Build an understanding of customers, how they want to be managed and what their potential may be.

Repeat purchase:
▌ ongoing
  management
 	
▌ managing
  dissatisfaction
	Let customers service (manage) themselves, but enable them to obtain personal service when they want it.
	Attempt to predict defections from customer feedback and contact analysis.
	Contact high value groups regularly.
	Manage key accounts actively (plans, aligned team, recognition).
	Manage dissatisfaction well.
	Encourage a no-blame culture throughout the organization.
	Do not underestimate the value of good customer service. In these days of choice and confidence to change, service experience is key.

Companies have improved their ongoing management of customers. The very strong focus of financial services and some other companies on retention and customer development is likely to be the reason for this. Also, more self-service (primarily via Web), more outbound contact strategies and an increasing recognition of the role of support staff in the customer experience are apparent across sectors.

Performance in managing dissatisfaction has slightly decreased. This is because many of the companies we have assessed are struggling with managing customers through several channels and are not able to cope with the increased complexity of contact at this stage, and the increasing volume of customer contacts.

WHERE VALUE IS BEING CREATED (EXTRACTED FROM HIGHEST-PERFORMING COMPANIES)

There are several areas where high-performing companies score better than others.

EXAMPLES OF BEST PRACTICES

Telecomms company: inbound enquiry handling framework

A European telecommunications company deals with hundreds of thousands of inbound campaign response calls each day. When it started planning a new call handling system to deal with most of these calls, it needed clear principles on the flow of an enquiry call (see Figure 7.1). It wanted consistency in the 'feel' of the calls handled by different call centres and to reflect its new brand values, listening and receptiveness. The call shape shown was developed and is still used as a reference point when designing call handling systems and scripts.

Open	Introduction of call handler by name and offer of assistance.

Demonstrate knowledge	Identify the caller and locate the record on the customer/prospect database whenever necessary. Demonstrate knowledge of caller by using information on the database (eg details of last contact).

Initial requirement	Identify and deal with prime reason for customer's call.

Campaign information	Seek campaign-related information such as promotion code or qualification information.

Further assistance	Offer assistance with anything else that the customer wants, emphasizing the breadth of enquiries that can be dealt with.

Cross-sell	Look for (often system-prompted) cross-sell opportunities based on information known about the customer.

Update information	Look for missing or expired information on the customer and update/validate.

Confirm action	Confirm all actions promised and timescales.

Close	Thanks for call.

Figure 7.1   Telecomms company: inbound enquiry handling framework

Table 7.3 Selected facts and figures from research

Acquisition: targeting, enquiry management, through to winback	
4% DO target new customers based on predicted lifetime value	Acquisition of new customers clearly has a long way to go. Only 1 in 20 companies with a database target prospects using 'allowable cost' based on lifetime value (that is, it has a target acquisition cost). Only 2% use any form of trigger (eg date, transaction, event) to prompt them to target prospects (this % is much higher for customers). Large-scale, untargeted campaigns are still the norm.
2% DO use trigger-based targeting to prospects	**War story: good targeting/poor service coinciding** A Range Rover owner visited her usual dealership to enquire about a new model and trade-in price for her current vehicle. She received an uninterested response. She called a few weeks later, because she had heard nothing from the dealership, and her phone call was put on hold for several minutes. She put the phone down and rang back, telling the receptionist what had happened and asking her to get the salesperson to call her back. She received a call more than a week later. Unfortunately for Range Rover, she had received a mailing from BMW about their X5 model, which she had already admired from afar. She had organized and been on a test drive in the week leading up to the Range Rover salesman's call. She had made the decision to buy the BMW, and had pleasure telling the Range Rover salesman just that! This is an example of how poor enquiry management and well-targeted competitive marketing coincide to change behaviour, a common combination and result.
40% DO have a defined enquiry management process	60% of companies do not have a measurable enquiry management process! Enquiry management throughout the world still performs poorly, whether the enquiry is on paper, via retail as in the example above, via the telephone or via Web. Recent research from the Hewson Consulting Group reveals that companies are slowly improving their management of online enquiries, although our research shows that only one in four companies handles Web enquires as well as it does telephone enquiries. Companies generating larger volumes of enquiries perform worse than those generating small numbers of enquiries, even when the percentage of valuable enquiries is similar. Just over half do not bother to identify opportunities to cross-sell on an inbound enquiry telephone call. Value can easily be created or destroyed with inbound calls. All leads cost money to generate, and poor lead management is another example of the ways companies are destroying value.
52% DO NOT actively cross-sell to inbound telephone enquirers	There can be problems when parties outside the call centre are involved, eg sales person, field marketer, agent or dealer. The feedback loop – passing the enquiry out to the third party, ensuring he or she receives it and actions it, and getting feedback for analysis – often presents a problem. Practical, simple systems can help here.
25% DO handle Web site enquiries as effectively as telephone enquiries	**War story: enquiry management** The dealers of a particular motor manufacturer took the concept of customer *ownership* to the extreme. Most had a clear ruling that once a prospective customer had established any form of contact with a salesperson, even if just to phone up to ask directions to the dealership, he or she was the 'property' of that salesperson. People walking into the dealership were asked whether they had spoken to a salesperson before. If they had, they had to wait for that salesperson to become free, even if other salespeople were available or were making cold prospecting telephone calls!

Table 7.3   (cont)

46% HAVE NEVER run formal Winback programmes and less than 1 in 20 do it regularly	Winback is a huge 'lost opportunity' in general and is consistently overlooked. Most companies still do not embrace winback programmes, even though our analysis shows that winback activities are normally very productive. **War story: winback** A financial services company frequently bought lists of names to use for outbound calling to set appointments for their sales people. It provided the names of current customers (but not lost customers) to the list provider to avoid buying names of existing customers. After a CMAT assessment, the company created a file of lapsed customers. It compared this to the 3,000 new customers it had gained over recent campaigns and found that 67% of the list had been customers in the past, with transaction records and (in some cases) with promotional consents already in place.

Early retention: welcoming, getting to know

6% DO have different welcoming strategies for different types of customer 26% say thank you to a new customer	Credit card companies perform well here and may spend up to 15% of their marketing budget on various welcoming treatments. However, just over 1 in 20 companies have different types of welcoming approach for different types of new customer. Even 'thank you' letters are rare – stunningly, just over a quarter of companies bother! Best practice here involves different welcome processes targeted at customers of different value. Also, best-performing companies monitor early customer behaviours so that they can ensure the relationship begins in the way it should continue.
15% DO have an information capture strategy for getting to know	There is weaker performance in *getting to know* customers even though 'getting to know' is already a low-scoring section. Only 15% of organizations have a strategy covering which information to capture for prospects and customers. Typically it is up to systems designers and campaign owners to decide what will fit on a screen. We estimate that less than half the information collected on customers is the right information, and that less than a quarter of information collected is ever used to improve the management of customers. Getting to know involves asking customers *clearly defined questions* about how they want to be managed (eg what information they want, what interests they have, which channel they want to be managed by, how often they want to be contacted), what their potential value might be, and what business they are doing with competitors. This information-gathering can be carried out across channels and over time (over a number of transactions).

Repeat purchase: ongoing management, managing dissatisfaction

48% WOULD NOT recognize a 'key' customer at every contact point	The principle of key account management is still not embraced in many companies. The exceptions are large high-technology or industrial product companies. Key account management can apply in varying degrees to many companies, in both B2B and B2C markets. Key accounts are often so valuable that they require (and sometimes demand) special investment and treatment. In most companies, key accounts are not recognized across all contact points.
17% DO communicate the account objectives for key customers	The idea of shared objectives across account teams is still only a concept for more than two-thirds of companies.

Table 7.3 (cont)

11% have a customer contact strategy that can be applied via database	More companies have an outbound contact strategy aimed at different groups of customers than in our last research period. Self-service is also on the increase.
52% DO NOT actively cross-sell to inbound telephone enquirers	Cross-selling is carried out for outbound activity rather than for RELEVANT inbound contacts in 8 out of 10 companies. One financial service company in Europe netted (eg after costs) a €5 million NPV from the first 12 months' activity by using branch-based system prompts.
6% USE triggers to predict defection	Less than 10% of companies attempt to predict defections, by using triggers such as 'second price enquiry in a week'; 'inactive account for 3 months', or 'normally orders every month, hasn't ordered for 6 weeks'.
	War story: ongoing management Mercedes-Benz was intrigued by the very different levels of satisfaction in the German and US markets. They looked into two call centres. They uncovered very different call handling. Both handled calls from women who had broken down on the way to pick up a child from school. In the German centre the call handler went through the process efficiently, firstly trying to qualify and isolate the problem to see if the problem could be rectified immediately before efficiently organizing a recovery vehicle as quickly as possible. In the US situation the first thing the call handler said was, 'Which school is your daughter at so that we can call and let them and your daughter know that you are delayed?' Management of dissatisfaction scores relatively highly but is still very focused on formal complaints rather than predicting and preempting dissatisfaction. Some companies have changed the way they see complaints, from negative to a positive input to service performance.
30% DO NOT check customer satisfaction after a complaint	**War story: ongoing management** A telecommunications company ran various high-cost and high-prestige customer events including golf, shooting and theatre visits. It decided to analyse the people who were invited to these events and, without telling the sales force the reasons for the question, asked them to score all the customers in terms of likelihood to defect. Virtually all the customers who had been invited to the next event had been classified as 'very unlikely' to defect. Other customers, classed as 'very likely' to defect, were not invited as they were considered 'a bit sensitive'.

Technology company: Web-based sales lead system

This company runs a lot of promotional activity and generated large numbers of sales enquiries. It has many sales channels with complex rules about which salesperson in which channel should receive which leads. It could not be sure which enquiries had been received and followed up, and it also needed to improve greatly reporting of the results of sales leads, so it used its intranet to host a Web-based sales lead system. The system allocated leads to the correct sales channel and person or outlet. It alerted recipients to new leads, and if they did not indicate that they had received the lead then it was 'repatriated' and reissued to another salesperson or outlet. The system also provides real-time monitoring and measurement of the performance of sales channels in following up leads, and of campaigns in generating leads that resulted in sales.

UK financial services company: monitoring welcoming

This regional financial institution marketed bank accounts, investments, savings, insurances, loans and mortgages. Its bank accounts were taken out by mortgage and savings account holders to support their 'main' product, and the bank account product line appeared buoyant. However, its customers normally had another account, from one of the 'mainline' banks, which they used for the majority of their financial transactions. So the profitability of its bank account business was low. It needed to make its chequebook and bank card 'front of wallet'. One programme it implemented was a 'welcoming programme' for bank account holders. This had two objectives. One was to inform customers about the advantages (for example, interest rates) of the product. The other was to monitor transactions over the first three months of the account and tailor different communication treatments to groups, depending on activity, to stimulate usage. This welcoming stage aimed to establish behaviours and attitudes before customers drifted into making the mental decision to keep this account 'back of wallet'. The programme was extremely successful, and more successful than other treatments designed to stimulate increased usage of the bank account later in the customer lifecycle.

Global chemicals company: key account planning

Figure 7.2 illustrates the dynamic account planning approach taken by this chemicals company when it wanted to standardize the way planning was conducted in each of its European business units. It did not want to implement a resource-intensive key account planning methodology but did want to achieve a change in the way of working. It also wanted an approach that encouraged input and involvement from as wide an account team as possible. Each step in the approach had clear descriptions of the scope but left the 'how' largely to the account managers. The approach was also an input to the development of technology support for an Account Management Excellence programme of which this approach was a part. As a result the system was closely aligned with approach.

On-line retailer: role of e-service

This company sold a range of durables, mainly in the IT area, to consumers and businesses primarily through the Web. The early success of the company was encouraging, but profit figures began to slip, even though costs were being reduced and hit rates maintained. The dip in sales was put down to increasing competition and an increasing abandoned rate for the online shopping carts. The company was smart enough not to react by reducing prices,

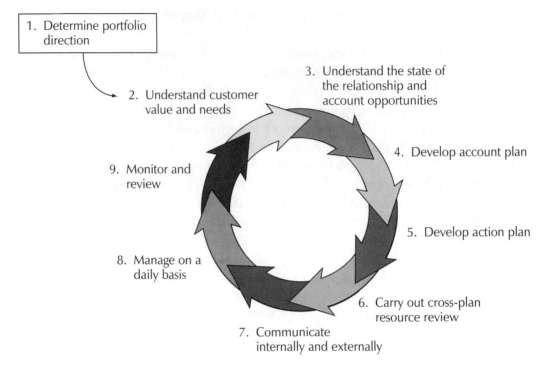

Figure 7.2 Chemicals company: dynamic account planning

but to look closely at its proposition, and why customers were (and were not) buying online. It realized that convenience, not price, was the main purchase driver among customers who purchased online. More than 50 per cent of its customers said that they purchased products on the net solely for convenience, and only 8 per cent said solely on price.

About 79 per cent of online shopping carts are abandoned before the checkout, more than the 65 per cent the company estimated to be the industry average. Its research showed that the reason for the abandoned carts could be traced partly to time pressures for customers and technical problems (for example, hung line), but mainly because of the complexity of the site and the passive nature of the shopping experience. Its research showed that customers liked the convenience of online but that they also liked catalogue shopping by telephone because it allowed a dialogue, some human feeling, advice, and specific answers to vague questions. They knew that retail-based face-to-face transactions for the same category of goods can lead to a better experience and three or four times the basket size revenue.

So the company adjusted its proposition around these findings. It integrated contact media, mail (catalogue, incentives, prompts to use), telephone (direct line, call me button and outbound order reminders to valuable customers, with their permission) and a redesigned Web site, which majored on the need for convenience, simplicity and relia-bility. Prices were gradually increased and although some price-based customers were no doubt lost, repeat purchasing by remaining customers has increased dramatically. It also utilized its greater customer understanding to develop simple cross-sell and up-sell rules, via the Web and the telephone, to create further value.

Hyundai: segmented customer magazine

Hyundai wanted a two-way dialogue with its customers, to find out what their new car needs might be and to feed this information to dealers to help deliver on this. For most motor manufacturers a magazine is an important element of the contact strategy for both prospects and existing customers. It featured articles on lifestyles and 'brand aligned' activities and enabled the company to gather information on customers (by enclosing questionnaires). In developing *Etcetera*, Hyundai's customer retention team took into account the effect of the widening product offering, including the sporty Coupe, on the changing make-up and interests of its target audience. It divided Hyundai customers into four segments, derived from behavioural and attitudinal analysis, data from satis-faction questionnaires, plus profiling. Hyundai and its publishers then developed four different versions of each issue of *Etcetera* to provide content relevant to the interests of people in these segments. As a rule 60 per cent of content is generic and 40 per cent plus a dedicated front cover is tailored by segment.

Six issues a year are now mailed to 110,000 customers under a personalized cover letter from each dealership's principal. Within the first year of launch the magazine generated 37,000 customer contacts via competitions, a feedback panel and the letters page (comments from which are fed directly into the Hyundai customer care programme). Any response generated by the magazine is followed up with an indi-vidual response by letter, e-mail or phone either by the magazine publishers or a Hyundai employee.

Manufacturing company: active complaint targeting

This large manufacturing company had four plants in the UK. The customer service manager at each plant was targeted with a maximum level of complaints for each month. The intention was to motivate staff in the plants to improve quality and customer satis-faction. The result was that plants simply stopped accepting complaints part-way through the month, when they had reached their target. Any approaches from customers after this time were called 'deviations' or 'incidents' but not complaints. This prevented them having to go through the formal complaints process and ensured that targets were always met. It became obvious that the real level of complaints was much higher than reported. It was also obvious that falling customer satisfaction levels were inconsistent with steady complaint levels. The organization completely changed its complaint targeting approach, removing the maximum target and effectively rewarding plant service managers for the number of complaints well handled. This dramatically increased complaints, which levelled out at double their previous level. Perhaps paradoxically, customer satisfaction rose sharply in line with the increasing complaint levels. Further analysis showed that no other major factor could have caused this improved satisfaction. It also showed that the satisfaction had previously been held down by a reputation that the organization had for being incredibly variable in the quality of complaint and issue handling.

The research shows that having acquired a customer, companies are neglecting to get to know them, which must have a detrimental effect on customer value. Furthermore, Winback is an area where companies have an opportunity to make a real impact, but focus in this area has declined.

NOTE

[1] Hewson Consulting Group (2001) [accessed 9 August 2002] *UK Scores on the On-line Doors: Results from HCG on-line survey* (May) [Online] http://www.hewson.co.uk/sistrum/crm management insights/stream7.htm.

8

People and organization

Neil Woodcock, Michael Starkey and Merlin Stone

The correlation between People and Organization and overall business performance is the highest for the whole of the CMAT model. This section continues to score well (see Table 8.1) and companies are clearly maintaining a focus on the role of people and organization in managing customers. Interestingly, there are signs that high scores in this area are correlated with low scores in the systems and process areas. Does this show that good people work hard to make up for deficiencies in processes and systems? Arguably, perhaps people with a strong customer management (CM) orientation – whether managers or customer-facing staff – enjoy a situation in which they are able to use their own skills and knowledge to manage customers, rather than relying on the more formal approach likely to be dictated by systems and processes. The corollary is that, perhaps, over-systemizing customer service has a negative effect on staff and reduces the quality of customer interaction and service.

Interestingly, the area where most value is being destroyed is in a section we call 'Creating the organization'. A fall in creating value can be attributed to falling organizational support for implementing customer strategies, customer management ownership

Table 8.1 People and organization

% score	Period 1	Period 2	Whether value is being created or destroyed
People and Organization	40	39	No real change
Creating the organization	43	38	Value being destroyed
Managing your people	40	38	Some destroying of value
Managing suppliers	38	40	Some creation of value

and, most alarmingly, a lack of senior management leadership. We believe this is primarily a reflection of cautionary or recession-based management. In this cautious business environment, companies appear to entrench into familiar strategies, become less flexible to change and 'leadership' moves from encouraging customer orientation to encouraging a cost driven productivity orientation. The reduction in CMAT scores could also be due, in part, to companies seeking to do more complex things in the area of CM, and this challenges their organizational structure.

Although organizations talk about how important employees are in delivering service, they do not appear to back this up with actions. For instance, recognition and reward structures rarely encourage staff to manage customers better. Training rarely covers CM competencies, except for those staff whose job is 100 per cent CM, for example, in call centres. Recruitment suffers from the same problem of a lack of competency recognition (knowledge, skill and attitude).

Performance in managing suppliers has increased. As organizations focus on their core competencies, partner with third parties, or outsource services, more third-party suppliers have become involved in CM. The scores show that companies have improved competencies in the way these suppliers are managed.

CHARACTERISTICS OF THE HIGHEST-PERFORMING COMPANIES

Here are some guidelines from best-performing companies for improving CM through people:

▮ Provide CM leadership with authority. Best-performing companies have leaders with clear responsibility, authority, understanding and determination to make good CM a reality in their companies.
▮ Ensure your organization encourages analysis of the customer dimension and decision-making focused on improving CM. Improved techniques for analysis, measurement and knowledge management allow companies to achieve higher-quality decision making in relation to CM. Though not many organizations are able to use these techniques, the ones that can tend to perform best.
▮ Align objectives relevant to CM throughout the organization. If CM plans identify retention, acquisition, penetration and efficiency objectives, these should be communicated to the groups and individuals who can make them happen. Mismatches can occur when CM planning is cross-functional, but objectives are set functionally.
▮ Recruit and develop the right people. The CM competencies of all people who affect the customer experience (this may include people in product development, marketing, sales, service, finance, administration, operations and technical support)

need to be defined. The right people need to be recruited, their competency gaps identified and their competencies developed. In customer-facing roles, some top-performing companies recruit staff based on their attitude to CM, believing that it is easier to develop an individual's knowledge and skills, rather than modify his or her attitude.

▌ Provide the incentives and reward required to encourage desired CM behaviours. In best-performing companies, employees believe that their salary and incentives match their customer management objectives and those of the company. This is a difficult area to get right, and employee groups can help determine it.

▌ Understand employee satisfaction and commitment. CMAT assessors aim to understand whether employees feel that the organization listens to them and reacts appropriately to their issues. There is a clear relationship between staff satisfaction, customer satisfaction and long-term company value.

▌ Manage partners and alliances well. High-performing companies score more highly in the area of supplier management.

EXAMPLES OF BEST PRACTICES

High street retailer: customer management leadership

This international company sold a range of pharmaceuticals and healthcare products, mostly through retail outlets, but also through the Web and its call centre. Its CEO understood the contribution CM could make to the company's value. The CEO appointed a board director to look after customer experience and service (CE&S). He gave her authority to work across all functions in the enterprise to ensure that they did what they needed to do to improve the customer experience for valuable customers. The CE&S Director tackled her job by working with the other directors and heads of departments, looking at all areas of the CMAT model. They developed a prioritized action plan of projects that would create both immediate and longer-term value for the company. The action plan included a variety of small projects in areas such as HR, IT, finance, marketing, sales, service, retail, call centre, Web, product development, and quality teams. Small projects were established, ensuring that results were achieved quickly and visibly, and project energy was maintained. Some of the projects involved quick wins, and this helped engage doubting senior managers.

She encouraged all managers to recognize and reward employee behaviours that were 'customer-positive', as the company called it. Appraisal processes and forms were adapted to reflect this, but it was decided not to introduce financial rewards and incentives. Customer-positive behaviours that were recognized included:

Table 8.2 Selected facts and figures from research

Creating the organization	
38% DO have a board level person with clear Customer Management responsibility	Many organizations now have a board-level executive who owns (and should spend most of his or her time on) CM. The proportion is rising rapidly – it was 20% only two years ago. This rapid rise is apparent because CRM has become a board agenda item and many companies are investing a great deal in it. But why is cross-functional executive leadership still not apparent? Nor formal research has been done on the impact peer pressure and consultants have on senior managers inexperienced in CRM. However, it appears that some are too willing to accept the latest theories and concepts without enough challenge and consideration of the practical implementation aspects. Proof of this can be seen in many of the other statistics presented in this book. **War story: leadership?** A US retail organization was adamant that a board director 'owned' customer management. However, when questioned, he admitted that he relied on others to drive this area. He did not understand that his role was to encourage enterprise-wide focus on customers. His performance objectives made mention of CM, but he admitted he was not appraised on this, or called to task for any failure in CM.
33% provide organizational support for implementing strategies	Organizational structures appear to increasingly hinder speedy decision making in CM. While this may be deliberate, to ensure people think through and formally justify their ideas, staff are often frustrated that they cannot react to market, competitor or customer dynamics quickly enough. Encouraging entrepreneurial thinking and collaborative groups may enable more ownership and faster reaction to market changes.
17% demonstrate consistent senior management leadership	In four out of five companies, managers do not actively and consistently reinforce good customer management behaviour (eg positive re-enforcement for good problem handling, good service, good piece of customer analysis, good measures, clearer customer-focused processes). However, in most companies there are examples of excellent leadership in customer management, so the picture is a patchy and inconsistent one. This illustrates the 'champion' nature of customer management: supportive management is down to individuals and their views on customer management, rather than a company-wide cultural norm.
Managing your people	
11% HAVE formally identified all the staff roles that impact on customer management	Although CM is beginning to be recognized at board level (see above), our research has found that CM is not recognized as a coherent set of skills and competencies to be used by a wide range of staff. CM definitions tend to extend to retail outlets, call centres, customer service and field staff but not as far as logistics, credit control, technical support, problem development, accounts and security.
30% DO NOT have a clear cascade of CM objectives	Impressively, over two-thirds of companies now enable staff to see, at least in part, how their job supports the company's objectives on customer acquisition, retention and value maximization. This helps shape their behaviours. **War story: people competencies may make up for poor customer-centricity** One organization that undertook a CMAT assessment was proud of how customer-friendly and service-oriented its staff were. However, the organization as a whole was not focused on customers in terms of processes, structure and even staff rewards. The staff spent much of their time making up for organizational failings by being customer-oriented as individuals. This increased frustration for customers and employees and reduced efficiency.
14% only HAVE objectives shared across departments	Sharing incentives across channels is still an issue. If a lead comes through the Web or call centre and is passed to a dealer or salesperson for follow-up, this can cause problems unless the contribution of both is recognized (see also Enquiry management in Chapter 7). Some companies find it too hard to tackle this problem and compromise by managing customers within individual channels, with a 'You came through to the call centre and this is where you'll stay, even if you are potentially high value' attitude!

Table 8.2 (cont)

Managing partners and suppliers	
26% DO NOT have a formal vetting process for customer management suppliers	Companies have improved their supplier management – probably because of the increased recognition in business today of the need to manage partners and suppliers who help define and deliver the customer proposition. This being said, just over a quarter do not have a formal vetting process for new suppliers.
39% DO NOT 'encourage' suppliers to buy from them	The reality of managing suppliers in many organizations is expressed by this quote from a senior procurement manager in a European telecomms company: 'I wish we spent as much time and effort selecting suppliers who actually deal with our customers as we do with those who provide us with wooden pallets.'
	Six out of ten companies encourage (a few politely insist) their suppliers to buy product from them.

- suggesting profitable service or promotional ideas;
- suggesting ways to enhance the customer experience through products and channels;
- identifying ways to deliver improved customer experience through people and systems.

Recognition was also given to branch staff who provided exceptional service to customers. They were used to recruit and train others. The overwhelming opinion in the company, confirmed by customer research, is that the company will realise significant additional value from this work.

Manufacturing company: customer management competency framework

Although this company had sophisticated HR processes and procedures, the discipline of CM was not formally recognized. This resulted in a narrow view of CM roles and competencies. This framework illustrated in Table 8.3 was their first attempt to map CM role and competency requirements and thence define a training and development programme for the company's new CRM initiative.

Table 8.3 Customer management competency framework

	Data entry accuracy	Complaint handling	Information analysis	Primary selling	Cross-selling and Up-selling	Creative communication	Managing suppliers	Managing projects	Face-to-face interpersonal skills	Customer persuasion	Information extraction	Opportunity identification	Telephone techniques	Understanding the organization	Understanding the market
Call centre agents	●				●					●	●		●		
Call centre team leaders		●			●					●	●				
Customer service agents	●	●								●		●	●		
Area sales representatives	●			●	●							●			●
Sales managers		●			●	●			●					●	
Key account managers				●	●	●			●					●	
Supply chain managers			●			●		●		●		●			
Technical support agents	●	●								●		●	●		
Dealer managers		●					●		●			●			●
Delivery drivers	●				●				●		●	●			
Credit control team	●		●							●	●	●			
Product managers			●			●		●						●	●
Campaign owners			●			●	●	●							●
Business analysts			●						●			●		●	●
Customer researchers	●								●	●	●		●		
Office receptionists									●	●	●	●		●	
Switchboard operators	●										●	●	●	●	
Board members		●				●			●	●					●
Security guards	●									●		●	●	●	

9

Information and technology

Neil Woodcock, Michael Starkey and Merlin Stone

Despite the continual investment in CRM technology, performance in this area overall is declining noticeably, as Table 9.1 shows. The evidence from the CMAT scores is clear: the overall scores for Information and Technology dropped from 40 per cent to 35 per cent, the biggest drop in any of the eight CMAT sections. Organizations are acquiring increasing quantities of data, from internal and external sources, without being sure what they are going to do with it and how they are going to maintain it. This results in 'data chaos'[1]. Customer trust and loyalty is undoubtedly being eroded through the collection of too much customer information (much of it irrelevant) and poor use of the data. Organizations are also investing heavily in technology without enough investment in managing data. They appear to be struggling to understand the impact and implications of data protection and privacy legislation.

A recent survey of CRM systems shows that overall customer satisfaction ratings[2] for CRM vendors are very low. The survey claims that world-class products and services routinely achieve Customer Satisfaction Index (CSI) scores in the mid-80s and low 90s.

Table 9.1 Information and technology

% score	Period 1	Period 2	Whether value is being created or destroyed
Information and Technology	40	35	Value destroyed
Acquiring customer information	49	43	Value destroyed
Managing customer information	32	28	Value destroyed
Current system functions	32	36	Value created
Developing new systems	52	38	Value destroyed

Good, but not outstanding performers typically generate CSI scores in the high 70s. However, the average CRM software package CSI score in this survey was 63.1. The survey reports 'Scores in the 60s or below are usually "panic-level" scores'. This average does not disguise some high-scoring products. The overall CSI range for all products reviewed was from 58 to 66. Ease of implementation was the most cited issue with CRM software. Most companies appear to be buying blind. However, on the positive side, we see from our research that companies are increasingly making CRM systems available to customer-facing staff and to customers. These systems are highly functional and increasingly relevant to the people that use them.

CHARACTERISTICS OF THE HIGHEST-PERFORMING COMPANIES

Best performing companies have:

▮ Improved data understanding. The requirements of European data protection legislation are forcing European organizations towards a much better understanding of the information they hold and ensuring that data is more accurate than in the past. This has the effect of creating customer databases that are more valuable than in the past.

▮ Increased visibility of customer data (to employees and partners). Customer information is now accessible to more customer-facing staff, and to key partners and intermediaries, than ever before. This is partly because of the possibilities the Internet and intranets open up for wider information sharing. This also leads to better updating of information and a wider understanding as to why data should be captured.

▮ Increased visibility of customer data (to customers). Some organizations make some or all of the customer information that they hold visible and maintainable to customers themselves. This enables those customers to take some control of their relationships and to maintain their own information (usually increasing its accuracy and value). It also reflects a maturity of operation, a willingness to release control, and the trust in customers implicit in this may contribute to the superior performance of companies that tend to do this.

EXAMPLES OF BEST PRACTICES

Motor company: business case for CRM system

A vehicle importer was frustrated by the dry, analytical approach taken in previous business cases, so it took a fresh approach, focused on hearts (Table 9.3) as well as minds (Table 9.4).

Table 9.2 Selected facts and figures from research

37% HAVE robust programmes in place to address data protection compliance 26% HAVE formal quality standards for imported data	Although virtually every organization assessed had a clear view that data protection was an issue (and that they could be fined for non-compliance), fewer than 4 out of 10 companies had robust programmes to do anything about this. Most take the '10% faster' approach: that is, you can drive as fast as you like on a highway as long as 10% of the automobiles are going faster than you are. Those are the ones the police are interested in, aren't they?
4% have an enterprise-wide customer management information plan in place	Information planning is very rare. Although a third of companies have some sort of information plan, normally this is departmental or functional. Only 4% have an enterprise-wide customer information plan. This point alone reinforces the silo-based nature of CRM.
11% HAVE customer databases that store planned activities as well as histories	About 1 in 10 customer databases store activity records that reflect customer plans (ie what is going to happen to customers) as well as what has already happened. This is an area where differentiation can be achieved in managing customers. CM systems are beginning to exploit this, with workflow-type functions provided to enable systems to support contact strategies.
9% have a clear framework for assessing CM technology with those responsible for the business case	Only 9% develop business cases that can be tracked over time (no wonder it is so difficult to understand the benefits of CRM!). A business case should set a 'stake in the ground' against which to measure progress. Business case benefits must be realistic, as unrealistic expectations can lead to sponsors being disappointed about progress. Over-claiming in business cases is one reason why CRM projects are 'seen to fail' by the sponsor. The system might actually be contributing well!

A few years ago, dealers did not follow up 60 per cent of centrally generated sales leads. To fix this without system support would have required a major culture change and workforce input. Customers received the same promotion irrespective of which car they had bought and when. Every time customers contacted the company, their details had to be re-entered.

Rolls-Royce & Bentley Motor Cars: planning for customer contact

Rolls-Royce & Bentley Motor Cars knew that they needed to provide a level of intimacy with customers over and above the level other motor companies achieve. However, they needed support from technology in driving the complex mix of contacts that they wished to achieve with each individual customer. All customers now have a contact plan. The activities in the plan include welcoming calls, satisfaction questionnaires, event invitations and even new product information. The plan is reviewed at each car purchase to

Table 9.3 Business case for CRM system: what the new system provided

Ref	Activity	Current capability	Delivered by new system	Possible workaround
1	Maintain customer information	Done reactively on outsourced database	Proactive information management with potential for customers to maintain their own	No, existing database is not accessible from and could not support Web access
2	Analyse customer information	Outsourced and chargeable each time it is needed	Yes, sophisticated analysis tools built in.	Chargeable and not accessible while outsourced
3	Develop customer segments	Done simplistically based on customers answering questions	Yes, segmentation could be based on behaviour and analysis as well as answers	Not until analysis done

Table 9.4 Business case for CRM system: main benefit types

Benefit category	Benefit
Additional revenue from acquisition	£1,300,000
Additional revenue from retention	£1,125,000
Additional revenue from development	£600,000
Future cost avoidance	£720,000
Short term cost savings	£250,000

prevent duplicated or inappropriate contact. It is also reviewed at 'life stage' events for the customer. Contact plans have been developed for other key customer management tasks as well, such as complaints. When a plan is allocated to a customer, each activity is added for that customer a predefined number of days after the plan start date. The activities then trigger the appropriate action on the relevant days, as if they had been added as individual activities. All activities also have a cost associated with them, and these costs are taken into account in calculating the cost of managing each customer.

NOTES

[1] Stone, M, Findlay, G, Evans, M and Leonard, M (2001) Data chaos: a court case waiting to happen, *International Journal of Customer Relationship Management*, **4** (2), pp 169–84.
[2] CRMGuru, Multi-function CRM software: how good is it? [Online: www.crmguru.com]. A 100-page report based on data generated by 2,200 software profiles from individuals who have used or evaluated CRM software. Using a rigorous methodology, vendors were rated on functionality, implementation, pricing, customer focus, and support.

10

Process management

Neil Woodcock, Michael Starkey and Merlin Stone

Performance in Process Management has not changed significantly, as Table 10.1 shows. The big issue here is that organizations still do not recognize customer management as a set of processes, driven out of the customer proposition, that need to be considered together rather than separately in different functions. This issue is reflected in scores in other sections; for example, proposition development scores are low (process scope and design should come out of proposition development), as are ' leadership' (for example, cross-enterprise authority over integration of processes) scores. The second issue is that organizations rarely actively examine the performance of processes, particularly from the customer's point of view, but also from the organization's own point of view. Individual activities are often measured against process standards, but little attention is paid to understanding whether the processes used to manage customers throughout their lifecycle meet the needs of the customers cost-effectively.

Table 10.1   Process management

% score	Period 1	Period 2	Whether value being created or destroyed
Process Management	30	31	No real change
Ongoing process management	32	29	Some value destroyed
Process improvement	32	35	Some value created

CHARACTERISTICS OF THE HIGHEST-PERFORMING COMPANIES

These companies integrate processes based on the proposition to improve CM performance. CM performance is weakened when CM processes are managed as a disparate set of functional processes rather than as a group of processes. This results in wasted resource and investment, poor systems support and dissatisfied customers.

EXAMPLES OF BEST PRACTICES

Utility company retail division: customer journey

This energy company (EC), like most of its type, has a set of CM processes that cover many contact points and interactions during a customer's lifetime with the company. It would have been easy to become tied up in the complexity of this and the need to adhere to all the regulations under which the company operates. The result would have been a loss of focus on the customer experience of dealing with EC.

For this reason EC wanted to ensure that it always focused on the customer when it made changes to its processes and procedures. So the entire experience of dealing with EC was documented in a simple flowchart (Figure 10.1) of the customer journey from being acquired as a customer, through retention activity (Figure 10.2), day-to-day dealings and even to being won back if the customer did defect to another supplier. The work was widely communicated within EC and became a focus for people who had to develop and change processes that affected customers. They knew that they had to ensure that the customer experience was always considered along with the operational measures and regulatory adherence.

Rolls-Royce & Bentley Motor Cars: customer management process documentation

Rolls-Royce & Bentley Motor Cars planned to grow its Bentley business through launching a new range of luxury sporting cars, breaking into new sectors of the car market. The challenge facing its CRM team was how to develop a new customer proposition to a new audience and then deliver it in a way that stayed true to the traditional brand values. A high-level process framework was agreed to capture and map all the touch points and 'moments of truth' in the customer experience (Figure 10.3) as it

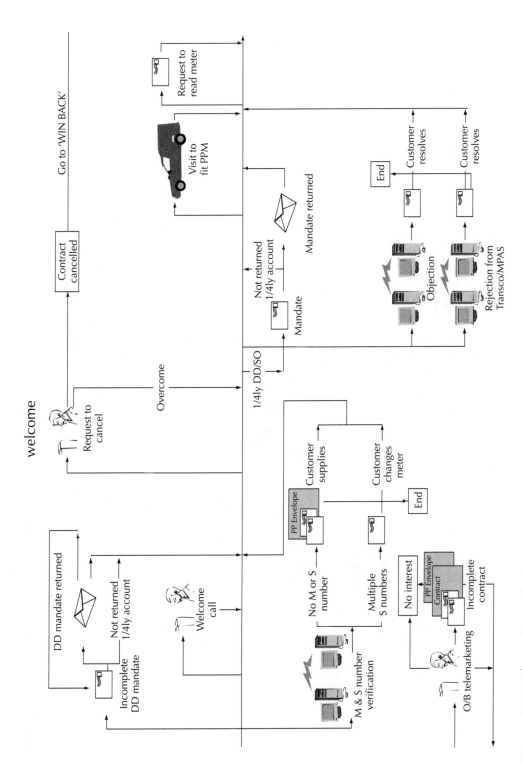

Figure 10.1 The welcome process

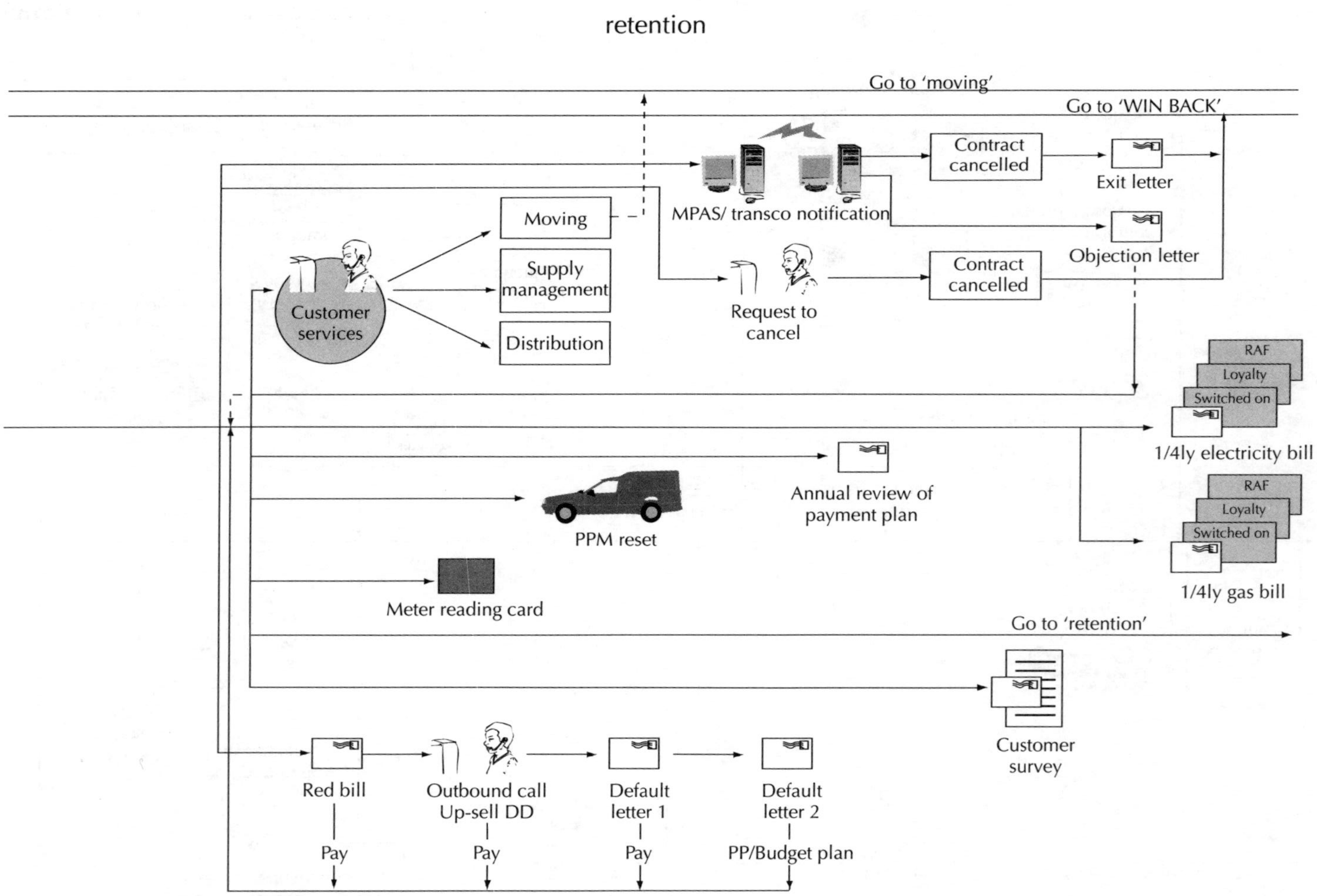

Figure 10.2 Retention activity

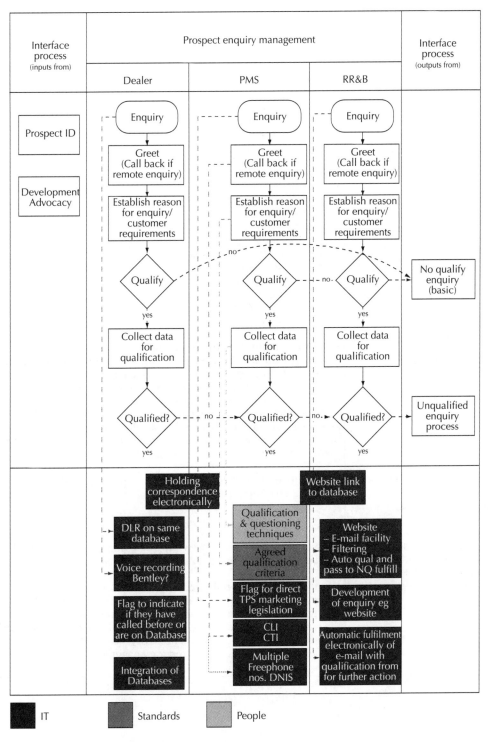

Figure 10.3 Prospect enquiry management

Table 10.2 Selected facts and figures from research

6% HAVE formally identified all customer management processes	Fewer than 1 in 16 companies have attempted to identify the wide set of processes that affect the management of prospects and customers. For example, the following processes may have an impact on customers: ▮ New product development and launch ▮ Product withdrawal ▮ Customer segmentation ▮ Contact planning ▮ Volume/margin forecasting ▮ Order processing ▮ Customer deliveries ▮ Returns and credits ▮ Enquiry management ▮ Prospect conversion ▮ Customer upgrade ▮ Key account management ▮ Complaint management ▮ Invoice payments ▮ Credit control ▮ Customer defection ▮ Customer return **War story: empowered organization?** One organization had an explicit policy within sales, marketing and service that it did not have any process documentation. It 'empowered' its people to do what was best for customers. In fact people started documenting processes for themselves, in their own way, and hiding the documents so that they were not seen. The assessment actually uncovered the fact that most staff felt uncomfortable about not having a process framework to at least give them a start point.
11% DO formally check for the organizational acceptability of their processes	Few companies check the acceptability of processes to their organization (their people).
13% HAVE got measures in place to look for radical change in customer management processes	Organizations are now more willing to review processes radically and be prepared to change (8%–13%) **War story: don't forget the customer** An organization had a very effective staff ideas scheme with substantial rewards for good ideas that generated step-changes in the way they operated. There were all sorts of category of idea, such as production, logistics and finance, but no category at all that vaguely accommodated a customer management idea.

happened at the start of the development process, and as it would be. The constituent processes in the framework were then developed by a cross-functional team to deliver the proposition across the touch points. The resulting processes were then fully documented and maintained via the Company's Quality Assurance infrastructure. Maps covered parallel processes operating in different channels, and documentation covered:

- the scope;
- ownership;
- stakeholders affected;
- process map and narrative;
- measures;
- people, standards and technology requirements;
- an assessment of risk.

11

Measurement

Neil Woodcock, Michael Starkey and Merlin Stone

The area has seen little change from period 1 to period 2, and as Table 11.1 shows, it has improved slightly.

Table 11.1 Measurement

% score	Period 1	Period 2	Whether value is being created or destroyed
Measuring the effect	35	36	No real change
Measuring customer management overall	31	30	No real change
Measuring the effect of campaigns	37	35	Some destroying of value
Measuring the effect of channels	37	39	Some creation of value
Measuring the effect of individuals	37	39	Some creation of value

Many companies now use systems to monitor the performance of different channels and the contribution of individuals to that performance, particularly those involved in sales and service. These are the two main improvement areas noted in our research.

However, campaign analysis performance has worsened slightly. This surprised us at first, but became clearer when we examined the detail. Although campaign reporting, ROI analysis and performance measurement have improved (mainly through the use of closed-loop systems), the formal learning from campaigns has not. This may be because of time pressures on campaign and marketing managers, meaning they do not have time to analyse results in depth and learn from the analysis. This implies that these companies are likely to continue to make the same mistakes, especially when experienced campaign and marketing managers move on.

CHARACTERISTICS OF THE HIGHEST-PERFORMING COMPANIES

The best performing companies:

- Are beginning to measure the relationship between customer behaviours and attitudes, CM activities and the effect on return on investment. These companies tend to have a hierarchy of measurement that links strategic measures such as ROI with CM measures. This enables them to begin to balance business performance with resource investment and different activities. Measuring a variable and recognizing (through whatever reward mechanism is appropriate) staff for their contribution to that variable is very powerful: the signal this sends to staff and partners alike is very clear.
- Measure the impact of different media on customers. One of the subtler characteristics of top quartile CMAT™ companies is their focus not just on the sales performance of different media, but on the role of different media and channels in the acquisition, retention and development process.
- Measure and learn from campaigns. The best performing companies make time to investigate what really happened in campaigns and then apply the learning in the definition of new activities.
- Measure the effectiveness of individuals.

EXAMPLES OF BEST PRACTICES

Utility company retail division: key performance measurement

This company needed to review the way it measured itself and its performance, both strategically and, after a CMAT, at the customer management level. It decided to focus on the REAP structure; although it is still early days, it now has a comprehensive framework in place from which to build, as more data becomes available. The framework, which is expected to be delivered in a Web-based computer application, provides for top-level indicators of business performance, focusing on the customer as well as the more traditional areas for measurement. A Red, Amber, Green approach is used to highlight where top-level measures are down against the targets set for them (see Figure 11.1). Access to various areas of commentary and other qualitative information will also be provided (see Figure 11.2). Users will then be able to drill down into top-level measures within each of the four main areas (retention, efficiency, acquisition and penetration) (see Figure 11.3) where more detailed measures are presented in the same format. Some of these measures will then provide further drill down and access to 'slice and dice' type functions to enable the information presented to be looked at in different ways. The work is still in progress but the clarity of the framework and care that has gone into its development makes this one of the best examples of true CM measurement.

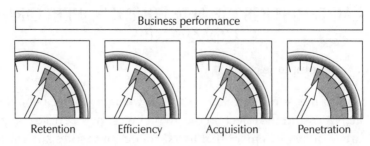

Figure 11.1 Dashboard: Level 1

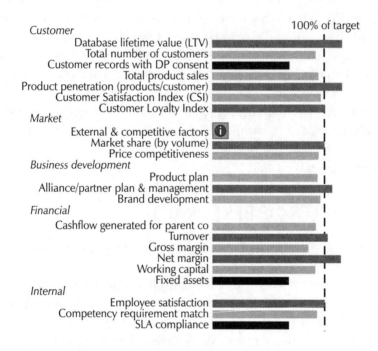

Figure 11.2 Dashboard: Level 2

NOTE

[1] Rackham, N, and Ruff, N (1991) *Managing Major Sales*, Gower, Aldershot.

Table 11.2 Selected facts and figures from research

Overall	
70% DO NOT have clear retention, efficiency, acquisition and penetration (REAP) measures in place 26% DO review CM measures at board meetings	Generally organizations are better at measuring specific things such as campaigns, channels and people than measuring customer retention, acquisition, penetration and cost to serve. Although 3 in 10 companies have some REAP measures in place, only 1 in 20 have measures covering all areas of REAP. This may be one of the reasons why only a quarter review CM measures at board meetings. Even this normally does not extend beyond simple statistics for new customers, complaints and customer loss numbers.
Channel	
22% DO understand the performance of their channels	More measurement of channel effectiveness (volumes and costs) is apparent.
Campaigns	
27% HAVE comprehensive and consistent campaign KPIs in place 17% regularly review marketing campaigns	Although campaign measurement has improved, campaign learning has not as this war story illustrates. **War story: campaign reviews** A financial services company had a clear five-step campaign planning and measurement process. The final phase was post-campaign review and transfer of learning into future campaigns. After over 20 campaigns had been run through the process, not one final review had been carried out. In fact an informal competition existed between campaign managers to see who could produce the most creative reasons to avoid such a review It is no surprise that a characteristic of best-performing companies is to make the time to learn from success and failure.
Individuals	
27% DO understand how account managers spend their time	Just over a quarter of companies understand how their sales account managers spend their time (field or call-centre based). A number of the 63% that do not have individual accountability DO have close supervision in a call centre environment, so they have a good idea where their telephone account managers are spending their time. Although we have not isolated the monitoring of face-to-face time versus call-centre time, from our figures it is likely that the monitoring of *face-to-face* people's time happens in less than 27% of companies. The impact of face-to-face contact is important in many industries (people buy from people; field sales spend is not declining). Research[1] shows that an over-emphasis on activity management in higher-value sales may drive down order values. Surely even in 'empowered' sales environments, monitoring of the field channel, which has the highest cost to serve and is most remote from head office, should be more widespread than this? **War story: focusing sales people** An oil company analysed how much time account managers spent with different types of customers. The policy was that that the field people would manage the high-value customers (As), would be twinned with the telephone team on middle-sized customers (Bs), and would not contact smaller customers (Cs), unless there was a major sale opportunity or a crisis. The results showed that the actual percentage time split was as follows; As 30%, Bs 40%, Cs 30%! This activity analysis resulted in some field management changes!

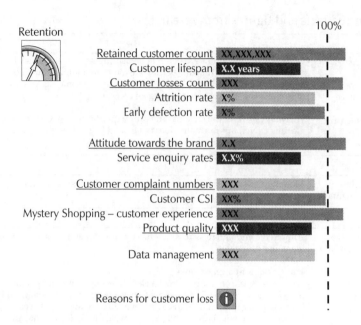

Figure 11.3 Dashboard: retention

12

The customer experience

Neil Woodcock, Michael Starkey and Merlin Stone

There has been a large dip in performance in this area, as Table 12.1 shows. The biggest drop is in understanding customer satisfaction and loyalty. Our research shows an increase in the use of customer satisfaction surveys, but a decrease in the research as to what underlies this satisfaction. Satisfaction is rarely a good indicator of commitment and repeat purchase.

Table 12.1   The customer experience

% score	Period 1	Period 2	Whether value is being created or destroyed
The customer experience	31	27	Value being destroyed
Understanding satisfaction and loyalty	34	25	Value being destroyed
Experiencing what customers experience	27	26	No real change
Using benchmarks	33	34	No real change

CHARACTERISTICS OF HIGHEST-PERFORMING COMPANIES

Here are some guidelines based on what our highest-performing companies do:

▪ Understand customer commitment, not just satisfaction. Business-to-business companies might try the CMAT Customer Loyalty Review Process; business-to-consumer companies might try the Loyalty Index, developed by the WPP group. Both help companies to identify the determinants of commitment, and the probability that valuable customers will defect or re-purchase ('loyalty').

▌ Find out how their company is really performing relative to its competitors, in 'moments of truth' and in all aspects of the customer experience. The customer experience is shaped in every contact with your company. Some experiences are more important to the customer than others and need to be handled more carefully. The best companies identify what these 'moments of truth' are for their key customers, how they perform during these events, set improvement targets for the customer experience, and measure and manage performance against these targets.

▌ In the areas that customers say are most important, benchmark against competitors and companies in parallel industries (those that customers take as their benchmark), set targets based on the best benchmarks, and measure performance against these targets.

EXAMPLES OF BEST PRACTICES

Industrial products: link between satisfaction and purchase behaviour

An international industrial product company (cutting tools and machines, smaller tools, consumables) wanted to understand the relationship between customer satisfaction (as they called it, but these were really indicators of commitment) and purchase behaviour. The analysis was carried out on both customers and prospects. The results showed the time lag between attitude and behaviour. The indicators of satisfaction (and dissatisfaction) needed careful definition. This company considers them so valuable that they cannot be discussed here, but they were determined through 'exit' interviews with customers who were leaving or who had left and 'entry' interviews with customers who were new or who had come back. Dissatisfaction indicators were plotted against behaviour, producing the curves in the diagrams in Figure 12.1.

Analysis showed that behaviour follows attitude. If prospects feel good about you then they might not buy from you immediately, but they are likely to in the future. Perhaps it will take a competitor's service failure to stimulate the change. If customers begin to feel dissatisfied, they might not defect immediately (although you might notice some loss of sales), but are likely to in the future. The company has used this analysis to predict defection, and to ensure that the acquisition programme delivers a positive attitude towards the company, so it can take advantage of any service slip-up in the incumbent supplier.

Table 12.2 Selected facts and figures from research

Understanding satisfaction and loyalty	
53% DO NOT understand the relationship between satisfaction and loyalty for their customers	Although the *weak* relationship between satisfaction and loyalty is generally understood, more than half the companies have not developed an understanding of the relationship between these two for their own customers.
60% DO NOT question what customers say compared with what they mean	Most companies carry out customer satisfaction surveys. The results are usually aggregated to provide a 'feel-good' indicator to senior management, with all of the real detail lost. These high-level aggregated scores provide little insight into the determinants of commitment and repeat purchase. The motor industry has a reputation for sending out satisfaction questionnaires at every opportunity, although the aim is often to monitor dealers rather than to understand what makes customers loyal. Only 4 in 10 look deeper into the satisfaction surveys to see what customers are really saying.
9% DO measure satisfaction by segment and/or value grouping	However, only 9% relate the satisfaction measure to the value and segment type of customers (see discussion of best practice in analysis and planning). The average satisfaction of a random sample of customers does not tell the full story and can be extremely misleading.

Experiencing what customers experience	
11% DO ensure that board members have regular and varied contact with customers	In only 11% of companies do board members have regular contact with a broad range of customers in 'business as usual' situations as opposed to golf days, executive briefings and the like. Without a formal programme, there are always good reasons why senior management avoid meeting customers in this way. **War story: senior contact** The members of the board of a retail finance company were asked in a CMAT feedback presentation who had seen a customer in any 'business as usual' environment in the last three months. None of them, in the previous three months had seen a single customer other than at a formal marketing event.
6% DO use event-driven satisfaction research	6% of companies do customer research focused on particular contact events or on events that are 'moments of truth', eg after a campaign; after an enquiry has been received (both converted and not converted); after a sales follow-up process; after the welcome pack; after a complaint; after a technical query. This, coupled with internal process measures (eg times to answer queries) should enable the company to see if the proposition is being delivered as promised. Although the sample size may be invalid statistically, if any issues are identified, deeper and/or broader investigation is possible.

Using benchmarks	
32% DO NOT know how they compare with competitors in terms of customer management	It is useful to compare your performance against competitors *and* against 'best of breed'. As an example, a major international airline that wanted to improve aircraft turnaround times did not focus on key competitors. Instead, it went to study how a leading Formula 1 motor racing team dealt with pit stop refuelling and tyre changes.
ONLY 6% of companies benchmark against best of breed non-competitive companies	**War story: benchmarking** A US bank, when asked if it wanted to take part in a benchmarking exercise, stated that it did not care who else was on the benchmark database and would only take part in the exercise if its major competitors were already benchmarked. This was despite the fact that all banks concerned performed very poorly in terms of customer management. How are companies with this attitude ever going to 'break out' of standard performance in their sector?
49% DO NOT encourage staff to experience the competitors' proposition	Over half the companies assessed encourage their staff to experience their competitor's offering to really understand the competitive experience.

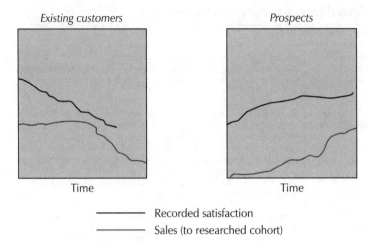

Figure 12.1 Satisfaction versus behaviour time delay

Retail finance company: competitor product purchase scheme

This company provided finance arrangements to purchasers of consumer durables manufactured by its parent group. As a benefit of working for the organization, employees were provided with low-cost finance for the company's products. However, this resulted in all the staff only having exposure to the in-house finance operation and not to competitor finance companies. It was also proving hard to organize mystery shopper research into competitor organizations that went all the way through to completing the agreement and experiencing the ongoing relationship. The solution was to launch a scheme where a proportion of employees using the staff scheme were asked to finance their purchases with competitor companies. They did this on the open market as if they were ordinary customers. The company ensured that they were no worse off than if they had received the company discounted rates, but in reality most participants negotiated better rates than their in-house subsidized rates. This quickly highlighted pricing issues with the company's own products. Over the longer term, participants of the scheme reported on all customer management activities of 'their' competitive finance house, enabling a clear picture to be built up of competitor tactics and strategies. This was fed into development of the company's own proposition and customer management activity development. It was also used as high-value internal communication material, with a constant stream of anecdotes on how staff were managed by competitor organizations.

13

The role of customer information management and usage in best practice customer management

Dave Irwin, Clarke Caywood and Iain Henderson

INTRODUCTION

One of the main challenges in implementing CRM projects is managing customer data. It is generally understood that to manage relationships with customers better, a business must start with a complete, accurate and appropriate view of the customer to establish and maintain a productive, relevant dialogue and relationship. Therefore, effectively managing and integrating the broad range of customer data for use in CRM is fundamental to project success. Yet, according to recent research detailing why CRM projects fail, the main reason is that the customer data is ignored.[1] To realize the potential of CRM fully, companies have implemented database marketing programmes over the past five years using data-trained graduate-level students. The leadership for CRM investment and installation seems to come from the IT function in corporations, despite marketing's early calls for databases with relevant customer behaviour data. Marketing managers now occupy the uncomfortable position of being most visible when the CRM systems are most likely to fail.

There are other issues that demonstrate the importance of how an organization develops and manages its customer information assets. The US Securities and

Exchange Commission (SEC), for example, now asks organizations to report on 'intangibles', such as acquisition and retention rates, or the overall value of a customer base. Such reporting is impossible without a thorough understanding of an organization's customer information. The practice of reporting on customer data assets is at an early stage, but one leading organization has already done so. When the financial analyst community begins to demand such reporting in a regular and consistent manner, the chief financial officer and the chief executive officer will be demanding the relevant outputs from the customer data warehouse.

In addition to the SEC reporting changes, there are also compliance requirements with federal and state privacy legislation. Issues of security, privacy and trust are growing in importance, particularly with the prevalence of Internet usage. 'Companies that will succeed over the next decade will be those capable not only of understanding their best customers, but nurturing those relationships and providing those customers with the comfort that their data will be used with integrity. This can only be achieved by taking a holistic approach to the processes and procedures for good data management.' [2]

One other critical customer data management issue emerging as significant revolves around an organization's ability to recognize its customers accurately so as to leverage the appropriate customer view for both analytical and operational purposes. The ability to recognize best customers and segment customer households to optimize retention and growth strategies requires an organization to start with accurate recognition of each individual. Then the organization must understand how those individuals make up each household across each product line in the organization.

The ability to recognize customers accurately enables companies to avoid the data fragmentation problem and accurately understand behaviour, profile and risk views of each customer household. This accurate view leads to analytics that are based on full information. This enables the most relevant and timely offers for cross-sell, up-sell, retention and touch-point management to occur, and each customer interaction to be tailored for maximum effectiveness. Business measurements are more accurate and robust based on this foundation, and broad-based decision making across many areas of the organization is improved through better, more meaningful information.

According to the Gartner Group, customer recognition is defined as:

> the ability to accurately recognize customers based on identifying infor-
> mation, and to synchronize all internal customer keys and pointers on a
> continuous basis. Customer recognition includes data models, real-time
> recognition components, high-volume batch processing components and
> associated interfaces. Its benefits include: first, providing a pre-built infra-
> structure for continuous synchronization of internal customer keys and

pointers and second, enabling instant customer recognition and consolidation of disparate customer information.[3]

The challenge facing many organizations today is the inability to recognize the customer. Inaccurate recognition of customers, because of poor data quality, completeness and accessibility, causes a ripple effect across an organization that degrades business performance and, if used for customer contact, undermines customer confidence in the value of the relationship with the corporation (see Figure 13.1). Given the increasing volumes of data across multiple systems, lines of business and channels, even small levels of data fragmentation can create significant downstream customer management performance problems. QCi CMAT assessments show that the reasons the management and use of customer information seem fraught with difficulty include:

▮ Limited control over too many legacy systems and an inability to pull together a single view of the customer.
▮ An inability to justify the ROI from data quality assessment and improvement projects, since payback is not easily quantifiable, particularly in its impact on revenue and profitability.
▮ The failure to deliver CRM improvements to specification during the previous year.

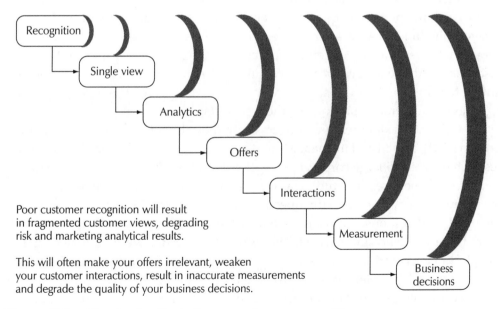

Figure 13.1   The ripple effect of poor customer recognition

▮ A lack of agreement among the marketing, sales and customer service teams on a common approach to CRM, so improvement is tactical rather than strategic.
▮ A lack of access to the internal skill sets needed to improve CRM implementation.

Given the benefits of best practice customer management, the push by the SEC to report on intangible assets – including customer-related information, increasing federal and state legislation concerning privacy, and the costs associated with poor management of customer data – an enterprise customer information plan has now become a strategic imperative for US corporations.

METHODOLOGY AND FINDINGS

Starting in October 2001, QCi and Acxiom Corporation investigated why organizations are finding so many difficulties in the area of customer data management and usage. The investigation used QCi's CMAT. For this study, a CMAT-Research (CMAT-R) assessment was used, which consists of a face-to-face interview lasting two hours with one or more customer management or marketing executives from each organization. This assessment uses an abbreviated subset of the full CMAT assessment. The full CMAT assessment would normally require four to six weeks and interviews with approximately 30 managers from each organization.

The CMAT-R assessment contains 49 best practice questions – a subset of the full complement of 260 best practices in the full CMAT assessment – and an additional set of Acxiom-sponsored questions focused on data management and usage. Whereas the full CMAT assessment requires evidence of progress to be presented about each customer management practice, a CMAT-R assessment relies on a discussion with the interviewee. As a result, scores from a CMAT-R assessment are quite often higher than the scores from a full CMAT, since the latter requires a rigorous examination of progress by the assessor(s).

The QCi and Acxiom research project centred on the role of customer data integration (CDI), as well as data management and usage in customer management. The research covered 15 large corporations with activities in the United States. With the exception of one case, this study was conducted using face-to-face interviews with the client organization. Specific questions pertaining to data management were included, and responses were recorded in the CMAT software. Responses were scored, analysed and summarized. The section level results were evaluated against the global benchmark and the sample average, and then compared against sector averages in which a relevant sector benchmark exists for the CMAT-R. The findings revealed that 46 per cent of the best practices examined in this research project would be unattainable without significant access to customer information. More detailed analysis revealed that even those best practices not directly using customer information are affected by it in some form.

GENERAL FINDINGS

Based on detailed analysis, the research uncovered the findings outlined in Figure 13.2. The CMAT scoring approach is driven by the distinction between 'intent, reality and effect.' For example, a score of 33 per cent represents intent, with pockets of activity driving the realization of customer management plans, but very little is known about the business impact. 50 per cent is a rough benchmark for acceptable business practice, while 100 per cent is the upper limit for a fully deployed and matured business practice that shows clear benefits. Figure 13.2 shows that the CMAT-R sample scored slightly lower than the full data set of US-based organizations in all but one of the broad section categories.

Generally speaking, US firms trail their European counterparts across the board in overall CRM performance and the results from this CMAT-R further confirmed this trend. The average total score of the CMAT-R sample set is 39, although there are some areas of exceptional performance demonstrated. To put this result in context, this level of score means 'some commitment, some progress'. Overall, some of the highlights from this broader report are on point in explaining key reasons why

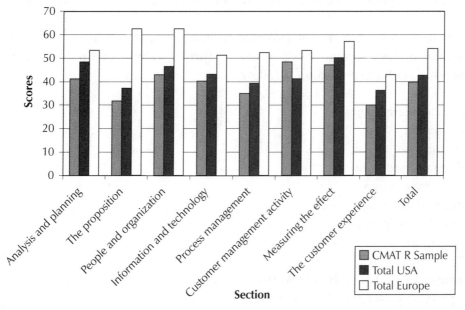

Figure 13.2 Comparison of CMAT-R scores in USA and Europe

performance is less than ideal despite increasing investments. These reasons include:

▌ Senior executive ownership and leadership is required, but is often not present.
▌ Too much thinking, too little doing: many CRM programmes get stuck in the strategy phase.
▌ The silo approach does not support building value through the customer management process.
▌ Larger organizations face a greater challenge in implementing customer management because of their scope.
▌ Education is needed but not made available across the organization at multiple levels.
▌ Poor project implementation leads to unrealized performance expectations.

Ultimately, large organizations in some sense must move mountains to change from product-centric to customer-centric behaviour. Phased implementation of interconnected and integrated programmes under an enterprise CRM strategy, with executive ownership, is proving to be a more effective approach. However, the foundation for being able to achieve this must be in place, and customer information management and usage is the backbone of that foundation.

INFORMATION MANAGEMENT AND USAGE FINDINGS

In order to evaluate the area of information management and usage more thoroughly, the analysis sections listed below are further defined and individual best practices are clustered by section as follows:

▌ vision and strategy;
▌ investment;
▌ resourcing;
▌ information content;
▌ information usage;
▌ information management;
▌ technology support;
▌ integration.

Our contention is that each of these performance areas (sections) can be a pocket of good practice in isolation, but their true benefits emerge when they are effectively integrated. In other words, an organization can demonstrate excellence in one or more of these areas; however, unless all areas are being actively improved, there will be barriers to achieving best practice. The Acxiom-sponsored subset of questions combined with pre-existing CMAT questions about information management and usage yield a total of 22 best-practice areas on the subject. These areas of analysis are designed to test how organizations currently compare with best practice in key aspects of information management and usage, and to indicate whether organizations are taking a wide enough view on the issue to enable future best practice.

The issues specifically tested in this research project and the average scores are shown in Figure 13.3. These scores reveal that there are many areas for improvement in customer information management and usage in support of CRM. Overall, the results indicate that there is a lot of work being done toward achieving best practice in information management and usage. There is also a growing awareness of the importance of better leveraging customer data in support of customer management to achieve real results, although the presence of an enterprise customer information plan is still one of the lowest scoring areas.

Another low-scoring area, appropriate access to customer data across the organization, is still a major point of contention for most of the organizations interviewed, who truly need broader, more complete and accurate customer data to be more readily available. Furthermore, access to certain analytical measures of customer

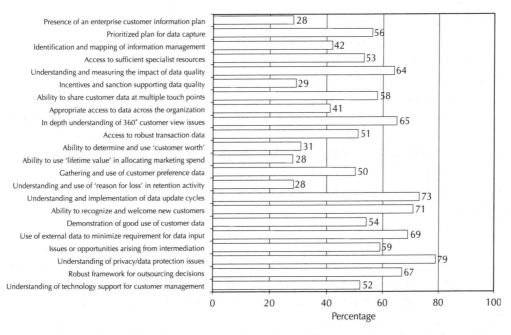

Figure 13.3 CMAT-R subset scores (based on 22 areas related to information management and usage)

value – customer worth, lifetime value or even reason for loss –was the weakest scoring area of the analysis.

To provide a more useful interpretation of the research findings, a set of best-practice information management and usage recommendations was created based on the research results, and they are discussed in the next section.

BEST PRACTICES

Taking the scale and scope of the customer management issues noted above, Acxiom and QCi jointly developed a series of best practices encompassed in an approach designed to support a chief information officer in developing an enterprise plan for managing and using customer information. The best practices can be pulled together into a broader quantifiable improvement plan. The plan details the short, medium and long-term improvements in customer information management and usage that an organization must undertake to best prepare its data assets for use in customer management. A sample of these best practices is outlined below. The Acxiom-sponsored subset of 22 detailed questions about information management and usage is divided into 10 best-practice categories derived from the CMAT-R results.

- Create an enterprise customer information management plan.
- Obtain resources to support the plan.
- Build measures of data quality.
- Define a single customer view.
- Collect transaction history data.
- Use customer data to understand customer worth, lifetime value, preferences and retention drivers.
- Build a customer infrastructure that supports recognition and welcoming of customers.
- Account for third-party data (intermediation).
- Understand privacy.
- Consider outsourcing business processes.

The individual best practices in information management and usage, and the findings from our sample to date, are detailed below. Each can be seen as a recommendation that, if implemented in isolation, would engender improvement; however, much more improvement is gained if the best practices are performed in an integrated effort across the enterprise.

Create an enterprise customer information management plan

Ensure that an enterprise plan for management and use of customer information is in place. All key stakeholders, with representation from marketing, sales, customer service, finance, operations and IT as a minimum, must feed the overall management plan from an enterprise view.

Organizations spend vast sums of money on managing and using customer information, and the customer database is often quoted as a major asset of the business. As such, it should be covered by a comprehensive plan that does this asset justice. Only one organization in the US study felt it had an enterprise customer information plan in place and actively being used. Only 4 per cent of companies in the global assessment base felt they had such a plan in place. In many cases, departmental plans exist (that is, in marketing or in CRM teams), but organizations find it very difficult to take an enterprise view of their data assets. Given the inherent value of customer data, this is something that organizations must address.

According to Scott Nelson from Gartner Group, one of the reasons CRM projects fail is because there is no plan:

> No one builds a house or a bridge, or anything that is the least bit complex, without a plan. Yet, most enterprises still undertake CRM with no idea of what they are hoping to build in the long term. One solution is haphazardly joined with another, initiatives come and go, and soon enthusiasm is waning throughout the enterprise. We recommend that enterprises create a three-year plan for their CRM initiatives, then tactically invest toward that vision.[4]

An enterprise customer information plan should be a core component of a CRM plan. An enterprise customer information plan enables corporations not only to respond more quickly to supporting and successfully executing CRM projects, but also effectively position the value of their customer base to the investment community.

Obtain resources to support the plan

Ensure that the resource requirements of customer information management and usage are sufficient to support the enterprise plan. Build into the requirements that this is a specialist area where employee development and sourcing may be constrained. Consider strategic outsourcing as a valid option.

Customer information management and usage, by their nature, include a range of skill sets that in the open market are in short supply. Therefore, organizations must ensure not only that they have sufficient resources in place to meet current business needs, but that succession planning is also in place. Only one of the organizations assessed felt it had this issue fully under control. The majority recognized the issue but had not yet confirmed plans to implement a robust process in this area.

Another reason CRM projects fail, as cited by Scott Nelson from Gartner[5], is that no attention is paid to skill sets. 'All the money in the world can't save a CRM project if, at the end of the implementation, it is put in the hands of under skilled and under trained employees.' He further states that it is necessary to 'educate employees on the CRM initiative and train them on CRM tools and technology to enable them to communicate with customers more effectively.' The same applies to handling the ongoing management of customer data, from sourcing and procurement through quality control, definition, security, integration, maintenance, accessibility and value measurement, just to name a few management areas.

Build measures of data quality

Build robust measures of data quality and take remedial action when necessary, including incentives and sanctions for your customer-facing employees.

Organizations should understand and measure the impact of data quality on the various customer management processes and build appropriate business cases for investment in data quality improvement programmes. These measures should include, for example, financial data on wasted marketing activity generated by poor data inputs. In addition, other less obvious process measures such as the amount of re-work undertaken at information-intensive stages in customer management processes should be included.

Customer-facing employees should have incentives and sanctions in place relating to information quality on the customer database, since these employees are best placed to capture and validate data. 'Understanding of data quality' as a key issue to be addressed scores well across the board in the US sample, but interestingly the question about incentives and sanctions sees a very low overall score, with only two organizations claiming to have them in place.

Data quality is the overall quality of the data content upon which a company bases its marketing and customer relationship decisions. There are four components to data quality:

▌ Data completeness: this is the percentage of all possible data sources and the coverage across all defined data fields a company has integrated into its decision support and operational CRM processes. If there is data about customers in 12 different operational data stores, then all of those sources should be integrated into the CRM system. However, this also refers to sources of outside data that may be available.

▮ Data accuracy: this is the overall accuracy of the data content identifying contact information and known data (internal or external) associated with each customer record. Once a company has all of the sources and fields identified and populated, then how accurate is that data content? In most companies, this answer will vary considerably with each source.

▮ Grouping accuracy: this is the accuracy with which a company can consolidate data from disparate sources. Once a company has all of the data sources identified and has performed the necessary hygiene to ensure that they are accurate, how well can the company identify and group multiple occurrences of the same customer in order to provide a comprehensive, accurate customer portrait?

▮ Data access: this is the speed with which a company can integrate its data and provide that data in a usable form across all decision support and customer-facing applications. If all the activities described in the first three components of data quality take months or weeks to complete, a company still will not be driving its CRM strategy based on the most recent information available.

Theoretically, a company can represent where it is in a 'data quality continuum' to improve the company's position constantly. Each improvement directly influences the effectiveness of a company's CRM strategy. The way a company manages its data quality is by using a set of processes called 'customer data integration' (CDI). This means the creation of a 'comprehensive customer portrait' based on business requirements and made available anytime, anywhere across the enterprise, as needed. These CDI processes handle extremely complex data management tasks and, in many ways, provide the foundation for the most important component to the overall success of a CRM strategy: an understanding of the customer.

For the past few years, Acxiom has been using assessment tools that contain data quality measurement components. Data diagnostics is the first step for building measures of data quality. Acxiom's Opticx® quickly provides a snapshot of how good a company's customer data is. For instance, in one Opticx test on a client's data, almost 64 per cent of the identifying information for customer records was good, but over 36 per cent of the records had data anomalies. Acxiom also provides a data quality index score that benchmarks performance against an industry average.

Define a single customer view

Build a detailed understanding of the issues around the 360-degree view of the customer prior to making commitments to build such a view.

This recommendation does not assert that an organization should already have built such a customer view; indeed our findings confirmed that very few organizations have such a view in place at this time. This chapter asserts that organizations should build an *understanding* of what such a view entails, enables and costs. There are significant differences in the cost and implications of the options, and it is vital that organizations are clear on their requirement before beginning CRM programmes to put a single view of the customer in place. In the US sample, we found that most organizations recognized the significance of the issue but tended to be inconclusive in their analyses and had not chosen a specific route to building this understanding.

Suppose an organization has been advised by its agency or technology supplier that it needs a 360-degree view of the customer in order to implement CRM activities. The reality might actually be entirely different, depending on factors such as industry sector, nature of customer base or nature of existing technology infrastructure. The point is that companies need to build the single view they need, and improve it over time as business requirements dictate. For example, a start-up e-bank sector might find it needs a complete view of its customers available in real time, and it might even find that this view is relatively easy to attain, as it has no legacy systems or unclear issues to resolve. Another organization that relies on an intermediary sales channel might find that while it desires a 360-degree view of the customer for market and customer analysis and planning, it does not immediately need to be in real time since it is being used in offline data mining.

So the 360-degree view is in fact a moving target, and the key is building an understanding of what is actually required by the organization, what can be done, and at what price. The end result is almost certainly different for every organization that goes through such an exercise.

Collect transaction history data

Organizations should hold and provide appropriate access to a minimum of three years of transaction history in a form that enables detailed analysis.

Three years typically represents two or more sales cycles, although industries such as automotive may require up to six years of data to achieve similar analysis outputs. Data should be held at the transaction level and should include a unique customer ID along with the date, product, volume, value and channel/outlet for each transaction. Ideally, it should also include the transaction margin. For analysis purposes, ZIP codes/post codes and customer segmentation related fields should also be accessible.

Overall scoring on access to transaction data is mid-range in the US sample; however, there are wide discrepancies across sectors. Financial services and telecommunications typically score well, and automotive less so. From the wider CMAT benchmark, only 28 per cent of companies have three years or more of sales purchase information.

Use customer data to understand customer worth, lifetime value, preferences and retention drivers

Use the customer data you hold to improve the customer interface(s):

▌ Understand and determine individual customer worth across your customer base.
▌ Use lifetime value data as key feeds into marketing activity.
▌ Gather and use customer preference data to build customer satisfaction and reduce operating costs.
▌ Ensure that retention activity is driven by all valid data available.

Presenting data already known to the organization at the customer interface is, if handled correctly, a way in which the customer can recognize the value in providing such information in the first place. It can also be a driver for personalized messaging at the interface, with all the benefits that it entails.

Two organizations flagged the capability to return comprehensive customer data at each customer touch point, adding significantly to the customer experience. However, the majority of organizations were unable to do so at all, or only in a limited number of contact channels. Limitations around customer data integration and the single customer view were the most common barriers identified.

Customer data should be used to recognize customers with multiple relationships and in some cases multiple addresses. Proper recognition of customer households leads to accurate segmentation and modelling. It also enables organizations to execute the most appropriate groupings for strategy execution. Across your business, it is vital to start with accurate recognition of each individual, and how these individuals make up each customer household in your base and across each product line.

Customer worth

An organization should be able to determine the worth of individual customers; combining sales margin, sales and marketing costs, management costs, logistics and service and so on. Armed with this information, an organization is able to make very robust decisions on marketing activity, including acquisition profiles and planned customer loss programmes. This capability scores very poorly in both the CMAT-R sample and across the CMAT database as a whole. This has a significant impact, since organizations are unable to conduct fully robust analyses, which drives further weakness in customer management activity and ultimately in measurement of success.

Developing this capability in practice is not as difficult and expensive as one might think. An individual, customer-worth figure based on informed 'guesstimates' built on top of a core of robust data is significantly better than not having one at all. Of course, CDI and good data quality capability improve the accuracy of the customer worth data, but the real key to progress in this area lies in a good analysis team and the senior management commitment to putting this key metric in place.

Customer lifetime

Organizations should recognize the potential length of lifetime of new and existing customers as well as their short-term value when allocating marketing budget and priorities. This should ideally be translated into an allowable cost per sale, which is a well-established metric in the campaign evaluation and review process. Scores in the CMAT-R sample, and in the wider CMAT data set, are very poor on this issue. One exception to that rule is found in the CMAT-R sample in the publishing sector. It is likely that inability to calculate and use lifetime value is a function of weakness in ability to isolate complete views of individual customers and possibly a weakness in resourcing of the analysis and planning function. Outsourcing this analysis to specialists, if needed, could be a good option in the short term.

Customer preferences

The gathering and use of customer preference data is a recent but powerful phenomenon whereby organizations invite their customers to advise them on preferences around communications frequency/channel/timings and so on. When gathered and implemented in a robust manner, customer preference data is a powerful retention driver and a significant contributor to reduced operating cost. One other point to note is that gathering individual preference data and then ignoring it or operating outside of the preferences shared is worse than not gathering at all. Communication based on customer preferences is a robust tactic in improving perception of the organization with regard to the privacy issues discussed later. Preferences are either overtly or by implication 'opt in', and thus in a safe zone so far as the customer is concerned. Two organizations in the sample showed a sophisticated understanding and use of customer preference data. However, the majority indicated that gathering and use of this data was at best sporadic and the data gathered under-utilized.

In order to support retention activity, reason for loss should be sought and stored on the customer database for every known customer loss. This may be as simple as a drop-down list of possible options, even though it will not be able to be completed in all situations. Given the business benefits of retention over ongoing acquisition, any supporting information for retention is valid. Similarly, event data, such as price inquiries, changing order patterns and lapsed accounts, can be used as possible predictors of defection. This best practice scored very poorly in the CMAT-R sample, with only two organizations claiming to have made significant progress in this area. Other organizations scored poorly even on recognition of the issue. Retention is a major issue that remains poorly addressed overall; from the wider CMAT data set, some 63 per cent of organizations still do not even measure retention rates.

Build a customer infrastructure that supports recognition and welcoming of customers

Build an infrastructure and set of processes that enables recognition of when a new customer has conducted a first transaction with the organization, and then trigger appropriate welcoming activity.

Such practice affects customer perceptions of an organization and helps build a platform for ongoing communications. In doing so, organizations should recognize and plan for the opportunity afforded by the 'welcoming activity' to capture data while the customer is receptive and build the capability to have ongoing, personalized communications with the customer based on his or her preferences, and the most cost effective channel for the supplier.

Organizations as a whole, in both the CMAT-R sample and the global assessment base, are handling this issue well, with the majority having robust welcoming programmes in place. While this is viewed as progress in comparison with QCi research in previous years, which showed that welcoming programmes were scarce, there is diversity in practice in the current sample. Welcoming activities today range from real time over multiple channels – using the opportunity to capture and validate preference data – to welcoming programmes that run offline, such as mailing campaigns that welcome a new customer who is actually an existing customer buying through another channel.

Organizations should be aiming at the former, with an understanding that a complete multi-channel solution will take time and may be reached incrementally. The infrastructure required consists of a core single customer view with a significant CDI capability to manage the recognition process for new, rather than existing, customers. The process also manages the data quality issues typically associated with large and complex customer contact solutions.

Account for third-party data (intermediation)

Take into account the impact intermediation has on your information management capability and be proactive in anticipating and resolving problems associated with exchanging data with this third party.

Intermediation, where a third party sits between an organization and its end customers, is an issue that has caused many organizations problems with gaining access to managing and using customer information.

For the most part, this issue is of less concern to most organizations than it would have been five years ago, even in the sectors where intermediation is the norm, such as brokerage, automotive and insurance. The majority of organizations interviewed now believe that these issues are well understood and are being addressed, typically through the development of joint 'win-win' marketing programmes between the parties, with the intermediator being encouraged to share data with the supplying organization.

Understand privacy

Understand privacy and its implications in all relevant geographies as both a threat and an opportunity.

This best practice contains a number of facets. From a narrow viewpoint, privacy implications can be seen as the legal constraints and processes that have emerged and will continue to emerge as the consumer privacy debate ebbs and flows. In this sense, the organization has no option except to conform, but it should be aware of the issue of potential impact far in advance through monitoring. The organization should be involved actively in the lobbying and approval processes that all such legislations go through. Our contention, however, is that best practice in this area goes well beyond the monitoring and implementation of legislative imperatives. Organizations should be analysing the underlying drivers buried beneath privacy. For example, are customers actually happy to share data with suppliers, but just do not like the current terms and conditions? Or is it invasiveness or distrust that is the issue? The actual drivers of privacy warning bells will inevitably differ significantly by sector. Organizations should understand what the real driver of the issue is in their own situations.

Most of the organizations assessed believe they understand and have acted upon the privacy issues they face in all geographies in which they have customers. Note this contrasts significantly with the wider, more European, multi-national focused CMAT assessment base, where less than 40 per cent of the organizations claim to have robust programmes in place to tackle the more stringent legislation-driven issues emerging. Far fewer are seeing privacy as a possible opportunity to build deeper, trusting relationships with customers. This begs the question, is the recent privacy legislation that has forced US-based organizations to take note of this issue only a forerunner of what is to come? Our view is that privacy – as an issue to which organizations must allocate resources – is only just emerging, and that many twists and turns have yet to appear.

Consider outsourcing business processes

Consider outsourcing of information management business processes when appropriate or beneficial.

Having a robust framework for determining whether to outsource information management activities is a best practice in which the majority of organizations assessed to date indicate they have made significant progress. Note that the resourcing issue is one of the key drivers in our definition of a robust framework for outsourcing decisions; it is not about cost alone.

CONCLUSIONS

The two companies that scored highest in this study are companies that have already taken significant action to make sure their customer information assets are properly managed and integrated. For example, the strongest performer brought together transactional data from multiple business and product divisions with non-transactional data – including contact history, demographics, and preference data – in a meaningful way. While this type of integration does not guarantee customer management success, it does enable these companies to understand and serve customers better. Specifically, the high scorers either had significant outsourced IT relationships that helped them prioritize and manage key data-related issues, or a well-designed information gateway that managed the data quality and integration across platforms.

At this stage we cannot take the data gathered and prove a causal link between best practice management and use of customer information, and successful customer management performance. However, the issue of information management and usage in support of customer management is not going to go away. In fact, we see it becoming increasingly significant and growing quickly as new channels and more transactions are carried out in ways which link directly to a customer record. SEC requests for reporting of customer information will also cause new demands to be placed on often already overburdened information management infrastructures.

Customer information is the fuel in the customer management/CRM engine. It is a key factor to many more facets of customer management than might appear obvious. In other words, customer management is not going to work without a strong customer information infrastructure to support it. Given the significance and scale of this customer information issue, as exemplified by the best practices noted above, we believe the first of our findings, develop and implement an enterprise customer information plan, is of real significance. Organizations must ensure that an enterprise plan for management and use of customer information is in place, and is used by all key stakeholders, with representation from marketing, sales, customer service, finance, operations and IT as a minimum, with an enterprise view. Without such a formal planning process, the likelihood of being tripped up by one or more of the many complex issues, or failing to take into account the requirements of all users, is a recipe for less than perfect solutions. Best practice in information management and usage is readily achievable by organizations. Perhaps the difficulty lies in taking a wide enough view of the issue, and a long-term, planned approach to making coordinated improvements.

NOTES

[1] Nelson, S and Kirkby, J (2001) *Seven Key Reasons Why CRM Fails*, Gartner (August 20).
[2] Stone, M, Findlay, G, Evans, M and Leonard, M (2001) Data chaos: a court case waiting to happen, *International Journal of Customer Relationship Management*, **4** (2), pp 169–84.
[3] Nelson, S, Singhal, W and Janowski, N (2001) *Customer Data Quality and Integration*, Gartner (November 26).
[4] Nelson, S and Kirkby, J (2001) *Seven Key Reasons Why CRM Fails*, Gartner (August 20).
[5] Ibid.

14

The Dutch insurance industry CMAT study

Hans Neerken and Roland Bushoff

INTRODUCTION

In the final quarter of 2001, BSN Nederland (a leading Netherlands business school which provides a general MBA and also an insurance-specific MBA), IBM Nederland and QCi carried out CRM benchmark research at 27 insurance companies, using CMAT-R, the research version of CMAT. Each company was assessed in eight different CRM related areas against best practices in these areas. This provided insight into the performance of each of these companies and highlighted differences between companies in their approach to CRM and in their results.

The results in this chapter are based on 27 participants. The group included general/property and casualty insurance, life insurers and healthcare insurers. Of this group, 9 dealt directly with retail customers, 13 sold insurance primarily via independent intermediaries, and 5 had other companies as their customers. In the analysis no differentiation was made between general, life and healthcare insurers, since this differentiation was not always clear-cut and there were no significant differences between these types of company in their CRM performance. Interviewees were mostly commercial directors or marketing managers. Each of the participants received customized feedback, in which his or her scores were compared to the average scores of all other participants. In addition, the scores were explained qualitatively, and recommendations were made for the next steps.

GENERAL RESULTS

CMAT-R not only gives general CRM achievements (total score), but it also sub-scores on the eight CRM related areas, which makes it possible to see how the scores in these areas compare with each other. The CMAT model has as an underlying hypothesis that the various areas relate strongly to one another and that the combination of these areas makes for successful CRM. A low score in one area can have a negative impact on overall success, even if other sub-scores are high. This is especially so if the lower score is in one of the more important areas, People and Organization, Measurement or Customer Management Activities.

The overall score for Dutch insurers was 37 per cent, with the highest 63 per cent and the lowest 17 per cent. A 100 per cent score would have been achieved if an insurer had claimed that it had fully implemented 'good practice' in all its aspects, with the effects clearly visible, and with some proof of this. An average score of 37 per cent implies answers varying from 'plans to do so' to 'implemented in isolation'. This means insurers were only at the very start of implementing effective CRM-focused changes and solutions and of reaping benefits from them. This finding is in line with research done in other parts of the world.

The low average score of 37 per cent in the Netherlands was less than the average CMAT-R scores for insurers in four other countries (average 53 per cent), but more than the average score of the 'full CMAT' research scores at insurers (average 28 per cent). Table 14.1 summarizes the scores.

DIRECT INSURERS SCORE BEST

The scores varied a lot, as was mentioned above. One would expect insurers with direct contact with retail customers ('direct insurers') to have a higher score than intermediary

Table 14.1 Overall scores

	Direct	B2B	Intermediary	Average
Targeting	45	40	36	40
Enquiry management	68	45	30	45
Welcoming	53	15	37	38
Getting to know / healthcheck	47	30	30	36
Ongoing management	37	39	35	36
Managing dissatisfaction	53	45	39	45
Winback	25	25	47	36

insurers. Direct contact makes it both more important and more feasible to take the wants and needs of customers into account. One would also expect that insurers with a large number of final customers would have implemented CRM more explicitly than business-to-business insurers. Most CRM for the latter takes place in the head of the salesperson managing the customer! These expectations were supported by the research. Direct insurers scored 43 per cent on average, while intermediary insurers scored 33 per cent and business-to-business insurers 39 per cent. The three lowest-scoring companies (17 per cent) were all intermediary insurers, but there are exceptions. For example, three intermediary insurers scored higher than the average for direct insurers. However, there was another difference in scores by type of insurer. While overall, direct insurers scored highest, this was not the case for Proposition. Business-to-business insurers scored highest in this area.

We must be careful in how we interpret these scores. Some organizations base their strategy on customer knowledge and want to serve customers as far as possible with individualized products and services. For this 'customer intimacy' strategy, one must have CRM in place. An organization with a cost-minimization strategy needs this less. Organizations operating in a niche market may also be less inclined to focus strongly on CRM. However, our research does not explore whether higher or lower scores correlate with a more or less explicit CRM-related business strategy.

For most participants the scores for the various CRM areas differed greatly. This implies that only few insurers had an integral approach to CRM that involved all the various areas. It also means that the results of CRM efforts might be negatively influenced by low achievement in one or more CRM areas.

ANALYSIS AND PLANNING

The spread of the scores here was comparable with the spread of the total scores: on average 39 per cent with a maximum score of 63 per cent and a minimum of 17 per cent. Almost all insurers stated their commercial objectives in terms of premium income and ultimate profit. Few insurers stated how they would achieve these objectives by acquisition of new customers and/or developing existing customers. Objectives in terms of (maximum acceptable) lapsing were almost never stated. Retention policies measured by customer segment, based on customer value, were nowhere to be found. This was remarkable since the relevance of retention activity and the optimum investment in retaining customers depend on the current (and future) value of these customers.

Although almost every insurer stored detailed transaction data over a long period, few actually analysed it for value development of customers or for lapse risk. From this study, it seems that only 'direct writers', who only know their customers from their databases, did this type of analysis of customer data.

We came across a best practice at one of the participants, which used data mining to predict lapse. These predictions were pretty accurate. However, it proved hard to use this information to prevent lapsing, because the letter triggered by lapse prevention activity increased the probability of lapsing as opposed to the situation where no letter was sent!

Particularly with business-to-business insurers and those selling through intermediaries, there was some insight into value per customer, and service is differentiated on the basis of this. This service differentiation consists mostly of some form of dedicated account management. Direct insurers who differentiate do so mostly by means of a glossy company magazine, sent to the more valuable customers. No companies had insights into individual customer profitability. Insurers who work with intermediaries and see them as their prime customers have most insight into what these various intermediaries bring in and what they cost to support. Most insurers – except for those who have just bought and implemented CRM software – do not have data on contacts with the customer. So most insurers cannot use this contact data to calculate profitability using activity-based costing.

Business-to-business insurers score well on understanding the competition. This is partly because customers do their own research to find the best insurance offers. Insurers need to have this knowledge themselves.

Planning of customer development scored highly, not only for business-to-business insurers, but also for intermediary insurers. Having fewer customers than the typical direct insurer, these insurers had high scores on questions that had to do with 'key account planning'.

PROPOSITION

The proposition is what binds an insurer to its customers. Obviously this is more than just the product. It is also the way in which (potential) customers are treated when they have questions about the product, during a claim or when a disbursement is to be made. When the proposition is developed, the customer's wants and needs should be known. Thorough communication of the proposition is vital. For this, there must be clarity regarding the customer benefits of the various proposition elements, and all employees who interact with customers must be aware of these benefits, so they can focus on them when communicating with customers.

In our study, the average Proposition score was 41 per cent, above the overall average of 37 per cent. This relatively high score was maintained (44 per cent) in the area of proposition development. Proposition communication scored an average of 37 per cent. In development, it was mainly the business-to-business and direct insurers that scored highly, with scores of 56 per cent and 54 per cent respectively. Intermediary insurers lagged with a score of 32 per cent. It seems that direct contact with final customers makes a difference.

In the area of communication, business-to-business insurers had a high score of 62 per cent. Direct insurers scored less, with 40 per cent, but intermediary insurers did even worse with an average of 25 per cent. Given differences in (communication) channels, this was not surprising. However, the differences are huge and this area should be of concern, especially for intermediary insurers. They need to do more to make the intermediaries aware of the benefits of their proposition.

Of the 27 insurers, 9 (33 per cent) said that they had no insight or only a very high-level insight into the wants and needs/loyalty drivers of their customers. No explicit research was being done into this. Given the increasing competitiveness in the marketplace, this is unexpected. Those who did formal research did it in different ways. Personal, direct contact with customers was an important source of information. Apart from that, many insurers participated in external research, or did their own research by customer panels, monitoring and exit interviews.

PEOPLE AND ORGANIZATION

This was one of the worst-scoring areas, with an average of 33 per cent. The score for management of people (29 per cent) was worse than that for organization (38 per cent). The intermediary insurers scored significantly lower (22 per cent) than direct insurers (36 per cent) and business-to-business insurers (33 per cent). In the area of organization, there are differences between the three types of insurer, but they are less significant. Intermediary insurers scored an average of 37 per cent, the direct insurers an average of 39 per cent and the business-to-business companies 41 per cent.

The low scores in the area of people management indicated that not much or nothing is being done for CRM in this area. In general, desired CRM behavioural characteristics were not specified, and neither was conformance of people to desired behaviour. Only 5 out of 27 (19 per cent) said that the necessary CRM competencies were part of job descriptions or were being made part of them. Only at one insurer were performance and merit systems focused on this aspect. In some situations employees were encouraged to take part in projects to extend their understanding and commitment to 'total service'. In the area of performance management, concrete and measurable targets were rarely defined for CRM, let alone cascaded to personal targets for managers and employees. Although several insurers said they had general CRM targets, only 2 out of 27 (7 per cent) had cascaded these. In the two companies where CRM performance was measured, there were no associated incentive plans.

Only 8 out of 27 insurers (30 per cent) said that their organization structure supported CRM. Scores were higher with the smaller insurers, where no walls exist between several departments and where employees are more concerned with customer well-being. For all the other insurers the structure is still too product-based.

Given this, one would expect few insurers to have allocated responsibility for CRM clearly at senior management level or to have management leading visibly in this area. The scores confirmed this, with only 9 out of 27 (33 per cent) of the insurers stating that this was happening.

INFORMATION AND TECHNOLOGY

This area is, among other aspects, about the quality of customer information. The quality of the data determines its usability. It demands specific attention. The scores in this area were lower than the average total score: on average 29 per cent, with a maximum of 58 per cent and a minimum of 2 per cent. As one would expect, the direct insurers scored higher in this area than intermediary and business-to-business insurers.

Most insurers were still struggling to create a single customer view. In many cases, customer information was stored in product administration systems. Particularly where companies had emerged from several mergers, no single customer view existed. One intermediary insurer had more Dutch intermediaries registered in its databases than exist in the Netherlands! Although customer files with name and address, interfacing with all other systems, were common, there was no insight into, for example, the number of products a customer had bought or the total premium per year across products. Only in one best-practice case was all customer information, including contact information, made accessible over all channels: call centre agents could see the type of information a customer had just asked for over the Internet.

PROCESSES

At 36 per cent, performance in this area was low. That this score is lower than the overall average score is attributable to a score of only 34 per cent for process management. Participants seemed to do little about formal identification and management of business processes that involve customer contact. This means that the prerequisites for structural improvement of these customer interaction processes did not exist. Processes were not formally identified, and there were no concrete and measurable targets from a customer's perspective. Also process performance was measured insufficiently. It is therefore remarkable that process improvement still had a relatively high score of 41 per cent. It seems that although the prerequisites are missing, this does not prevent insurers from trying to make process improvements. This is most strongly seen with business-to-business insurers who scored 54 per cent. Direct insurers scored lower with 46 per cent, and intermediary insurers lagged with 33 per cent.

Only 9 out of 27 (33 per cent) had service level agreements for CRM. In 6 cases (22 per cent), no formal initiatives existed. With the others, there was much variation: ranging from having identified processes, but doing nothing with them, to not having identified processes or formal targets, but still making ad hoc improvements.

CUSTOMER MANAGEMENT ACTIVITIES

Here, direct insurers scored higher on average (47 per cent) than the intermediary (36 per cent) and business-to-business insurers (35 per cent). It was remarkable how many times the minimum score of 0 per cent appeared for the various customer management activities.

Many insurers only welcomed their customers by sending out with policies a brochure giving the customer additional information. However, one direct insurer welcomed every new customer and asked him or her for additional information, varying from family composition to holdings of other policies. A customer sending back this information was rewarded with a pen. Subsequently the company called the customer to discuss neglected risks, on the basis of the information submitted. Though this approach seems aggressive, the company seemed to have found the right tone of voice, so customers appreciated this welcoming. For the insurer this programme was very profitable, especially in selling legal cover.

Most insurers did nothing or almost nothing to get to know their customers better. Most customer data was simply copied from policy documentation: name and address, policies and premiums. Even this information was not always easily accessible.

Almost every insurer managed customer dissatisfaction through a process and/or a system for complaint handling. However, almost everywhere a complaint was only a complaint when stated to be as such by the customer.

Almost no winback activities existed. With one exception, no companies registered the reason for lapse on the customer database.

Intermediary insurers, for whom customers (mostly only intermediaries) represent much more premium than for just one policy, scored higher (47 per cent) than the direct insurers (25 per cent). Surprisingly, business-to-business insurers scored only the same as direct insurers.

MEASUREMENT

Of all eight areas, this scored highest with an average of 43 per cent. The relatively high score in the area 'measuring customer management' (45 per cent) was probably due to the long tradition of marketing and sales budgeting, and the increasing focus on measuring retention, acquisition and 'wallet-share'. Only business-to-business insurers performed slightly less well. They scored 38 per cent, compared with 47 per cent by intermediary insurers and 46 per cent by direct insurers.

Scores were highest in the area of monitoring the effect of campaigns (56 per cent). However, measuring distribution channels scored lower than the other subjects at an average of only 34 per cent. Only a few insurers knew revenues, costs and margins by distribution channel. However, the direct insurers scored higher in this area with an average of 44 per cent, compared with 28 per cent for intermediary insurers and 29 per cent for business-to-business insurers. Direct insurers seemed more conscious of the variety of distribution channels and the margins available, perhaps because they tend to work on tighter margins.

Measuring employee performance scored relatively poorly with 38 per cent. With the exception of employees with sales responsibility, setting targets for employees with customer interaction was very limited. Performance was weakest for intermediary insurers.

CUSTOMER EXPERIENCE

As in other CMAT studies, customer experience was one of the areas with the lowest score: 32 per cent versus the overall average of 37 per cent. Most participants undertook research into customer satisfaction (average score of 47 per cent). However, research based on the customer experience at 'moments of truth' was done much less often, and 11 participants said this did not happen at all, or only at the lowest level. Mystery shopping was done only by a handful of insurers. So despite the high attention given to CRM, this attention was not focused on an understanding of what customers want and how they experience the company.

CONCLUSIONS

Slightly more than half of the insurers who participated in this benchmark research were focusing on a new way of approaching customers. Many were at various stages of implementing a CRM system to support this new approach. For them, a single customer view is key. Enriching this total customer view with relevant, possibly derived, customer information such as customer value, customer wants and needs, and contact history is not on the 'to do list' of most insurers. Only the direct insurers and some intermediary insurers have really progressed here. Most insurers were very focused on customer information and have a long way to go, and may be neglecting other CRM areas, such as insight into the wants and needs of the customer, the capability of employees to serve customers, or continuous improvement of customer-facing processes.

Insurers should move their focus away from package selection to an organization-wide CRM vision. which is not an issue for just the marketing or IT department, but needs to be initiated and supported by the board. The starting point for such an organization-wide CRM vision is not the architecture for implementing CRM IT, but the wants and needs of target customers. At many insurers, insight into the latter was weak.

15

Trends in customer management

Neil Woodcock, Michael Starkey and Merlin Stone

Global CRM spend is forecast to increase dramatically in the next five years. Consumers are steadily becoming less loyal, or at least happier to switch suppliers. Direct mail, telemarketing, face-to-face selling and television are the media of choice for most companies, with the most expenditure and steady growth forecast. Call centres will undergo a great change in the next few years and move away from the factory sweatshop image to a more service-oriented culture.

CUSTOMER MANAGEMENT SPEND IS INCREASING

Gartner predicts[1] that worldwide spending on CRM will reach US $76.3 billion in 2005, up from the US $23.26 billion achieved in 2000. Licence revenue will continue to be around 16 per cent of this total revenue. The North American share of spending will drop from 67 per cent to 48 per cent of total spending during 2000–5, as Europe and Asia increasingly focus on customer relationship management. What is driving this increase?

Supply-side complexity

Companies are faced with many choices in customer management. The larger the company, the more complex the choices. The choices include:

■ Product and product variations (although products are becoming more similar). Product marketers have done a good job of providing subtle variations to differentiate their products from those of competitors. The difficulty with this is maintaining the product line with the increased cost of development and brochure ware.

- Channels: which channels to use to access which customers – retail, outbound/inbound call centre, kiosk, intermediary, direct sales force, Web, wireless (for example, SMS), and mail.
- Segment targeting: which customers to target for which products.
- Choice of partners: which partners to choose for which products, segments and channels, and at what level of the supply chain.

Is it any wonder this increased complexity is confusing to marketers, and to the consumer? This is clearly one reason why IT vendors have had such an easy time selling to companies who are desperate for a solution to sort out this complexity. In reality, it rarely does.

Demand-side promiscuity (and control by customers)

Customers are quicker and happier to switch between suppliers. They are more positive about changing suppliers: they embrace it, often seek it, and are confident about it. They are more demanding of their existing products and suppliers and less accepting of error (although very loyal customers can be very forgiving). Globalization, deregulation and easy access to the Web enable consumers to seek the products they want. They can seek, source and purchase the product and leave without ever talking to a salesperson.

Bob Tyrell[2] described the conditions for 'exit' behaviour in social relationships and how this relates to buyer behaviour and loyalty. Individuals are more confident about making their own choices, partly because they have access to many more information sources than previous generations. They demonstrate their new confidence by:

- accessing the company how, when and where they want to;
- controlling the relationship and not wanting to feel controlled;
- asking to be valued and treated specially, particularly if they are a valuable customer;
- switching suppliers if they feel aggrieved, or if they receive unfulfilled or disappointing service 'promises'.

The Henley Centre's report, *The Loyalty Paradox*,[3] demonstrates that while companies often talk about their need to manage relationships with their customers, few customers use this language or indeed behave in this way. According to Frederick Reichheld[4] of Bain and Co, 'Between 65 per cent and 85 per cent of customers who defect say they were satisfied with their former supplier'. Reichheld suggests that sometimes customers stay because they are locked into long-term contracts or because they are unaware of competitive offerings. Reichheld proposes[5] the 'Loyalty Acid Test', which is a set of surveys that measures the loyalty of customers, suppliers' employees and other corporate stakeholders. The Loyalty Acid Test addresses the basic question: does this organization deserve your loyalty?

TRENDS IN CUSTOMER CONTACT CHANNELS AND MEDIA

In this section we investigate changes in media usage in the UK and United States, and from our own research provide some insight into what companies say about their future use of media.

The overall message is one of a healthy observation and testing of new media but no big change for the foreseeable future. Telemarketing, direct mail and television advertising are by far the most important media in terms of expenditure and will continue to be so for at least the next year, and probably longer. These traditional media continue to flourish even with the introduction and growth of the new media. In the UK telemarketing accounts for around 25 per cent of overall expenditure, followed by direct mail with about 20 per cent and television advertising with about 17 per cent. In terms of intentions over the next five years, spend on interactive digital media is forecast to grow sharply and is likely to erode telemarketing and mail spend, but we expect to see steady, rather than dramatic, change because the adoption of interactive techniques will not be widespread for some time. In any event, the interactive dialogue is likely to generate telephone and direct mail usage as part of the sales cycle. In the United States, a similar trend is emerging: the traditional media continuing to grow steadily. The Web and e-mail are growing rapidly and beginning to challenge spend on traditional media.

In our research, companies were asked which channel or media they see having most impact on sales in the next 12 months. Personal selling (face-to-face via sales people, dealer, agents, retail outlet, branch) was number one in most industries except consumer insurance, mail order and telecommunications, where the telephone was the number one selling medium. Direct mail and telemarketing normally came in as the number two or three most important medium. The Web has an increasingly important role in pre-purchase information searching. The use of online media for customer servicing is still not widespread. The implication here, again, is that media use is not changing quickly.

Despite the arrival of new media such as the Internet, e-mail, interactive television and the short message service (SMS), the impact so far has not lived up to the hype. Mail is still the second most important medium in terms of spend and is still growing in both the UK and the United States. Our research confirms that 'new media' are not yet significant components of the communications element of the marketing mix. Companies expect direct mail volumes to grow in line with other media. The US Direct Marketing Association (DMA) census states, 'direct mail continues to confound predictions of its decline in the electronic age. In fact, it has shown particularly strong growth in the face of increased competition.'

In the United States, the DMA suggests[6] a cautious approach to new media on the part of the traditional US direct marketers. The reasons are twofold. First, Christmas catalogue mailings are planned and budgeted up to 14 months ahead, Second, the DMA predict Internet-driven direct marketing sales will grow 50 per cent a year to US $84.4

billion by 2004, catalogue sales will be greater at US \$125 billion (6.1 per cent growth per annum), and direct mail will do even better with US \$723.8 billion (8.6 per cent growth). Traditional marketers will not ignore the Internet, but they will also continue to refine and retune both catalogue sales and direct mail.

A paper[7] produced by the DMA gives insight into the future of e-commerce media:

97 per cent of DMA members have a Web site in comparison with 90 per cent a year ago (1999).

- Of these, 60 per cent have e-mail marketing capability.
- 51 per cent conduct e-commerce sales and purchase transactions online.
- Business-to-consumer organizations are more likely to transact online.

The Web is becoming an important medium for international transactions, as it respects no frontiers.

- 56 per cent of all companies accepting orders online accept and fulfil orders outside Canada and the USA (70 per cent for B2B sites).
- 65 per cent of those indicate that transactions from overseas customers account for 10 per cent or more of all their transactions.

US marketing companies[8] are cautious about e-mail marketing and so use it mainly for customer retention rather than for prospecting. One approach is to use 'permission marketing' and only send e-mails to those who have opted in to receiving them. According to Forrester Research, 77 per cent of marketers send e-mail to customers who have asked for it. This is the opposite of 'spam'. Forrester estimates that by 2004 US marketing companies will be sending 210 billion e-mails a year. Seth Godin[9] describes organizations using what he refers to as 'interruption marketing' to get people's attention. Interruption marketing, Godin argues, is the enemy of anyone who wants to save time. Godin proposes 'permission marketing' as an alternative, which offers potential consumers the opportunity to choose to be marketed to. Volunteers are more likely to pay attention to the message. Permission marketing encourages people to take part in interactive long-term campaigns and be compensated for paying attention to the message. Godin says, 'imagine your marketing message being read by 70 per cent of the prospects you send it to (not 5 per cent or 1 per cent). Then imagine that more than 35 per cent respond. That's what happens when you interact with your prospects over time, with individual messages, exchanged with their permission over time. Permission marketing is anticipated, personal, relevant'. One company that uses 'permission marketing' is Omahasteaks.com, which sells beef and other food products online. Since 1995 it has built up a list of 500,000 names from people who have ordered from the site, requested information, taken advantage of on-site giveaways, and from purchasing opt-in names from list builders. Less than 1 per cent of these self-targeted consumers opt out.

The advantage of both e-mail marketing and direct mail is that they are less intrusive than telemarketing. Consumers can decide for themselves if and when to read messages.

Every six months the Hewson Consulting Group and eGain conduct an Online Service survey of UK organizations who advertise their presence with either an e-mail address or a Web site address. The results for the fifth survey[10] in May 2001 showed for the first time an improvement in service, with the Internet 'black hole' (where enquiries are not responded to) shrinking by 74 per cent. Now only 9 per cent of sales leads are being ignored entirely. The report says, 'Getting online service right is not a philanthropy but a hard-nosed business imperative with a high pay back. Much evidence indicates that good online service increases sales: both initial and repeat. For example, in the US financial services market, potential investors receiving an accurate e-mail response within one hour appear to be some 75 per cent more likely to purchase.' The report finds that only 1 in 20 companies are offering levels of online service that are likely to increase sales.

Hewson states there is now hard evidence of how poor online service affects offline business adversely. They quote Jupiter Media Metrix who recently reported that inadequate online customer service can cause 72 per cent of US online customers to reduce their spend in retail outlets, as well as to refuse to buy online. The survey shows that the biggest opportunity in online marketing for most companies is based on focusing on the early stages of the customer lifecycle: for example, by improving pre-sales service to hot prospects. Wendy Hewson, Research Director of Hewson Group, says, 'the current state of play in the UK is so feeble that the 1 in 20 companies who manage online sales leads well have an opportunity to win business in a channel with little real competition'.

One of the biggest changes we are likely to see over the next few years is in the management and organization of call centres. The stated rationale for setting up call centres is usually to improve customer service and reduce costs. However, instead of creating value, call centres may actually destroy value by increasing costs and reducing customer service. Call centres will receive increasingly adverse publicity. Customers cite long waiting times, incessant music, operatives who are not empowered, incompetent advice, and low call-closure rates: all these yield a negative experience and leave customers feeling bad about the service they have received. Apart from having a material effect on satisfaction and no doubt retention, poor call centres also increase the cost to serve (because several calls have to be made to answer one problem) and decrease the likelihood of cross-selling to the customer. One of the common roles for a call centre is to handle queries and problems, which as far as customers are concerned are normally one of the 'moments of truth' by which they judge a company. The call centre therefore has a high impact on the creation or destruction of value.

Our research confirms that good (competent customer managers) companies are likely to set up good call centres (good in the eyes of the customer), and bad companies, bad ones. In these 'bad' companies, although call centre managers may talk about service, their prime concern, encouraged of course by their bosses, is often cost (that is, the call centre is intended to lead to increased efficiency and cost reduction). Examples of this are the measures that staff are subjected to: for instance the number of calls taken or made, time per call, break time taken, call wrap-up time, call preparation time, and occupancy per cent. Although these are obvious measures for measuring productivity, they are also measures that get in the way of customer satisfaction and employee motivation. John Seddon[11] states, 'this is to argue for economies of scale, a feature of scientific management thinking which led to the development of large scale mass production systems at the turn of the 20th century. It would appear that the same thinking is adapting the technology of today to the same design – that of the factory.' Scientific management thinking was developed by F W Taylor and used by Henry Ford for mass production to reduce the costs of manufacturing automobiles. Many call centres are run on this principle. Call centres were introduced to provide differentiation, but when measured on operational measures can result in commoditization. Many 'bad' call centres have become little more than low-skilled 'sweat shops', with high employee attrition rates and poor morale. This is because they have been designed and managed according to F W Taylor's principles of 'mass production' – they are factories.

However, there is evidence that world-class organizations have moved away from mass production thinking towards the concept of systems thinking, which demands breaking down vertical functional silos so that all units collaborate and work together as one system. John Seddon of Vanguard Consulting argues that if customers experience what they require and no more and no less, service and efficiency will be optimized. Providing good service really does cost less. Seddon differentiates between 'value demand', the things you are there to do for the customer, and 'failure demand'. These are calls the customer has to make because the organization has not done something or has not done something right for the customer. The Vanguard report argues that the best way to design a call centre is to use a systems thinking approach. Management can do this by looking at the organization from the outside in and using methods that focus on value to the customer rather than production and units of work. Customers do not like having to wait a long time for the telephone to be answered, being kept waiting in a queue, then being greeted by a seemingly uninterested operator. Outside-in thinking leads to an understanding of the real nature of demand and precisely why customers call in.

NOTES

1 From a presentation by Michael Maoz's, Gartner Spring Summit, March 19–21 2001, Gartner Research, Chicago.
2 Tyrell, B (1998) Customer futures: implications for relationship marketing, *International Journal of Customer Relationship Management*, **1** (2).
3 Henley Centre (1994) *The Loyalty Paradox*, Henley Centre, UK.
4 Reichheld, F (1993) Loyalty based management, *Harvard Business Review* (March–April).

5   Reichheld, F (2001) Lead for loyalty, *Harvard Business Review* (July–August).
6   Online: http://www.the.dma.org/library.
7   US Direct Marketing Association (DMA) (2000) *Direct Marketing, the Internet, and the Survival of Direct Mail* (September), DMA [Online: http://www.the-dma.org/library/whitepapers/dmandinternet.shtmel].
8   DMA (2001) *Spam's Good Twin: If e-mail is done just right, people will want to receive it. Really* (September), DMA [Online: http://www.the-dma.org/library/whitepapers/spams-goodtwin.shtml]
9   Godin, S (1999) *Permission Marketing*, Simon & Schuster
10 Hewson Consulting Group (2001) *UK Scores on the Online Doors: Results from HCG Online Survey (May)*
11 Seddon, J (1999) *The Vanguard Guide to Transforming Call Centre Operations*, Vanguard, Buckingham.

16

The business case for customer management

Neil Woodcock, Michael Starkey and Merlin Stone

There is a strong correlation between business performance and customer management (CM). Most benefit is gained from viewing CM as a system, or value chain. On some commonly used measures, the scale of benefit varies widely. For instance, companies can expect to gain between 2 and 50 per cent increases in turnover from improving CM. A more reliable guide is that companies can expect a 400 per cent return on investment from well-managed programmes. However, the benefit and the payback period vary greatly with the company's maturity in customer management and the size of the investment. Lower-quartile performers need to invest more, and take more risk, to achieve high levels of benefit.

THE CORRELATION BETWEEN CUSTOMER MANAGEMENT AND BUSINESS PERFORMANCE IS CLEAR

In our report 'The customer management scorecard: the state of the nation'[1], we discussed several approaches that have influenced and shaped our thinking and can help create customer value. These included the Deming Prize, the Malcolm Baldridge National Quality Award, the EFQM Business Excellence Model, the Balanced Scorecard, and the American Customer Satisfaction Index (ACSI).

Professor Peter Doyle of Warwick Business School[2] refers to how managers have sometimes confused maximizing shareholder value and maximizing profitability. Doyle states that the two are completely different and that:

Maximizing profitability is short term and invariably erodes the company's long-term market competitiveness. It is about cutting costs and shedding assets to produce quick improvements in earnings. By neglecting new market opportunities and failing to reinvest, such strategies destroy rather than create economic value. Strategies aimed at maximising shareholder value are different. They focus on identifying growth opportunities and building competitive advantage. They punish short-term strategies that destroy assets and fail to capitalise on the company's core capabilities.

There is a close correlation (0.88) between the Dow Jones and the ACSI. Researchers at the University of Michigan Business School[3] claim that market value added (MVA), stock price, and return on investment are highly related to the ACSI. Their research shows that companies with the top 50 per cent of ACSI scores created an average US $24 billion in shareholder wealth while firms with the bottom 50 per cent of scores generated only US $14 billion. An article[4] by Michael Lowenstein describes how the ACSI shows that satisfaction scores for airlines, banks, department stores, fast-food restaurants, hospitals, hotels and telephone companies are all down. Lowenstein suggests the reasons for this include cost reduction pressures, reduction of investment in human factor in favour of technology, and the attitude of senior management, as it shapes the culture, structure, systems and processes within the company.

Further evidence[5] that the implementation of best practice and quality management principles has an impact on the bottom line can be found in a recent study conducted by Dr Vinod Singhal of Georgia Institute of Technology and Dr Kevin Hendricks of the College of William and Mary.[6] Their five-year study of over 600 quality award winners concluded that award winners achieved significant improvement in operating income, stock value, sales revenue, return on sales, asset growth and employment. The researchers tracked performance over five years, from one year before the award to four years after receipt. Compared with a control group, award winners achieved a 44 per cent higher stock market price, 48 per cent higher growth in operating income and 37 per cent higher growth in sales revenue.

QCi commissioned research[7] to examine the correlation between how well a company manages its customers and business performance. It showed strong correlation (0.8) between good customer management performance and business performance (Figure 16.1). In other words those companies that look after their customers and are truly customer-centric are more likely to return better financial results. This research indicates that a system approach to customer management is likely to lead to stronger business performance. This is shown in Figure 16.2, which shows how the overall CMAT score (the score of how well companies manage customers) and scores for each element of the CMAT model correlate with business performance.

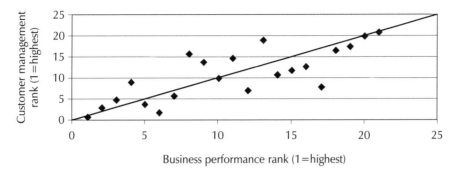

Chart shows a powerful 0.8 correlation between the way a company
manages customers and its business performance

Figure 16.1 Correlation between customer management performance and business
performance

The highest correlation is with the overall CMAT score itself, implying that greatest
business performance is likely to be achieved by carrying out a number of 'priority' activities across the whole model: a first pass across the model if you like. This approach is likely
to be more beneficial than focusing deeply on one area, such as analysis and planning.
While correlation does not necessarily mean causation, all the combined evidence from the
various performance studies suggests that striving towards best practice across the
'system' delivers a sound return on investment.

An integrated approach is required to create maximum value

These studies show that it makes sense to work with a system approach, and specifically
across the CMAT model, rather than to work deeply in one area to the exclusion of
others. Why is this the case? Because the compounded benefits of action (across the
enterprise) will lead to a scale of benefit tactical approaches themselves cannot achieve.
For instance, there is little sense in having excellently motivated people with clear objectives managing customers who make a loss for the company. There is no benefit in
having a clear proposition aimed at the wrong customers. There is much more value to
be gained from measuring activities than just running them without measurement.
There is no point having an excellent IT system if it contains the wrong data and people
are not competent to use it, or the customer experience of IT being used is poor. There is
less value in managing enquiries well if the targeting programme is poor, as the boxed
example shows.

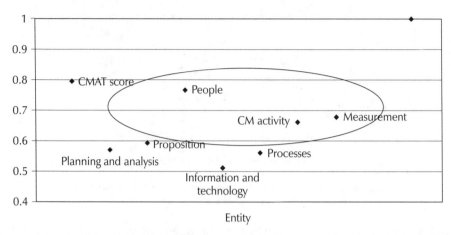

Figure 16.2 Which areas are most important?

A company improved its enquiry management process (through improving the competence of the enquiry handlers, and changing the incentive programme) so much that actual 'sustained sales' (that is, enquiry conversions that were not later cancelled) increased from 6.5 per cent to 10.6 per cent, with little change in average sales value (US $550 to US $535). This process improvement created value for the organization. However, the analysis and planning process did not recognize high-value prospects, so targeting programmes were not focused. Work was carried out in analysis and planning and targeting areas, and pilot campaigns showed that both conversions and average sales values were increased (to 14.3 per cent and $710 respectively) through better-targeted programmes. This simple example shows that value creation can compound between stages of the model, in this case from analysis and planning, targeting and enquiry management.

However, cross-enterprise planning and business-case development rarely happen because planning and budgets are still mainly carried out on a functional or departmental basis. It is therefore more difficult for a company to coordinate this work so that more value can be created. We provide some insights and guidelines on programme planning in the next chapter, but in this chapter we go on to look at the prize from customer management for companies today.

IDENTIFYING THE MAIN BENEFITS

This chapter does not cover the detailed building of business cases. Instead, it provides some rules of thumb for calculating the scale of the benefit that can be achieved. Our insights have come from analysis of:

▊ various reports which estimate the scale of the benefit;
▊ CMAT score and company performance;
▊ experience of tactical and strategic projects in which our clients have been involved that led to an increase in CMAT scores;
▊ a few successful projects running over three years where the business cases have been tracked.

To determine the potential benefit, you must take into account the following:

▊ The turnover of the company, which influences the scale and variety of potential benefits.
▊ The size of the investment made: we have identified a ratio for return on investment (ROI) which is remarkably similar for a number of different companies.
▊ The maturity and competence of the organization in customer management. This affects first, the size of the investment needed; second, the potential prize; and third, the expected timing of benefit. These in turn determine the project risk.

BENEFITS AS A PERCENTAGE OF TURNOVER

Few companies that track benefits from CM projects find a relationship between the level of benefits and a particular percentage of turnover. The best one will get are ranges. Some idea of the possible benefit can be gleaned from the Hewson Group[8], who have reviewed various studies of the results of implementing CRM systems (though systems are, as we have seen, not the most important factor). As a caveat, they note that it is very difficult to assign benefits in this way. We concur with their reasons, which are that:

▊ There is rarely baseline data before a system is implemented.
▊ There are many other independent variables at work.
▊ Many benefits are soft and therefore hard to quantify.

None the less, they argue that CM programmes make a significant difference.

A convincing estimate of the benefits on offer comes from Insight Technology Group, which examined the effects of CM programmes where they are followed through to completion. Insight Technology identified that companies had achieved benefits (actual results) in five key areas, and these were the upper limits of the benefits achieved:

▊ Revenue increases   42 per cent;
▊ Sales cost decreases   35 per cent;
▊ Sell cycle reductions   25 per cent;
▊ Margin improvements   2 per cent;
▊ Customer satisfaction   20 per cent.

QCi business case tracking analysis (actual results) shows similar overall benefits. It shows that turnover increases of between 2 per cent and 58 per cent are possible. In a detailed study over three years for three different companies, QCi found the relationship of the benefits achieved to a company's turnover to be variable and unpredictable. CM improvement is likely to increase turnover, perhaps substantially, but is not directly related to it.

There is some evidence that smaller companies or business units can achieve greater benefits than larger companies. Singhal and Hendricks[9] state that most small firms believe that performance excellence is more relevant and applicable to larger firms. However, their research showed that small award-winning firms achieved on average 63 per cent increase in operating income, 39 per cent increase in sales, 17 per cent increase in return on sales, 21 per cent increase in employment and 42 per cent increase in assets. For each of these metrics the smaller award-winning firms outperformed the larger ones. Another interesting outcome was that high-capital-intensive award winners do not perform as well as lower-capital-intensive award winners. Great is small?

In summary, benefits as a proportion of turnover are potentially very large, but their variability implies that they clearly do not tell the whole story and should not be used alone to build a case for CRM investment.

THE SIZE OF THE INVESTMENT: THE 4:1 RULE

The data from four business cases from different international companies tracked over three years showed the remarkable similarity in ROI across three very different businesses and a close match for the fourth.

Note that in the above example:

- ▊ Size is turnover at the start of the period, and all benefits are calculated in NPV terms.
- ▊ CM investment as a percentage of turnover is exactly as stated.
- ▊ Benefit as a percentage of turnover is the total net benefit across the three-year forecast period.
- ▊ ROI is defined as the total increase in revenue relative to the total additional investment applied.

Table 16.1 appears to show a relationship between the level of investment and the benefits from improved acquisition, retention and development. (There are no general rules for efficiency gains, as these depend so much on how efficient the company was before the investment.) That is, in general, revenue increase is around four times the original investment. Though this is a small sample, this figure is consistent with projects we have implemented. So we suggest that if a business invested US $50 million in CM, if

Table 16.1 The size of the investment: the 4:1 rule

Company	Turnover	Sector	CM investments as % of turnover over 3 years	Benefit as % of turnover	Return on investment (ROI)
1	$~700 million	Computer supplier	2%	8.5%	4.3
2	$~7 million	Financial services	15.5%	52.6%	3.4
3	$~11 billion	Telecomms	0.5%	2.1%	4.1
4	$~600 million	Travel	1%	8.3%	4.2

the project is managed properly it should expect a US $200 million return. This is a useful rule of thumb, but it does not guide a company on how much it should invest. It also disguises the relative benefits to be gained from companies with a different starting competence in customer management. This is where our maturity model can help.

THE ORGANIZATION'S MATURITY AND COMPETENCE IN CM MANAGEMENT

Figure 16.3 shows the ROI planned for a number of companies at different stages of customer management maturity. How CM investment pays back varies by the company's CM maturity. Companies that manage their customers especially badly are likely to see a much greater benefit but from a higher level of investment, over a longer period of time. They have more to invest and more to gain.

Lower-quartile performers

Lower-quartile companies (for example, low CMAT scorers) are likely to operate a classic product organizational model with strong product management disciplines and a focus on product sales. There will be a limited focus on the overall proposition, and their approach to marketing will not be focused on customers. Companies towards the top of this quartile believe that better coordination in CM will improve customer satisfaction and loyalty. However, customer management in these organizations is likely to be 'champion-based' (enthusiastic individuals), and senior, cross-enterprise leadership not apparent.

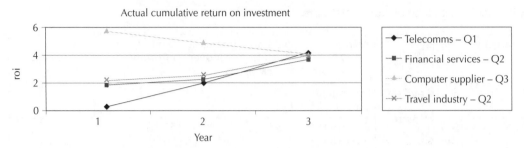

Figure 16.3 Maturity and the time dimension

Table 16.2 suggests that these companies need to invest heavily in infrastructure and programmes. Careful project planning is needed to allow the achievement of quick wins that help justify continuing investment, but net benefits will be more apparent towards the latter stages of, say, a three-year programme. With the short-termism commented on earlier, does this imply that poorly performing companies are unlikely to invest in customer management because the payback is in two or three years? If they do not invest, our correlation work (see Figure 16.1) shows that they will continue to under-perform from a business perspective. At best they become targets for hostile merger or takeover activity. At worst they could go out of business.

The investment in these companies should not be biased towards IT systems, as it often is in practice, but should be applied across the enterprise for all aspects of CM. Our CMAT work shows that companies at this stage benefit from making the customer management process more robust, but the net benefits should be reinvested in developing infrastructure. Steady investment for these companies is not an option. However, relative performance might not increase if competitors are also investing from a more advanced starting point. The decision facing senior managers and stakeholders in these businesses is to look long and hard at their market potential, and either invest significantly to achieve a step-change in customer management, or divest, sell or merge. Commitment, strong leadership, higher investment and careful project planning are required to generate attractive benefits over time.

Higher-quartile performers

Highest-quartile performers will be high business performers. They will already have a well-developed people and systems infrastructure and a mature, customer-centric culture. All of the characteristics of top-performing companies mentioned in this book will be in place. These companies 'know who they are', what they offer and which customers they are managing. They are flexible in their planning, and their decision-making ability allows them to react to market changes quickly. Their IT systems and

Table 16.2   Indicative estimate returns

Customer management performance	Likely investment level needed	Likely main investment areas	Likely ROI year 1	Likely ROI year 2	Likely ROI year 3	Overall ROI (simple average over 3 years)
Lower quartile performer	High	Whole model	1	3	7	3.67
Third quartile	Medium–high	Whole model	2	3	7	4
Second quartile	Low–medium	Measurement, activity, proposition, IT	3	4	5	4
Highest quartile performer (est)	Tactical	People, activity, customer experience	4.5	5	5.5	5

culture will be customer-focused, so that, for example, their databases will contain the full customer 'context' across any channel and transaction, data capture will be consistent across channels, a common set of business rules will apply, for example offering prompts as to how an individual contact or transaction should be handled, irrespective of medium (that is, on the Web, in the call centre or sales force, in partner intermediaries or in retail outlets). The business rules help identify issues and opportunities, and rather than being given to uninterested agents will be used by empowered service staff as the context demands. The benefit for these companies from further investment in CM is likely to be lower overall, because they have already achieved a great deal. We have no evidence of ever-increasing benefits from CM investment. These companies, and there are not many of them today, receive a good rate of return from smaller, often tactical initiatives, but these higher returns are from a smaller investment.

Maturity and the time dimension

Figure 16.3 shows cumulative ROI, to the end of the first, second and third years. A rising line indicates that ROI has increased, year on year. A flat line indicates that the effect of investment remains constant, while a descending one (as in the case of the computer supplier) suggests that there is some degree of diminishing return at work. The match between quartile and ROI pattern is not exact. However, the idea that emerges is that poor CMAT performers (quartile 3 or quartile 4) need high initial investment, which will be followed by slow initial gains and major gains after two to three years. Those already performing in this area will show quicker initial gains (the infrastructure to capitalize on gains is already in place), but, the level of investment will not change much year on year; so benefits tend to follow a steady rate, rather than leap up dramatically at any point in time. The major overall implication that we have identified across numerous forecasts is that it is likely to take time for the full effect of CM to be delivered (though this is not always the case).

Table 16.2 gives indicative estimated returns. Please treat it as a guide only as it is based on a small number of detailed tracking studies. We have not yet seen a top-quartile performer.

Note: when comparing this table with Figure 16.3 above, the figures quoted here are our estimates for ROI within an individual year, while the final column (average ROI over three years) corresponds to the final points on the graph. Table 16.2 illustrates much more starkly what we believe to be the differences in effect between CM investment applied to top and bottom-quartile companies. For instance, in Year 1, we expect bottom-quartile companies to show no or little return on investment. This closely matches our experience. Bottom-quartile companies have invested little in their customers, so the first year or two can be a very expensive catch-up phase, followed by quite exceptional ROI in year three and beyond. Here we quote an ROI figure of 7. Note that the end benefit (that is, average ROI) tends to converge for organizations starting at different levels of maturity. This is because companies in low quartiles are moving up the maturity ladder, so that spend in Years 2 and 3 is more akin to spend within a company that was already more mature.

Net benefit by customer maturity

From the comments and data above, the graph in Figure 16.4 can be prepared. The graph takes into account the maturity of a company (in terms of the way it manages customers) and level of net benefit it is likely to achieve initially. It is an S curve, showing that companies moving from the third quartile to the first quartile have the most to gain from customer management. Top-performing companies (and there are not many of them as CMAT-Results show) can squeeze incremental advantage from customer management, but their main business growth areas are likely to lie elsewhere. They have a good return on a smaller investment.

Business benefits: two worked examples

A financial services business unit has a turnover of US $500 million. It has scored 20 per cent on a CMAT assessment, which means that it is at the low end of the lower quartile for its sector. Target benefit is US $100 million (averaged over three years). Applying ROI criteria from the table (ROI = 3.67), it needs to invest about US $27.5 million over three

Smoothed results will give an "S" Curve

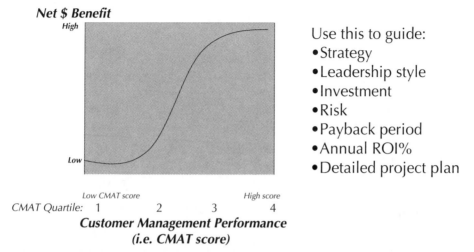

Net $ Benefit

High

Low

Low CMAT score   High score

CMAT Quartile: 1   2   3   4

Customer Management Performance
(i.e. CMAT score)

Use this to guide:
- Strategy
- Leadership style
- Investment
- Risk
- Payback period
- Annual ROI%
- Detailed project plan

Figure 16.4   QCi maturity model

years to obtain this. Assuming this investment is split evenly between the years (US $9.2 million per year), it should see returns of:

▓ US $9 million in year one (in fact an ROI of less than 1, so the investment is producing a net loss);
▓ US $27.2 million in year two (which means the investment is beginning to pay back);
▓ US $63.6 million in year three (which is a very handsome payback).

The investment is high, so the risk is higher, particularly in the first period of the project, but the eventual net benefits are also high.

A second company also has a turnover of US $500 million. However, it has scored 75 per cent on a CMAT assessment, which means that it is just in the top quartile overall. Target benefit is US $100 million (averaged over three years). Applying ROI criteria (ROI for this quartile = 5), it needs to invest US $20 million over three years to obtain this (27 per cent less). Assuming this investment is split evenly between the years (c. US $6.67 million per year), it should see returns of:

▓ US $30 million in year one (an immediate payback);
▓ US $33.3 million in year two (continuing payback; similar to year one);
▓ US $36.7 million in year three (continuing gradual rise in payback relative to year one and year two).

This company has a lower investment and a much lower risk associated with the payback.

Another way of looking at this is that a company that stays in the bottom quartile will have to make about 4.5 times the investment of a similar-sized top-quartile company for the same return. However, as its CM performance improves, it will need to invest less.

SUMMARY BASE DATA USED IN QCi RESEARCH

The companies illustrated in Figure 16.3 are:

▮ a computer supplier;
▮ a financial services provider;
▮ a telecomms company;
▮ a travel company.

Some of the figures that describe their actual and forecast performance have already been given. The base data are repeated and expanded upon here for clarity. At first sight, there does not appear to be a clear pattern. However, this shows how different approaches to CM can take different times to work. The telecomms and financial services companies both wanted to develop CM from a position of little previous investment in it. They therefore needed to invest heavily in systems – call centre and database – before they saw any payback, so the cash flow for both was very negative in year one. As the implementation proceeded, so the benefits began to flow, leading to a better ROI in years two, three and beyond.

In the case of the computer supplier, the situation was quite different. This company was mature in CM terms. It had already invested heavily in systems, and scored quite highly on CMAT for its customer-handling capability, so many of the proposed measures related to making better use of existing CM assets. A good return was possible using CM techniques, but the company was starting to reach saturation in its market. Getting higher returns from CM would only be possible if it entered new markets.

The travel company lies somewhere between these two extremes. Already fairly customer-focused, it shows fairly speedy payback on investment in year one – an ROI greater than 2 – with slow growth after that, finishing at a perfectly respectable ROI of 4.2 across the whole three-year period.

An analysis of payback for lower-quartile companies shows just how little benefit is delivered until the third year: in fact, between 60 per cent and 70 per cent of total benefit does not come through until then. It underlines the need for CM initiatives to be viewed as at least a medium-term investment. Companies that score poorly on CMAT should not look for any net benefits in the first 18 months. Although benefits may begin to flow in that time, they are really quite small. In all cases, there is evidence that the ROI improvement in specific countries or sub-segments of the overall market could be significantly greater.

The main outcome here is the remarkable consistency in forecast benefits, relative to CM development. There is a range, from ROI of 3.4 to 4.3. However, these appear to be close to the extremes, suggesting that CM investment should aim to repay approximately four times the costs within three years of implementation.

NOTES

[1] Woodcock, N, Starkey, M and Stone, M (2001) The customer management scorecard: the state of the nation, *Business Intelligence*.
[2] Doyle, P (2001) *Value Based Marketing: Marketing strategies for corporate growth and shareholder value*, Wiley, Chichester.
[3] Online: http://www.bus.umich.edu/research/nqrc/acsi.html.
[4] Lowenstein, M (2001) Customer service in decline, *Marketing Business* (October), p 12.
[5] http://www.oklahomaquality.com/benefits.htm.
[6] http://www.oklahomaquality.com/benefits.htm.
[7] Woodcock, N (2000) Does how customers are managed impact on business performance?, *Interactive Marketing*, **1** (4) (April/June).
[8] See www.hewson.co.uk.
[9] http://www.oklahomaquality.com/benefits.htm.

17

Guidelines for successful CRM implementation

Neil Woodcock, Michael Starkey and Merlin Stone

Many companies aim to implement complex customer management (CM) strategies, and this increases the risk of project failure. We have shown that companies' CM is not particularly robust, even though the prize for success is large. The chances of achieving success can be increased if a company follows some simple guidelines. Plans are often inflexible. They are often based on little accurate knowledge of the company's situation. Activities should be prioritized from the beginning. They should build on the strengths and remove weaknesses. Prioritization should be based on factors most likely to affect business performance. Projects should be kept short with a clear business focus. The programme should be managed, not just individual projects. To help you do this, this chapter ends with a checklist for CM programme management.

CM PROJECTS ARE FAR MORE LIKELY TO FAIL THAN SUCCEED

Many CM programmes started this year will fail! The dangers of very large projects are particularly acute, any CM project greater than US $15 million is almost certain to fail.[1] The biggest shortfalls between expectation and reality are in customer service and responsiveness, staff productivity and business management. Specific targets and expected results are rarely achieved: around half of those companies in a PA survey[2] sought to streamline and integrate business processes, or improve productivity. In reality, only 5 per cent felt that progress had been made in this area. Organizations end up with systems that are poorly aligned with business needs. Companies often maintain that they ended up with a system that does not support the business need. This is usually due to an unclear definition of requirements (possibly due to an unclear business model) or poor project control. This leads to 'scope creep', so system requirements are never actually finalized.

Nick Hewson of the Hewson Group believes that recently there has been some improvement[3] in CRM project implementation. He feels that the failure rate for tactical CRM projects will be in the order of 30 per cent to 40 per cent, but around 60 per cent for those with a strategic focus. Sales force automation (SFA) projects are most likely to fail, mainly because sales people can resist or hinder implementation – they can even refuse to use the software – as opposed to call centre staff.

The commonest reasons for CM project failure[4] appear to be:

▌ Failure to think through the business strategy and model.
▌ Not dealing with the basic problems of the organization. (Listening to employees would help here!)
▌ Too much focus on technology, too little on data and skills.
▌ Objectives unfounded on knowledge of the organization today, its capability to change, and receptiveness of customers to different ways of being managed.
▌ Absence of skills to deliver the programme.
▌ Not having done it before, there is no knowledge of how and where to start.
▌ Choice of wrong partners to support the project.
▌ Failure to integrate the different aspects of CRM in a 'joined-up' manner, partly because senior management do not view the idea holistically, and because organizational structures create problems.
▌ Setting aggressive timescales.

PROJECT IMPLEMENTATION TIPS

The following approach to CRM project development appears to give the best chance of success:

▌ Take a phased, steady approach to CRM development, not big bang.
▌ Develop a vision of the future, but do not make it too detailed too soon.
▌ Know where you are starting from. Be clear and unemotional about how well you manage your customers now.
▌ Focus on a few easy actions that will lead to increased profitability quickly: cherry pick key actions and quick wins.

▌ Listen to staff: remove what they see as the basic barriers to managing customers better.

▌ Right from the beginning, manage the programme by outputs as well as inputs, to ensure that what you expect to happen with customers does happen, or at least to understand why it does not.

▌ Measure and build on phase one in future phases.

▌ Accept willingly and unemotionally any challenges to your longer-term vision, whether they are challenges from others in your organization based on their analysis or ideas, or performance challenges identified during the early stages of implementation.

Let us examine some of these points in more detail.

A phased, steady approach to CRM development

In our work over the last 15 years, we have identified the following two basic models of programme planning for implementing CM:

▌ *Big bang*: moving as rapidly as possible to implement CM principles across the business. This generally only works for 'greenfield' businesses. Success is very rare, and normally only works in businesses that are direct-only or single distribution channel businesses, usually with simple product ranges, where strong central control can be used to ensure implementation.

▌ *Steady progress*: moving steadily towards a CM vision, while recognizing that the vision will continue to change. For larger companies, often with a background of several partly successful CM initiatives, this is usually the better option. Very strong programme management disciplines are required as the series of projects is rolled out across the business. It is usually best to start with pilot projects to establish possibilities and capabilities, before rolling out CM activity to the rest of the business. Tough choices have to be made about where to start, and indeed whether parts of the business should be left untouched. Eric Abrahamson of the Columbia Business School has been studying for many years how organizations change. He argues[5] that in order to change successfully companies should stop doing it all the time.

Develop a vision of the future, but do not lock into detail too soon. Know where you are going, at least in outline

Establishing the vision is normally the starting point. This should cover markets (segments), competitive positioning and your broad approach to distribution channels.

Unless your company is a start-up, or is changing its CM approach as part of a much wider change programme, the vision need only be in outline.

Look at the relative attractiveness and size of different sectors and the company's competitive differentiation in each one. This will help you determine your future direction. What communication and distribution channels will you use to reach out to each segment? Will this change for different product groups? What proposition do you need to find and keep target groups, and how will you ensure the organization behaves in a way that can deliver the proposition?

Know where you are starting from

If you do not know this, it makes planning the route very difficult indeed. Not knowing your company's competence in managing customers is a major reason for CRM project failure. Figure 17.1 shows the percentage of companies where the senior sponsor view prior to the assessment was within 10 per cent of the actual score. Companies who do not know their starting position build future corporate competencies on shifting sands rather than a solid foundation. It is usually only companies who are good performers already that know what is wrong and what needs to be done.

One of the commonest findings in CMAT assessments is the difference between management intention (and belief) and reality. We have called it 'the great customer management illusion'. Just as alarming is the fact that 67 per cent of senior managers do not give clear, visible leadership in achieving excellence in customer management. Lack

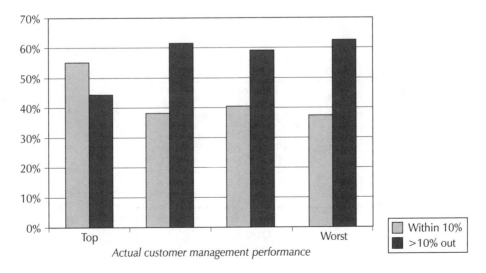

Figure 17.1   Sponsors' estimate of CMAT scores

of clear visible leadership is particularly evident in poor-performing companies. Those with the worst CMAT scores (and therefore the worst business performers) are the ones most likely to believe that they are good, and the ones least likely to welcome 'bad' or critical feedback.

Cherry pick key actions and quick wins: use a clear prioritization process

To select the components of the first phase of a project, you need to prioritize the activities or tasks identified in the business case. The prioritization process involves examining the following elements:

▌ expected net value of benefit over three years;
▌ expected timing of benefit;
▌ probability of benefit being achieved (which takes into account 'ease of implementation').

The matrix in Figure 17.2 has two axes. The x-axis (horizontal) looks at the net financial benefit of the project while the y-axis (vertical) looks at the probability of achieving the benefit. All projects in the top right corner of the matrix should be considered for the first phase of any CRM project. For these projects, the matrix implies that there is a good probability of achieving relatively high payback for these projects. Table 17.1 shows an 'ease of implementation' scoring system. For each of the possible activities, the ease of

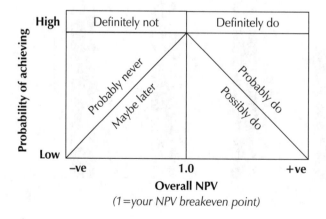

Figure 17.2 Financial benefits and probability of achieving the benefit

Table 17.1 'Ease of implementation' scoring system

Scoring system				
5	4	3	2	1
Score 5 if:			*Score 1 if:*	
• culturally easy to implement (likely to be readily accepted by senior managers);			• culturally very difficult to implement (unlikely to be readily accepted by senior managers);	
• can be set up quickly (<1 month);			• will take over 6 months to set up;	
• is low risk (cost);			• is high risk (cost);	
• is low risk (in terms of achieving stated benefits);			• is high risk (in terms of achieving stated benefits);	
• reliant on simple system functionality.			• reliant on advanced system functionality.	

implementing them is important in determining the probability of the benefits being realized. This helps the programme manager score the activities on the 'y' axis.

The first phase should contain a blend of quick wins and longer-term capability development. The quick wins will give confidence to the sponsor, senior team, project team and others, help engage doubters, and encourage sponsorship for longer-term investments. As our chapter on business cases showed, the payback for lower-quartile companies is two to three years, but well-constructed plans can produce benefit each year.

Manage the programme for outputs from the beginning: minimize payback time and investment

The first phase of the programme should last no longer than about six months. Costs should be limited before some payback is witnessed. This applies even in the largest companies with the largest systems projects. Some may find this controversial, but the strong evidence of project failure justifies this. Projects with first phases longer than six months or with very high costs will be a leap of faith: there is a chance they may work, but they are more likely to fail.

Listen to staff

Ensure enough resource is allocated to training, coaching and measurement. In many systems projects, too much time and resource is spent on systems development and formal training. Companies should consider more post-implementation coaching. What is the project trying to change? Post-implementation, the programme manager needs to ensure that the project is working. People should be coached to ensure they understand and can apply the new ways of working. Management must listen to feedback on why people find it difficult to deploy, and then make changes to ensure easier programme deployment.

Measure and build on the first phase

Measurement should cover employees' and partners' behaviour and attitudes towards the required change. This may involve researching your own people and partners, as well as customers. The same measurement process that identified where the company was starting from should be used to identify whether improvements actually have been made.

Prepare for future phases

Later phases of the project cannot be planned in detail at the outset. Future phases should be relatively flexible, based on the vision and actual performance in earlier phases.

Manage the programme, not just the project

QCi uses a programme management checklist (Table 17.2) for determining the likelihood of programme success and for identifying where changes are needed. The checklist is normally 'scored' using a simple red/amber/green flagging system. This is defined as:

▓ Red: an area of high risk to the programme. Significant issues have not been addressed. Failure to do so may endanger the whole programme.
▓ Amber: an area of moderate risk to the programme. Significant issues have only been partially addressed, less significant issues may have been ignored.
▓ Green: an area of low/no risk to the programme. Best practice has been observed, or alternatively, issues have been identified as irrelevant to the success or failure of the programme.

The checklist is completed via interviews of key project and user staff, and by looking at project documentation. A report can be produced recording the positive and negative observations, and risk factors.

Table 17.2 QCi programme manager's checklist

Check item	Positives	Negatives	Risk level
Project scope			
1.1 Clear objectives overall.			
1.2 Realistic deliverables / accurate reflection of business case.			
1.3 Real change to business.			
1.4 Adequate focus for change management.			
1.5 Areas for potential conflict.			
Project financials and business case			
2.1 Robust business case. Accurate financials.			
2.2 Access to sufficient budget. Short-term budgetary constraints.			
2.3 Short & long-term deliverables / parallel strategies.			
Project team			
3.1 Senior and supportive programme leader.			
3.2 Supportive senior champion.			
3.3 Coordinated by a steering group of senior managers. Clarity of roles. Full buy-in.			
3.4 Overall delivery entrusted to senior experienced programme manager.			
3.5 Programme team have full implementation authority.			
Project management			
4.1 All key stages in project identified and planned. Sub-projects?			
4.2 Right project structure.			
4.3 Clear and unambiguous business measures in place.			
4.4 Clear prioritisation process.			
4.5 Current position benchmarked.			
Managing implementation			
5.1 Informal network to identify blocks / barriers. Dependencies identified.			
5.2 Key influencers identified. Are they advocates?			
5.3 Right skills mix internally. Too much outsourcing?			
5.4 Sufficient skills to maintain project momentum.			
5.5 Have we identified the right supplier(s)? Are formal procedures in place?			
5.6 Is momentum maintained by documentation and communication?			
5.7 Internal communication in place.			
5.8 Benefits identified for all key influencers.			
5.9 Thought given to holistic implementation.			
Reviewing and maintaining performance			
6.1 Right balance between coaching and training. Skills being passed on.			
6.2 Is attitude and behaviour research planned relative to implementation?			
6.3 Scope within the project to test and refine alternative approaches.			
6.4 KPIs being developed relative to project needs.			

Accept challenges to the longer-term vision

Very few markets are stable or predictable enough for you to be certain that the first phase of your programme is 100 per cent correct, especially if the first phase includes research and analysis of customer behaviour and value for the first time. Your findings will be likely to change future phases of the programme, accept this and continually review your vision and objectives.

NOTES

[1]   KPMG, 2000.
[2]   PA Consulting (2000) *Unlocking the Value in ERP*, PA.
[3]   Telephone conversation with one of the authors.
[4]   Woodcock, N, Starkey, M and Stone, M (2000) The customer management scorecard: the state of the nation, *Business Intelligence*, Chapter 6.
[5]   Abrahamson, E (2000) Change without pain, *Harvard Business Review* (July–August).

Part 2

Measurement, systems and data

18

Return on investment on e-CRM

Mark Cerasale, Merlin Stone and Julie Abbott

INTRODUCTION

The challenging economic conditions of recent months have forced a heightened interest in return on investment (ROI). This chapter aims to examine the ROI on e-CRM. The 'e' in this acronym was originally the 'e' from 'e-business', but as our understanding of the relationship between CRM and the supply chain has developed (see Chapter 25), so the 'e' has come to mean 'enterprise'. However, much of the thinking and experience of e-CRM relates to the use of Web technology to facilitate information flows within and between companies, so it is quite helpful to consider the 'e' as being both electronic and enterprise! This chapter will analyse the business case for using the Internet to improve marketing, sales and customer-support activities. This chapter presents quantitative information, such as the benefits of e-CRM as published by organizations in many industries. It also includes qualitative information gained from extensive research by the authors and their first hand experience of e-CRM.

The four main phases of e-CRM transformation are publishing information, interaction, transaction and integration. The success of e-CRM depends on the propensity of the organization, its customers and its partners to change, and the level of investment available. Each of these is unique to each organization. ROI on e-CRM depends on whether e-CRM transformation can actually be achieved. The key benefits of e-CRM are cost reduction, increased revenues, better cash flow management and an improved customer experience. The major costs of e-CRM are in purchasing technology, in the services required to integrate new and legacy systems and in organizational change and programme management. Generally, the greater the degree of transformation, the greater the potential benefits. This is shown in Figure 18.1.

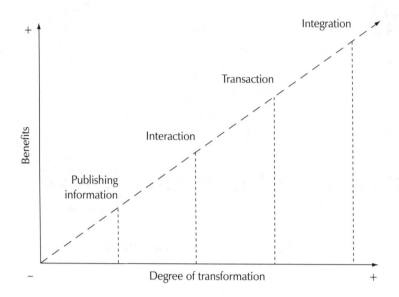

Figure 18.1 Transformation and benefit

E-CRM IS CRM ENABLED BY INTERNET TECHNOLOGIES

CRM is the cycle of activities (see Figure 18.2) by which an organization analyses its customers, targets potential customers, makes them aware of its offerings, acquires those customers, manages interactions with them, delivers value to them, develops a relationship with them over time and resolves their issues when things go wrong. These are often described as customer acquisition, customer development and customer loyalty activities, and in most organizations are performed by marketing, sales and customer support divisions.

While some companies are purely Web-based, the vast majority are not. Most corporations are 'bricks and mortar', and more and more are becoming 'bricks and clicks'. That is to say, increasingly they are using the Internet to improve performance in research and development, manufacturing, human resource management, enterprise resource planning, procurement, supply chain and customer relationship management. CRM is performed across all customer contact channels throughout the extended enterprise. It is performed indirectly via dealers or retailers and directly via call centres and field sales forces. Technology, including pervasive computing devices such as mobile phones and Web sites, is often used to enable effective CRM. The Internet is an enabling infrastructure that allows CRM performance improvements across all customer management channels.

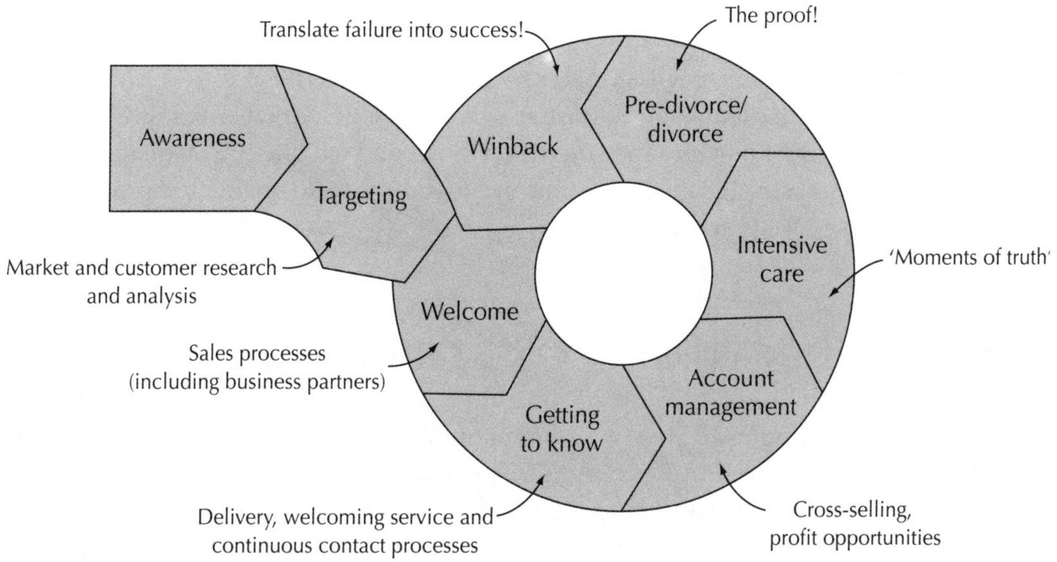

Translate failure into success!~ | The proof!

Awareness

Winback

Pre-divorce/
divorce

Targeting

Market and customer research
and analysis

Intensive
care

'Moments of truth'

Welcome

Sales processes
(including business partners)

Account
management

Getting
to know

Delivery, welcoming service and
continuous contact processes

Cross-selling,
profit opportunities

Figure 18.2   CRM cycle

BACK TO BASICS FOR AN E-CRM METRIC

Since the dot.com bubble burst and many markets have moved further into economic recession, many organizations have gone 'back to basics' to restore their fortunes. Their business strategies and subsequent transformation programmes aim to improve business performance so as to improve shareholder value. Many organizations are returning to traditional means to restore shareholder value, cost reduction, increased revenues and better cash-flow management. They aim to improve customer loyalty by improving their customers' experience because they understand that customer loyalty increases shareholder value in the longer term.

However, at any one time many projects are being planned in most organizations, but usually there is not nearly enough capital or resources to support them. As budgets are cut, business leaders must make tough decisions about which projects to proceed with. As a result, predicting ROI is essential for justifying investments in transformation programmes. The metrics for measuring a transformation programme depend on its objectives. The metrics used to measure the success of e-CRM transformation programmes should relate to cost reduction and increased revenue, cash flow, and customer satisfaction and loyalty.

LEARNING FROM THE MISTAKES OF THE PAST

During the dot.com boom, speed to market was viewed as critical for e-CRM success, particularly though not exclusively in business-to-consumer markets. Web-site hits were regarded as key e-CRM performance metrics. However, Web-site hits, registered users and 'eyeballs' did not survive the test of time in isolation, and do not feature prominently in today's ROI on e-CRM business cases.

DETERMINING THE ROI ON E-CRM IS CHALLENGING

Focusing on the ROI on e-CRM serves a number of useful purposes. It forces business leaders to focus on the main programme costs and benefits. It guides them towards better decisions on the scope and phasing of the initiative. It helps articulate the size and nature of the prize from the very outset, because quantified financial benefits tend to rally support particularly at the highest executive levels. However, most organizations find it hard to measure this ROI. There are hard and soft costs and benefits to consider. Soft benefits such as improvements in customer loyalty, while often articulated in terms of customer satisfaction, can be measured in many ways. Customer behaviour may be unpredictable, while customer relationships are complex and therefore difficult to measure.

Measuring e-CRM performance is also difficult because it usually cuts across numerous processes, functions, geographies and organizational silos. Few corporations appear to have put in place performance tracking and measurement systems. Even fewer publish their results, either within their own organizations or externally.

THE CHANGE REQUIRED IS GREATEST ON PEOPLE, ORGANIZATION AND PROCESSES

Making product information available on a Web site does not mean that customers or the field sales force will use it for gathering information. Providing online commerce may not in itself be enough to convince customers to change their buying behaviour. First and foremost, e-business is about business and any e-transformation programme should reflect that. To determine the ROI on e-CRM accurately, one must consider the business impact of the planned transformation. A good business case should include process re-engineering, organizational change and programme management costs in addition to the cost of purchasing, implementing and supporting technology.

PUBLISHING INFORMATION

Many organizations have moved much of their technical literature and marketing information or 'brochure-ware' on to the Web. The cost of producing hard copy brochures is often high, particularly in high volume business-to-consumer markets. Product and technical information changes regularly, while the cost of frequent print runs to keep information current can be prohibitive. The results are often higher costs or fewer print runs. Online publishing provides customers with access to up-to-date information, at any time, wherever they might be. For organizations operating in distant global markets, the cost of distributing information can be high. As a result, brochures are often in short supply or out of date. Customer satisfaction can be damaged if customers have to wait for accurate marketing brochures or technical data. When photocopies are used, presentation is often poor and brand image can suffer.

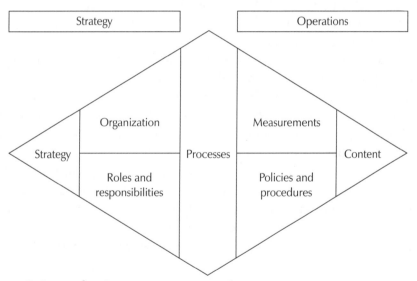

Figure 18.3 Relationship between strategy and operations

Some customers, when buying books, are prepared to use the Internet for research, to ask questions and to transact. However, most use the Internet to perform part of the buying process, that is, for information gathering. When consumers move from the information-gathering phase they often return to traditional channels such as retail outlets to complete the process. Many consumers prefer to touch and try products before buying. They still value the physical 'shopping experience'. Business customers often prefer to question a call centre representative or receive a visit from a salesperson before placing an order. To facilitate transition to the Web, customers can be offered financial incentives, that is, a 2 per cent discount on Web purchases versus offline and added value through Web-only product configurations.

INTERACTION

Online interaction enables consumers to personalize how they access information, configure and compare products, ask questions, conduct searches such as locating dealers, check delivery status and enter online user group discussions. This improves the customer experience and provides new opportunities to cross-sell products and services. Customers often value access to information that is specific to them, such as their account history and invoice records. Appropriate security must be in place for the customer to have enough confidence to access information in this way. Customers and business partners might also have to be trained to use the new service, which further increases cost. To be successful, 'self-help' should be introduced as part of a managed organizational change programme.

One of the commonest forms of online interaction is e-mail. For e-mail to succeed, it is essential to have appropriately trained and available support staff who can access information and respond to inquiries in a timely and accurate manner. It is quite common for organizations to publish service levels on Web sites and combine the Internet with telephone support so that customers do not feel their correspondence is going in to a 'black hole'.

The ability to personalize, configure and compare products can be provided by stand-alone applications and configurators. As the volume of online customer interaction grows this approach becomes less cost-effective and more difficult to manage. It is increasingly common for systems to be integrated into back office systems and 'Web enabled' so that customers view and access accurate information in real time.

TRANSACTION

Internet usage has grown exponentially in recent years and online commerce has grown accordingly. Business-to-business (B2B) e-commerce is projected to outgrow business-to-consumer (B2C) e-commerce. Organizations can monitor customer buying behaviour and responses, and tailor appropriate offers and propositions. Added to this, increased online functionality, such as product comparisons, has meant that the consumer buying experience has significantly improved.

Business intelligence technology can be used to track, analyse, evaluate and examine highly complex customer behavioural patterns and trends. Customer information can be accumulated and used to mass-customize marketing activity and enable predictive marketing based on real data. For example, a leading Canadian retailer has increased by a double-digit percentage the spending of shoppers who are shown personalized cross-sells based on their purchase history when paying online.

INTEGRATION

The phase of e-CRM transformation requiring perhaps the greatest amount of change is integration. In many organizations, invoicing, credit checking, billing and financing are performed manually, or at best they are partially automated. There are often major opportunities to reduce costs in these customer-facing activities. By integrating systems, many organizations achieve 'straight-through' processing which enables them to reduce manual intervention significantly.

Re-keying information or 'swivel chair operations' are still commonplace. People make mistakes and these errors tend to drive consequential loss: for example, an error in an invoice might generate a delay in a customer paying a bill. If that invoice is for several hundred thousand dollars, the cost of that outstanding money over several weeks might be several thousand dollars. Therefore, e-CRM integration and straight-through invoicing improves cash-flow management and reduces costs.

Integration of information technology systems requires processes, organizations and people to be aligned. Successful organizations often establish a management system so that all parties understand the strategy, their respective roles, responsibilities, organization, processes, policies, procedures and the agreed measurement systems, as shown in Figure 18.3.

E-CRM FOR COST REDUCTION

A major opportunity for cost reduction is in publishing marketing and technical information. The cost of publishing information online is significantly lower than publishing by traditional means, that is, hard copy brochures. IBM saved between 10 per cent and 20 per cent in supplying brochures online. E-target.com recently reported that significant savings could be achieved in preparation and dispatch of results data to customers. A reduction of US $1 per result was achieved and delivery speed was reduced from two to three days to instantaneous.

Web-enabling systems and providing 'straight-through processing' reduces costs. One packaged consumer goods company selling through distributors achieved a cost saving of US $50 per order processed. At Cisco Systems, 81 per cent of queries are handled online. Estimated savings are US $150 per transaction. IBM found that the time to enter a customer order reduced from 30 minutes to 5 minutes and time to respond to enquiries reduced from 15–20 minutes to real time. In 2000, IBM handled around 99 million customer transactions involving self-help services, up from 14 million in 1998, and achieved a saving of US $20 per customer on self-service information enquiries.

The Internet is increasingly used to reduce the cost of distributing advertising material. IBM found that the cost of downloading a television advertisement was approximately US $50 less than the manual process, that is, transfer to tape and courier.

Many divisions in an organization purchase their own Web services or Internet technology either internally or from external 'boutique' suppliers. As a result it is often difficult to manage the digital brand because each department controls its own Web site, often in isolation, and there is little reuse of Web content. This disparate approach also creates inefficiencies in Internet infrastructure. IBM achieved a reduction in costs of between 10 and 20 per cent by consolidating its infrastructure.

E-CRM FOR INCREASED REVENUES

E-commerce enables organizations to enter new markets, both geographical markets and new segments, which were previously uneconomical to enter with traditional channels. Web selling also makes it feasible to sell low-margin products in mature markets and still retain a healthy profit. In 2000, IBM sold US $12.3 billion in goods and services over the Web, up from US $3 billion in 1998.

Sales force productivity can be improved by publishing information and by providing commerce online. IBM's experience shows that 15 to 25 per cent of face-to-face time could be returned to its distributors by using the Web in this way. This efficiency could be used to enable the sales force to sell higher margin solutions, or to lower costs by reducing the sales force.

Web-based interactive marketing produces response rates five to six times higher than classic direct marketing. SKF, the Swedish manufacturing conglomerate, has achieved a 25 per cent increase in service-related revenue from using its e-CRM systems. In the same way, Quick and Reilly, a financial services company, achieved a 50 per cent improvement in lead conversion, 67 per cent increase in average revenue per sales person, 10 per cent increase in customer retention and 5 per cent improvement in cross-selling.

E-CRM FOR IMPROVING CASH-FLOW MANAGEMENT

'Straight-through' processing reduces error rates and reduces returned orders, leading to improved cash-flow management and lower costs. One product manufacturer selling through distributors achieved a reduction in error rate on electronic orders of between

1 per cent and 4 per cent with an average cost per error of US $120. IBM found that the time taken to arrange business partner financing reduced from two days to two hours, the percentage of its orders manually shipped reduced from 75 to 0 per cent and invoice accuracy was raised from 70 to 98 per cent. First Service Networks, a facilities mainte-nance company, reduced the time between service request and technician despatch by 25 per cent. They reduced billing, invoicing and collection cycle times by 50 per cent and reduced total paperwork and status phone calls by 75 per cent.

E-CRM FOR IMPROVEMENTS IN THE CUSTOMER EXPERIENCE

E-CRM leads to an improvement in the customer experience and in customer retention due to the availability or ease of Web sales. Honeywell Industrial Control improved customer delight from 92.3 to 98.1 per cent and has achieved a 15 per cent reduction in call-centre personnel costs. IBM increased its customer satisfaction by 5 per cent by effective implementation of the e-channel. The average order configuration time at Asyst Technologies, a high-tech company, has dropped from 25 days to 2 days in one product group, and they have achieved a 50 per cent reduction in delayed deliveries. AT&T Digital Broadband achieved a 20 per cent reduction in the number of calls that require call-backs, a 50 per cent reduction in customer hold time and 75 per cent reduction in backlog of service requests.

THE COSTS OF E-CRM ARE IN TECHNOLOGY, PROCESS, PEOPLE AND ORGANIZATION

A typical e-CRM transformation programme consists of several interrelated components including technology procurement, systems integration services, and organizational change and programme management. The cost of hardware and technology infra-structure should include computer hardware, middleware and applications software. The infrastructure can be purchased outright or as an outsourced service provided for a recurring fee. Telecommunications and technology, such as routers and hubs, should be included and extra bandwidth may be required. Systems integration costs will constitute a significant proportion of the total cost of an e-CRM solution. The middleware and appli-cation software must be configured and perhaps integrated with existing back office and external customer and partner systems. Costs will increase if multiple geographic loca-tions are included.

One major cost often overlooked is data management. This involves providing accurate information to the customer-facing environment. Customer databases, account records and technical data are often stored in disparate systems and so are often incomplete. Many organizations address this problem by creating 'data marts' and subsequently create mini investment cases to introduce further data management capability.

If the implementation is complex, significant programme management resources may be required both from within the organization and externally. The ROI case may depend completely on delivery of the solution on time, to budget and with the required functionality. Delivering an e-CRM solution requires coordination between IT staff, business leaders, business users, customers and suppliers, and therefore appropriate investment should be made.

Many organizations also overlook the importance of organizational change management, and as a result reduce it to a minimum. They then realize their mistake when low user adoption rates and lower than expected ROI are measured later. The organization needs to understand why it is changing and that the change has an appropriate level of management sponsorship. A communications plan is essential.

An e-CRM solution usually requires significant change in roles and responsibilities. IT staff must be trained in supporting the new applications and infrastructure, customer support staff must adopt new service levels, marketing staff must learn how to use new applications and sales staff must adapt to new tools and processes. Customers and business partners will be required to alter their established ways of doing business.

Appropriate investment should be made in designing new processes and organization. While many software applications contain a core set of predefined processes, which may be targeted to an industry or process, technology is purely an enabler and consideration should be given and investment made in process, organization and people requirements particular to a specific industry or market.

CONCLUSIONS

Much has been written about CRM and e-CRM and this chapter has attempted to take a path through this, basing the text on 'real-life' implementation. A recurring theme in this book is the frequency with which CRM approaches fail from a customer viewpoint because of their inability to integrate the customer touch points, the lack of customer-centric process design and the failure to provide real customer benefits.

The main reasons for this are:

▌ poor understanding of, and focus on, customers;
▌ lack of involvement of, and input from, customers;
▌ rewards not related to customer objectives;

▓ thinking technology alone is the solution;
▓ lack of properly designed, interlocking processes;
▓ poor quality data and information;
▓ poor coordination between many different departmental projects;
▓ absence of business staff on the CRM team;
▓ late formation of the team;
▓ absence of measurement of benefits;
▓ lack of testing.

Empirical, quantitative evidence resulting from projects involving the authors and other CRM consultants and vendors shows that if the projects are approached in the correct manner with rigorous planning in all affected areas, along with the correct budgets and top-down commitment, then an e-CRM project will almost certainly deliver the expected ROI and other benefits within the projected timescales. This will happen with the minimal loss of staff morale and customer satisfaction.

19

UK data warehousing and business intelligence implementation: general and retail

Merlin Stone, Julie Abbott and Tony Dobbs

INTRODUCTION

In this chapter, we summarize briefly the state of play regarding the penetration of data warehouses and business intelligence systems in companies across a range of industries in the UK. Following this, we present a short case study that describes an example of a successful implementation of a business intelligence solution that supports CRM in a major retailer. We draw upon the results of a recent IBM-sponsored qualitative study in order to emphasise the points made[1].

THE CURRENT STATUS

The amount of data collected by most UK firms is increasing rapidly. This is creating a need for businesses to use tools to view the data, dissect it, and of course understand it. Users of the resulting information include managers at various levels as well as analysts and, increasingly, more junior staff whose job requires them to understand precisely what is happening in one part of the business. At all levels, staff need accurate information in a form that can be easily understood and quickly acted upon. In the past, many of these kinds of decisions would have been made either without analysis or using out of date information. Companies today are increasingly relying on applications from leading analytical tool vendors and enterprise software suppliers such as IBM.

As the UK's leading companies embrace the Internet as a core part of their business, suppliers are introducing applications and toolkits that can extract data from Web-enabled business processes and make it accessible for decision making. In some cases they can even make the business decisions without human intervention. In the area of customer or Web analytics, aggregation and interpretation routines are used to create a much clearer view of each customer and/or group of customers as well as track, profile, and illustrate the habits of individual visitors to a Web site.

Data plays a crucial role in most companies, but there are some industries that need to analyse very large amounts of data from different sources quickly and accurately. Modern manufacturing plants generate and store huge amounts of data from ERP (enterprise resource planning systems) and other transaction-based systems. Often many different systems store and analyse data relating to the production of various items or substances, for example stock levels, delivery schedules, customer orders, prices paid, product return rates, product development schedules and the like.

If these systems do not communicate with each other, or if there is no single point from which to approach all of this data, it is impossible to find accurate answers to questions such as 'How will a 5 per cent drop in production of a particular product in a specific month affect company profits?' and 'Which are our most profitable customers?'

The majority of the data in most manufacturing companies covers manufacturing, logistics and financial areas, rather than market information and customer data (although both the latter are important). Financial services companies, however, see service operations and customer information as mission-critical. Retail banks and insurers usually have millions of customers. It is not easy to predict how changes in areas such as consumer behaviour, the performance of financial markets and government policy will affect business. To benefit from all the data they have collated and stored, these companies need to:

1. Extract the data they have from its different and varied sources.
2. Transform it into a consistent format.
3. Load it into a repository, for example, a data warehouse.
4. Find a way to analyse the data so as to give decision makers at all levels and in different units the support they need to make better business decisions more quickly than their competitors. (Typically this entails using business intelligence software, ranging from advanced reporting suites to statistical packages.)

THE RESEARCH RESULTS

The research[2] indicated that in most financial services and manufacturing companies, the following conditions held:

1. Senior management were committed to the idea of data warehousing.
2. The board was involved in decisions.
3. Just under half of all companies have a true data warehouse: the larger the company, the more likely this was.
4. Most companies relied on external consultants, and valued their role, although this was not necessarily correlated with the perceived success of the implementation.
5. Two-thirds of companies were generally satisfied with their data warehousing implementation, but financial services companies were more dissatisfied than manufacturing companies.
6. Satisfaction was most strongly correlated with the perceived quality of information in the warehouse.
7. Most respondents considered their investment to be justified.
8. Under half of respondents were using business intelligence tools. Most of these were used to analyse data from ERP and CRM systems, and nearly half were using these tools to analyse data from CRM systems.
9. Almost two-thirds of the companies have not been able to measure the return on investment (ROI) from their projects. Several companies that have been able to measure ROI were only able to do so because the reporting and analysis tools just implemented gave them a clearer view of the benefit of many business initiatives.
10. Most companies that have implemented business intelligence solutions were happy with the investments they have made in this area.
11. The most common problems to overcome contacts were related to business culture eg moving to a data-supported view of how to make decisions and, indeed, to manage the enterprise.

THE CASE STUDY

This case study, which is anonymous for confidentiality reasons, shows how a very large retailer uses data warehousing and business intelligence tools to improve results from its approach to customer relationship management.

Company X is the largest retailer in its category in the UK. It needed a campaign management system that would enable it to target customers with relevant, timely marketing programmes. It uses traditional market research to understand why its customers shop in its stores, and why they make particular visits to branches. Today, it knows a great deal more about the individual preferences of a high proportion of its customers, thanks to its loyalty card.

Its customer relationship management (CRM) approach for its loyalty card is based on a DB2-based data warehouse that uses integrated analysis for querying, reporting and data mining. It is also integrated with a campaign management system, developed by IBM. The campaign management system allows targeting of customers for specific programmes based on how they have accumulated their loyalty points.

With several years of individual cardholder transaction records and a selection of non-cardholder sales records to provide a comparison with cardholder behaviour, the size of the database created a performance challenge. Flexibility was also essential. This was achieved by storing data at the lowest level of granularity so that users can build it up to any level they require during analysis. Another important aspect is that the company's commercial analysts have quick, real-time access to all of the data without having to make special IT support requests. The database is structured to support the analytical process.

Currently a large team of full-time analysts, as well as a separate team of direct-marketing experts, use the system. From the point of sale data, the company already knew what was being sold, where and when. Now it can determine what different groups of customers are buying and monitor their behaviour over time. Using the IBM solution, direct-marketing analysts are now able to develop target customer profiles without having to first create a separate extract of data and are also able to base these profiles on the full richness of information held within the DB2 database. Analysing purchasing trends by shoppers over time also provides the company with a new view of its traditional product categories and departmental divides.

This retailer can now also see how much shoppers buy in specific product categories. Monitoring purchases over time also helps identify buying patterns that can fuel further marketing efforts. For example, customers may buy a particular product from the company, but it can now see if they also buy related products. It can then determine whether it is more profitable to encourage existing customers to buy more products in a certain category than it is to attract new customers. The company combines its basic customer demographic data (age, gender, number of children and postal code) with externally available data. However, the real power of the business intelligence solution comes from being able to combine this information with detailed purchase behaviour data. This new knowledge base is used to support business decisions outside the marketing arena.

An analysis of how its customers shop in a group of stores in a particular geographical area has led to a greatly improved understanding of the role different outlets play within that area and the range of goods that should be offered across them. For example, its stores have typically been grouped and merchandised according to their physical size. This leads to competition between large and small outlets in the same area. The company learnt that its most valuable customers shop across many stores in their area. So rather than having them compete against each other, the company now manages them as local areas.

The incremental sales generated by the data warehousing and business intelligence system have paid for the initial investment, but long-term value is coming from the application of customer insights across the business. The company has already proved that it can add significant value from doing this.

This is in line with wider research in the implementation of CRM[3], which shows that a steady approach, with strong measurement, pursued consistently over a long period, is much more likely to lead to profitable outcomes.

CONCLUSIONS

We can see that across many industries in the UK today, there is a growing need to understand the business more in order to compete in a fast-changing marketplace. Knowledge is key, something that companies are becoming more aware of, and they are therefore implementing business intelligence solutions in order to gain that knowledge rather than make assumptions.

It is widely believed that 80 per cent of all assumptions about the customer are wrong, but as we can see, in the past many decisions were based purely on assumption, as accurate information was not available or the information was out of date. This often resulted in customer dissatisfaction and low employee morale, as staff felt under pressure to deliver excellent customer service but had no tools to help them do this. Qualitative research carried out in the UK[4] showed that marketers in particular felt that more information helped them to do a better job: but it had to be accurate and timely, as bad data hindered campaigns and the marketers felt their efforts were then largely wasted, leading to a loss of morale.

Businesses are now in a position to take full advantage of the technological breakthroughs, not only at the client end via the Internet, but at the heart of the company's information systems through their data warehouses and large array of business intelligence tools. The more these systems are used, and the information fed back in a closed-loop process, the more value can be gained from them.

Companies that were drowning in data but had no information suddenly find that they have the knowledge base that they need to move their business forward in an ever more competitive environment. Not only can they now give their customers the excellent products and services required to meet their demands, but their employees are likely to have much higher job satisfaction, leading to higher quality service to the customers (an area discussed at length by Daffy[5]) in a virtuous circle that should lead to higher profits for the company.

NOTES

[1] Networks IT Marketing (2002) *Data Warehousing and Business Intelligence in the UK*, Spotlight.

[2] Ibid.

[3] Stone, M and Woodcock, N (2001) Defining CRM and assessing its quality, in *Successful Customer Relationship Marketing*, ed B Foss and M Stone, Kogan Page, London.

[4] Abbott, J (2000) Data, data everywhere and not a byte of use, *Qualitative Market Research*, **4** (3), p 182.

[5] Daffy, C (1996) *Once a Customer, Always a Customer*, Oak Tree Press, Dublin.

20

Using advanced data analytics to improve customer management

David Selby and Julie Abbott

INTRODUCTION

In tough economic times, many companies cut costs by simply reducing their marketing spend. Although on paper this might seem a desirable approach to cutting costs, the timing for this is less than desirable. Consumers' expectations are continuing to rise due to increasingly sophisticated advertising campaigns focused on brand and service, while at the same time they are discovering that they have virtually unlimited choices in areas such as retailing, telecommunications and financial services.

Businesses that cut back marketing efforts risk severely testing customer loyalty. Such actions may reduce profitability (exactly the opposite of what they are designed to achieve) by sparking sales declines, widespread attrition, and an inability to capture the very people most likely to become prized customers in the future.

In many industries, low-cost 'lean' players have demonstrated that, by controlling operational costs, they can grow market share, often by using more profitable direct-sales channels such as the Internet or call centres. When it comes to marketing, they have not always reduced spend, but they have made better use of their budgets to attract customers' attention.

Improving marketing results while minimizing marketing expenditure, increasing return on investment in marketing, can be achieved by combining operational customer relationship management systems with an entirely new dimension of customer intelligence. This can increase customer satisfaction, stimulate purchases, increase loyalty, and retain valued customers, while controlling costs. It requires combining analytical techniques and computing technologies that enable businesses to communicate with individual customers, regardless of contact channel, by offering service and purchase suggestions that reflect precise buying habits, needs and desires, preferably in real time. Knowledge of the customer is key, but ability to use this profitably via closed-loop CRM systems is rare; as Hirschowitz points out, 'no matter how sophisticated a company's ability to generate customer insight, it will deliver little value without the processes in place that exploit this understanding to build stronger customer relationships.'[1]

IBM has developed and proved an end-to-end solution called Enterprise Customer Analytics (ECA) which consists of sophisticated mathematical techniques and advanced models (including feedback loop) that, when combined with effective operational customer relationship management (CRM) systems, can significantly improve marketing results. This chapter describes the journey to implementing a sophisticated operational relationship management system as proposed by ECA

TREATING THE CUSTOMER AS AN INVESTMENT

In many companies, customers are not viewed as longer-term valuable assets but just as prospects for the next contact list from which to make the next sale. When a company starts to think of customers as valuable assets, it can justify investing in individual customers so as to get the best from them. English noted that 'Businesses fail when management focuses too much attention on today's immediate needs, such as quarterly profits, at the expense of solving tomorrow's problem, such as discovering and satisfying customers' emerging requirements.'[2] ECA is designed to show the customer base as a portfolio. Viewing marketing as an investment, rather than focusing on the better performing groups alone, ensures a more equitable distribution of funds across the customer base. The typical approach of selecting customers for campaigns continually saturates the best customers with offers, whereas ECA spreads the marketing budget more evenly over the customer portfolio.

Most marketing systems use a point in time (that is, a campaign by campaign) logic when investing marketing dollars. We call this 'vertical logic'. With ECA the effect of one campaign on another is taken into account before an offer is presented, creating a 'horizontal logic'. This process generates a customer management plan for each individual customer. This plan is continually re-evaluated and designed to feed campaign management with a set of offers that maximizes the return on investment for each customer, as shown in Figure 20.1. ECA involves planning and managing customers to a budget. Where most event-based marketing triggers an action whenever an event is seen, ECA first evaluates if this is the best use of the marketing budget for this individual.

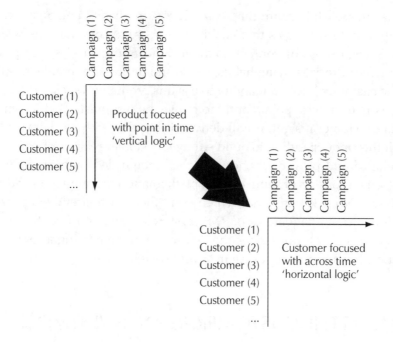

Figure 20.1　Vertical versus horizontal logic

SINGLE-ENTITY VIEW

Customers should believe they are dealing with one integrated firm, rather than a disjointed set of business units which only take ownership of a customer for those interactions relating to their particular part of the business. The integration facility of ECA enables this via a real-time data management system which utilizes a data store incorporating operational data-mining models to generate ever-evolving propensity scores and a living customer behaviour profile which is shared by all the customer touch points. While customers interact with a firm, an ever-evolving customer behaviour profile develops, giving each touch point hard accounting data (for example, on what was spent or invested) and soft facts (such as attitude to risk, price sensitivity) which are used in conjunction with powerful technology to generate personalized messages for each individual customer. You really understand me. Ultimately, ECA provides a mechanism to enable customers to acknowledge that the firm understands them and meets their needs, ensuring that they continue to do business with that supplier. Figure 20.2 shows how the ECA structure achieves this.

ECA links e-commerce and traditional, multi-channel business intelligence practices, and shows that combining novel Internet capabilities with existing, proven IT fundamentals, including data warehousing and data mining, results in an integrated solution that can be applied to both Web and traditional channels. ECA offers what may be the

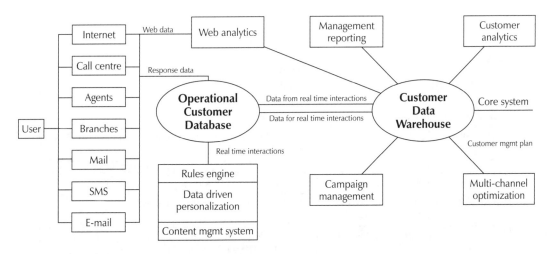

Figure 20.2   ECA reference architecture

most exciting customer relationship development since either e-commerce or advanced analytics first appeared: a closed-loop, 360-degree customer relationship process that grows increasingly intelligent with each interaction. Assessing the dynamics of every promotion and channel interaction continually generates intelligence that refreshes and enriches ongoing relationships with customers, enabling businesses to optimize the lifetime value of each one individually.

IMPLEMENTING ECA

The road map to a complete ECA implementation is designed to be incremental and provide return on investment (ROI) at each step. A short description of these steps and the expected ROI can be found in Figure 20.3.

Step 1: Assess customer management practices

The CMAT diagnostic process described in the early chapters of this book is designed to help companies assess their current customer management (CM) capabilities in order to:

- develop a holistic CM strategy;
- set priorities;

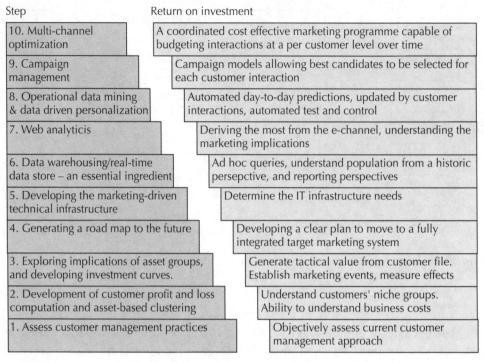

Figure 20.3 Ten steps involved in developing ECA

▍ build business cases for CM projects;

▍ build consensus for creating a customer-centric organization;

▍ provide a benchmark against other organizations.

Carrying out a CMAT provides data on the quality of the infrastructure (people and organization, processes, systems, data) required to support ECA.

Step 2: Asset clustering, valuing the portfolio

Generating a profit and loss account

For each customer, a profit and loss (P&L) account is established. The P&L establishes the criteria for dividing customers into a set of asset groups, a loose grouping of similar, but not identical, customers. This P&L calculation must be agreed at an executive level. To achieve this P&L a set of cost elements is derived using a variety of mathematical techniques. These elements are of two types, direct and indirect. The indirect elements can represent potential. Examples of both types of variables are given in Table 20.1, an airline

Table 20.1 Profit and loss variables

Direct elements	Indirect elements
Age	Number of miles flown
Sex	Number of purchasing channels
Marital status	Mixture of products used
Nationality	Number of products used

industry example. Note that in some industries, the construct of an accurate P&L is not always possible. The airline industry is a good example. It is not possible to exactly assess the profitability of each seat sold on a departing aircraft, so proxies and average passenger fares are used. In pure direct marketing and certain other industries, calculating a customer P&L is more straightforward, but it is harder to allocate acquisition cost. The value of referrals is often overlooked, as is the value of retention, for example.

Asset clustering

Discovery tools rather than query tools are applied to the per-customer profit and loss account from the previous step, to break the customer base into clusters of similar but not necessarily identical customers. Further tools are then applied to the asset model to allow it to be operationalized. This model can be installed in a data warehouse, allowing the continued assessment of the customer base. The inputs and outputs of asset clustering are illustrated in Figure 20.4. The P&L is designed to utilize existing elements in the company's ledger system. When sophisticated mathematical transformations are performed on existing data, new data elements are generated which lead to further insight into each

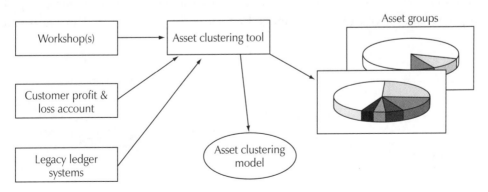

Figure 20.4 The asset clustering process

customer. This study also provides useful input to the design of the data warehouse and identifies a business case for embarking on such a course. Recommendations can be made both on data quality issues in ledger systems and on which other data elements should be collected and maintained in a data warehouse. For an existing warehouse, these recommendations help identify any shortcomings in its design.

Asset clustering vs. RFM

Most current industry clustering approaches are based on RFM (recency, frequency and monetary value). The result of using the RFM method alone is usually to identify and then saturate the best customers with contacts, thereby reducing the contact stream to lower-spending, less frequent, but perhaps high-potential customers. Asset clustering is mapped back to these dimensions (RFM), allowing an easy transition from RFM-based marketing to asset-clustering based marketing.

Step 3: Exploring the implications of asset clusters and budgeting

Several business re-engineering steps can now be taken. As is shown in Figure 20.5, the asset clustering can be enriched by survey data. If none exists, or for some reason none can be joined with the customer base, the research department can conduct focus groups and the resulting information can be used to add depth to the clusters. The appointment of cluster managers can also be explored. The job of a cluster manager is to manage the needs and wants of each of the individual clusters located by the discovery process. There should also be a cluster manager whose main responsibility is to look after customers who are new to the company. These customers are too new to show allegiance to any cluster; however after enough activity, they will migrate into one of the existing clusters or form an entirely new one.

Each cluster manager is responsible for growing the customers assigned to him or her. The operational asset-clustering model can also continually sift the dormant groups for hidden potential that can then be managed accordingly. As illustrated in Figure 20.6,

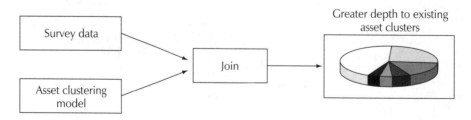

Figure 20.5   Survey data enriches existing clusters

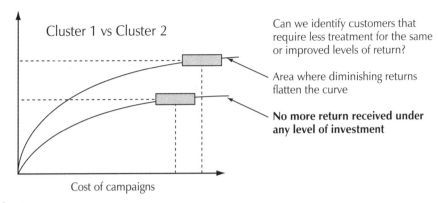

Figure 20.6   Optimal investment curves

investment curves may be calculated at this stage, giving a clear indication of the optimal investment point for each group. Once the groups have been established via a discovery process, they are operationalized in the data warehouse to allow customer migrations to be understood. Ultimately asset curves should be replaced by a customer value index, which allows a much more accurate analysis for budgeting and decision making at a customer level.

Using asset clustering for tactical targeting

By now, an understanding of the customer base that encompasses its historical brand perception, product usage, and demographics should have been achieved. To enhance return on investment, some tactical targeting may be done. For example, a cluster demonstrating a propensity to buy premium (higher margin) products might form the basis of a campaign that encourages it to sample a premium product at an introductory reduced rate. In the long term, asset clustering should be valued for its strategic direction and budgeting, but not as an ongoing customer targeting approach.

Step 4: Strategic direction setting, developing a road map

This area requires strong focus by the firm's executives. By using the historical perspective derived from the existing data, they can establish any required changes in offerings. These might include different levels of service or different levels of offering. To help in executive direction setting, sources of profit need to be recognized. For example, does the Pareto principle (20 per cent of the customers giving 80 per cent of the profits) apply here? Equally, an understanding of the levels of customization, by product, service, or delivery, needs to be achieved. At the end of this phase a clear road map is produced to take the business forward from the current position to where it needs to be in the future.

Step 5: Developing or enhancing a marketing-driven technical infrastructure

Infrastructure development includes assessing the current system architecture and defining requirements to support the strategy. A series of technical assessment, impact and cost/benefit analyses is conducted, along with systems implementation planning, to determine how best to support possibly massive online data volumes, evolving data types, and perhaps new media such as wireless communication. The outcome is a technical plan for merging online and existing data sources, including operational data, and translating that information into meaningful, relevant customer interactions. Architecture requirements differ significantly from those of traditional analytical or customer intelligence systems. Real-time decision making requires new capabilities, including transaction behaviour sensors, unique technical features, and Internet-based technologies, coupled with advanced database marketing capabilities, including pattern recognition and mathematical transformation techniques that exploit the vastly varied data on which the Internet thrives.

Step 6: Data warehousing/real-time data store: an essential ingredient

After collecting data and transforming it into insightful matter, the organization needs to focus on its storage and retrieval to ensure it becomes a useful corporate asset, delivering useful results to both customer and company. In many companies some form of data warehouse already exists, and the approach is to validate the existing warehouse for its ability to satisfy the management plan produced in step 4. Business data is a corporate asset that can become a corporate nightmare if not treated with the right stewardship and structure. Certain data types require focus to ensure that they enable accurate and sound corporate decision making. Examples include campaign information, campaign responses, customer characteristics, channels used and cross-product behaviour, as well as the more obvious customer details such as name and address. Traditional retailers have been quite effective with warehouses organized by location, time, product, promotions and price. With the introduction of the Internet, more dimensions are necessary such as traffic sources, online behaviour segments, and content or image categories. Data warehousing methods provide the foundation for building a historic record of both product performance and more importantly, customer behaviour. This record of behaviour provides a vital piece of information for the generation of analytical models that can predict the propensity of a customer to respond to a Web page or direct mail offering.

To make decisions and effect change, one almost always needs historic data: a record of previous responses. It is the basis for future modelling processes and becomes the foundation for the corporate decision-making environment. Importantly, it allows us to create a view of the customer before a significant event, such as a Web page or kiosk screen presentation, or a direct mail offering. These events stimulate consumer behaviour and provide important ingredients for predicting behaviour of consumers before an event and analysing the state of the consumer population after the event. With this evidence – a prior view and a response to a stimulus – sophisticated data-mining algorithms can be used to generate models that predict the customer's next behaviour. This prediction can then be applied to other customers within the same cluster.

Management reporting is the basis of any good data warehouse installation. It provides basic day-to-day health checks. Reporting must of course be based on business needs.

Obstacles to customer-centric data warehouse implementations

The following can be obstacles to customer-centric data warehouse implementations:

- **Completeness of data.** There might be issues with data completeness because of the range of sources of customer-related data. Thus, for a customer loyalty system, base data might have passed through a central data collection agency and the transaction data through the EPOS or teller system. The data warehouse might then be faced with the problem of transactions appearing before the related base customer data.
- **Quality of data.** Errors might be discovered in data collected through transaction systems because this data, though collected for some time, might never have been used for customer-centric analyses and hence is not proved 'clean'. Errors are defined as incomplete, missing, or wrong data.
- **Data volumes/performance.** Transaction data volumes can be enormous. Performance of data load and inquiry functions must be considered in the design of the data warehouse and technical infrastructure. To address this, activities such as volume prototyping and performance guidelines for coding need to be built into the project plans. The batch window is almost always the limiting factor in these environments.
- **Privacy legislation.** Customer data privacy is a topic that every company needs to be aware of, not least because of evolving legislation. These issues range from the opt-in versus opt-out issue to consumer health insights derived from drug, vitamin and supplement purchases.
- **Business rules.** As rules for calculating business figures are determined during requirements gathering and design, repetitive calculations are frequently found: processes and data with similar names within one company, perhaps by different

departments. These need to be understood and rationalized prior to solution implementation.

ECA requires the implementation of a real-time data store, as this is used to maintain continuously updated customer behaviour profiles. This data store is connected by a messaging system to prevent it becoming a single point of failure in the system.

Step 7: Web analytics

The Web analytics phase involves both design and implementation steps. First, online analytics requirements are assessed, along with the various tools available to support the strategy and decipher aggregate Internet traffic patterns. Once a real-time solution has been established, a company can begin capturing and analysing customer preferences, identifying predictive indicators that can be applied to boost Web sales and create other optimal marketing approaches. By deciphering Internet traffic patterns – both on a specific Web site and as aggregated Internet data beyond a company's boundaries – businesses can discover where traffic originates, which visitors are the most profitable, and which marketing approaches are the most effective for each customer type. Businesses can deepen their understanding of the graphics, text, promotional offers, navigation options and numerous other variables that impact online sales. The resulting information can be used to optimize overall Website navigation and determine the most effective ways to reach finely categorized customers. When combined with other enterprise customer analytics components, these insights can be extended to other marketing channels. These insights help structure which key performance indicators should be included in the customer behaviour profile for the Web channel.

Step 8: Operational data mining, and data-driven personalization

Whereas the previous Web analytics step focuses mainly on piecing back together Web sessions and inferring some business intent by the customer, the process known as 'data-driven personalization' actually prescribes rapid responses. This component is one of the cornerstones in ECA. Data-driven personalization synthesizes online and offline transaction data to generate comprehensive, continually improving customer views. Advanced analytic models, tightly integrated with a business rules engine, automate the process of evaluating and responding to individual preferences and habits. The results are real-time, informed profiles that enable businesses to anticipate and react appropriately, by personalizing Web, call centre, IVR, intelligent Kiosk, and other experiences for each customer and prospect. Identifying and maintaining such visitor profiles – updated in real time during each interaction – is central to data-driven personalization.

Operational predictive models and a business-rules engine, which makes response decisions based on logic supplied by the models, are applied to each emerging profile, providing each visitor with an individualized, optimal interaction point experience. Specific personalization campaigns and other interactions then can be measured with a test and control management system, enabling businesses to optimize every customer's lifetime value. Simply put, the more an organization knows about a customer, the more personally and effectively it can treat the customer.

Step 9: Applying cross-channel campaign management to improve results

Campaign management establishes the tools and techniques for tracking, analysing and taking appropriate action at every stage of a Web-based or multi-channel marketing effort. Campaign management solutions typically include tracking and mapping campaign information to fine-tune the results. Unlike standard solutions, this stage – in combination with the multi-channel optimization phase – enables businesses to act simultaneously across marketing channels and to influence Web results in real time. This step addresses, for various customer classes, such questions as whom campaigns should target, which channels are optimal, and how effective campaign content is within those channels. Features may include channel interface management, communication content management, calendar management, and cost and budget recording.

Step 10: Multi-channel optimization

The multi-channel optimization phase helps maximize individual customer relationships across all marketing channels. By tracking each customer's interactions at every channel selected, businesses can forecast precisely what to offer, when, and through which channels to meet that individual's unique needs and preferences. Messages can also be tailored to each customer, a process that fosters loyalty while serving corporate sales and profitability goals. Also known as 'horizontal marketing', this component treats marketing activities as continuing customer investment rather than as one-time or relatively short-term campaigns. Businesses can generate risk/return curves that determine when customer types cease to be profitable or, conversely, when in their life-cycles they are expected to become profitable. Accordingly, businesses can determine when and how much to invest in each customer, and when not to invest, or they can evolve to use a customer value index function to determine an optimal investment point at a customer level.

Saturation: the relationships between promotions and channels

The interaction of promotions is an extremely important component of any marketing automation approach. Cannibalization, or saturation, describes that portion of a promotion's sales that are consumed by a follow-on promotion, while the original promotion was still generating sales. Similarly, a portion of the follow-on promotion's sales is consumed, or cannibalized, by the previous promotion. After close investigation, it is believed that three forces move this cannibalization effect:

▐ A product component: how similar are the promoted products?
▐ A promotion type component: how similar are these sequential promotions?
▐ A time component: how close together in time are these promotions?

Sometimes the combined effects of the promotions create a positive effect on revenues, while other combinations create a negative effect. The key to understanding the effect on an individual customer is to evaluate the total promotional strategy. The amount of cannibalization increases when similar promotions with similar merchandise are created fairly close together in time. The more time between the promotions, the less the cannibalization effect. Dissimilar promotions, with unlike merchandise, will have very small cannibalization effects. By evaluating the total strategy, an understanding of the incremental gains or losses due to multiple promotions can be developed. This information is used to seek out the optimal strategy for each customer or customer cluster.

The impact of saturation in the Internet-only business applications remains an open issue. Though inexpensive, volumes of unwanted e-mail will create a noxious effect on customers. Also, such issues as opt-in versus opt-out and other privacy controls need to be considered in the firm's promotional strategies. Direct-mail firms that are now using the Internet as a new channel are seeing some positive interactions. Mailing of catalogues referencing the Web site is driving site traffic, and the resulting sales appear to be incremental. Analogously, Web sites referencing the catalogue are driving new productive prospects.

CONCLUSION

A new standard of customer intelligence is emerging, one that is changing marketing, sales and service, as we know it today, helping to create a 'customer feedback loop' with each individual customer. The customer and the business together redefine what it means to participate in a commercial relationship.[3] Why? New information technologies, business models and competitive pressures are driving the need for more relevant, intelligence-driven customer transactions and experiences. Equally, good fiscal policy toward customers is essential; getting the best possible productivity for each dollar spent in marketing is a requirement in such a tough economic climate.

Every interaction channel a company uses to contact customers should address customer demands and needs in an efficient and capable manner. Deep analytical techniques need to be applied to truly understand customer preferences, needs and behaviour. Only by demonstrating that they know and value their customers can businesses deliver the highly personalized offerings and services that differentiate them from competitors. The notion is to treat customers as individuals and optimize interactions with them across touch points by providing consistent, high-calibre, real-time customer experiences. This approach can build loyalty, sales and profitability company-wide.

While the notion may sound simple, building such a capability is complex. Figure 20.7 brings it together. The 10 steps discussed above, ranging from strategy development to multi-channel optimization, thoroughly address every step of creating, evaluating and implementing an effective solution. The result is an integrated system that can deliver the best new technologies and analytical intelligence practices possible.

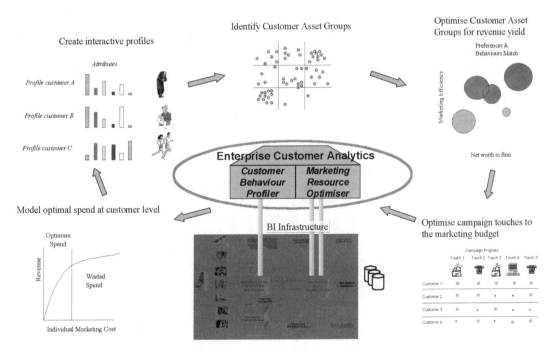

Figure 20.7   The overall approach

NOTES

1 Hirschowitz, A (2001) Closing the CRM loop: the 21st century marketer's challenge: transforming customer insight into customer value, *Journal of Targeting, Measurement and Analysis for Marketing* **10** (2), pp 168–78.
2 English, LP (1999) *Improving Data Warehouse and Business Information Quality. Methods for reducing costs and increasing profits*, Wiley, Chichester, p 339.
3 Peppers, D and Rogers, M (1997) *Enterprise One-to-One*, Piatkus, London, p 13.

21

Applying IT in customer management

Bryan Foss, Thorsten Gorchs, Juergen Uhl, Divya Verma, James Richie and Merlin Stone

INTRODUCTION

Lately, the technology available to companies planning to manage their customers better has greatly improved. In this chapter, we outline the basics of systems selection, review some of the difficult issues associated with setting up an integrated CRM systems capability, and outline some future technology developments that will make a difference to how CRM is managed in the next few years.

THE BASICS OF SYSTEMS SELECTION

A few years ago, the process for buying and using this technology might run more or less like this.

Planning and strategy

This involves deciding why, when and where you want to manage your customers better, setting your objectives – how much better you want to manage your customers – and determining your targets. For smaller as well as larger companies, this is not easy. Smaller companies may use as many communications channels for managing customers as larger companies. These include sales force, distributors, direct mail, telesales and tele-service, field service, counter service, the Web, e-mail, and direct contacts with company management or other staff. The main improvement areas include direct mail (better targeting and response management), outbound telemarketing for prospecting or customer development – up-selling and cross-selling, inbound tele-service – ensuring customers get better service when they call in, and improved sales force management.

In-depth diagnosis, programme planning and budgeting

This is more detailed investigation, to see what is feasible, when, what processes need changing, and what budget should be allocated, for systems and all the other work involved. Priorities must be set.

Development of a systems brief and package selection

This involves developing a separate brief for each systems component, such as a customer contact system (often split into sales and service), a marketing database, a marketing campaign management system, a system for selection and targeting, and a system for analysis (to see what has worked).

Package installation

This involves installing packages on existing or new hardware, entering relevant data, testing that the package works, or that two or more newly acquired packages, perhaps a marketing database package and a sales force management package, actually work together. Staff issues include training and motivation.

Package running and maintenance

The use of packages needs to be overseen, to ensure they are used (at all, and then correctly). Limited package customization may be required. Data quality must be monitored and usually improved. Problem solving may be needed. New staff have to be trained. New releases of the packages may need evaluating.

RECENT CHANGES

Today, the major changes have been to the amount of experience companies have with using CRM, and the changes that have taken place in the packages available. There are more people around with experience of implementing one or more aspects of CRM. More people understand what can be achieved and how fast. More people have the knowledge and skills required. This applies to both business users and IT people. This can instil greater confidence, but it can also – dangerously – create over-optimism about what can be achieved in what time. Knowing more does not necessarily make it easier, but it can help to avoid some failures!

Fully integrated CRM 'suites' such as Siebel, PeopleSoft, SAP and Kana, which go well beyond the original domains of sales, marketing and service into supply chain and partner management (so-called enterprise relationship marketing), have made a big difference to what companies can do. So while the first two steps above are more or less the same, the possible scope of CRM has increased greatly. The last three steps have changed, not only because of improvements to the software available, but also because of a tidal wave of new capabilities permitted by:

- the enhanced processing speed and reducing storage costs of computer systems;
- the ability of telecommunications systems to transfer data and become integrated with data systems;
- the range of devices allowing staff to interact anywhere with customers, and allowing customers to access companies almost anywhere.

Learning from experience

Smaller companies can and should learn from the experience of larger companies – or indeed those that have simply made good progress. The 'tidal wave' of new capabilities has produced a surge of investment in CRM technology, with good results for some companies. Companies have been able to acquire new customers more selectively, retain them more securely, develop them (via cross-sell and up-sell) in directions that are mutually appropriate, handle problems more securely and in a more customer-oriented manner – all this more cost-effectively. But not all companies that have used the CRM approach have achieved such results, as the first few chapters of this book show. For every company that succeeds in CRM, there is at least one (some would say two) that has spent a lot on systems, marketing and service strategy, and organizational change without benefit.

Why is this so? Because many companies assumed that CRM systems by themselves produce the desired result. They learnt too late that other areas must be changed too. These include:

- Analysis: how the company understands what is happening with its customers, their behaviour, attitudes, responses, purchases and so on.

▌ Planning and strategy: how the company decides what it wants to do with customers, in particular how it plans to manage them.

▌ Proposition: how the company turns knowledge of customer needs and company capabilities into a market and customer proposition.

▌ People: how staff who manage customers (whether in stores, offices, call centres, on customer premises or on the Web) need to change how they work.

▌ Processes: how plans are translated into actions that can be replicated and scaled up.

▌ Data: what data you have about your customers now, what its quality is, where it has come from and whether you can legally use it to improve how you manage your customers.

▌ Measurement: how actions and their results are measured and how learning and improvement occurs.

The earlier rush towards CRM applications as the sole solution now appears to be waning. Businesses are beginning to recognize from their experiences and those of others that project success (measured in business success terms) results from an appropriate focus across analysis and planning (including analytics), incentivizing change of people and processes, appropriate integration of channels and closed loop business and systems operations.

IMPLEMENTATION

Put together, all the above factors determine how a CRM approach needs to be implemented. So in the rest of this chapter, we first summarize the steps you need to follow to deploy the CRM approach successfully, from planning through to systems acquisition and implementation. This is followed by an in-depth discussion of the key requirements for getting a positive rate of return on your investment in CRM systems.

Here is a very brief summary of the steps:

1. Set up a CRM team, composed of people from the different areas involved in managing customers. Make sure you get input from them at all stages of the process.

2. Do a simple audit on your customer situation. Most companies will of course benefit from the CMAT approach, which is the theme of this book. The very smallest companies may wish to compile their audit from the coverage of this book. This means answering questions such as
   - How much do your customers buy from you, and what are the trends?
   - Why do they buy from you? Why do customers you want not buy from you?

- What is the situation with your main competitors? Who are they, and who is being particularly successful in winning customers and developing and retaining them? Why?
- How would your customers like to be managed?
- How much is it costing you to manage different customers or types of customer? Are any making you lose money?

3. Decide which customers you want more business from, which to retain, which are not worth keeping and which new customers you want.

4. Decide how and when you want to change the way in which you manage your customers to achieve the required effect. Decisions here may include changes to frequency and scope of contacts with customers, and to the communication channels you use.

5. Decide what you are prepared to spend and over what period. Try to find businesses that have been through this process. If you are considering a CMAT, take up client references. Use their advice to help set your expectations.

6. Develop an implementation plan, with actions, accountabilities and budget allocated over time. Involve the staff who are going to be responsible for delivering change.

7. Find ways of evaluating or testing your approach before you decide on systems. This may involve adapting existing systems and even adding manual processes. Find out whether customers really do respond positively to your changes.

8. Decide what systems you need. Many systems suppliers understand businesses' need to be sure that changes will work, so they support early implementations of different modules of their integrated systems. You can outsource some aspects of customer management, because outsourcing suppliers have benefited from technology improvements, so it is easier to set up their service for smaller customers. Outsourcing can be considered as a short or long-term solution.

9. Develop a brief for systems suppliers. Ask around in your business community to see which companies have a track record of success. Consult the trade press. Browse the Web too. Smaller companies should realize that many companies have adapted systems targeted at larger companies for use by smaller companies. Smaller companies should normally deal with resellers. Software producers generally focus on larger companies, using other channels for small company markets. The key to successful implementation is a business partner that works with you, not just sells you software (CRM in a box).

10. Send your brief to a selection of these companies.

11. When you evaluate their responses, listen to their advice about what you are planning to do. Make your initial programme plan part of the brief – this gives suppliers the opportunity to comment on feasibility.

12. Ask for references from companies similar to you – whether size, sector, main business applications supported by the system. Find out whether they succeeded in implementing changes similar to yours.
13. Make your choice.
14. Review your programme again with your chosen supplier, and get their inputs into the programme. Modify it with them, involving your people in any changes. Set clear milestones for both the installation and use of the system. Gain responsibility and delivery commitments from the selected supplier / s.
15. Implement the programme and start to manage your customers better.

This is a simplified set of tasks – the bare minimum. If you cannot afford consultants (this applies to some larger companies today, not just to smaller ones) or systems resellers, emulate this process by yourself. Try to hire someone who has implemented CRM in a similar company. If this guide is not enough, there is lot of help available cheaply. Many books, research reports and other publications are available at low cost – the co-authors of this book have produced several. So browse CRM forums and publishers' Web sites. Look for reports on what works and on what does not. If you exercise due diligence, you will almost certainly get good results.

BUILDING AN INTEGRATED IT CAPABILITY FOR CUSTOMER MANAGEMENT

Introduction

One of the main tasks of today's chief information officers (CIOs) is to get their IT department into the position of being an internal adviser to help their business create and sustain innovation cost-effectively through creation and deployment of new information management capabilities. Using IT to innovate in the business is becoming very important in virtually every business sector. The focus today is more on the enterprise's IT capabilities and how these can be exploited for business benefit, rather than on underlying system considerations.

So what capabilities are required to make IT a business innovator? The results of CMAT research discussed earlier in this book, and our project experience with clients, suggest that failure to integrate IT and business capabilities, and failure to integrate different areas of IT, lie at the heart of most failures to innovate or to gain return on investment (ROI) from customer management programmes.

The most severe problem is failure to integrate business and IT. Poorly defined processes, organizations, and governance rules and structures are the main causes of this. Other issues are more specific to IT, including the heterogeneous technologies, lack of architecture, or application landscapes that undermine an integrated approach. It is the CIO's task to build the primary capabilities that help to overcome these integration issues.

It has been highlighted by Bloor Research[1] that the market for application integration products and services, including middleware and corporate portals, will soar to a staggering $10.5 billion by 2006 according to Gartner Dataquest, as more companies focus on linking existing and new technologies.

The following sections will outline these integration issues and discuss the capabilities necessary to improve integration for business success, and propose measures to acquire these capabilities more rapidly and with acceptable risk.

Business and systems integration (or not?)

Most industries are being reshaped by IT in different ways, because software applications can now be developed and assembled to support a very wide range of business processes. This means that IT has a greater role to play in the development and support of new and enhanced business capabilities and processes. This raises a number of problems, but has also led to various methodologies being introduced to solve them. These are discussed below.

Mapping business needs to IT development and delivery

Many companies are under enormous pressure to reduce or contain costs while maintaining operational resilience and quality. Many also experience tension because of pressure to transform the business through local (sometimes tactical) initiatives, even though it may be clear that cost reduction, improved operational resilience and higher quality can best be achieved through shared infrastructure. Companies must continue to modernize their shared IT infrastructure, but in stages and when fully justified. There is greater realization that business assets now include data stored in computers. Customer management and (in some industries) compliance with legal or regulatory requirements is requiring real-time or near real-time processing and consistency of operational management. Still, within many companies, business and IT are too often disconnected organizationally as well as intellectually. IT is often grown from and oriented towards particular internal functions, departments or market sectors. Requirements that cross these boundaries, such as customer management and risk management, are hard to satisfy. A new level of cooperation and teaming is required between business and IT. However, prioritization, cost and value delivery for new IT projects are also important, and these are usually harder to achieve when systems cross boundaries.

Management of cost and value from IT projects

Pricing for profit is increasingly dependent on IT capabilities. This is partly because more accurate pricing requires transparent process costing, and IT services are an increased proportion of process costs. This means that both production transaction costs and IT investments must be identified and calculated. Where pricing calculations form part of an investment decision, IT costs (local and shared) should in principle form part of a business case and ROI calculation. Although this may sound obvious, few IT investments are assessed in this way.

Business gets value from IT projects in four main ways: efficiency, effectiveness, market expansion and advantage creation. Efficiency and effectiveness create value by automating business processes, making them more efficient (using less resources) or making them more effective (leading to greater impact). Cost reduction pressures have been the traditional justifications for IT outsourcing and cost reduction (the traditional 'your mess for less' strapline). Market expansion and advantage creation represent innovation value, now considered as the main differentiator for new-style IT outsourcing propositions. Examples of IT value justification include acquiring new customers, opening new markets, improving cross-selling to existing customers, and enabling creation of customized services and products and enabling faster product design cycles.

Business impact of technology

IT can create new channels for managing customers (such as requesting data using mobile devices or digital television services). These channels may also be introduced by companies to reduce the cost of customer management and other internal business processes, sometimes making certain customer segments profitable for the first time. These examples show how new technologies can create new business value. This requires the identification and understanding of technologies and the determination of the benefits for the business.

Capabilities

IT as the service provider for business

CMAT results show that IT is an important enabler of CRM. To meet the requirements of the business, the IT services group must consider itself as a service provider. To act as a service provider requires both a clear description of the service offerings and a reasonable pricing of that service offering. The service offering description is a service catalogue with service packages, which include single service elements with service-level agreements and corresponding prices for each service package. This offering must be accompanied by IT processes for providing the service package to the agreed service level, for communicating the selection catalogue to the business divisions, and for administering and modernizing the catalogue. Further, the IT service divisions should be able to support the business divisions in calculating the business case (see below) for an appropriate IT service package in each situation.

Business divisions and users need help in specifying and checking the offerings of the IT services group. If the offerings do not meet the requirements, the business can reject the offering and use another service provider. Here, the conflict between localized budgets and objectives versus the need for shared infrastructure for cost reduction and operational resilience can become apparent.

It is important that business managers understand at least the critical success factors for IT project involvement. This can help to ensure that change programmes run as seamlessly as possible, with responsibilities correctly allocated. Those programmes proving to be most successful share a common governance system, rather than creating a blame culture between business and IT.

Process-oriented application development and integration of IT systems

CRM systems exist to support business processes. Today's application selection and development methodologies allow excellent mapping of business process requirements and design to application selection and customization. Depending on the kind of new systems to be selected and customized or created, different techniques can be used. The focus may be on connecting existing process elements or on implementation of new process elements, or entire new processes. Too often the focus is only on adding new elements, when it can be far more effective (for ROI) to replicate or scale up existing implementations, or integrate existing capabilities to create closed-loop operational control.

Where a pre-developed application is selected and customized, much of this component work is already structured and provided by the application vendor, so the customization process can then focus on closing any gaps. Over-customization (for example, making the new application fit very closely with existing business processes) should be avoided, as this delays implementation and reduces ROI. It may also be more effective to customize (beyond the essential gaps) once the application has been deployed and experienced. Some packages are so functionally extensive that customization may be simply to restrict function use, at least in the early stages of implementation. Companies have been concerned that having paid once for the function, they are paying again to disable it while delaying implementation and ROI from wider deployment.

John Smith of IBM Global Services Quality Assurance[2] suggests that experience from package implementation reviews shows that programme risk appears to increase dramatically with the degree of 'package customization' attempted. It appears to be wise to execute a rapid and lightly customized implementation first, which partially links the package into the existing business processes. Few code changes are made to the package and limited interfaces are implemented between the package and existing operational systems. Additions and adjustments are made to the business processes over time to better match the optimal business process support of the package and its interfaces to other systems within the organization. This approach is not initially popular with business units or end-users and demands board-level support for ruthless prioritization and control of user requirements. However it has proven to be most effective in achieving business success and ROI.

Ability to develop a business case for each new IT project

In calculation of the business case three parts are normally considered. First, the scope of cost and value are defined. The following layers for the scope discussion can be identified:

▮ Operations cost avoidance (eg improved efficiency in internal IT operations).
▮ Development cost avoidance (eg by using standardized architectural patterns and components, or shared infrastructure).
▮ Improved IT process efficiency (eg through usage of simplified data maintenance).
▮ Business process efficiency potential (eg through fewer processes, replicated processes, by improved focus on customer segments through better data quality).

Second, the financial calculation method must be selected. Net present value seems to be the favoured option here, although various forms of this calculation are available. Businesses are increasingly implementing standardized methods and models for assessing project value in a comparative manner.

Third, each business case calculation needs data. This requires transparent information on current costs. Normally, IT infrastructure costs for hardware and software are well known. If not, comparable industry values can be used. It is harder to calculate the costs of implementing particular software packages; usually these costs have to be estimated.

Too frequently risk management does not form an integral part of the IT business case. It is always easier to make a theoretical calculation and to spend money than to ensure that ROI is achieved! Many of the factors that affect the ROI outcome are external to the project or company. They need to be identified and evaluated as potential risks to project and payback success, allowing relevant risk mitigation actions to be implemented where appropriate.

IT strategy based on a global requirements management process

To meet the business needs of single and associated projects, especially when planning to take advantage of shared infrastructure to deliver cost reductions and operational resilience, a well-defined IT strategy and supporting architecture must exist. This IT strategy is the basis for deriving IT initiatives and concrete IT projects. The IT strategy defines the large-scale action plan (programme) and includes products to the business (IT services offerings) and IT business areas, platforms, architectures and technologies, methods and tools, competencies and IT processes that are the basis of a shared but responsive infrastructure.

The IT strategy definition must be based on a proper business requirement identification process. IT requirements cannot be defined independently from business requirements; business process requirements and IT solutions must be developed jointly and coherently. In customer management projects it is common to translate business needs too quickly to IT application selection, ignoring the importance of people, processes and other key issues, which usually have a more immediate effect on project success or failure. The business model used by CMAT also provides a strategic guide to these factors.

Enterprise architecture management and IT governance

A consistent and well-managed approach to governance for customer management activities and underlying systems transformation is required for programme success. This should provide a consistent view of prioritized business processes across the organization, and requires an overall view of all IT systems involved in that programme. This is important for the technical, business and financial success of the programme. A good architecture enables the exploitation of existing systems in conjunction with new application investments. The same architecture must support all the initiatives of the company (not only customer management) in an integrated and shared manner. The architecture must also provide the basis for future developments, although in many cases future technologies and technology applications cannot yet be envisaged. A good architecture will achieve these objectives through use of sound integration technologies, enabling flexible and prioritized integration of data, real time and other messaging, on-screen applications (eg portal and portlet) and workflow concepts. Industry data models and common interchange standards (eg XML) have an increasingly important role to play here.

Enterprise architecture management includes the analysis of the current application portfolio and the identification of areas for improvement, and the definition of a unique business, application and infrastructure architecture across the enterprise. The management of processes to create this unique view with the relevant architectures is called IT governance.

Poorly integrated technology

Issues

Most of today's enterprises have to deal with a heritage of poorly integrated technologies. By 'technology' we mean all aspects of applications, platform categories, operating systems and middleware including application servers, transaction monitors, user interface platforms, messaging and extract–transform–load middleware, database management systems, or programming language environments. A company may have a variety of products within these categories from different vendors in different releases.

Reasons for poor integration include the following. For application selection or custom application development, the major issue is the lack of coordination of (internal) development efforts. The trend to moving responsibility for application selection or development towards business units often has the undesirable effect that each project team makes its own technology decisions, undermining enterprise flexibility, cost reduction and operational resilience. But even without this general trend, development often becomes dispersed within the enterprise.

Second, for the integration of application (component) products, the major issue is the dependency of each such application component on a given technology, or the application component may bring its own technology components, making the problem worse.

In considering the consequences of poorly integrated technology, we need to distinguish whether the technology is used 'locally' to applications or whether it serves as a shared application integration platform. With the increasing need for application integration, there is a trend to view more technologies as potentially local to application components (eg a programming language/environment or a database system). The application component then only reveals its interfaces in a way that is neutral to these technologies (eg as WebServices with only functional interfaces). Varied, poorly integrated technology local to applications leads to increased cost of ownership, including (additional) investments in skills, licences, maintenance, or bug tracking. It can also make integration of application components much harder and more expensive, and might even completely undermine the business case for such integration. With the growing demand for e-business solutions which span a single enterprise, poorly integrated technologies create additional problems, for example in inter-business processes.

Capabilities

The capabilities needed to address the above issues fall into two categories: first, those used to unify technology and architecture decisions within the enterprise wherever feasible, and second, those used to manage heterogeneity where necessary, since it may be too idealistic (or naive) to aim to avoid heterogeneity completely.

The first category requires process and architectural capabilities. The most important process requirement is for strict architecture and technology management processes and for a delegation of decision responsibilities, which is enforced by these processes – the governance model. There are very different approaches to such models, depending on a company's organization and culture. The introduction of a particular model usually requires organizational and cultural change. Models include a centralized technology management department with decentralized development units (where development may take place in the business units), a centralized development unit ('production line') including technology management, or decentralized development with technology/architecture boards.

If an effective architecture management process is in place, the remaining threat to uniformity of architecture arises from technology evolution. Evolution, including the evolution of technology standards, is still extremely dynamic, with significant new technologies being introduced every year. Many evolutionary steps do not introduce significantly new architectural principles, though. Consider, for example, the chain of DCE, CORBA, EJB (as part of J2EE) and WebServices. All are models for distributed computing, all have to reinvent, replicate or reuse solutions to the tough but common problems of security and transaction handling in distributed environments, but none introduce significantly new architectural principles. For in-house application development, it is therefore good practice to separate application logic completely from the underlying technology, for example, by encapsulating specific technology through an extra software (architecture) layer or by using code generation techniques that generate flexible mapping between application code and the current technology. Thus, architecture can remain stable (evolve through upward compatibly) for some time, while technology that implements the architecture may well change. Typical architectural decisions that enable this flexibility include separation of user interface and application logic, and separation of components via interfaces.

The second category, management of heterogeneity, requires a component-based approach to application architecture with an enterprise-wide standard for integrating application components. Components themselves may then use any basic technology as long as it is encapsulated within the component. Integration of components must be enabled on two levels: on the functional level and on the user interface level. On the functional level, the major integration mechanism is provided by message-oriented systems with added capabilities for message routing and data mapping. XML, the de facto data standard in this area, is being extended with functional capabilities through SOAP (simple object access protocol) and WebServices. It is more important to focus on the general architectural capability of separating application components with well-defined interfaces than to focus on one specific technology. Once such interfaces are conceptually defined, it is mostly simple to map them to different technologies, be it CORBA, EJB, or WebServices. More and more application products expose their functional interfaces to enable their integration on a functional level, despite potentially heterogeneous under-lying technology. On the user interface level, (tight) integration is much more difficult, since most off-the-shelf application components do not expose their user interfaces as separate entities. However, this may change in the future, since with the increasing need for business workflows, application systems will need to be broken down into activities that can be triggered separately, including functionality and user interface. Another promising trend is the move of user interfaces towards pure Web technology and shared portals. This requires more sophisticated Web user interface elements and, more important, the separation of Web page content from sequencing control.

Managing technology heterogeneity for off-the-shelf application products while providing the necessary integration capabilities depends on imposing requirements that products publish their interfaces and provide a component based approach to their overall architecture, from a functional, but also from a user-interface point of view.

Collaborative, operational and analytical functions

Issues

The distinction between the collaborative, operational and analytical functions is clearly recognized in CRM, where all three need to combine in a closed-loop approach for business success. Collaborative functions support the communication with the customer via Web-chat or, more traditional, e-mail, telephony, face-to-face or intermediary support applications. Operational functions provide (ideally the single point of) access to customer data and are the basis for automating customer or product marketing and serv-icing tasks. These are the 'systems of record' or 'legacy systems' (where the definition of legacy seems to be that the system has achieved production status!). Analytical functions provide data consolidation for analytics, mining for segmentation, trends and predic-tions in customer behaviour, often using complex mathematical models. Analytical func-tions can also provide measures on the effect of CRM initiatives, thus closing the loop.

It is easy to see that the potential for poor integration of these three dimensions is huge. It starts within one category, for example, contact tracking and reporting being separate for the different channels, and extends to systems across different functions. As a result, the enterprise often has no consistent view of its customers along all three dimensions, which is often obvious to the customer. Moreover, poor integration of analytical and operational systems may break the controlling and learning loop described above.

These dimensions clearly apply not only to CRM but to other, if not all, areas of the business. Collaborative applications extend to process flows between front, middle and back office within the enterprise as well as flows between the enterprise and business partners, service providers or suppliers, respectively. Analytical functions extend, for example, to risk management applications. Operational functions cover all tasks being automated within the enterprise.

An enterprise cannot afford to use more than one architectural approach, as its systems would otherwise remain disconnected, or to have disjointed processes (as an example) for customer and risk management.

For example, channel integration is threatened by poorly integrated collaborative and operational applications serving different channels, like call centre, e-mail, Web transactions, face to face and intermediated customer contact. Channel integration requires the delivery of current, accurate, and consistent data from (typically many) operational to (one or more) analytical systems. Automation turns collaborative into operational tasks, requiring a flexible and seamless integration of collaborative and operational systems.

Capabilities

In the CRM systems market, several vendors offer integrated (or suite) packages that contribute to more than one dimension, and sometimes all three dimensions. However they still do not provide a complete and integrated solution for a complex enterprise. Where packages do not fulfil the integration capabilities discussed below, the reliance on a single vendor makes it harder to enhance the application landscape with products from other vendors or with custom-developed components over time, as new business requirements and priorities emerge.

The authors of this book have written much on the relevance and required integration of collaborative, operational and analytical CRM functions for ROI achievement. This topic is covered in our previous books.[3] Most vendors and service providers suggest an enterprise application integration (EAI) platform to solve the complex integration issues found in complex enterprises, while simpler solutions can be relevant to smaller businesses. An EAI is needed to integrate applications from different vendors that have not been designed specifically to communicate with each other or with pre-existing and future systems.

Applications to be integrated must provide some functional service interfaces. These interfaces should be 'transaction-enabled' or, technically speaking, support a 'two-phase-commit' protocol, so they can be safely combined with other 'industrial strength' application functions. Ideally, these interfaces should follow some standard, like SOAP/ XML, or CORBA, probably also supporting industry data exchange standards such as IBM's IAA or IFW in financial services. Second, application components must notify interested parties of relevant changes or, at least, provide customizing facilities for adding such notification capabilities. This is particularly important if data in separate systems has to be up-to-date and consistent – an increasing requirement of real-time business operations with personalized customer management capabilities. Today, many systems are integrated via batch updates, violating the data currency requirement for some critical business purposes. Finally, if application components are candidates for integration into people-based processes and workflow, or simply integration on the desktop of a single user, they should provide user interfaces that can be controlled on the level of elementary activities (or functions), such as 'create a new customer', or 'approve loan'. If this capability were absent, integration of application components within a more global workflow would require the custom development (or redevelopment) of user interfaces. The first and second capabilities are found with many application systems on the market; the final one is currently rather rare, but is becoming more common with the penetration of Web or portal interface components, allowing single access points to multiple systems for employees, partners and customers.

As far as the overall application and system architecture is concerned, the major capabilities are multi-channel enabling, and the separation of largely context-independent activities as the basic granularity of application components. Multi-channel capability, in turn, is mainly enabled by a clean separation of logical activities and physical user interface. Activities should be modelled in a way that does not anticipate which user interacts with which activity. This provides the flexibility to have an activity executed by a client via different channel devices, by call centre staff, or also automatically. (Note again the point made above that the trend is towards automating more manual activities.)

From a data architecture point of view, integration will rarely be seamless. Attempts to move towards an enterprise-wide, redundancy-free data model have mostly failed, since the data architecture gets too complex if it tries to address all different aspects of the enterprise. It is therefore advisable to have local data architectures for different domains, probably introducing some well-managed redundancies, defining which application component is responsible for managing which data, and defining a proper mapping between these models to allow consistency of key data across the architecture.

Industry data models play an important, central and intermediary role in supporting effective customer management. The most obvious, and now proven, uses for industry data models are:

▌ Development of a 'single customer view' (in fact a single business view, of all customers, products, channels, alliances etc) for analytical uses. This is normally known as a data warehouse, and provides the base for providing consistent views and extracts (data-marts) of the same core data for various marketing, risk, profit, finance, measurement and scorecard applications.

▌ Development of a 'single customer view' (in fact a 'party' view of customer and eventually all other personal and business relationships relevant to effective customer management) for operational (system of record) and collaborative (integrated multi-channel) purposes.

▨ Development of data mappings for data interchange (eg XML formats) and other integration standards, including combined portals and portlets.

Industry data models provide the required common ground for consolidating shared data and sharing data dynamically as required. Industry data models also provide the shared home for data content that enables customer risk and profitability insights to be combined with offer and response information. Without this additional industry profit and value data, and without the integration of analytics, operational and collaborative function, isolated CRM application components may be deployed to target responsive customers of any value and fail to deliver the anticipated ROI. Figure 21.1 shows a typical high-level architecture (IBM financial services example) for successfully integrating analytical, operational and collaborative processes, functions and systems in this manner.

Batch and on-time execution integration by synchronous or asynchronous operations

Issues

There are various styles of system in use today that have been implemented over many years. First we have systems that work in batch mode: that is, the input data is pre-batched and processing tasks are run sequentially within a defined time frame, for example overnight, weekly or monthly. Second, there are systems that take immediate input requests, process those individual tasks immediately (eg credit risk control system or dialogue applications) and respond in real time to the requester or user.

Many businesses require these previously disparate systems to be integrated to form a single business process. Some operations previously implemented as batch need to be carried out in real time due to a business requirement for an immediate response. A financial services example could be that funds are transferred between accounts immediately and made available for the next transaction to take place. 'Straight through processing' is a term now commonly used to represent immediate data validation and update.

Capabilities

The integration of the activities (functions) of the business process chain must be implemented using both mechanisms, by synchronous as well as asynchronous operations. Synchronous operations are applicable if the operation result can be delivered immediately. The asynchronous method may be appropriate if the calculation of the result requires additional input that requires some time, so the result cannot be delivered immediately. Asynchronous activity may be preferred if the action must be carried out in

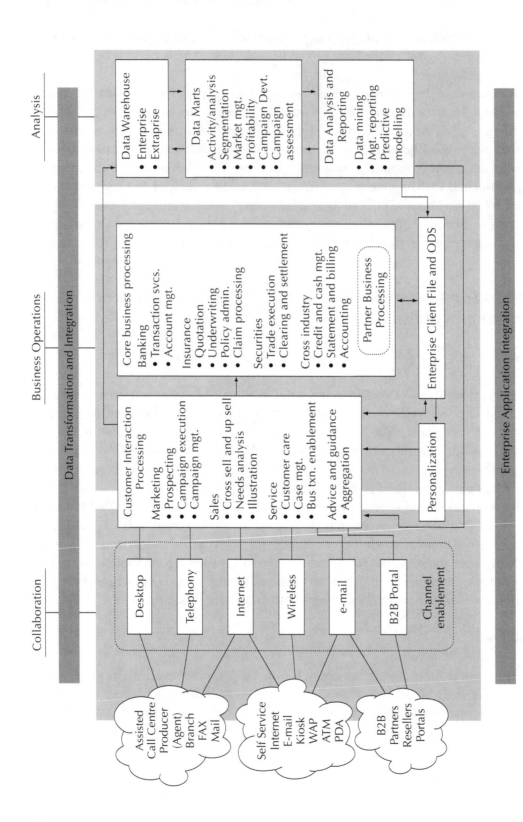

Figure 21.1 The customer management value chain

near real time (the results made available almost immediately, perhaps in seconds or even minutes).

In each case the synchronous and asynchronous activities (functions) of the process value chain have to be connected. For integration of these activities a uniform system model is needed that brings the different styles together. This might be a (work) flow-oriented approach that retains the sequence, consistency and rigour of the process value chain, for example ensuring completion of multiple update stages for various sources of customer data. Thus, this integration can be accomplished using appropriate workflow management systems.

Another approach is the use of enterprise application integration methods. Here, an integration broker allows a bus-like topology for connecting different activities and a minimal number of interfaces and connection between the components. The integrator itself (eg IBM's Websphere Integrator) can enrich data and transform them into another data format. Compared with the workflow management system approach, this method has the disadvantage of fixed process chains and the necessity of implementation of some control and data flow between the activities.

An easy way to connect systems is message queuing, allowing the integration on a synchronous and asynchronous systems basis. Such connections are characterized by guaranteed delivery within defined time intervals and without delivery duplication. However, these systems have traditionally not included control-flow management and have required a unique data format between sender and receiver. These combined requirements have now been addressed by the most recent integration developments, as in IBM's Websphere business integration product suite.

Integration performance needs to be considered, because more functionality (as in the case of the use of workflow management systems) requires a significant overhead of (system) management operations. So in cases with high performance requirements it makes sense to implement a special process management system, based on defined (fixed) process flow criteria and a state machine.

Many integration methods are able to satisfy the requirement of the on-time execution of activities. However the best integration methods and tools can rapidly and flexibly combine analytical, operational and collaborative systems for effective customer management. The same integration methods can also integrate existing systems ('legacy' or operational), current systems purchases (such as CRM components or suites) and future systems elements, so far unknown.

Integration summary

Integration of analytical, operational and collaborative systems is needed to deliver substantial ROI from enterprise and closed-loop customer management projects.

Current integration methods and tools can deliver the function needed to consolidate past, present and future systems within a single consistent architecture. Industry data models are essential for managing customers for profit, through integrating analytical and operational customer databases and supporting consistent data sharing for integrated channel management and closed-loop operations. Although integration issues are tough to tackle, and need to be addressed in a prioritized business transformation programme, it is now possible to balance accelerated delivery of short-term business requirements with delivery of a flexible, shared infrastructure for cost reduction and operational resilience.

FUTURE TECHNOLOGY TRENDS

Introduction

Information technology is a field in which innovation is constant and relentless, as we have moved over the last 100 years through mechanical, electromechanical, vacuum tube and discrete transistor to the integrated circuit of the current paradigm. Moore's Law offers the most widely recognized evidence of the growth rate of technology; in 1965 Intel's Gordon Moore predicted that the number of transistors per integrated circuit would double every couple of years. Moore forecast that this would continue until at least 1975; in fact it has continued through to today. Storage density offers another example of this trend; mobile hard disk drive densities have shown growth rates of 100 per cent per year. There are obstacles to this relentless progress however; Moore's Law has relied on a manufacturing technique called scaling in order to shrink transistors, but we are now approaching the limits of scaling, as key transistor components such as the gate insulator are reaching physical limits. Components are approaching atomic layers of thickness; further shrinking would degrade performance. The history of technology indicates, however, that as each generation of technology reaches its limits, new breakthroughs are discovered.

This constant technology innovation has exerted a strong pressure on the costs of physical assets, yet IT spending by businesses continues to grow. This paradox is rooted in two key factors. First, the physical cost of assets accounts for a falling proportion of businesses' IT costs; IBM research indicates that the labour cost of supporting storage systems is approaching three times the hardware cost. Indirect costs such as helping colleagues informally can account for 60 per cent of the total cost of ownership for PCs.

The second reason that IT spending has not fallen in response to falling physical costs is that the increasing business demands placed upon IT have matched or exceeded the improvements in technology. Increasingly complex business processes, globalization and e-business have all driven the demand for more effective IT implementation and optimization. It is these business demands that account for the developments in deep computing, pervasive computing, e-sourcing, continuous operations, bandwidth, universal access and security which are addressed in this chapter.

Bandwidth

Bandwidth is defined as the information-carrying capacity of a communications channel and is usually expressed in Hertz (cycles per second) for analog circuits and in bits per second (bps) for digital circuits. The most popular development within bandwidth technology is broadband, a term that has many meanings, but was coined originally to describe a channel with more bandwidth than a standard voice grade channel which is usually a 48KHz link.

There are two main contenders in the broadband access market: cable and digital subscriber line (DSL) technology. Traditional cable companies, aiming to increase their revenue by providing voice telephony, high-speed Internet access and interactive programming, have built broadband cable networks.

Cable is easy to install and get running, and cable operators are trying to bring down the cost of installation by selling their cable modems through retail channels. DSL on the other hand is being promoted by telephone companies that historically have copper-based local access networks. Subscriber numbers for DSL have recently exploded in Europe and this is primarily for three reasons: first, the telephone companies have improved the logistics of providing service to customers; second, there have been significant price cuts for the service; and third, customers now have the option of installing their own DSL connections.

The development of increasing network bandwidth will enable new applications and drive significant increases in Internet usage penetration. As a result, an increasing number of profitable customers will have high-speed access anywhere – in their home, office, hotels and anytime – even when they are mobile. Organizations will also be able to provide richer and more relevant content to various devices, and hence they will need to think harder about the services they want to offer. Moreover customers will have a choice of more channels such as phone, Web, television, or a new device, and hence businesses need to think about what the interface will be. The carrier's backbone network will be able to support these initiatives, as most of the optical fibre that has been laid in recent years has been used to speed up the backbone network, almost creating a glut of capacity ensuring its abundance and cheapness.

However, one of the greatest impacts of this new technology will be felt on mobile workers, who work from both their homes and offices. Fast data speeds and no need for reconnection will help reduce the time spent accessing data services and waiting for downloads. Real-time connectivity will allow them to react quickly to customer enquiries. The always-on fixed cost element makes this a highly cost-effective solution for those workers who need remote access. Businesses will be able to forge closer links with suppliers, enabling real-time inventory control and easier stock ordering. Moreover, broadband access technologies will allow smaller businesses to cover a wider geographic scope, enabling a pan-European or global strategy to be employed more efficiently than was previously possible.

Performance and capacity

Advances in data storage and technology make it practical and economical to store quantities of data that would have been unthinkable a few years ago. For example, when USAA began scanning documents and mail back in the 1980s, it was considered to be a major technological breakthrough in storage cost. Today, a consortium of banks has formed a check-imaging archive to store large numbers of documents efficiently, hence further slashing storage costs and crossing another threshold in this rapidly developing area.

This reduction in storage cost is further made possible by the emergence of new systems such as autonomic computing. An autonomic system is an entire system – devices, networks, file systems, data objects, and software – that manages itself and achieves business objectives. Such a system uses detailed knowledge of its components, current status, ultimate capacity, the extent of its 'owned' resources, those it can borrow or lend, those that can be shared or should be isolated to govern itself.

The storage cost of this highly efficient system is 20–80 per cent of typical total server purchase cost, where storage personnel cost has historically been approximately three times the purchase cost of storage. The autonomic manager can perform tasks today done by an administrator in storage management to achieve overall objectives. This includes reports on availability and performance, moving data for performance, provision capacity, backups and restoration and commissioning new hardware, thus improving availability and response time and data integrity.

Advances in the field of shared IT resources are further improving the performance of an organization's technological infrastructure. One of the latest developments in this field is the emergence of grid computing, defined by Platform Computing as 'the coordinated, transparent and secure sharing of IT resources across geographically distributed sites'. Grid computing will give companies the ability to share computing resources such as software applications, data, storage and computing power both internally over the intranet and externally over the Internet. By tapping into the enormous reserves of under-used computer power, organizations can deliver cost-effective computer resources on demand. It is estimated that only 5 per cent of the capacity of PCs and 20 per cent of servers deployed by enterprises are used. By using the idea of grid computing – which is taking under-utilized IT resources, such as PCs, workstations and storage devices, adding a management software layer that can pool, manage and allocate these resources dynamically, and then enabling users to call upon these shared resources as they need them – this usage level can be raised to 80 or 90 per cent, which will help companies increase revenues, save costs and improve their time to develop and market products.

Pervasive computing

Pervasive computing will enable 'anytime, anywhere' access to information via devices that will pervade our environment. Pervasive computing will be supported by powerful non-PC gadgets, in cars, homes, clothes and accessories, and these devices with highly integrated hardware and software will become dominant means of information access. The initial steps towards pervasive computing have already taken place with the increasing performance, storage and display resolution of hand-held devices such as mobile phones and personal digital assistants. As a result, individuals can now carry out more complex transactions such as micro-payments, undertake useful browsing, and receive high content and larger volume alerts on these devices. However, enabling pervasive financial applications is all about reliable business infrastructure and not just gadgets and stand-alone Web servers. New programming models and tools are creating strong linkages between clients, Web services and back-end applications. Pervasive plat-forms are emerging as potential control points in the end-to-end connected client server infrastructure. Support of multi-modality (such as voice and text) by the development environments also enables synergies among the platform segments.

Pervasive computing and its enabling infrastructure increase the channel choices that the consumer has and affects a business's channel delivery strategy. It is another impetus to force businesses to move away from silo-based organizations towards integrated channels and start thinking holistically of their business-to-consumer, business-to-business and business-to-employee capabilities. Most importantly, they need to realize that the increased functions, features and connectivity of these non-PC devices are not just add-ons to their existing channels and capabilities but will have a significant impact on their enter-prise infrastructure.

Continuous operations

Traditionally businesses thought in terms of disaster recovery when considering how to restore centralized data centres in the event of natural or man-made catastrophes; the emphasis was on backup of data off-site, and planning was in terms of how many hours or days it would take to recover. This disaster recovery mindset has been replaced by a continuous operations approach, in which businesses must be able to maintain core business processes continuously, before, during and after catastrophe strikes.

The shift to continuous operations has been driven by two major developments over the last 10 years which mean that the data centre approach to business IT of the 1980s, in which computing was something in the background which provided information to help people doing the business, has been replaced by a paradigm in which business cannot function without IT. The first development has been the growth of enterprise resource planning, supply chain management and customer relationship management, which have combined to create an environment in which businesses can no longer function without access to the applications and data run on these systems. The second major development driving the shift to continuous operations is e-business: companies selling on the Web must be operational 24 hours a day, seven days a week. There are already well-publicized examples of revenue losses in millions of dollars from real-time systems failures.

The implementation of continuous operations is critical for most businesses, but must be considered carefully. Ensuring continuity is an expensive business and should be applied on a targeted basis: any company that implements a single business continuity strategy across the organization will either be spending money unnecessarily or failing to provide the needed levels of continuity for the truly critical processes. IBM has identified a logical approach to implementing business continuity. First, identify the business processes that are crucial for competing in that business area; next identify all the capabilities (skills, knowledge, physical facilities and IT) needed to perform those critical business processes. Finally, analyse the risks associated with these capabilities and determine how to manage them. Options for managing those risks will be to accept, mitigate or transfer, depending on how critical the capability and risk is.

Critical success factors in ensuring continuous operations include rapid fail-over facilities housed and powered separately from the main production equipment, access to a pool of skilled support staff, effective use of techniques such as database and disk mirroring and electronic journaling, and ensuring suppliers are able to replace physical assets quickly in the event of a facility-wide incident. Riding above all these however, is the need for the business to recognize that continuous operations has become a critical business, not purely IT, issue and must be managed by all executives, managers and employees – not just by the IT manager.

E-sourcing

E-sourcing is defined by IBM as 'the delivery of standardized processes, applications and infrastructure over the network, as a service, with both business and IT functionality'. Three key characteristics differentiate e-sourcing services from traditional outsourcing: first, the services are shared among many companies; second, they are standardized rather than unique to one business; and finally, they are scalable so that usage and pricing are managed on a utility basis. Companies that use e-sourcing are able to buy process, application and infrastructure capabilities, such as purchasing, e-commerce solutions and storage, in the quantity and at the time that they need them.

E-sourcing has become a realistic business proposition due to the development of what IBM describes as an 'e-business infrastructure'. The e-business infrastructure is underpinned by three key trends. The first of these trends is the growth in network capacity as a result of heavy investment by telecommunications companies in recent years. Second, the architecture of computing now enables disparate groups of networked devices to operate as a single system; Extensible Markup Language (XML) facilitates data exchange between devices through tagging of content in standard formats, independent of operating platform. Finally, hardware platforms such as servers and storage systems are able to support multiple users, with each user's processing and data held securely and separately in virtual spaces, while running on the same physical machine: this is crucial for those organizations providing e-sourcing services.

E-sourcing offers a series of benefits to businesses, and this explains why it is moving from an interesting concept into a business reality. The first benefit is financial: rather than investing large sums to build new capabilities and then waiting to see whether the resulting business benefit justified the initial cost, businesses are able to receive (and pay for) e-sourcing services as and when their business demands it. For any business with cyclical demand, such as toy retailers at Christmas time or financial product providers at the end of the tax year, the ability to buy additional capacity for short periods of time is of significant financial value. The second benefit is simplicity: rather than manage complex programmes to develop new capabilities internally, businesses can focus on their core business while gaining new capabilities rapidly through e-sourcing. The third benefit is access to innovation: individual businesses can rarely afford to keep up to date with every marketplace innovation in applications, processes and infrastructure. E-sourcing providers, however, have the ability (and in order to be competitive, the obligation) to innovate constantly and improve the e-sourcing services they provide.

There are a number of concerns, however, which must be addressed for e-sourcing to achieve its full potential. Security is the primary concern of users. Data is one of the most valuable assets many businesses have: they will need to have confidence that that data will be managed securely and with due regard for privacy concerns. Second, e-sourcing at this stage remains a largely unproven concept: most businesses will need to see specific services and references from other organizations that are already enjoying the benefits of e-sourcing. Finally, there are technology issues to overcome: technical standards have yet to be agreed, implementation approaches proven, and performance demonstrably equal to or better than existing levels.

Deep computing

IBM defines deep computing as a number of complex calculations being performed on massive amounts of data, in order to support business decisions. The field of supercomputers is often confused as being synonymous with deep computing, but in fact supercomputing is just one of four key areas in which developments have enabled the emergence of deep computing. Supercomputing, thanks to ongoing developments in processor speed and parallel design, continues to advance: IBM delivered ASCI Blue, capable of almost 4 trillion calculations per second, in October 1998, while today ASCI White at peak performance achieves 12 trillion calculations per second. Assuming supercomputing continues to develop at the same rate, by 2014 or 2015 a supercomputer will have the computing power of a human brain.

The second key development underpinning deep computing is in the field of algorithms. Well-designed algorithms offer an alternative to brute force in computing solutions to problems. For example, when trying to find the word 'zebra' in a dictionary you could start on page one of the dictionary and keep reading until you find it, or you could start at the Z section: a probabilistic indexed algorithm looks for matches only in those places it is likely to find them.

High-performance software is the third element in the deep computing field. To achieve high performance levels, supercomputers require highly complex architectures, comprising multiple layers of registers, caches, discs and memory. In order fully to exploit the physical components of the supercomputer, high-performance software designed specifically to suit the supercomputer's architecture is vital.

The final component of deep computing lies in expert domain knowledge. Without an expert understanding of the nature of the issue being studied, high-performance software incorporating complex algorithms on powerful supercomputers simply enables business to go round in circles, albeit very quickly. Deep computing is dependent on expertise, often from multiple disciplines to channel the technological power into delivering business benefit.

Deep computing has been applied in a variety of instances. In the USA, IBM worked with Farmers Insurance Group (part of the international Zurich Group) to perform data mining on 35 million records from over 2.4 million policies spread over 7 different databases in order to improve pricing policies for different risk groups. Deep computing analysis revealed 43 individual business insights, including the counterintuitive finding that certain 'high-risk' sports cars, if owned in conjunction with at least one other vehicle, are actually far less risky. One individual insight generated in excess of $2million profit for Farmers. Southwest Airlines were struggling to manage scheduling for 270 planes, 3000 pilots, 4500 flight attendants and 2400 departures per day, and meet regulations and individual preferences. Using deep computing, IBM and Southwest Airlines were able to apply a volume algorithm to reduce the scheduling process from three to four weeks down to a few days. The airline was able to reduce aircraft downtime, flight costs, and most critically improve the quality of life for employees by reducing crew work hours.

Deep computing is a key IT development for businesses that need complex calculations to be done on massive quantities of data, whether that is in operating complex processes that need to run more efficiently, gaining business insight from vast quantities of data or performing cognitive modelling.

Security and privacy

One of the biggest barriers to online purchasing is fear about lack of credit card security, followed by a desire not to disclose personal details online and distrust of Web retailers. Distrust of the Internet is an issue that online banks have faced from the onset, and their greatest challenge lies in convincing their customers that their online operations are secure and trustworthy.

Online banks use a variety of security systems in their quest to ensure that their operations are well protected. These include passwords and PIN codes to identify and authenticate users as well as smart cards with embedded chips incorporating the customer's personal data. In the recent past, increasingly sophisticated biometric systems have developed: these can be used to identify individuals using their unique physical characteristics. Scientists are using this approach to make digital signatures more secure by developing a system that recognizes not only the handwriting but also the speed, pressure and acceleration of the writing in real time. Hence while hackers might be able forge a signature, it is far more challenging to copy the signature flow. Similarly, if these systems are built into the computer mouse and keyboard, the computer will be able to detect if someone else is using it.

Encryption systems that use complex algorithms or keys to scramble data play a key role in all online banking security systems. The most widely used system is Secure Sockets Layer (SSL), which encrypts data travelling between the customer's system and the bank's server, or between secure internal servers. Firewalls and intrusion detectors can be used to provide good protection to the bank's internal server. Authentication software can also be used to control what online customers can see and do: the stronger the authentication, the more you can do. For example it can help determine how much money an individual can transfer.

Hence, though there have been substantial advances in the field of data protection and security, these give rise to another challenge for the online bank, which is to strike a balance between security, cost and convenience in determining their preferred combination of security options. The sophistication in technology does give the bank more options in the level of security that it wishes to provide. It will however need to assess the level of security that it wishes to provide against the transaction cost on its online channel. For example, though smart cards can be made secure by using biometric information, such as fingerprints, and provide the bank with useful customer information, they require readers, resulting in a hardware cost. Moreover, the bank would need to provide the customer with not only the reader but also the relevant help and support services.

The greatest challenge, however, will remain in maintaining the customer's perception of the online channel as being a safe one, as all it will take is a story of a hacker transferring funds from accounts or their personal information being shared publicly to make customers reluctant and wary of giving online banking a chance.

CONCLUSIONS

In this chapter, we have ranged widely over various issues relating to implementing CRM systems. Starting with a simple view of how to go about the process of system selection, we dived into the details of techniques of systems integration, often all too easily dismissed by non-systems managers but absolutely critical to implementation of large-scale systems. We then concluded with a review of how technological developments are likely to affect CRM and related systems. In all, the story is one of increased opportunity combined with increased complexity, with the hope that in the end, company and customer will be happier with the result.

NOTES

[1] See www.it-director.com.
[2] A selection of his papers is on www.iee.org.uk.
[3] For example, Chapter 10 of Gamble, P, Stone, M and Woodcock, N (1999) *Up Close and Personal: CRM@Work*, Kogan Page, London; Chapter 7 of Foss, B and Stone, M (2001) *Successful Customer Relationship Marketing*, Kogan Page, London; and Chapter 18 of Foss, B and Stone, M (2002) *CRM in Financial Services*, Kogan Page, London.

22

CRM's Achilles heel: understanding the customer

Raymond Pettit

INTRODUCTION

Now, more than ever, companies are keenly aware of the tremendous benefits associated with understanding current and prospective customers from an economic, attitudinal, and behavioural perspective. Seeing through the 'lens of the customer'[1] has emerged as a requirement rather than a 'nice-to-have'. Strategy and management gurus, such as Fred Wiersma, lament the 'lack' of customers in such a consumer-rich world.[2] Competitors abound, information is in abundance (but quickly becomes useless), and consumers seem to have less and less time to make informed purchasing decisions: these are but a few of the reasons for this paradoxical situation.[3]

In an attempt to address this complex issue, many companies have embraced customer relationship management (CRM) as an important element of their corporate strategy. To help enable these CRM strategies, investments in customer-facing software applications have occurred with the fervent hope that better service and more efficient interaction with customers would occur – at every conceivable touch point. To achieve that objective, however, requires a thorough strategy development process that takes into account numerous variables in order to optimize the fit between organizational and customer needs; that is, it is not just a technological exercise. To date, most companies have just not taken the time to completely:

- develop the strategic role for CRM;
- build the information foundation;
- develop and prioritize tailored and customized offerings;
- implement and execute at the 'front line', directly with the customer.[4]

This has resulted in 'choke points' that clog the effectiveness potentials of the system (see Figure 22.1).[5] At the most fundamental level, companies have rolled out CRM applications as independent, nonintegrated solutions and generally only from an IT vantage point. The result, all too well documented,[6] is that most organizations that have implemented CRM technology have not achieved the competitive advantage they expected. The primary reason is that most investment in CRM has been in developing the essential IT structure and technical architecture – not on focusing on understanding and relating to the customer as a means to improve customer satisfaction, loyalty, and profit (Figure 22.2).[7]

What has clearly emerged is a strong need to focus on the customer – the customer-centric imperative – and a wide array of companies that say they do just that. But the reality and the vision are clearly not aligned. It would be safe to say that few companies have employed the extensive research and analytical processes presented in Figure 22.3 that could maximize and optimize the CRM solution.

WHAT HAPPENED TO THE CRM 'VISION'?

CRM brought the compelling promise that businesses could personalize, please, and profit by most of their customers nearly all the time by deploying a software solution. By

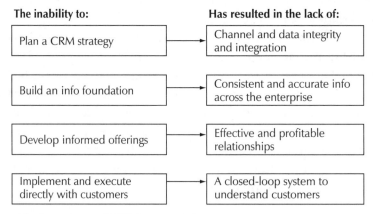

Figure 22.1 Chokepoints of CRM potential

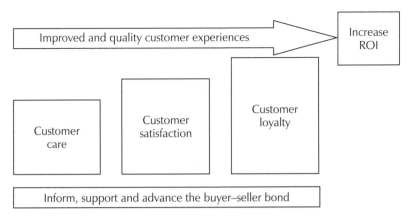

Figure 22.2 Customer satisfaction, care and loyalty

focusing on the satisfaction of customers, organizational efficiency and effectiveness would increase, and more importantly, profits would rise. However, as Lincoln observed, you can only fool some of the people some of the time. While rare success stories have emerged, CRM has not yet delivered on its ultimate promise – the transformed and improved customer experience. Why not? The answer is buried in a complex mixture of naïve and somewhat misleading attempts to embed CRM as a 'silver bullet' solution.

While generally improving the organization and efficiency of sales and service through sales force automation and call-centre productivity systems, companies have largely missed the boat to the destination called 'business success'. Absent is the piece that allows companies to best understand and utilize their customer information in order to approach a more personalized, long-term relationship. This is the piece that is strongly

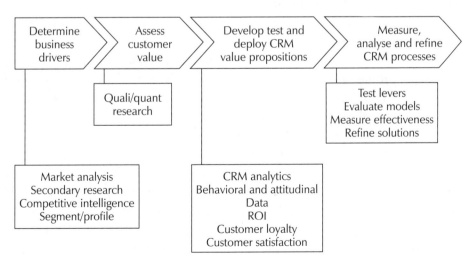

Figure 22.3 CRM optimized for effectiveness

connected to better customer care, potentially deeper loyalty, and improved return on investment (ROI). Indeed, missing is marketing and marketing research, primarily in the measurement and study of customer satisfaction.

CRM began as a solution for providing more efficient customer transactions, but has not evolved into a process by which companies can foster more meaningful customer interactions. Today, the challenge is on to take the next step – to focus on building lasting and profitable customer experiences at all interaction and transaction points to increase the probability that customer and brand value can be maximized.

In hindsight it is evident that many companies assumed that just 'adding on' new technology would enhance customer relationships. The fallout of this assumption is all too clear today. To make matters worse, many companies now face the unsettling situation of having too much data, analytic techniques that quickly outpace the ability of the company to use them, and no guidance in optimizing this new-found customer 'intelligence'. In many cases, businesses are left with sophisticated tools that offer little real value. The bottom line is that few companies today are optimizing CRM to create lasting customer relationships and build superior brand value. Thus, many companies are not realizing any returns on their CRM investments.

WHERE MARKETING AND RESEARCH FIT IN

Customer insights are critical to the personalization of specific sales, marketing and customer service interactions. By understanding and managing customer segments (segments based on a thorough study of customer behaviours and attitudes), market research techniques can help improve the cost effectiveness of call centres and sales forces and inform customer retention and cross-selling activities.

With the advent of CRM, however, an emphasis on harnessing customer insights at all customer interaction points and – more importantly – translating those insights into better customer experiences has emerged. This situation, while holding much potential, is hampered by a proliferation of fragmented contact points and a lack of conviction that a problem exists. Thus, the more creative and analytical aspects of marketing and research, which can make better use of rich customer insights to create improved experiences across customer channels, have yet to blossom.

Yet companies sense at some level that marketing and research contributes most when it converges completely with operational CRM applications. Marketing insights and analysis can be used to develop data-driven business decisions, among other things. Improved marketing campaigns, relying on enriched customer insights drawn from behavioural and attitudinal databases, can be targeted to increase brand value and potentially boost profits. In short, marketing is waiting to be revitalized, through extracting the maximum value through research and analytic thinking to understand customers and by using this understanding to guide actions. When integrated fully with sales and service efforts, market research completes the CRM solution.

As would be expected, the widespread demand for analytical applications is being led by CRM initiatives. Entrants to the CRM software scene, coming from many disciplines, directions, and perspectives, are beginning to make inroads via a focus on 'improving CRM'. While many are totally technology-driven, some are not. For example, the rather large global market research industry is casting an eye toward what it fears is a rapidly growing competitive threat to its established activities and intricate network of long-standing relationships.

If we step back and cast a discerning eye at the big picture facing businesses today, a universe of processes, procedures and tools falling under the broad category of 'business information' can be discerned. This can range from software, such as enterprise resource planning (ERP) and CRM solutions, to syndicated research that companies buy off the shelf from analyst firms. Deep in the mix can be found the activities and services of what we identify as the market research industry, a complex panoply of custom, specialized and syndicated services, with a modicum of database, online and technology-enabled efforts.

What sets the market research industry apart is the ability of its 'product', whether it is a report, a presentation or raw data for further analysis, to deliver fresh insights regarding how customers/consumers think, feel, perceive or intend to act. The objective, of course, is to enable marketing, advertising and sales efforts to 'meet the mark'; to better deliver to and serve customer needs, desires and requests; and to drive insight where it is needed most – at the front lines. What is occurring is that new competitors from the overall business information community are also – rightly or wrongly – saying the same thing.

The array of firms involved in 'healing sick CRM systems' is staggering. It includes the major CRM software providers themselves, all the way down to one-person consulting shops with a 'unique' take on measuring the ROI that CRM is purported to deliver.

CRM providers and consulting integrators

CRM itself, although fundamentally a technology-driven software solution, is also an approach to serving customers to best retain, satisfy and maintain profitable ongoing relationships. However, CRM analytic solutions – primarily advanced, automated approaches leveraging the collection of data on individuals – have arisen that seriously purport to inform advertising and marketing users of the CRM system about the customer: the who, when, where, and what to build profitable relationships. Consulting integrators too have taken on the mantle to make CRM systems 'work'. The end result is that the CRM decision maker – often the chief marketing officer (CMO), chief technical officer (CTO), chief information officer (CIO), or even chief executive officer (CEO) – believes/trusts that these systems are essentially delivering a 'closed-loop' process, when the reality is that nothing of the sort is occurring. Identifying this gap between belief and reality, based on evidence, is a key objective of any CMAT assessment.

Business intelligence and online analytical processing (OLAP) tools

These tools access the data warehouse, data mart, or operational data store that a company erects for a variety of efficiency and effectiveness reasons. Originally deployed as a part of ERP solutions, they have migrated quite nicely to use with CRM software, and are sometimes embedded or can be purchased as a stand-alone package with connectors to the CRM system. While there is nothing wrong with what OLAP does, it is not a substitute or solution for finding out what customers are thinking, feeling or saying. OLAP tools are a way to get at, examine and manipulate historical data about transactions (or in ERP solutions: financial, manufacturing or inventory data). They do not tell a marketer or advertiser anything new about consumer attitudes, behaviours, or propensity to purchase the latest BMW.

New-technology-driven CRM analytic players

Generally, these are research solutions of value and use to marketing and advertising professionals that were built from the ground up to be technology-enabled or based. Almost without exception, they have been involved primarily with the online world of e-commerce, Web traffic measurement, site statistics, online advertising and branding, and profiling or segmenting of online visitors. A number of large global market research firms contribute here, building off successes and experience with traditional media. However, with the downturn in the 'new economy' fortunes, there are fewer and fewer companies attempting this. There is also increasing demand to integrate these analytics with others in the traditional or core business, to provide a more comprehensive and multi-channel view.

Pure play online firms

The attempt in this category is to supplant – although today it is more to supplement – traditional market research techniques using extraordinarily sized 'pseudo-panels' of respondents accessible online.[8] In one way, these efforts have been the 'guinea pigs' for learning about the efficacy of this approach and for ways to work around various methodological deficits of the online sample universe. Few attempts have been seen that try and make the 'leap' toward being a CRM analytical solution.

Database and direct marketers

Database and direct marketing companies are cut from the same cloth as CRM companies. The analyses that these firms use to maximize the marketing effort are of direct interest and usefulness to CRM optimization, with methods often proven over many years. It is surprising that these two 'cousins' have remained so distant from each other, although transition examples include Peppers and Rodgers who were first direct marketers, before they jumped into the personalization space.

Major consultancies

While mentioned above, consultants also continue to look for 'silver bullet' data integration projects on a grand scale, essentially bypassing easier and potentially equally effective solutions. One has developed a practice dedicated to data warehousing and CRM analytics which uses aspects of the market research toolkit to enrich and amplify CRM integration solutions. Another is exploring the online market research space. Another trend, found in smaller, niche consulting firms, is the 'after the fact' attempt to institute ROI metrics that assess the efficacy of system implementations. While everyone seems to agree this is the 'year of optimization', the way to achieve this varies greatly.

Syndicated research and expert analyst firms

While primarily evident in the IT sector, certain syndicated products have become de rigueur for CRM firms to automatically purchase. Expert analysts are proliferating with a 'buzzword per month' to try to garner interest in ways we can improve CRM systems.

Global marketing communications conglomerates

These large umbrella organizations also have bits and pieces within the agency stable that increasingly are 'doing' CRM improvements. Many of the advertising, marketing, communications and direct marketing fingers inside these organizational networks have their own in-house CRM or relationship management improvement staff, and more frequently these are being linked up (via technology, Web, and intranets) to further extend and keep the function in-house and away from competitive 'outsiders'.

Enterprise Applications Integration (EAI) firms

A few players with 'very' big solutions are attempting to tie the whole ball of data wax together. Still missing, however, is what to do with all this data once it is merged and accessible to anyone at anytime. Thus, the pendulum swings back again and we may well have a 'three-peal' – ERP, CRM, and then there was EAI.

THE 'SOLUTIONS' PLAYING FIELD: WHAT'S GOING ON

So what is the configuration of the CRM analytical solutions space? As mentioned above, the number of entrants is staggering and diverse. The primary efforts are on addressing the CRM chokepoints:

█ one view of the customer;
█ consistent and accurate customer information across the enterprise;
█ closed-loop customer interaction;
█ multi-channel data integration.

Ironically, these are (or were) precisely the 'sell-in' points CRM companies used originally.

At the most basic level, it appears that CRM clients are asking for two things: first, 'I want to understand my customers better', and second, 'I need to have an articulated strategy (including the much touted ROI metric)'. While the 'insight' that emerges from analysts that CRM will not work without cultural change in the organization may appear like solid advice, the fact of the matter is companies know this and are struggling with it. The CRM implementation orders that were handed down from the CEO a few years ago are now in the hands of the CMO or CIO to make them work. At the marketing, sales, and customer service personnel level, the deficiencies of not having a plan in place are a daily fact of life.

Similarly, the inability to 'close' the highly touted loop with CRM software really centres on not having the proper techniques, processes, protocols and methods in place to understand the customer that can be tied back to the CRM system. This includes not just 'hearing' their feedback, but in garnering insight about their attitudes, feelings, and perceptions across the board.

The major portion of this chapter will discuss the following analytical CRM solutions providers and what they are doing that have emerged from my recent research:

█ **CRM majors** have obviously heard what clients are saying and are frantically at work to develop 'analytic solutions'. Some are achieved through suite integration of analytics from mergers or acquisitions, others through internal developments – although these developments often prove to be beyond the core competency of those companies.

- **Point CRM 'solutions'** companies actually comprise overlapping and somewhat undefined thrusts:
  - those growing from the online market research and customer feedback direction;
  - slightly broader customer experience management (CEM) and customer value management (CVM) efforts.
- **Market research firms** – given their pedigree and history – have assumed a somewhat defensive posture, in most cases. The problem here is that – except for those firms who delved into online market research (MR) – most MR firms are not technologically savvy. In addition, their network of contacts and relationships within their client base (although it is huge) tends to be involved at the 'front lines' and not necessarily consumed with the CRM initiatives or even systems in place. Thus, there is a reticence to even explore this area, and the resultant 'head in the sand' situation makes the 'CRM' arena even more mysterious that it actually is.
- **Consultants and integrators** appear to be focusing here on where the 'biggest' opportunities are and the fact that they are tied in, generally, to a fairly high executive level. Thus, their solutions centre on things that CEOs, CIOs and CMOs are struggling with:
  - 'Let's integrate all your sources of data': long-term projects with a potential for huge payoffs (certainly for the consultants); although some services suppliers have proven to be very practical and focused on delivering 'CRM in stages';
  - 'ROI': strategy, planning and measurement consulting that probably should have been done at the earliest stages of planning a CRM implementation, with increasing client pressure to deliver ROI at every stage and from previous CRM project expenditures.

One additional segment is somewhere between the CRM majors and other efforts. Called EMM (enterprise marketing management) systems, they are intent on taking the very important and difficult area of marketing and attempting to automate, as much as possible, this function across the enterprise. Firms such as Protagona and Aprimo have arisen, that essentially are taking a technological step tempered with the fact that so much of what is needed for success in marketing is located in people's heads, as well as in corporate documents, external research and knowledge, and organizational management processes, techniques, and history.

Thus, at the most basic level, the EMM thrust is to use the technology to enable marketers to take full advantage of the entire store of 'corporate knowledge' contained in a business (or from 'best of breed' companies) via an automated system that supports communication, collaboration, interaction, learning and knowledge management. Buried somewhere in there is the proposition that customer understanding and relationships will be enhanced as a result – and that EMM represents the next 'evolutionary' step of CRM. Unfortunately, it is so early in the 'evolution' of these companies, that it is difficult to assess whether they are on target or not.

Data analysis redraws the CRM landscape

As companies demand better tools to exploit growing stores of customer data locked away in CRM systems, CRM companies – and many others – are rushing to add analytical capabilities to their applications. The push for better data understanding is creating a convergence between traditional business intelligence, market research, and CRM, as transactional CRM vendors integrate business-intelligence functions through internal product enhancements or via third-party support. Some argue that bolting on analytics to operational CRM could create more work for enterprises. Where CRM customers are concerned, integration should be the key word driving vendor feature sets. However, some observers believe the integration trend could render business-intelligence vendors unnecessary, whereas others point to new opportunities for enterprises to finally realize solid ROI from costly CRM implementations. What is missing, of course, is still the capability to actually turn the data into insight beyond the technology enhancements, and the need for marketers and business people to go beyond OLAP to get at questions they really need answered about the who, why and what of customers.

How analytics fit into the big CRM picture

Already a variety of companies are focusing on one or more aspects of analytical CRM, such as trying more clearly to pinpoint customer preferences, customer attitudes and customer opinions, and feeding that into critical processes within the overall CRM picture. While these companies each have a different focus, each has in common a heavy reliance on translating traditional market research processes and techniques via enabling technology that 'fits' within CRM systems.

As more companies centre on their existing customers, they are learning that there is a gaping hole between their CRM system and their ability to understand customers. While the idea of gathering more detailed customer feedback across a CRM environment and actually using it seems like common sense, it is also clear that the larger applications vendors are not yet convinced. Where the leadership and impetus will emerge to drive customer understanding and the application of that knowledge is difficult to predict today.

THE 'CLOSED LOOP' BREAKDOWN

From an engineering perspective, any continuous process can be controlled easily enough. What is needed is a 'feedback controller' that measures the process variable, determines if it has deviated too far from a desired setting, applies the necessary corrective effort, checks to see if the error is minimized, and repeats as necessary. This closed-loop control procedure will eventually have the desired effect provided the controller is sufficiently patient.

Unfortunately, patience is not generally considered a virtue in process control. A typical controller will apply a whole series of corrective efforts well before its initial efforts have run full cycle. The option of waiting for the process to play through every time the controller makes a move generally leaves it 'offline' for so long that the controller becomes virtually useless.

On the other hand, a controller that tries to eliminate errors too quickly can actually do more harm than good. It may end up over-correcting to the point that the process variable overshoots the desired settings, causing an error in the opposite direction. If this subsequent error is larger than the original, the controller will continue to over-correct until it starts oscillating from 100 per cent effort to 0 per cent and back again.

This condition is commonly called closed-loop instability. An aggressive controller that drives the closed-loop system into sustained oscillations is even worse than its overly patient counterpart because process oscillations can go on forever. The process variable will always be too high or too low. Worse still, in the mechanical world, the oscillations can sometimes grow in magnitude until pipes start bursting and tanks start overflowing.

In the business world, and particularly in marketing, we are continually involved in processes that have a beginning, middle and end. In fact, CRM software has been designed to support a 'closed-loop' process, usually described as a three or four-step process such as plan, implement, evaluate, or plan, test, deploy and analyse. The problem, not unlike the description of a mechanical process presented earlier, is that darned 'controller'. In the real world of marketing, if we use a controller at all (a dubious assumption), the timing of adjustments (based on feedback, analysis, inspection or research) is usually off. In fact, in the majority of cases and places, there is no 'controller' present. This results in the 'closed-loop' breakdown effect, shown in Figure 22.4.

The 'controller' in the CRM process is a person who takes the mass of feedback generated from a campaign or action, analyses what happened, and (theoretically) feeds insight or adjustments back to the appropriate place. The intent is to take the learnings and 'optimize' or improve the marketing, sales, or call centre process the next time. High on the list is trying to understand more about customers: how many responded (counts); determining if that was a success or not (compare); and 'why' they may have responded or not (analysis). If these three simple actions are taken and not 'fed back' to the appropriate place, then this is where the 'closed loop' breakdown occurs.

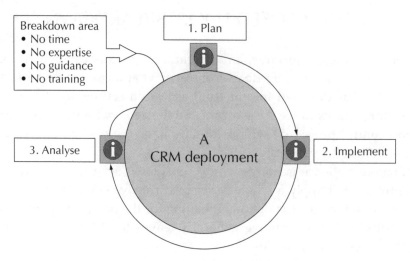

Figure 22.4   The closed loop breakdown

CRM software cannot provide a 'closed-loop' or 360-degree view of the customer. It takes some sort of 'controller', usually an analytical person, to either initiate the 'corrections' to the process to ensure it is on track, or – in the case of human systems and processes – try to improve it. It is simply the 'analysis' function that software cannot accomplish. Further, the 'insight, feedback, results' must be 'applied', either by the analyst, or by 'reporting' to the people who can make the necessary changes to optimize the process.

What a seemingly small issue – yet what large implications. I would venture to say that this tiny detail has been a cause for failure in many CRM implementations. The logic is so good from a mechanistic perspective. Yet when deployed in a human system, it breaks down.

So what to do? Fortunately, there are numerous efforts out there to correct this problem. The popular conception that an AI analyst could be the closed-loop 'controller' in CRM systems (automated analytics) is a long way off. That said, for such a small 'defect' in the CRM system, there are an extraordinary number of 'ways' to fix the problem that are being advanced.

A universe of CRM analytic solutions

Figure 22.5 depicts a breakdown of the various categorical players in the race to improve CRM via an 'analytical solution'.

Although it is clear that a lot of people know that 'understanding customers' is vital to CRM success, it is less clear what the best approach is. Most suppliers, if not all, are coming up with better ways to get data in a form that could yield insightful analysis – but none

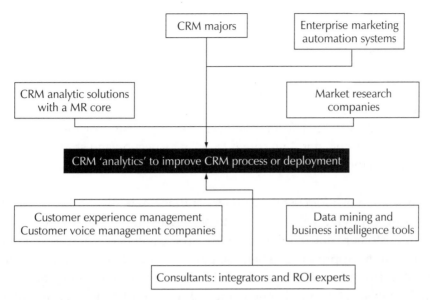

Figure 22.5 Current analytic CRM solution space

appear to take the next step in ensuring that it gets acted on, optimized, or used to benefit, or – the most optimal way to accomplish the goal of better understanding of the customer.

Companies that are addressing CRM weaknesses

A few niche suppliers are trying to take what are essentially market research functions, such as the ability to collect survey data, and embed the results and/or data collected into technology-enabled systems. One company has focused exclusively on embedding this function within a call centre infrastructure. Others have targeted the customer experience management space via a captive online panel where they can execute a number of research and tracking exercises.

Technological progress now happens on such a continuous and rapid basis that it can be hard to stay aware of, let alone assess, the implications of many of these developments. And yet new technologies must be tracked and evaluated in terms of their potential for commercial exploitation. Anything less could mean abdicating competitive advantage. A particular mindset is currently maturing and converging to support a significant improvement in CRM capabilities. The ability to collate, analyse, and deploy more and more information about individual customers and segments of customers, and utilize the information to anticipate or respond to them, is becoming a primary force in optimizing CRM solutions.

Customer-centric insight: how it is driven

Becoming customer-centric is an increasingly popular goal for many companies, and there are many ways to achieve customer understanding. Some believe that it comes from thoroughly understanding customer (dollar) value and (potential) profitability. Others see 'customer value analysis' (CVA) as a means of understanding the complex set of buyer needs and desires that forms the basis for purchase decisions. Still others maintain that customer understanding comes from an inspection and study of segments of customers based on their behaviour, or perhaps their lifestyle and attitudes thrown in for good measure.

What is the best approach for customer understanding? Actually, all three – customer profitability, customer buying values and customer segmentation – have a place under the umbrella of customer-centric understanding. The challenge is to understand the differences between the approaches, when to apply them, and how to derive strategic and tactical value from them. This function is often the responsibility of a skilled researcher and analyst who can also be stationed at a point to influence, guide, or support informed actions.

Customer profitability

For many companies, a fervent belief exists that all customers are important, and all should be treated equally. While this makes for a good public relations or vision statement, it ignores the relationship of customer value to company profit. All customers do not contribute the same value to a company. A simple analysis can reveal surprising insights into relative customer value. In general, the Pareto principle applies, in which about 20 per cent of customers represent about 80 per cent of total revenues.

Recognizing the importance of a small segment of highly valued customers translates into several imperatives. First is managing the cost to serve customers. While a reasonable level of customer service is appropriate for all customers, it makes sense to balance the cost of serving a customer with the current or potential value of that customer. Combining this principle with customer preferences can drive customer profitability, customer satisfaction and company value.

The second imperative is product strategy. Too many companies make the mistake of managing product offerings based on the perceived needs of the entire customer base, rather than tailoring offerings to the needs of those customers who actually drive profitability. Measuring only the value of customers at one point in time is not sufficient. What about customers who have spent a lot in the past but are not currently spending at that level? What about customers who are not currently valuable but will likely be so in the future (such as college students)?

Customer lifetime value (CLV) analysis provides an approach to measuring customer value over time. CLV captures the net present value of the future stream of revenues less the costs associated with a customer. The CLV formula also helps to identify the factors that drive value creation, including the costs and benefits of acquisition efforts, up-sell and cross-sell marketing, and retention activities, as well as the impact of customer referrals. Although more easily measured when applied to an aggregate customer base, CLV can be a valuable measure of customer profitability. It clarifies the extent to which a company should invest in marketing, sales and service efforts, and at the individual level guides how much should be spent on a given customer. CLV then becomes a useful guideline for making quantitative resource allocations, especially in investments such as customer databases, customer analytics, customer interactions, and other CRM-related resource decisions.

Customer values: why they buy

A second approach to customer-centric understanding is to determine why customers make specific buying decisions and then incorporate that knowledge into specific marketing and service strategies. This involves:

▌ identifying the key values that drive customer behaviour;
▌ understanding customer preferences and the trade-offs people are willing to make;
▌ segmenting customers based on their values and decisions;
▌ developing product, channel, pricing, service strategies and value propositions that best serve those segments.

The resulting value-based segmentation can support strategic imperatives including overall corporate strategy, revenue enhancement, cost reduction, process improvements, and increased customer responsiveness.

Typically conducted by surveying a representative sample of customers, a values analysis identifies the key elements that drive purchasing, and measures what is truly important to customers by asking them to make trade-off distinctions. Trade-off research uses conjoint analysis to measure the decisions customers face in actual purchase decisions. By asking a customer to choose between a pair of options, and by conducting multiple paired comparisons, weightings are determined for each variable to discover their relative importance in the buying decision.

When a trade-off analysis of this sort is conducted, it is critical that an analytic researcher with business/consumer knowledge is involved. To include all the factors that are likely to influence the customer's decision and to combine the factors in ways that make sense to the customer and reflect their actual decision process is a combination of science, art and experience. Not choosing the right path runs the risk of missing a critical driver of customer behaviour, and producing misleading results.

When the analysis is successfully completed, customers are then grouped into segments based on their responses. For example, a segment of customers might value transaction speed and be willing to pay a premium to get it, while another segment's behaviour might be driven by channel preference, and a third segment might be motivated by low price. The most important values for each segment can be identified, leading to an understanding of what matters to all customers as well as what matters to specific segments.

A closely related approach known as customer value analysis (CVA) also focuses on understanding a customer's key buying factors, by incorporating the choices customers make in coming to a decision to buy. It balances the relative importance of each buying factor, the rating of how well each competitor delivers on the key factors that drive the purchase decision, and how the buying factors, importance weights and relative competitive performance are changing over time. This approach is based on the idea that customers make buying decisions based on a complex set of decisions between product and service attributes and cost. It can be used to better understand customer satisfaction by looking not only at a customer's satisfaction with a particular company's offerings but how well those offerings stack up against competitive offerings. It can also serve as a leading indicator of competitive threats and inform strategic measures to counter those threats.

Customer behaviour segmentation

A third approach to customer understanding is the use of behavioural segmentation, particularly the analysis of customer data found in customer databases. Database segmentation addresses a critical methodological weakness found in a customer values analysis: the inability to assign segment membership efficiently to all customers.

Unless all customers can be scored in some way, the application of customer value metrics in an efficient and effective way is impossible. Segmentations based on surveys are actionable in a strategic sense, but their value is extended when the survey results can be imputing back to the total customer population. A combination of database segmentation and customer value surveys can deliver a more robust means of deploying customer-centric understanding that can drive marketing, sales, and customer service quality initiatives. And with the addition of data mining, customer databases can become an even more potent source of customer-centric understanding.

Behavioural analysis can generate insight into customers because it reveals what customers actually do – not just their propensity or their stated attitudes. This analysis presumes the capture of transactional data – products or services purchased, how much, when, sales versus full price purchases, and so on – as well as demographics, lifestyle and life stage data, when available.

Effective behavioural segmentation starts first with a set of business requirements, and an understanding of the critical business issue to be resolved. This shapes the choice of variables used for the segmentation and can produce a meaningful outcome. Many companies have used attitudinal segmentation approaches to customer understanding, and continue to use the segmentation to drive advertising, marketing, and brand strategies. In fact, attitudinal and behavioural segmentations can reinforce each other. Attitudes, perceptions, and feelings drive behaviours, and behaviours in turn confirm what people actually do. Both attitudes and behaviour can provide valuable customer insight, but differ in their application. Attitudinal segmentation is primarily survey-based and tends to inform broad strategic decision making, such as market positioning. Behavioural segmentation can be either survey-based or database-driven; however, in data-driven segmentation all customers are placed in segments. As a result, behavioural segmentation drives both customer strategies and targeted action.

A common mistake in performing segmentation analysis is mixing demographics, such as age, gender, or marital status, into a behavioural segmentation. This tends to cloud the resulting segments, and can sometime render them useless. A 'cleaner' approach is to define pure behavioural variables from the database, chosen for their business information value, and use these variables in the segmentation analysis. Then these derived segments can be 'profiled' at the level of demographic data available. In fact, hypotheses about drivers of the behavioural segment can be tested here. Thus, the behavioural segmentation supports a stratified study of attitude and needs culled from surveys, such as, what are the drivers of value in Segment A and how do these customers look, think and live?

Another useful aspect of segmentation is the ability to score every customer with segment identifiers and profile information. This requires a data-mart or store that contains all the necessary information used to derive the segments, and the information used to profile the segments. Analysts can run segment-based multivariate techniques to produce models capable of predicting customer response to marketing, sales or advertising actions, campaigns or offers.

After the model is completed, it must be deployed. To avoid a closed loop breakdown, sales and marketing personnel should be guided and assisted by analytic experts to use the models, set up the campaigns and test them, and retain and make sense of the outcomes. This evaluative information, in particular, must be fed back into the data stream (store or mart) to train better models. Campaign protocols enforce the use of the models and a measure of their effectiveness. Without careful proofs, metrics and 'learning' in place, the success of a new modelling approach may suffer. It is clear that an analytic person (or persons) with business knowledge is required to make this happen effectively.

The end results of segmentation analyses can be used to build a set of customer portfolios. Each portfolio will have its own set of priorities and directives. For example, a service-seeking segment might require a company to develop special services and better quality programmes. A 'newbie' segment might require education and extended assistance. A low-value segment might need careful migration to a higher-value segment. The point is that the segmentation portfolio becomes the framework from which all CRM activities are defined, studied and improved.

A long-term but elusive goal of many companies is to take better advantage of the mass of data they possess about customers. Particularly as CRM systems afford the capture of precise behavioural data, survey-based attitudinal segmentation can become a cornerstone for effectively informing and tagging all customers in the database with some degree of accuracy. Complex multivariate models can link attitudes to behaviours. These models are then applied to a complete customer base for full coverage and guidance of business tactics. While not perfect, the resulting 'imputed attitudes' do approach a much better and quantifiable 'understanding' of the customer. Segmentation is one pillar of customer insight. It is a robust organizing structure on which to build marketing actions. It also enables experimental validation of marketing ideas and strategies, and allows for the development of customer portfolios to be managed at a specific and detailed level. Segmentation is not trivial, nor is it inexpensive – but it is a solid step toward a more customer-centric enterprise.

CUSTOMER EXPERIENCE MANAGEMENT SOLUTIONS: CRM LOOKS IN THE MIRROR

Customer experience management's (CEM's) premise is that every time a company and a customer interact, the customer learns something about the company. Depending upon what is learnt from each experience, customers may alter their behaviour in ways that affect their individual profitability. Thus, by managing these experiences, companies can orchestrate more profitable relationships with their customers.[9]

CEM, in short, is contextual. It gathers information about interactions between company and customer, and analyses the dynamics that are present. Thus insight, wisdom and understanding can be fed back to the company in a closed-loop system which (in theory) makes optimal use of every opportunity to influence customer behaviour.

As CRM is more widely used, its weaknesses become more apparent. As Gurney states, 'CEM's strengths lie in precisely the areas where CRM is weak. By focusing on the experiences of customers and how those experiences affect behavior, CEM examines both the quality of the company's execution and the efficacy of the result. It aligns customer needs with the company's ability to fulfill those needs, leading to business relationships that are mutually beneficial and that both parties – company and customer – are motivated to improve.'[10]

How customers interact with us

A well-designed CEM initiative begins by defining precisely the types of customer behaviour the company wishes to influence, recognizing how customer needs and expectations change at different points in their lifecycle, and planning experiences that will positively influence customers. CEM is difficult because it seeks a high level of precision. It requires upfront thinking to define the customer behaviours, how to best influence them, and then align marketing messages, performance standards, training content, employee incentives and measurement systems to realize these goals.

How you do CEM

The foundation of a CEM system is based on information captured about individual customer interaction, dialogue, and experience that is analysed and fed back to the organization in some usable way. The information can be gathered from surveys, from qualitative (observational) studies, or from incoming calls or e-mails to the company. At the next level of sophistication, the data can be integrated with other customer data on hand. But the key in CEM is to have real (or near real) time capture and usage of the incoming flow of the 'customer voice'.

Next, this data needs to be turned quickly into useful information to guide actions. Perhaps the best arena to accomplish this is in the service organization (call centre or customer service). In addition to providing guidance to call centre personnel (for example, to cross-sell or up-sell an incoming caller), information must also loop back to training programmes so that knowledge and performance deficiencies among employees are directly addressed. Further, CEM programmes may extend this linkage to employee and manager incentives.

Finally, a fully developed CEM programme incorporates key metrics related to CEM success, such as retention rates, average purchase amounts, store sales, and complaint and resolution rates. The strength of a CEM system is in its ability to help people continually align their performance with customer needs and behaviours, enabling companies to make small, day-to-day adjustments as well as track enterprise-wide changes, trends, or successes.

Alignment is critical

The concept of 'continual alignment' is critical to CEM because it allows the system to function as a practical, front-line business tool that effects change on a consistent basis. A comprehensive CEM system deals with many crucial points of alignment. Among the most important are these:

▮ **Company message with customer expectations**: Is the brand (advertising, marketing messages, etc) consistent throughout all phases of the customer's experience? What do customers expect of the company? Is it consistent with expectations?

▮ **Customer expectations with company standards**: Are standards consistent throughout all interactions with the company? What do customers expect? Is it consistent?

▮ **Company standards with training content**: Does quality training align with company standards? What are employees expecting?

▮ **Training content with front-line execution**: Does training content align with executing directly with customers?

▮ **Front-line execution with rewards and incentives**: Are rewards supporting quality service motivation via alignment with day-to-day execution?

A robust CEM programme offers more than an online customer feedback system can provide. Although follow-up surveys to recent customers, typically conducted over the Internet (with 'instant' results provided through online graphical reporting) are important, they address only a portion of the scope of CEM. CEM tools and methods also include:

▮ **Customer feedback:** Both survey and real time capture of the 'customer voice':
  – telephone interviews, generally as a follow-up to call centre service;
  – e-mail invitations with a link to a Web-based survey;
  – Web site 'pop-up' surveys;
  – interactive voice response (IVR) surveys;
  – face-to-face interviews;
  – e-mail customer service (text) messages;
  – IVR (text) data.
▮ **Performance audits and monitoring**: Metrics to support and track performance, while feeding back measures to drive improvements.
▮ **Learning management:** Taking the results of analyses to drive 'improvement' programmes.
▮ **Incentives**: Taking and using the results of analyses to drive incentive, evaluation or compensation programmes.

The idea that customers can be managed strategically is not new. Companies have always tried to optimize their customers' experiences through advertising, store design, lighting, music and, of course, quality service. Although the term may be new, CEM has for many years been a fundamental approach to doing business.

Fuelled by technological advancements, which have expanded the range of services available to customers – and simultaneously led to escalating customer expectations – a number of fundamental changes have occurred in the business environment. The changes have been affected by the fact that although there are now more services and products available than ever before, customer satisfaction is at an all-time low. CEM is a philosophy, approach and strategy that can help to make the interactions between companies and customers more rewarding through utilizing customer dialogue and understanding as linchpins for relationships.

ANALYTICAL AND MARKET RESEARCH INTEGRATION

The evolution of CRM analytics

OLAP (online analytical processing) tools first appeared in the early 1990s as part of ERP systems. These systems analysed data from a variety of sources within organizations, and did not necessarily focus on customer data. Financial reporting and analysis, budgeting, planning, and sales reporting and analysis were common OLAP applications. However, most of these applications required aggregated data in order to achieve reasonable, timely access. This became a point of frustration for marketers because the real 'critical learning' was in the more intricate details – for example, 'Which customer is likely to churn?'

At about the same time, a new class of data mining applications was gaining popularity. Like OLAP, these tools were designed to analyse data from a variety of different data sources. In addition, the data-mining tools were explicitly designed to discover valuable findings while handling the huge volume of data stored within the transactional database or data warehouse. Unfortunately the new data-mining tools did not easily deliver the detailed insights that corporate users wanted.

As a consequence another new class of technology has emerged: analytical CRM. Analytical CRM attempts to blend the ease-of-use characteristics of OLAP with the insight afforded by data mining tools. Most recently it forms part of an application suite that enables easier business application of the results. It is no surprise that this market is large and growing at a rapid pace, since companies are now beginning to realize they are sitting on a wealth of information that is just waiting to be tapped.

While the potential benefits of analytical CRM are compelling, companies should be aware of the complexities and potential challenges when selecting and implementing these applications. Market researchers can be the guides. Knowing that successful analytical CRM implementations are built on a solid, customer-centric transaction database that integrates information from all customer touch points is fine. But knowing what data is important, what data means, and what insights can be garnered from analysis is far more useful. Thus, market researchers need to be up to date with a technology infrastructure that can be optimized for sophisticated analysis, and support real-time deployment and delivery of results. It is clear that executives believe that today's insight is today's opportunity.

The (near) future: real-time analytics and reporting

As companies continue exploration of analytical CRM, with counsel and guidance from analytical professionals, and reap incremental benefits, the next step will be away from periodic reporting and analysis to executing real-time analysis and connecting results to action. The next wave of analytical CRM is already being discussed, and is based on real-time analysis. This has the potential to allow companies to interact with their customers intelligently and expeditiously across all channels.

The ability for analytic CRM applications to drive process improvements in operational systems is substantial. As a result, the mainstreaming of online market research is a vital component for exploiting and mediating:

▮ multi-channel data integration: call centre, sales force, wireless and the Web;
▮ delivery of market research's core values: insight, recommendation, and counsel;
▮ an optimized environment for delivering directly to the corporate desktop;
▮ tight synchronization between analysis, insight, and execution;
▮ the ability for companies to be equipped to react and refine in real time through a robust data delivery system filtered and monitored by an analytical partner.

Coupled closely with the mainstreaming effect is the trend toward deploying the widest variety of research techniques possible using an online infrastructure and system. Together these two trends combine to impact and extend the potential for global organizations truly to deliver in step with the clients they seek to serve.

The deployment of enterprise software for customer understanding

As consolidation and globalization continue for both client and supplier, it will be imperative to have analytic procedures and software capable of performing across the enterprise. Building on the natural advantages the Internet network holds, the customization of research, online data collection and storage, the widespread communication of results and data, and the flexibility of open-source solutions can combine to create an integrated research network known as 'enterprise software for market research'. This system delivers not only on the back end – procuring results and collecting, accessing and storing them – but also on the front end: new ways to deliver desktop analytical capabilities to the client, and Web-enabled reporting and publishing schemes. These combine to allow the full range of market research processes to be delivered to clients anywhere at any time.

The online enterprise market research system gives the market research supplier the ability to manage and deliver the complete continuum of research. All aspects of research coverage can be achieved in an integrated manner: from qualitative research to branding studies to online surveys to varying types and degrees of access panels to data mining and business intelligence exploration. This full range of services can be managed, deployed and utilized in one integrated system.

Business organizations of all shapes and sizes are embracing Internet technology for many reasons. At the very least, the explosion of Web use on both the consumer and business level has promoted new ways to advertise, market, sell and communicate. One of the primary by-products of this has been the generation of massive amounts of data – and the need to collect, explore and make sense of this information.

While it is tempting to rely on software and technology shortcuts to handle this overload of information, the road to gathering customer knowledge and delivering insights to clients is still a combined effort of tried and true market research and analysis techniques, and creative use of new tools and processes. The key to useful and actionable research still lies in the proper use of appropriate data collection methods and thoughtful, high quality analytics. Instead of embracing online research without question or in a fragmented way, clients benefit most from the control and integration of new technology and traditional research.

However, the Internet and related ways of collecting data have also opened the door to new information gathering, analytic and delivery possibilities. Researchers can now offer customized research approaches based on data-mining techniques and / or the integration of market research, CRM analytics and database technology. In the vast majority of cases – especially in the CRM space – this serves to enrich the overall market research process and add needed value and business intelligence at key customer touch points.

E-RESEARCH AND BUSINESS

E-research is a practice concerned with all approaches to analytics and market research, both qualitative and quantitative. From focus groups to standard research instruments to advanced data mining approaches, techniques are utilized to make sense of market research and business data and information. The key component, however, is that the management, deployment, collection and access of data is integrated and carried out using enabling Internet technologies.

Business is enhanced by an integrated e-research approach, since not only is the full range of research available to attack problems and assist in informing solutions, but lower cost and efficiency are built into the system. By utilizing the e-research approach, enabling technology opens the doorway to an integrated system of data collection and delivery not possible in the past. However, and this is key, none of the value-added analysis and insightful delivery of recommendations and guidance need be sacrificed. Quite the opposite is true. E-research lends itself particularly well to being embedded into intimate client delivery platforms. Thus, in combination with original custom research results, new features, such as searches, libraries and related syndicated reports can be delivered directly to the client desktop. The range of information can include raw data for additional, ad hoc desktop analysis to fully completed and polished reports, as well as tracking, both syndicated and proprietary, that complements the whole package.

The five components of e-research

The five components of e-research support a thorough approach to the informed business intelligence needs of clients. They trace the following research path:

▌ Web site, marketing and advertising assessment protocols;
▌ positioning, strategy, and branding studies;
▌ online market research surveys;
▌ online advisory, business or consumer access panels;
▌ business intelligence tools and data and Web mining.

Web site and related assessment protocols inform about the sales and marketing channels and the impact/perception of advertising/marketing campaigns. They sharpen business focus and assist in fine-tuning both online and offline messages. In addition, they can begin to address branding and positioning issues in the total market-place the consumer inhabits. Without a doubt, this step is one of the most important to business success, but unfortunately one easily overlooked or passed by in the rush to 'get to market' or 'expand globally'.

Positioning, strategy and branding studies follow closely from assessments. These studies identify and explore competitors' strengths and weaknesses, help businesses devise and test creative strategies, and examine the power, perception and awareness that branding can bring to the mix.

Online market research surveys are deployed to allow businesses to get to know customers – a key step in CRM. With online surveys – just as with traditional market research surveys – actionable business information can be gathered towards improving service by better meeting the needs of customers. Custom surveys form the basis for best understanding people's perceptions, attitudes, feelings, and intent.

Online advisory, business or consumer access panels are key ways regularly and effectively to track critical business issues/trends, customer perceptions, and changes in attitude and satisfaction toward product, service or industry. In addition, the nature of online panels and the online environment affords quick collection and assembly of research data. As the consumer privacy issue rages, and more and more restrictions to data collection appear, access panels, particularly of a global nature, may be the only legitimate way to approach and reach people for marketing and advertising research purposes. Enabling technology is key here as well, since the better integrated and managed this key resource, the more likely it will yield valuable results that can be delivered to clients.

Business intelligence (BI) and data/Web-mining techniques are coming of age quickly. These highly sophisticated tools allow exploration of warehoused data in real time, segmenting and profiling of customers (including integration with corporate or third-party databases), and the construction of predictive models. Increasingly these tools are incorporated in CRM or eCRM software solutions. However, they currently represent only a small portion of assessment, and are often the most complicated solutions available. In addition, attempts to 'template' them for ease of use are not likely to generate the best results. While not typically thought of as tools within the market researcher's tool box, the enterprise market research system does bring the capability to use business intelligence and data/Web-mining tools within the knowledge worker's domain. Precisely since analytical CRM is notably weak at the moment, and CRM firms generally do not carry the sort of expertise needed to carry out a high quality market research function, this is a key area for competitive consideration that many firms are currently exploring.

Web site and marketing/advertising assessment

Many Web efforts suffer from a lack of attention to the user. Recent research has shown that most sites fail basic reliability and consistency tests. Web usability and navigability – although deemed important by experts in Web design – are often neglected. Finally, too many e-business sites suffer from a 'lack of identity'. Advertising and marketing efforts are making valiant attempts to build online brand and awareness. However, without a thoughtful study and understanding of basic business fundamentals, no 'idea' – no matter how compelling – can flourish for long.

The first stage of 'need' in building business insight often resides in the exploration of basic business issues through the use of qualitative research and focus groups. Additional sessions can range from the truly scientific (for example, the tracking and measurement of eye movements) to 'softer' assessments, such as group critiques and explorations of a variety of Web site designs, advertising creative and positioning issues. This is often followed by Web site design that is assessed and studied through usability and navigability tests.

The insights, results and observations made in focus groups, both on and offline, provide the grist for the next step, which is creatively and deeply to explore positioning, strategy and branding issues: that is, to begin to enter the realm of customer knowledge, the who, why, what, where and when of your business.

Positioning, strategy and branding studies

A variety of methods is available to construct the legs on which a business stands. All require an inordinate sense of the competitive set, practical experience within an industry or market, and extreme creativity to enable the development of new and exciting ideas. All customer knowledge begins by understanding what your brand says to people, how and where it is said, who sees it, and why it makes them respond. All advertising should be an outgrowth of how research and analysis helps you determine position and strategy within your brand's effect.

Positioning studies make use of competitive market analysis, critical looks at what constitutes the strengths, weaknesses and uniqueness of your business proposition, and how to best 'place yourself' for success. Strategic studies are similar, but are often done to test the success or failure of a 'position' you have devised, or to explore multiple ways of achieving strategic success.

Finally, branding and brand perception studies bring a qualitative, often 'hard to measure' property into play. The key in studies of this nature is to have a robust research plan that can adequately measure perceptual and attributional changes. This often requires a creative combination of research and statistical methodologies to achieve useful and actionable results.

Online surveys

Once an advertising or marketing plan has been adequately tested and developed – and positioning, strategy and branding have been addressed – businesses need to learn continuously about their customers, visitors and prospects. This is the essence of CRM: constantly making the best use of customer interactions and data to improve communications, message and service.

While Web-mining tools exist that 'automatically' track and report on information found in Web log files, they are limited – and do not constitute the whole picture by far. Just as valuable – and usually more useful – is the deployment of online surveys that gather important information businesses need to inform their customer 'relationship': satisfaction, awareness, usage, attitudes, behaviour and the like.

Deployment of online surveys can be accomplished in a number of ways: by e-mail invitation, by Web site 'pop up', and by formal invitation through letter or phone. Online surveys can be timed to appear at a certain place in a Web site, or to capture every 'nth' visitor. Results can be merged with stored data from Web site registration forms or data on databases in a corporate warehouse or data mart.

Since the collection of data and feedback is so rapid in the online environment, such deliverables as real-time reporting, tracking reports delivered directly to the desktop, and online report publishing provide valuable and actionable business intelligence in a familiar form to marketing, sales and executive divisions.

Advisory, business and consumer access panels

An access panel is a dedicated group of specific users, clients or advisers who agree to provide substantive feedback on a regular basis. Access panels are no different from traditional advisory, executive, business or consumer panels that provide business leaders and strategists with useful and critical research information.

Developing an access panel can require an extensive evaluation and search process to best reflect the population of interest. They can also be expensive to maintain and manage. Once created, however, access panels can be housed in an attractive password-protected Web site that serves as 'home base' for the administration of timely or mission critical surveys of great value to research clients. Access panel management and maintenance assures a continuous supply of opinions, attitudes and information that can be accessed to address business issues, perceptions and concerns. In addition, access panels are valuable as devices to track important metrics over time.

On the buy/sell side, access panels can be used to test products, concepts and positioning strategies. With the advent of online focus group technology, participants can be chosen from the panel and group results can be immediately analysed or mapped to other information about the panel member. Thus, a synergistic and valuable qualitative/quantitative potential is built into the system.

Business intelligence and data/Web mining

Web mining is more than the automatic counting of Web clicks, or even when/where someone 'clicks off' on a Web site. Data mining is more than building automatic cross-sell models to deploy against a database list. While valuable, these approaches tell us little about the 'who, what, where, why and how' questions that need to be answered effectively to drive the customer relationship building process. Relying on 'the numbers', while ignoring important attributes and information contained in 'knowing about your customer', can be extremely misleading.

Web and data-mining tools handle extremely large quantities of data – too large for a human analyst to consider – and search for patterns, associations and relationships. Data mining enhances traditional and advanced market research approaches by employing a bottom-up approach. Data-mining tools can measure individual customer/visitor-level behaviour and help make sense of a vast assortment of variables. In addition, Web mining incorporates data collected from log files, online surveys, information contained in corporate or third-party databases, and can supplement software solutions such as online analytical processing tools.

Increasingly, data and Web mining are being integrated into a larger process termed 'knowledge discovery in databases'. While many variations of the model exist, it is essentially an effort to tie the entire business process together into a coherent whole built around the customer. The net effect is efficiency and effectiveness in communicating and building customer relationships, and forms the essence of the 'one to one' business revolution. The elements consist of:

▮ data warehousing and data-marts;
▮ target data selection: getting at the data you require;
▮ cleaning;
▮ preprocessing;
▮ transforming and reducing data;
▮ data mining;
▮ selecting models;
▮ evaluating and interpreting models;
▮ consolidating and using models.

Data gathered as a by-product of Web activity and behaviour, consciously collected, used and mined, is another potent facet in the overall picture. These solutions show great promise, but currently are both limited and extremely complicated to structure and implement. In addition, the relationship to original survey data is often difficult to ascertain. They remain, however, a potential area for extending customer analytics that is viable and possible within an integrated data collection system.

The five components constitute a framework for approaching the continuing and necessary research necessary to drive business success. Businesses can enter the research protocol at any step. Market research suppliers can and do offer some or all of the services described. Increasingly, however, it is clear that this continuum of research services can be delivered most effectively, creatively and efficiently via an integrated online channel and embedded, linked or merged into a variety of CRM systems.

CULTURAL AND ORGANIZATIONAL CHANGE: A REALITY IN ORGANIZATIONS

Why it is important

Figure 22.6 is a multi-dimensional picture of the four major components of CRM. While the operational, analytic and strategic facets are currently addressed, the cultural aspects

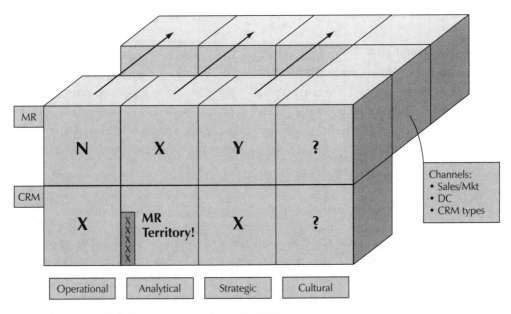

Figure 22.6   A multi-dimensional view of CRM

– change management, organizational cultural adjustments, and the like – are in a relatively virgin state.

Yes, it is precisely in this messy human sociological frame that the 'make or break' of CRM systems will occur. While the whole science and field of 'organizational development' exists, it has apparently not been translated well enough for tech-driven solutions companies to access. Management knows and deals with the 'day-to-day' factors that drive success and failure on a regular basis. CRM is no different.

Why it is overlooked

Given that 'everyone' understands that the cultural frame is so important, the obvious question is, 'Why is it overlooked'? The answer is a complex mixture of human nature, habit and, to a certain extent, the extreme cost (dollar and psychic) necessary to grapple with the issues here. It is much easier to go with a 'silver bullet' solution than do the necessary work to achieve 'real success'. Yet the nature of business, management politics, and continuing investor pressure work against going down the 'path less taken'.

Ironically, certain (but rare) CRM success stories have arisen (almost as folklore at this point) that are solidly built on such old fashioned concepts as 'leadership', 'taking the high road', and 'preparing and moving the entire company through change'. When the tide will turn and businesses will realize that the 'silver bullet' is best 'bitten down on' while one does the hard work necessary for success is anyone's guess.

CONCLUSION AND OUTLOOK

In all fairness, CRM has filled an important need as a technology for automating many of the necessary functions of the front office. Efficiency and cost savings have been its by-words. Indeed, the current CRM software offering grew from an effort to bring together primary business process areas to enable an integrated view of customer data. However, managing customer data is not the same as managing customer relationships. To date, CRM benefits have been focused more on the technology and less on the customer.

Whither CRM?

In addition to working toward the goal of efficient customer-centric business processes, the next step will be about actually optimizing customer understanding to inform better relationships and experiences.

There are three imperatives that must be addressed at this point in time: improved customer understanding, component/process integration, and strategic thinking, planning and action. From the perspective of CRM weaknesses, improved customer understanding is the driving factor. It is supported by the ability to integrate new analytic components and processes into the system, and the ability to infuse strategy, guidance and analytic expertise at numerous points in the CRM process.

Improved customer understanding

In most cases, customer understanding is based on a study of a business problem. The first time a client is engaged, a dialogue and dance begin that can end abruptly or continue for many years. Customers stay invested only as long as the company maintains and demonstrates an understanding of their needs, wants, psyche and desires.

Thus, many businesses have discovered that the path to cross-sell and up-sell opportunities is supported through the ability to access and analyse databases that capture customer needs and interests, in addition to their transaction history. The dialogue and information gathered from customers provides companies with the raw data to act and move with insight toward market trends. In addition, individual customer attitudes are flags and alarms that companies need to attend to. Bottom line: understanding customers can reap big rewards.

Component integration

Components for successful CRM are more than technology-based. But they must be assembled to optimize a strategy and process for dealing with complexity. While it is vital that technology components be built for rapid change, equally important is the infusion of human guidance, expertise and analytical processes to optimize the systems.

A modular software approach can isolate business rules from the operational software code so that changes can be made quickly through the system. As well, analytic processing, guided by protocols and definitions, enables better usage and greater capacity to adopt and change. However, a human element – the brains of a system, for example – must be evident to ensure the loop is closed, the customer-centric focus is sustained, and the system can work seamlessly. A form of process consulting is needed, either internally developed or externally applied, to achieve success in CRM.

Strategic thinking, planning and action

Perhaps the biggest missing link in CRM today is the unwillingness to spend the necessary 'think time' upfront to concretely plan for CRM. This includes numerous areas of study, planning measurements and evaluations, establishing benchmarks, and scoping and addressing the business problems evident to the company.

Every company is different, and each industry suggests an optimal mix of growing strengths and minimizing weaknesses in the effort toward CRM success. For example, SFA's original orientation – to improve sales force efficiency – is at odds with another primary orientation: sales effectiveness. Efficiency is volume-oriented – it enables an individual salesperson to handle more opportunities with the expectation that, as more opportunities are processed, more deals will result. In one industry this logic may make sense, but in another effectiveness, or even efficacy, is the key.

What's ahead

Some of the more promising trends involve new technologies that capture direct customer dialogue that can be infused and merged with a variety of quantitative data. This ability to blend the customer voice with a wide variety of other internal and external data, properly chosen, is powerful. It enables the measurement of customer input and the generation of insight to better address the CRM optimization issue.

Large market research firms, often global in nature and with a vast network of established client relationships, are beginning to show signs of interest in running the gauntlet as CRM solutions providers: not necessarily in the tech-driven, but more so in the data-driven sense. The market research industry has many analytical talents that are poised right at the nexus of CRM, data mining, and improved understanding of customers. It will be interesting to see if this notoriously conservative and slow-moving industry can shift gears fast enough to grab what appears to be an outstanding opportunity to become leaders in data insight.

New entrants into the CRM space are deploying innovative applications that support solutions to new business problems generated by operational CRM. Many ways to collect, merge and access data exist, and the book is not closed on unique ways to approach this. Flexibility, and an ear to the ground to capture what both client and customer are thinking, are needed for success.

Regardless of where technology takes us, it will be necessary that software, strategy, analytics and people achieve the balance needed for success. Once these facets are in alignment, companies can begin to reap the larger benefits of CRM that are based on the concepts of customer centricity and optimizing customer understanding.

NOTES

[1] Johnson, MD and Gustafsson, A (2000) *Improving Customer Satisfaction, Loyalty, and Profit*, Jossey-Bass, San Francisco.

[2] Wiersma, F (2001) *The New Market Leaders: Who's winning and how in the battle for customers*, Free Press, New York.

[3] Ibid.

[4] Johnson, MD (2002) Growing Pains, in *Financial Times Next Generation Business Series: Customer Relations*, ed S Chowdhury, Financial Times, London.

[5] Ibid.

[6] Lee, D, Mangen, D and Thompson, B (2001) *Multi-Function CRM Software: How good is it?* FrontLine Solutions, High Yield Marketing, and Mangen Associates [Online] www.crmguru.com/crmstudy.

[7] Monster, RW and Pettit, RC (2002) *Global Market Research in the Internet Age: Leveraging technology for market measurement and consumer insight*, John Wiley, Singapore.

[8] Göritz, AS, Reinhold, N and Batinic, B (2000) Marketforschung mit Online Panels: State of the Art, *Planung & Analyse*, **3**, pp 62–67.

[9] Gurney, P (undated) *The CEM Concept*, Kinesis [Online] www.kinesis-cem.com.

[10] Ibid.

23

Managing public sector customers

Merlin Stone, Alison Bond, Roger Clarkson, Peter Hayes, Peter Lavers, Clare Traynor, David Williams and Neil Woodcock

INTRODUCTION

Public sector organizations have as large an impact on customers' lives as private sector companies. In many countries, public authorities are trying to extract lessons from the first 20 or so years of private sector experience of CRM. They are asking questions such as:

▌ What are the lessons from the private sector? Has the private sector itself learnt from its own lessons?

▌ Are the lessons from the private sector relevant? If so, which are most relevant?

▌ Which models of customer management in the private sector are most relevant to different public sector operations? Does the answer to this question depend on the size of the public sector operation, or whether it is central, regional or local? Does it depend upon the objectives of the particular public sector operation; in particular on whether it offers customers full or partial options about whether they are to be managed (such as law enforcement, criminal custody, tax payment, versus higher education, employment or information services)?

▌ What does comparison with the private sector reveal about the main opportunities for improving levels of service while containing cost, or for saving cost while maintaining levels of service?

- Does the change towards more customer-focused ways of doing things have to be handled differently in the public sector, whether because of the political dimension, because of unclear, conflicting or rapidly changing objectives, because of the dominance of cost as an issue, or for any other reason?
- How can progress in the chosen direction be maintained, perhaps accelerated?

The track record of applying measurement-based CRM ideas to the public sector is relatively short, so although we have included two case studies at the end of this chapter, rather than try to present a perfect model of how public sector customers should be managed, we have instead used this chapter to review some of the areas public sector managers need to explore before and during application of CRM ideas to their domain. This chapter does not pretend to do anything more than provide a helpful summary of the main issues, and suggest to public sector management how it can learn (or not) from the very varied and problematic experience of the private sector in applying the ideas of customer management.

The term 'public sector' conceals an enormous variety of activities, such as:

- defence;
- law and order;
- foreign affairs;
- industrial – whether as a direct government activity, as a regulator or provider of support services;
- revenue raising, eg taxation;
- providing income, eg pensions, social benefits;
- transport, whether infrastructure – airports, roads, traffic signals, testing, surveillance, or direct provision of public transport services;
- postal and telecommunications services, regulation, infrastructure support;
- control over airspace, airwaves;
- health service provision, and inspection and audit or private provision;
- welfare, eg infrastructure and services: old people's homes, day centres, provision of access or funding;
- education, leisure, arts.

Functions include:

- servicing clients: identifying need, attuning service, delivering service, quality check;
- developing service capacity, eg physical facilities, teams, systems and data;
- raising finance, eg taxation, fines, borrowing;
- control processes, eg laws, regulations and codes, governance, boards of trustees, political members etc, entitlement/exemption validation or withdrawal, issuing identification documentation, enforcement;

▌ organization and human resources, eg recruitment, selection, allocation, motivation, qualification, quality control.

Just as in the private sector, interaction between customers can be classified as case processing, involving in-depth diagnosis of need/qualification and possibly protracted interaction, or as transaction processing, involving relatively quick interaction with a very large number of standard cases. In practice many situations are some mixture of these two. However, the two have very different process, human resources, systems and data needs.

Examples of case processing include:

▌ child protection;
▌ legal aid;
▌ tax returns;
▌ hospitalization;
▌ prosecution for serious offences;
▌ treatment of chronic disease;
▌ housing;
▌ planning authorization;
▌ inspecting/testing compliance (eg weights and measures, health and safety, education);
▌ entitlement to education/loans;
▌ security/accident incident management;
▌ complex licence allocation;
▌ complex complaints and queries.

Examples of transaction processing include:

▌ benefit payment;
▌ routine inoculation;
▌ simple licence allocation, eg driving, motor vehicle, broadcast reception;
▌ automated tax collection;
▌ routine complaints and queries.

THE CHALLENGE

In many countries, central and local governments and other public bodies are focusing on open government, improving citizen access and enhancing the quality of the services provided, while retaining the strong traditional focus of government on cost-effectiveness. These new foci manifest themselves in various initiatives from central and local government and other public agencies. They include:

▌ provision of electronic access;
▌ improvement in citizen service provision and management;
▌ ensuring that social exclusion does not occur when new initiatives are implemented, and that those in need of help or service actually receive it, rather than those who take most quickly to new channels of access.

The challenges this new direction poses to governments are:

▌ engaging the external environment after years of inward focus;
▌ determining what the current situation actually is, before formulating new initiatives;
▌ establishing the current level of citizen service provision, including the development of acceptable measures and measuring tools;
▌ identifying where the gaps exist in the service provision;
▌ directing resources in the most cost effective / prioritised way to improve the service.

Meeting these challenges is made more complex by a number of other factors, including:

▌ increasing customer expectations, caused by the performance (and perhaps sometimes only the promise) of the private sector;
▌ the rising numbers of lobby and other pressure groups;
▌ increased confidence of customers in using the media to put pressure on government for better treatment;
▌ the need to use new channels of communication and distribution to reach customers who have had problems accessing government services through traditional channels, while ensuring that these new channels can work in an integrated manner with older channels;
▌ the need to observe the government's sometimes very tough general requirements affecting how customers are managed in either sector, eg data protection law;
▌ the need to manage new relationships with the private sector service providers who are involved in some way in this change, usually as agents.

SPECIAL ISSUES AFFECTING PUBLIC SECTOR CUSTOMER MANAGEMENT

A number of special issues affect the inter-sector translation of good practice. These include:

- The existence of differential/unequal information between providers and clients in service delivery, particularly where provider is more expert than customer/citizen can ever hope to be, either because of life-stage (education), knowledge (eg health), or because of costs of information access. Some examples are health, law and education. This often applies to the costs/difficulties of applying general information to specific cases.
- Many activities are associated with dealing with problem/extreme rather than average cases (law, welfare, education, health), and the aim of government is to prevent people needing the services, when they do need them to ensure that they get served quickly and efficiently, then to minimize the need for the service to be used again. Government bodies can focus heavily on prevention and lose sight of the fact that some people will not respond and then need support and help. If they over-generalize, people can fall through the net completely and form part of an underclass who are not serviced and are outcast.
- Externalities exist: that is, the act of providing/receiving service affects others than the recipient of the service. Road congestion is the obvious example, but the same applies to any queue for a scarce service. However, social interdependence in the act of service consumption therefore causes greater social benefits than private benefits to suppliers, and can cause much greater social costs to citizens than private costs to suppliers.
- There is concern about the influence of distribution of income and assets on ability of individuals to take up or benefit from services, so the 'value of the customer' is measured by other criteria than money, eg 'need', or 'social priority'. In some life stages money ceases to become the benefit it is in others, as it becomes impossible to buy the level of care that is required by the individual.
- Customers often cannot exit, so they need to be given voice (for example, through representation).
- There is also concern about the provision of access, choice and redress.
- Many governments see the role of the public sector as providing socially important interdependent, non-marketable services for social optimality, particularly where market tends to produce non-optimal results.
- Often there is a relationship of trust and agency between provider and client. The idea is that the citizen trusts a professional supplier to do what is right. However, this has been called into question, and the question applies to both correctness of service and quality of service.
- In many public sector operations (eg health services), the service is delivered by professionals, with their own interests and agenda.
- There is some tendency of the professional to mystify the customer so that the customer cannot independently judge the quality of service, particularly where the customer has no choice or right to data showing the quality of the service delivered.
- Many public sector organizations are considered by government as its agent in helping it meet its objectives for the citizen. However, the agency may develop its

own set of objectives that conflict with the government's. In other cases, the provider is supposed to be the agent supposedly acting on behalf of the citizen, but again may develop objectives of its own.

█ Quality of service is an issue, and particularly where there is no competition, independent bodies are needed to monitor quality. This leads to the question of who vets the vetters without the vetting becoming an onerous amount of red tape to the providers. There has to be room for trust in a system that is becoming heavily geared towards policing.

█ Consultation as to what services should be delivered is often highly biased, with activists influencing the nature of service provision.

█ Lack of proper research means that customers' needs and experiences are rarely properly understood.

█ The process by which the public sector allocates its benefits is often by rationing and queues as a substitute for the price mechanism, rather than by some socially optimal selection process.

█ In cases where central government provides resources and frameworks and local agencies deliver, there is a process break between who does the analysis and planning, and then decision making, and who implements, or delivers. This can lead to delivery failure.

INTER-SECTOR DIFFERENCES

Generalizing from private sector experience must take into account the many differences that exist between public and private sectors. In practice, great differences in customer management requirements and practices exist within the private sector, limiting the transferability of experience. In either case, overlooking these differences can prove very expensive, sometimes to the extent of leading to complete programme failure. These differences relate to:

█ The type of service/need, ranging from large commercial organizations gaining permissions from public authorities, to private individuals applying for and then receiving a state benefit. A simpler distinction is between revenue raising and expenditure.

█ The nature of transactions/cases, ranging from a one-off transaction (eg request to inspect land registration), to bursts of many transactions (eg that take place when a relative dies), series (eg submission of regular tax returns) and continuous (eg receipt of education, intense medical care). In some cases, individuals' occasional transactions are translated into continuous relationships by the use of a specialist private sector agent, who handles the needs of many individuals: for example the accountant handling tax returns, the lawyer requesting land registration or planning information.

▪ The degree of variance in cost to serve between individuals with the same requirement. This in turn often relates to their education level, previous experience, whether they use an expert agent and other factors. For example, an experienced customer may 'know the ropes' and how to get served quickly, or on the other hand how to defer an unwanted public intervention by a series of interventions which cause public sector re-work.

▪ How the service is delivered: for example whether it is local, regional or national, whether it must (for various reasons) be delivered face to face or can be delivered using other channels such as the telephone, mail or the Web.

▪ Whether the service is effectively part of a series of interactions performed by several agencies for a customer with a given need (eg the involvement of medical and care authorities in helping the elderly), and how these agencies interact with each other (including whether there are legal limitations to their doing so).

▪ The relative importance of the interaction to both parties.

▪ The degree of customer involvement in the delivery of the service that is possible and/or permissible.

▪ The extent to which the interaction is initiated by the customer or by the public supplier.

▪ The extent to which legal/enforcement issues are involved.

▪ The risk to the individual and/or to the public sector of mismanagement of the situation, which can include anything from threatening the customer's well-being to causing a politician to look ridiculous.

UNDERSTANDING THE CUSTOMER

Despite these problems, we believe that some classic private sector techniques can be used to reduce the difficulties of managing customers. For example, although there is immense variety in the types of situation managed, the private sector uses the technique of segmenting (classifying customers into groups which share certain characteristics) and managing them appropriately. Although in the private sector this approach carries risks of stereotyping and misclassification, there is no doubt that it has made it much easier for large companies to meet the many and varied needs of customers, even if the classification is quite crude. Some examples of the variables used to segment include:

▪ High, medium and low-value customers, with the risk of misclassifying possibly dealt with by identifying customers likely to move between categories. Value may be defined commercially, for revenue-raising operations, or by need for expenditure operations.

- High versus low cost to serve, including perhaps the operational management required to meet the need: time, resources.
- Volumes of transactions/interactions, overall and by category of contact.
- Fundamental nature of the customer. This might be by general psychological characteristics (eg confident or subservient), or by characteristics related to the service in question (eg level of previous education or IQ for a school, health record for a medical service).

It is often forgotten that segmentation is a creative process. In the end the public sector, like the private sector, is faced with a large number of people who are individual customers. Segmentation is designed to make things easier to manage, for the customer and/or supplier. Thus segmentation might be used just to understand the variety of customers and their needs, even if the service provided to all customers is the same. It is used perhaps to determine what the service features should be, or how many customers are over or under-served. It might be used for tactical management of customers, for example to determine why the immediate needs of a particular group of customers are not being met. Or it might be strategic, to show that the way the service is organized is not meeting the needs of a priority group of customers, and how service delivery should be redesigned.

TRANSLATING EXPERIENCE BETWEEN SECTORS

Our view is that most customer management techniques are not sector-specific, but they need to be translated into the context of each sector. This also applies within each sector, for example in translating from education to health, or from insurance to banking. In some cases the translation is linguistic, in others much more substantive. It is also our view that once customer management is broken down into a series of components, the translation is much easier and more legitimate. So here is our suggestion as to the main translations from good practice in the private sector. These have already been fully documented in one of the authors' works, which are based on QCi's Customer Management Assessment Tool, which among other things breaks customer management down into 260 attributes.[1]

These are the main comparisons between public and private sector customer management, phrased in terms of CMAT definitions:

- The value of the customer often transforms to the need/priority of the customer.
- In many cases, the aim is for the customer's need for the service to be identified, and then to process the customer so that ideally he or she will not need to be reprocessed in the same way, or so that the customer will not need a more expensive or intense

service, or to ensure that the customer never needs the service (a version of de-marketing). This may make acquisition and retention issues the reverse of the private sector customer management cycle at the end and beginning, though delivering service activity is virtually the same.

▌ In many cases the service is provided by a public agency acting on behalf of a central government department. In some cases this has been triggered by the emphasis of separating purchasers and providers, but there are other roles such as enablers and regulators. This makes intermediated customer management a very common process in the public sector. In some cases the central department will have other agencies dealing with other associated aspects of the customer, while other government departments will use yet other agencies. Even for a particular customer's case, a particular government service might be just one of several that will be dealing with the customer's case (as in child protection cases, where police, medical services and social services are learning to cooperate). We know that failure in interagency cooperation can be catastrophic in such cases, but just processing the customer efficiently without contacting the other relevant agencies could be the worst thing to do. These other agencies could be regarded as the private sector defines partners or channels. Key areas are likely to be interagency processes, information systems/data and organization/motivational issues.

▌ Many public sector organizations work with their customers through a series of communications initiatives, analogous to private sector marketing campaigns.

▌ Private sector customer targeting and acquisition often become translated in the public sector into identifying and serving those needing help or likely to get into problems.

▌ In the public sector, customer retention might be translated into the need to serve the customer so well that customers do not need service again, or at least one of similar intensity, or can be moved to a different type of service provision.

▌ Objectives and accountabilities tend to have more dimensions in the public sector than in the private sector, as do incentives and motivation. However, the extent to which this is so in the private sector must not be underestimated.

▌ In the private sector there is a strong focus on important or high-value customers (although this is often mistaken, as profit objectives can often be met better by serving large numbers of medium or even low-value customers cost-effectively, while controlling risks of escalation in individual cost to serve). In the public sector, this sometimes can be translated into customers with intense/special needs, high priority and so on.

▌ In the area of public sector customer development, further action may be required, such as transfer to a different agency, need for further clarification action, so there may be a need to focus on how processes, systems and so on work to support this.

▌ In some public sector situations, some staff may be private professionals or professionals on special contracts, and might need to be managed as internal customers, possibly even using private sector norms.

▌ Understanding the offers of competition in the private sector can become understanding offers of parallel agencies, plus competitive or partner private sector agencies.

▌ The buying cycle may be best seen as a cycle of needs.

▌ Customer loss in the private sector might change in the public sector to users dropping out of the system (whether or not they are entitled to receive continued service), or perhaps to lapses in communication when it is required. The need to win back customers in the public sector depends on the definition of lost customer (eg failure to take up entitlement).

DELIVERING BEST VALUE LOCAL CUSTOMER SERVICE TO THE UK CITIZEN

The public sector CRM vision

Since 1997 the public sector has focused on delivering high quality, appropriate and timely services to the citizen. However, we are still in the early stages of a long journey, as the following milestones demonstrate:

▌ **1997**: Traditional one-to-one communication with citizens supported by departmental applications. Citizen-focused data was limited and in silos, making cross-departmental or joined-up services impossible to deliver without implementing costly, dedicated staff.

▌ **2001**: Having embarked on the process of joined-up service delivery, the public sector today has the tools at its disposal and is beginning to offer multi-channel access to a consistent standard of response, with appropriate service delivery at the point of contact. This is being supported by contact centres offering multiple services, contact tracking and management; e-forms and scripting,[1] linking back to integrated back office systems.

▌ **2005**: The government's own target for the delivery of e-enabled services. We should see integrated cross-departmental cooperation, with multiple services available from a single contact, with the integration and delivery of partner services where appropriate. This will be supported by integrated legacy and citizen data; the use of data mining and other analytical tools to support improvements to services; and Web and community portals with workflow processes improving the ease with which citizens navigate new services and achieve the required service.

▍ **Future**: Looking further ahead, the ultimate goal is to achieve a holistic view of the citizen. Employees will be empowered and enjoy an inter-agency (including non-public sector) approach to casework. Communication will be through a variety of channels, and field staff will have online around the clock access to information and resources. By this stage customer knowledge will be core to the community and service planning processes. Underpinning this holistic citizen view will be fully automated systems with interdepartmental access to citizen data, as well as online access by citizens to community data. Mobile telephony, interactive television and smart cards will enable this. Throughout these developments, the principles and technologies of CRM will leverage new technologies and changes in organization structure and process to provide a platform for delivering improved services and supporting the constant evolution of new services to meet the diverse needs of a changing population.

Becoming customer-focused

With electronic service delivery high on the agenda, local government in the UK is rapidly cultivating a customer-focused ethos. Supported by customer relationship management (CRM) systems, one-stop shops and citizen contact centres (providing information and access to services) are prime examples of the modernizing initiatives now gaining momentum. However, simply implementing a call centre and CRM system is not the solution to the delivery of integrated, joined-up services to the citizen and will not enable the public sector to meet the modernizing government agenda. Simply automating existing processes results only in small, short-term efficiency gains. A significant step-change in the approach to service delivery is needed. By taking a strategic view of the way in which citizens are dealt with at the point of contact – using knowledge and systems to deliver as much service as possible at the point of contact, and learning about customer needs and service effectiveness (rather than just providing a single contact for registering service demands) – the public sector can use CRM as a driving force for improvements and changes to services in line with evolving citizen needs.

The public sector does not manage its citizens well as customers (although the perception of individual delivered services can often be high). However, customer service was at the top of the political agenda during the mid-1990s, as the previous long-term focus on improving efficiency through cost cutting gave way to a new approach to delivering the right citizen services.

The causes of this shift in emphasis were twofold. First, the past decade has seen a sea change in customer behaviour, with high expectations of service delivery, a shift that is also being felt throughout the public sector. Second, the cost-cutting policies of the previous decade had reduced inefficiency and improved effectiveness, but there was a growing realization that the next step in service improvements required the public sector to work differently. Improved efficiencies paved the way for enhanced service delivery, but it has become apparent that, as society changes, new service delivery mechanisms are needed to meet the evolving needs of the citizen, while retaining a focus on efficient and cost-effective delivery. With the dramatic increase in Internet usage, combined with growing adoption of interactive television and mobile telephony, there is also huge potential for new means of accessing service and as a result, the need to be ready to intercept the potential of the development of new routes for customer access.

Forward thinking local authorities in the mid-1990s initially embraced this 'customer focused' approach, although they adopted different methods. One authority introduced customer service 'advocate' personnel who took on the citizen's issue – be it housing, social services or benefits – and then followed up that issue on behalf of the citizen, with the appropriate department. Others began to explore the concept of improved interagency and cross-departmental communication to create a coherent approach to service delivery. This increased efficiency by reducing the duplication of processes. This approach to service delivery received a boost with the arrival of the new government in 1997. It was at this point that 'joined-up government' and citizen-focused delivery mechanisms achieved centre stage. Now, government funding is dedicated towards projects that deliver the modernizing government agenda. Indeed, the Labour Party's election manifesto implied that those organizations not delivering 'customer focus' would be most under threat.

The result of citizen-focused initiatives has been huge growth in one-stop shops and citizen contact centres. These have clear customer service goals and attendant benefits in smooth service delivery. In addition to addressing improved customer demands, one-stop access points provide an opportunity for a step-change in customer service and critically, an opportunity to re-engineer and change accepted ways of working.

With an increasing emphasis on joined-up government, the focus for the delivery of citizen services is on partnership – interdepartmental, cross-agency and with the private sector – aimed at delivering the right services at the right time. There are huge opportunities for providing a coherent citizen service that not only ensures the right service is delivered at the right time to the right person but also, by enabling tight cooperation between relevant agencies, results in reduced duplication and improved cost control.

A fundamental element of the customer services programme is to provide multi-channel access to these services, with Internet kiosks and interactive digital television expected to play a future role in ensuring inclusive access across society. Indeed, the explosion in technological functionality that has occurred over the past five years has been recognized by the government as providing a significant opportunity for changing the way in which it interacts with the citizen.

However, it is important to recognize that automating existing processes will not deliver citizen-centric services. As those local authorities that have implemented one-stop shops have discovered, there are some fundamental organizational issues to address if the public sector is to achieve the desired level of service. This requires a fundamental rethink of the way services are delivered to the citizen in the UK. The UK Government targets for e-enabling processes by 2005 are established and represent a significant challenge. But correctly implemented, a strategy that enables the delivery of citizen-centric services can provide a significant building block towards achieving this goal.

The role of customer relationship management

There is about a three-year lag in public sector adoption of CRM, with many public sector managers now applying the term to any customer-focused initiatives and interactions. One benefit of this time lag is that lessons have been learnt from many of the mistakes made in leading-edge private sector implementations. These can now be avoided in the public sector. Of course, the public sector definition of a customer differs greatly from the private sector definition. In the public sector, however, the situation is very different. The emphasis is on improving service across the board, rather than on segmenting and targeting customers according to profitability. CRM enables the public sector to enable improved customer access, to provide better service at the point of access, and to track the progress of customer problems/concerns more efficiently. Key public sector CRM benefits include:

▌ Managing the initial customer interaction, be it via telephone, in person or e-mail: a CRM approach enables a consistent delivery of information to the citizen.
▌ Prompting action to address customer need: using workflow processes, any citizen enquiry/problem prompts appropriate action by one or several departments.
▌ Tracking customer interaction throughout its full lifecycle to provide total visibility. Each enquiry generates a contact history, enabling both authority and the customer to keep a track of the situation without the need for the customer to repeat the enquiry and name and address details.
▌ Providing information for further analysis, to enable services constantly to be assessed and re-focused in line with evolving needs. For example, if a citizen calls requesting a house repair, an integrated CRM approach delivers key information from the outset. The citizen is told the current status of house repairs, length of the waiting time and when to expect an initial inspection. Indeed, with an integrated system that incorporates back-office information from the housing department, an initial inspection appointment can be made immediately. A reference number is then allocated to this request and, should further calls be required, the status of the repair process is immediately visible.

Today, CRM is focused on delivering customer service at the point of access. As few as 10 per cent of local authorities are achieving this goal. However, several have merely automated existing processes. While delivering short-term efficiency gains, such implementations do not provide a platform for further exploitation of CRM technologies, namely analysing the information to support further changes/enhancements to service delivery, both internally and through partners. The key to achieving this is a fundamental shift in organizational thinking that actually supports real citizen-centric services, rather than placing a unified customer service front end on fragmented back-end delivery. Looking forward, once CRM has enabled the delivery of coherent, consistent services, service planners will be able really to exploit the information captured by CRM applications, to gain a deep understanding of the services required and how the needs of the citizen are changing and evolving. This will help improve efficiencies through geographic focusing of services or changing of customer group definitions. With the emphasis on increased private/public sector cooperation, such information will be invaluable in assessing where each can deliver the most appropriate and effective services.

Having set a target date of 2005 for the delivery of e-enabled processes, the UK Government is working towards the delivery of online services, but many challenges remain. In Spring 2001, ukonline.gov.uk, the online citizen portal, was formally launched. However, while it provides a central point of access into government services, there are several key elements of the solution yet to be developed, most notably identification and authentication to enable personalized service delivery, as well as local or service specific portals. These too must also be supported by e-forms in a consistent manner across government.

Such challenges are not insignificant. However, by using CRM to transform the service delivery through face to face and telephone channels, local authorities and government agencies can create an environment that can then be replicated online as the technology infrastructure comes into place. Before services can be delivered coherently online, it is important to understand what citizens require; how they want to interact with the public sector; how inter-authority services can work together. CRM implementations that move beyond simple process automation to embrace new ways of service delivery provide a fundamental step in delivering e-enabled services to the citizen. Once interdepartmental cooperation and integration have been achieved and there is a robust, secure technology for identification and authentication, CRM can drive processes through the customer interaction lifecycle to provide a holistic customer view.

The challenges in introducing CRM

Today some 30 per cent of local authorities claim robust customer service strategies, but less than 10 per cent have actually implemented a joined-up service approach. It is the need for a fundamental shift in thinking that creates the challenges in CRM implementation, yet without that shift the goals of the modernizing government agenda and joined-up service delivery cannot be achieved. The challenges include:

▌ **Organizational change.** Fundamental organizational issues need to be addressed to achieve the cultural change to enable successful citizen-centric service delivery. Customer service requirements must be assessed and understood before internal processes and working practices can be amended to enable the service delivery. Cross-organizational cooperation requires a high profile sponsor and often some external challenge, to drive service delivery away from traditional stovepipes towards a citizen-centric model.

▌ **Cost.** As ever, funding is also a major issue but there are clear return on investment (ROI) measurements that can be used to cost-justify the investment. Additionally, with the overwhelming focus of the government on improved delivery of public services, projects without a modernizing government/service delivery focus cannot gain funding. ROI measures of improved performance and cost savings or displacement can be achieved. Market research can be used to monitor the number of lost calls that are now reduced, as well as customer perception of service quality. It is important to remember, however, that while consolidating separate customer service points into a one-stop shop can deliver economies of scale, the attendant rise in the quality of the service tends to prompt a significant increase in its use, which may then require additional staff to be employed.

▌ **Technology.** There are excellent CRM applications in the market that are mature and proven. However, to deliver citizen-focused services they need to support access to integrated back office systems supporting a range of service areas. The CRM application will handle scripting,[1] contact management and tracking, but it needs knowledge management principles to enable staff to pull knowledge from diverse applications to meet customer needs. So, in addition to the complex process of integrating legacy applications, introducing call centres and supporting Web access, CRM solutions also need to address knowledge management and workflow. To compound the issue, such solutions need to support not just telephone requests and letters but increasingly, electronic forms (e-forms), all with the same levels of service and according to predefined response times.

The government is working hard to introduce best practice – such as in call centres – to provide guidance and advice. There are also a number of standards initiatives under way to aid this process, such as the Electronic Government Framework and Web Guidelines which establish mandatory standards for the usability of government services, including Web navigation and transactions.

Citizen services in action

In spring 2001 the ukonline.gov.uk portal was launched as the principal entry point to online government information and services. Content on the portal is organized around the needs of the citizen, using 'life episodes' to enable users to access all the information they need about a particular event without having to understand the workings of government or departmental delivery structures. Such life episodes include death and bereavement, moving home, and pensions and retirement. In addition to powerful search engines and real-time government news, the portal also includes easy-access pages to support the visually impaired or those with low reading skills.

The contact centre

This chapter has emphasized the fact that while CRM solutions are a fundamental component of delivering joined-up citizen services, dropping a CRM solution into an existing set of customer service processes is not going to achieve long-term modernizing government goals. The contact centre is a first implementable CRM step towards the new citizen service vision. The centre is an organizational entity focused on customer service at the point of contact, and provides a range of services supported by clear operational objectives.

Conclusion

A CRM solution provides a platform for improved services to the customer. Critically, it provides a building block for the delivery of e-enabled processes as demanded by the government by 2005. This can, however, only be achieved if an organization takes a strategic review of its approach to delivering customer services and changes its internal culture to achieve cross-functional service. Simply automating existing processes using CRM solutions will provide short-term efficiency gains, but without transforming service delivery there is no building block for e-enablement.

Too many public sector call centres offer a 'one number' solution that provides the citizen with an immediate response but has no depth or knowledge with which to resolve issues: it is simply fielding calls. By creating an integrated contact centre that exploits the sophisticated elements of CRM technology such as scripting, call tracking, information and integrated line-of-business systems, the entire customer interaction is tracked from start to finish, problems are resolved quickly, with fewer calls, and the level of service offered is unprecedented.

This integrated approach delivers better customer processes that can be e-enabled easily to meet the government's targets. CRM is not just a means to add a short-term fillip to existing, sometimes poorly regarded, services, but actually provides an opportunity for a fundamental step change in service delivery and a platform for future development towards multi-channel services based on a holistic citizen view.

MEASURING CUSTOMER MANAGEMENT PERFORMANCE

Evidence from CMAT and other studies is that measurement is essential. Without what might be seen as the relatively simple indicators of success in customer management enjoyed by the private sector (revenue, profit, customer recruitment, retention and development, cost to serve), the public sector sometimes needs to develop a wider variety of measures. However, most private sector measures can be translated into measures for the public sector, with adjustment to take the context into account. These measures include:

- customer value, present and future;
- service levels to customers;
- take up;
- cost to serve;
- customer acquisition, retention and development;
- loyalty/commitment;
- customer attitudes;
- customer responsiveness/conversions;
- process performance.

In the next section, we examine three case studies of the application of measured customer management techniques in the public sector. It is noticeable that all three are from local authorities. This is because, as we have noted above, local authorities seem to be the public sector organizations in the UK that have made most progress with implementing more customer-focused approaches to customer management.

CASE STUDY 1: PUBLIC SECTOR CMAT

In its public sector derivative, CMAT provides a quantitative measure of the way that customers and citizens are managed in both the commercial and service areas of a public body. In commercial areas, such as leisure and entertainment, public sector organizations are considered to be very similar to other commercial bodies. In areas of public service, such as benefits and highways management, the values and objectives of the organization are clearly recognized as being different, and this is fully taken into account in the assessment methodology. The assessment is in two parts. It addresses over 160 good customer management practices expected to be performed centrally by each organization (each council in this case). It then covers almost 100 practices that could be done differently in each service delivery department (planning, leisure, libraries and so on).

Public sector CMAT is in the earliest stages of its implementation, so we are unable to show many results. What follows is an anonymized version of a study that had just been completed at the time of writing. The assessment was of three local councils, one at a higher (county) level and two within the county (district level), carried out using a new, bespoke public sector question set. QCi worked jointly with the three councils to test the approach, methodology and suitability of the new question set in relation to public sector needs, and would like to thank them for their input. Consignia sponsored the project.

The project team defined three service types that provided the focus for the project:

▌ generic services, where all customers should receive that same level of service irre-spective of need;
▌ needs-based services, where customers receive services dependent on their needs;
▌ mutually beneficial services, where authorities also receive financial value from service provision.

The departments involved are shown in Table 23.1. The main findings are listed below. Scores are confidential, so they are not given.

▌ There was a laudable degree of customer focus and service ethos in the assessed authorities.
▌ However, the philosophy of customer management as described above was not currently being practised.
▌ The organizations of all three councils were structured around their products (the services offered to customers), with the result that the customer focus was not joined up, other than in their attitude amongst front-line service staff.
▌ This engendered a mindset of delivering the here and now to prescribed standards, rather than the more proactive management and generation of opportunity. Of course, with the complexity of the authorities' business model, there is an advantage in the relative simplicity that a product focus brings to the equation, with the downside being the inevitable silos that result.

Table 23.1 Departments involved

	Authority A	Authority B	Authority C
Generic	Procurement (planned but not completed)	Planning	Planning
Needs-based	Enquiry management	Enquiry management	Enquiry management
Mutually beneficial	Libraries	Leisure	Leisure

▮ To illustrate the point, an entrepreneur moving into the locality, with particular requirements, would have to deal with up to 24 people in the authorities to fulfil statutory requirements, plus spend many hours filling in forms (often duplicating the information).

▮ While it is unrealistic to expect to deal with one person for all these requirements, it was universally agreed that it should be significantly fewer than at present.

▮ Only a handful of individuals within each organization really understood the customer management philosophy and they saw that it could be extremely powerful.

▮ There was political reluctance to offer differentiated services to different customers.

▮ Senior management could not be sure how wholeheartedly to adopt customer management, as little value or needs analysis had been done. Therefore, although the theory appears sound, the practical application of it would prove difficult.

▮ The main areas that came out strongly in the assessment across all organizations are process management, people and organization, and the central enquiry management function. This appeared to be because of centrally generated initiatives such as Best Value, People First, the Charter Mark applications and compulsory competitive tendering (as was). In these areas good practice had been determined and then, through audit and assessment, was looked for with rigour.

▮ It would be easy to view some of these initiatives as 'obstacles to be got round', but it is to all three authorities' credit that the general view was one of recognition and acceptance that they did raise the standards and generate customer focus.

▮ The three organizations scored less well in analysis and planning, developing the service offering, information and technology, and measuring the effect. Since the basic value/needs analysis, segmentation and resource allocation based on needs had not been done, it was hard to score well here. It is these sections that represented the greatest gap, possibly the largest learning, and perhaps the biggest opportunity.

▮ In service management, one aspect missed was the application of key account management (KAM) principles. Intuitively staff knew who the most important customers were, but the reactive nature of the organizations means that there was little or no formal work being done to really drive the relationship more to the mutual benefit of the local authority and the customer.

▮ Sales and marketing as functions within the three organizations were not in evidence to anywhere near the same degree as in commercial sector companies.

▮ Marketing was predominantly viewed as a public relations function, with a little marketing communications (brochure and leaflet production) included.

In conclusion, the three organizations were evidently progressive and forward thinking. There was a willingness to consider, learn from and even perhaps adopt new thinking. Some stated that they had a strategic intent to actively take on customer management. The assessment showed that they had excellent foundations upon which to build, while the weaker areas were readily identifiable and possible to improve swiftly. The final message is that the customers of the three local authority areas assessed can be said to be looked after by their public sector representatives as well, if not better than, by the majority of private sector organizations whose services they also call upon.

The overall conclusion from the first application of public sector CMAT was that the adaptation from private sector CMAT, using specialists in public sector management, followed by a pilot with organizations to be assessed, where they were able to finalize the form of customization, proved successful.

CASE STUDY 2: THE COST OF CUSTOMER MANAGEMENT

A recent study by Quadrant Consultants and Royal Mail, with five local authorities, focused on the local government administration of housing and council tax benefit in Great Britain. The study focuses on this large and growing £600 million activity, where all involved want to do better for claimants. The key facts about this activity are as follows:

▮ 4 million customers or claimants.
▮ 17,500 staff in local authorities.
▮ 27 million items of post involved.
▮ 33 million phone calls received.
▮ Overpays £1.1 billion pa.
▮ Recovers all but £250 million each year.
▮ A claim costs £82 to administer.
▮ One in 10 applications arrive correct.
▮ 30,000 evictions each year, up 12 per cent from 2000 to 2001.
▮ 90 per cent of evictions are due to housing benefit arrears.

Quadrant used their Baseline Evaluation cost-benchmarking tool to evaluate housing benefit cost to serve. Participants in this Royal Mail / Quadrant Baseline Evaluation study were:

▮ Blaby District Council.
▮ Charnwood Borough Council.
▮ Hinckley and Bosworth Borough Council.
▮ North West Leicestershire District Council.
▮ Oadby and Wigston Borough Council.

The programme included process mapping and cost to serve apportionment, and benchmarking between the participants. It was concluded in April 2002. The process mapping enabled re-engineering of local authorities' efforts to manage the flow of funds, because

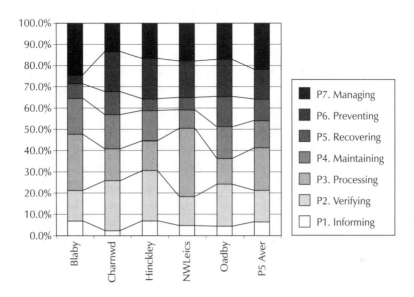

Figure 23.1   Process breakdown and cost benchmarks

it could be seen for the first time how costs build up in customer terms rather than in terms of traditional functional budgets. Departmental costs were converted into customer process costs, allowing management to see where processes were cost-effective and where to allocate resources. Though many local authorities found the process difficult, the Baseline Evaluator tool also helped determine what happens to fixed or indirect costs if they use alternative contact management channels for part of process.

Figure 23.1 gives the cost comparison, showing the top-level process breakdown.

Cost per process, for customer and contact management, could be highlighted and benchmarked with large-scale comparisons. For example, it was found that a £20 application process for housing and council tax benefit might be a generous resource compared with the usual lower 'cost to serve' for national activities (compared with Post Office averages). Centralized contact management schemes like passports, driver licences, motor tax applications and television/radio licence applications have been processed for less than £10. Admittedly these transactions normally require less skill than a housing benefit/council tax first time claimant 'assessment', but that part of the process map might best be managed at a local level.

CASE STUDY 3: SERVICE TO THE ELDERLY

One of the most significant recent trends in customer service has been the move away from face-to-face care to remote service using a variety of channels. This has allowed many more customers to be served, using fewer people. Though remote servicing can be impersonal, with suppliers being one step removed from customers, it also allows for a less intrusive personal experience for customers. However, there is one category of services where this type of mass service will probably never come to dominate. These are services that we shall probably all need. We have little choice about who provides these services to us. We need them at a time when we might least be able to control or influence the level of service we are given. We usually need them after years of using remote services, of making active choices, of being in control and of not accepting second best. They are the services we need when we become old and possibly dependent.

For the public sector, caring for older people is becoming increasingly demanding. People are living longer. Resources to care for the old are in short supply. We live in an ageing population more geared to the young and active, to those with their own cars, rather than to the elderly. The elderly largely live on fixed incomes, and although some are lucky enough to have inflation-protected pensions, most do not. However, the state will not provide unlimited increases in resources to care for the elderly – in fact the trend is in the opposite direction. This poses the question who should receive the services: those with high needs or those who have some prospect of a healthy, enjoyable old age, or both.

For one council, Spelthorne Borough Council, understanding and delivering care for the elderly has become a very high priority, simply because of the rapid ageing of its community. As with many boroughs in the southeast, its population is an ageing one. The population has decreased over the last 30 years but in recent years the proportion of older people has increased. Most want to stay in the area, but many people's relatives have moved away, in some part due to the high cost of housing. Spelthorne is gearing up its services to cope with this demand, with less money and fewer staff to go round.

Spelthorne's work has led to its receiving Beacon status from the government, for its work developing 'Independent Living for Older People'. This award recognizes the council as a centre of excellence and requires it to disseminate best practice throughout the country, to other local authorities and relevant organizations. Spelthorne has held open days, presented at conferences and invited groups from other authorities to visit it and discuss/view first hand the services that it provides.

Spelthorne's main centre is Staines, Middlesex. It is near Heathrow Airport. Proximity to the airport is relevant because it leads to a lack of people to deliver the individual personal care needed by the more frail elderly. The airport with its high wages and glamour lures away many of the people who might otherwise work in the care sector, leaving few to offer services to people who needs lots of assistance. Good schooling and high house prices mean that many of the young find well-paid jobs elsewhere in the country and abroad, leaving their families behind to fend for themselves, as they become older and reliant on a fragmented community and overstretched services. The many older people with no local family to support them locally need help from the overworked and sometimes undermanned voluntary sector and publicly funded services. In Spelthorne, the growing number of middle-class, home-owning families suffer the most. They often have too much capital to qualify for means-tested services, but fixed incomes too low to afford private services they need, like home helps and gardening. Paradoxically, those on lower incomes with local family may be able to access help more easily. They are more likely to qualify for means-tested services too.

Many of the techniques used by the private sector to deliver service where demand has increased dramatically in a short time cannot be used in this sector. A call centre cannot usually help an elderly person take a bath or move food from plate to mouth. However, not everyone needs this level of care. Many older people are active and fit and need services that allow them to stay this way. This is Spelthorne's main focus.

Given these trends, Spelthorne wanted to identify how these trends were affecting the need for care for older people, and what sort of organization, culture and processes would ensure that needs were met. Despite being a borough council without social services responsibility, Spelthorne spends about £2 million per annum on various services for the elderly. Key services include the provision of day centres, meals on wheels, community transport and a personal alarm network. Where possible Spelthorne uses technology-based solutions to provide a more personalized service, and it is planning services for customers who have a history of choosing quality services and increasing expectations.

For their more dependent customers, Spelthorne is using mini call centres in the shape of SPAN, the Spelthorne Personal Alarm. This is open 24 hours a day and combines the latest in computer technology with a caring staff who take calls from elderly people if they fall or hurt themselves. However, it provides more than an emergency medical response service. Customers call for many reasons, such as needing a reliable plumber or electrician, checking to see that a meal or a carer is on the way, or finding out how to deal with a bogus caller. SPAN works closely with the voluntary sector and social services to ensure that individual needs are met. It is a successful combination of technology with caring people who us a network of resources to find and provide solutions to most problems.

For the more active and fit, Spelthorne is designing services to meet the needs of the next older generation. The traditional image of a day centre for the elderly, with bingo and functional food, has disappeared. In its place are centres where the focus is on enjoying life and keeping active. Social inclusion is a key issue. Spelthorne sees the need to be ready for a generation of older people who are used to having busy lives and choosing and using quality services. The aim is to ensure that as people become older they are able to continue being active, so minimizing the need for high-dependency services. The centres aim to provide a family-type support system and environment, alleviating some of the problems associated with diminishing family support.

A key question is whether these and other Spelthorne services are meeting the needs of all older residents. Older people are not a homogenous group. To ensure that customer needs were being met, Spelthorne realized it was important to listen to a representative mix of people. ABA Research was briefed to help with this, and set itself the task of listening to all the segments of the older people in the borough, not just the ones who were most accessible (those who were able to get out and about, or who responded to telephone calls or letters). A number of segments were identified (see Table 23.2). Focus groups were conducted for each segment. In some cases, having single-sex groups made discussions easier and freer. The same applied when it came to those who lived alone, had family support or had access to a car and could get around easily.

Just conducting the research was challenging, especially the groups for those with higher needs. In some cases it took 45 minutes to get everyone into the room and the same to help them leave. We could not have groups lasting any longer than an hour because of the frailty of the respondents. Some respondents hardly leave home and have almost hourly care to keep them living in their own homes.

We were surprised by how well informed people were, and by the willingness of people to get involved. People were delighted that we wanted to listen and were keen to influence the process. We learnt about the urgency of decision making in areas where it might be slow. We began to understand how to communicate with people whose access to normal forms of communication was limited. We understood the benefits which modern technology and call centres, backed up by caring staff, can bring to the quality of life of this group – making staying at home, rather than going into a home, a real option for even the most frail.

Spelthorne Community Visitors, who check the equipment three times a year, try to ensure that when more help is required their clients can access the relevant services. This includes obtaining help in claiming attendance allowance, how to access Spelride, the community transport service, become users of day centres, apply for meals on wheels, and referring clients to social services if their needs increase. Spelthorne has a database of members for Spelride and for day centres. This makes it easier for the various services to keep in touch with their users, when the need arises. Visitors use the visit to generally assist the elderly with any daily living enquiries. It is a successful combination of technology with caring people, using a network of resources to find solutions to most problems.

The research showed that different groups of older people access and view Spelthorne's services in very different ways. Customers in every other sector are changing their wants and needs, and so are older people who need to access services from councils and public bodies. To enhance services to these groups we can learn from many of the customer management techniques used in other sectors. So the lessons from Spelthorne's experience are these:

Table 23.2 Segmentation approach

Segment	Specification	Main findings
Independent active	*Aged 55–65* *Drivers – fully mobile* *Currently receiving no care*	This group think the council takes very good care of them. They use the day centres and can get themselves around and so find everything very convenient.
Partially dependent	*Aged 65+* *Require occasional support* *Some with mobility difficulties* *Drivers and non-drivers* *Living alone/not alone* *With/without family support*	This group finds getting around the borough the biggest issue. The council has its own transport system for the elderly and disabled and this is a real life-enhancer for this group. They often rely on local churches and charities for additional help. Those without local family support are often worse off than those with less money but with local supportive families.
Receiving care	*Possibly using council services* *Require regular support from others* *Mobility difficulties* *Some with modification to their homes*	These are high-need residents, who need a varied, hands-on care package. Call centre elements work well when they use the alarm and if they are able to use the council's own transport service. Many are confined to their homes and use meals on wheels and council carers to allow them to stay there. The research identified a need for a strong relationship between the voluntary sector, social services and the council. This relationship is vital as this group find it hard to manage different service providers as well as to stay in their own homes. Many also rely on support and help from their families to resolve service provision issues.
Voluntary sector	*Voluntary service providers, via Spelthorne Borough Council*	This group see the acute problems being faced by overstretched services in the public sector. They highlighted the problems that occur when cases are referred to them. They feel that they are people's last hope of assistance. The level of stress felt in all sectors of care for the elderly is most obvious in this group.

▌ Seeing the old as the new generation of customers is an essential mind-shift. They are not a problem to be managed, but a group of customers with reasonable needs. They have paid taxation for a lifetime, and may still be paying, and they have strong customers' rights.

▌ Today's older people are better informed about their needs than their predecessors, and have more experience of taking action themselves to ensure that these needs are met. This can make them more demanding, but also makes them more responsive to self-service. For this reason, self-service works in this market like any other.

▋ Understanding different kinds of needs is important: this is not a 'one size fits all' market. Classic techniques for understanding customers must be used. Market segmentation is essential – it helps ensure better targeting of resources.

▋ Services can be designed that people want to access. These may be remote services or face-to-face, such as day centres offering computer time or tuition.

▋ Technology can be used to deliver more personalized services, whether remotely or face-to-face. The first Internet generation is moving into retirement, but its members may not want to sit at home browsing by themselves.

▋ Customer management tools and new communication channels can be used to save time. This can then be used to deliver the one-to-one care that will always be required.

▋ The new elderly are not all poor, but they do need help. If they do not get the help they need, they might not be able to change supplier except by moving to another area, but they can change who manages the supplier, by voting. In some areas, their ballot box power will be crucial to electoral success.

For Spelthorne the next stage is to develop an action plan for the future delivery of services for older people. This will include a shift towards community centres as opposed to day centres, opportunities to 'enable' older people so that they do not miss out on the technology revolution, and a review of where resources are currently targeted.

NOTES

[1] See for example the following:

Stone, M, Machtynger, L and Woodcock, N (2002) *Customer Relationship Marketing*, 2nd edn, Kogan Page, London.

Stone, M, Starkey, M and Woodcock, N (2000) The customer management scorecard, *Business Intelligence*.

Stone, M and Foss, B (2001) *Successful Customer Relationship Marketing*, Kogan Page, London.

Woodcock, N, Starkey, M, Stone, M, Weston, P and Ozimek, J (2001) *The State of the Nation II 2002: How companies are creating and destroying economic value through customer management*, QCi, London.

These books document an extensive programme of research into customer management carried out by QCi together with its leading business partners such as IBM, Ogilvy, Royal Mail and others, using QCi's Customer Management Assessment Tool.

24

CRM strategy and implementation in telecommunications

Rob Mattison, Len Tiu Wright, Julie Abbott, Andy Brown, Dave Cox, Mike Faulkner and Merlin Stone[1]

PART 1: CONTEXT AND METHODOLOGY

In part 1 of this chapter we present some methodological fundamentals and show how to apply this methodology to map business intelligence infrastructure against CRM processes and how to optimize these processes. In part 2, we present some telecommunications case studies illustrating different methodological points.

The telecommunications turning point

By the end of the 1970s the telecommunications market seemed to have reached saturation. However, from the middle of the 1980s, pushed by several generations of technological revolution and market deregulation, a new period of exponential market growth started. One of the most important characteristics of this 'turning point' is the rate and nature of the change. Telecommunication companies find themselves changing their understanding of their markets, their technology and their regulatory environment constantly. The industry and the companies within it are forced to constantly reinvent themselves.

Many structural changes associated with the turning point have been completely redrawing the telecommunications industry. The movement from monopoly to competition has been reshaping the typical telecommunications company's business structure. Pricing process is market-based instead of cost-based. Outsourcing, for example of network management, is very popular, to minimize the operational costs. With many competitors in each market, the demand for human resources, especially in marketing, is very high. Finally, we are undergoing a declared market war between the different business lines and/or technologies to acquire and retain customers.

The telecommunications industry is engaged in a number of different battles, each one with a particular history and strategy. At present we have at least three very important battles in place: the voice battle between the wire line and wireless, the message battle between cellular and pager, and the data battle between wireless, wire line, cable and satellite. The situation inside each battle is very chaotic and complex to analyse. However, we can identify some significant trends inside each battle.

The voice battle

In the voice battle, we can identify at least two very important worldwide trends. The first trend shows the movement from the corporate market to the mass market in the wireless industry, and the second one shows the possible substitution of wire line by wireless. The movement toward the mass market has been creating cost challenges and changing the CRM processes structures. Many carriers will have to enlist the aid of complex and expensive database CRM tools simply to identify their customers, now concealed among the masses. Now the wireless companies are using many CRM and sales strategies (prepaid, one-rate plans) to acquire new good customers and to deepen the relationship with them. However, one of the most important effects of this movement is a decrease in average revenue per user (ARPU), forcing companies to try to increase their wallet share.

In developing countries the numbers tell the same story, showing that these countries are leapfrogging intermediate technology, going straight to use of state of the art wireless technology and following developed-country trends. Prepaid cards, traditionally an option for the credit challenged, have become ubiquitous even in wealthy markets such as Germany. Another option that has influenced the exponential growth is the CPP (calling party pays) protocol.

One of the effects of the prepaid strategy is the difficulty companies have in identifying prepaid customers. Many times billing systems do not store data about these customers, transforming them into huge anonymous segments. This means that these customers will be harder to identify when carriers try to market news and information services (wallet share improvement campaigns) or unified messaging (fax, e-mail and voice mail). Those add-on applications will be necessary to increase minutes per use, which have been declining, as more mass consumers become wireless users.

The message battle

The major players in this battle belong to the wireless industry. On one side there are cellular phones including PCS (personal communication systems) and on the other side is the pager industry. The major trend in this battle is the replacement of pagers by cellular phones. In many countries we can observe a decrease in the growth rate in the number of pager subscribers; in other countries like Japan the absolute number of pagers has been decreasing since 1996. European pager manufactures have begun to exit the business. Ericsson has closed its pager production operations and Philips has sold its paging business. There are two major causes for this message revolution. The first is the CPP system which turned the cellular phone into a real alternative for classical inbound users. The second cause is the appearance of digital cellular phones with message capability. In general experts agree that the pager industry will not disappear in the medium term but will change its current format, including a market redefinition. New technologies like ReFLEX systems (two way paging technology) are starting to make this a reality.

The data battle

The data battle is the most complex and may be the most important. The complexity of this battle starts with the huge number of players, including wireless, wire line, satellite, cable and companies from different industries such as the computer industry, all trying to define the standards. The data battle is probably the most important because if we consider voice transmission as a particular case of data transmission (IP telephony, cable phone), this battle could include part of the voice battle. We can split the data battle into two sub-battles, the first focused on mobile data transmission and the second on no-mobile data transmission. To get a better sense of the mobile data transmission sub-battle, imagine a salesperson or an executive, out of the office, trying to connect his or her notebook with the company intranet. He or she can use wire line or wireless technology to make this connection. Forecasts are showing an exponential growth for this kind of mobile data transmission. In the no-mobile side we can imagine a similar person trying to access the Internet from home or from the office. In this case, he or she still has the same first two options (wireless broadband for instance) but technologies like ISDN, DSL, cable modem or satellite dishes (PC Direct) can also be chosen to make the connection.

THE VISION

Telecommunications companies around the world have been trying to adapt themselves to every new market force, constantly changing their organizational structure in order to react quickly and remain competitive. They expect that the changes will stop and the chaos will decrease in the short term. However, this is unlikely to happen, so companies need to continue to adapt. We suggest that a necessary condition for success is to optimize core CRM processes and establish a competitive advantage in each one. The four core CRM processes are:

- wallet-share enhancement (increase revenue from existing customers);
- acquisition (new customers);
- affinity (customer loyalty);
- retention (preventing customer churn).

Each CRM process has four steps:

- Prioritization and goal setting: deciding what to focus on and building teams that pursue those objectives.
- Modelling: performing segmentation, scoring, and other kinds of analysis that help CRM decide which campaigns to develop.
- Campaign development: choosing, creating and preparing the advertising medium and the message to be delivered to customers, as well as running tests to validate the CRM assumptions.
- Campaign execution: actually sending the messages through the respective media.

Prioritization and goal setting

The CRM process has to deal with many different sources of input, feedback and impetus. In fact, in most telecommunications firms there is so much input, from so many different sources, with so many different and contradictory objectives, that it is easy to lose control over the whole process very quickly. This step may be extremely dysfunctional in some organizations, nonexistent in others, and well run in only a small percentage of cases. Most of the major challenges to the execution of the CRM process occur here, in the area of prioritization and goal settings. During this step of the process, the major components of a CRM plan are assembled. These steps involve identification of sponsors, creation of projects, assembly of teams, identification of objectives, and identification of constraints.

Modelling

Once the project team has been assembled and financed and the objectives have been clearly stated, the team moves from prioritization and goal-setting mode into modelling mode. A model is a proposal of the method that will accomplish the sponsor's objectives and the mathematical proof that shows the proposed solution is reasonable and viable. The goal of modelling is then is to develop a plan, or a series of plans, that will accomplish the goals. The modelling process is where most of the analytical disciplines are employed.

Campaign/programme development

Once the modelling process has been completed and the decision has been made which model to use, the job of CRM shifts from the modeller to the campaign developer. Campaign developers turn the model into a specific, executable plan. There are several processes involved in campaign development.

▌ Media and message finalization: deciding on the specific message to use and how it will be delivered.
▌ Media selection and negotiation: choosing specific organizations and individuals to deliver the messages and negotiating the cost of delivery. Media selection is often influenced strongly by the time frame for the message, or the target group.
▌ Prospect targeting and list scoring. In the case of direct mail and telemarketing, one of the main jobs of the campaign developer is to select the list of prospects and to determine which specific people on that list will be targeted.

Campaign execution

Once the campaign for a given time period (monthly, quarterly or annually) has been developed, the marketer will be responsible for setting it in motion. It may involve nothing more than making a phone call to the advertising agency, or may be as complicated as initiating and monitoring the day to day activities of a call centre or mailroom operation. Once the message is delivered, the company is ready to analyse the results.

THE FORCES

To continue our effort to construct a logical structure to represent the core CRM processes we need to understand all sources of influence and how they impact these processes. We can categorize the major sources of influence in three different forces.

The support force

The support force works as a floor for the CRM processes. We can split the support force into three different components:

- techniques: specialized processes, procedures and techniques such as optimization, data mining and data;
- telecomms CRM skills: specialized skills needed to manage the whole CRM process;
- technology: the systems tools and data collection necessary to make this happen.

These components could actually be broken down further into different sub-components. For example, the technology component could be divided into a query system, to include the OLAP tools, data warehouses, data-marts and all the legacy systems; analytical systems for all of the optimization, data-mining systems and tools (this sub-component is very important for defining the optimality of many parts of the CRM process); and finally process management systems, to include systems such as campaign management. The implementation of this particular sub-component is very complex because of the complicated trade-off between the tool and the internal processes of the company. When a telecomms company buys this kind of tool it is really buying a process that often does not match its current CRM processes.

The motive force

The motive force works as an engine for the CRM process. This force is responsible for pushing the whole process forward. The more important components in the motive force are:

- corporate strategy and goal setting;
- competition;
- new technologies and innovations;
- market (customers and prospects).

The influence of the motive force within the core CRM processes is both very important and difficult to analyse. Companies often construct dedicated mechanisms to help them to understand fully all of the different components and how they affect their business environments.

The spoiler force

To understand the spoiler force we need to think of the spoiler on a race car, an accessory that adds to traction and steering capabilities, but can also slow down the car's progress based on its angle and how it is used. This spoiler force can be used to help or hinder the company's CRM progress. Components of the spoiler force include:

▌ regulation;
▌ network infrastructure;
▌ operations.

Each one of these components has an enormous influence on the CRM core processes. For example, network infrastructure can work against marketing by creating a physical constraint for any acquisition campaign, or can work as a competitive advantage, helping marketers in the same kind of campaign.

PART 2: CASE STUDIES

Part 2 of this chapter uses four anonymous and two attributable case studies from European telecommunications companies to illustrate the points made above, concentrating on how information technology in the form of the Internet and business intelligence solutions have enabled large businesses to focus on the customer as well as on their products and sales levels. CRM is an attitude that has to pervade the company, but it needs a solid foundation of knowledge of customers. This knowledge comes not only from customer-facing employees but also from the vast amounts of data collected by companies today. It is the technological infrastructure that allows this knowledge to be distilled from data about customers and their interactions with the company, and this facilitates better business decisions and encourages customer loyalty and retention.

Many telecommunications companies are now attempting to use CRM techniques to focus on the development and retention of higher value customers. The cases below show changes in marketing thinking and tactics towards customer acquisition and retention. Each company has used new ways to reach customers and to monitor and reduce the costs of managing customers through products and systems harnessed to the Internet. Effective customer support is delivered online. The short cases illustrate how traditional telephony companies and a new-entrant cable firm have applied new technologies to winning and retaining customers in the residential telephone market. They are based on large global telecommunications companies.

COMPANY W

Key activities

Company W is a wholly owned subsidiary of a major telecommunications company, focusing purely on digital wireless communications. It is one of the largest mobile communications companies in the United States, with a digital coverage of over 83 per cent of the country and has almost 13 million customers. It is growing fast, adding over 1 million customers in the first half of 2001.

Improved ability to understand customer needs and detect fraud

The company has installed a data warehouse solution that is continuously updated with call records (rather than having them updated in batch mode at specific intervals), and this gives the call centre operatives the ability to service customer requests with the latest information at their fingertips. The data warehouse can detect network problems even before operations staff are aware, enabling fast resolution and an increase in customer satisfaction, improving customer retention. Fraud detection is also improved, as call records reach the data warehouse within 30 minutes and they are continuously queried in order to detect potential fraud. This enables early containment of revenue losses and is also a deterrent to thieves stealing phones.

Future plans

The take-up of mobile communications is nowhere near saturation point in the United States and the company expects to expand its call centre facilities and data warehouse to accommodate market growth.

COMPANY X

Key activities

Telecommunications services, mobile communications, satellite communications, networking solutions, Internet service provider.

Market position

Market deregulation has resulted in many regional telecommunications companies starting up in competition to Company X. Therefore it has branched out into product areas that complement its core competencies, give opportunities for cross-selling into its existing customer base, and take advantage of the new and fast-growing youth markets.

Improved knowledge of customers and prospects

The use of a business intelligence solution that included data mining to drill down through the enormous amounts of data held has enabled Company X to gain valuable insight into its customer base and combat the increasing competition. Key areas concentrated on are increased customer retention, cross selling, attrition and loyalty building. The company now has an in-depth understanding of how its customers use the various products and services on offer and can therefore build some very targeted loyalty programmes. The systems also enable the company to understand why the best customers defect to competition, and allow its marketing teams to put in place counterpromotions to encourage them to stay. The company also uses targeted promotions to encourage competitors' customers to move across to it when they fall into the higher value segments of the market.

Measuring effectiveness

A key aspect of the CRM system is measurement. Detailed analysis of the outcomes of contacts enables the company to understand which are its most effective campaigns, which products and services are the most successful, and what are the effects of key aspects of customer service such as fault reporting.

Future plans

The business intelligence solution is still very new. It was used first by the company in fixed-line telephony, and it is now being applied in other key areas such as mobile and cable. The company does not expect huge improvements overnight, and accepts that CRM needs the entire company to participate, which can take some time to happen. The IT systems enable customer-facing departments to have the knowledge they need when in contact with customers, and permit rapid analysis of data to help the company understand the behaviour patterns of its customers and then determine their needs. Long-term strategies are now in place to ensure that the company remains customer-focused and flexible in the long term.

COMPANY Y

Key activities

Telecommunications services, mobile communications, IT solutions, Internet service provider.

Market deregulation

The monopoly position of Company Y was challenged. Market deregulation brought forth competitors, now numbering over 100 regional telecommunications companies. Cable operators took market share from Company Y, especially in urban areas. By the year 2000 other companies had taken 21 per cent of the market.

Hangover from years of monopoly

Company Y had a bureaucratic structure and had problems responding quickly to new technical developments and competitive events. There were frequent changes in senior management and thus in direction and style of leadership. Limited attention was given to customer retention, with consequent gradual and persistent loss in market share. New-customer-acquisition policies suffered from uncompetitive pricing structures, un-innovative product ranges and competitive retaliation.

Improved customer focus and relationship marketing

A customer campaign and analysis team was established. A data warehouse with data mining software was set up to provide the necessary analytical techniques. Data mining was used to support market segmentation and in-depth customer profiling. This contributed to improved rates of response in direct marketing campaigns because of greater accuracy in the use of customer data. The company studied customer attrition and this led it to simplify pricing structures, reduce prices, and give greater choice and increased value to its customers. Telephone calls are now made to existing customers on a regular and rotating basis to check satisfaction with the company's service, and to give information about new offers and to encourage their uptake by customers. Relationships with customers have been improved by a systematic approach to improving greater customer care and monitoring.

The company has invested in market and consumer studies, and created new customer databases. These are updated by including responses from existing customers. More effective targeting of market segments has led to new offerings being designed for residential customers, such as inclusive call allowances. There are add-on benefits including a free answering service that stores messages for up to 20 days to all residential customers, some of whom could be busy on other calls or logged on to the Internet. Those using the new options now constitute over 50 per cent of the company's call traffic. The company's best tariff compares well with other competitors. Joint schemes with television broadcasters, such as the bundling of television services with telephony with more than 70 channels, have helped it to diversify from its traditional telephony market. The company has also now won back many of its lost customers.

Exploiting online presence

A strong online presence has made it easier for the company to cater for the increasing number of residential and business customers, for example for information and billing inquiries, handling of faults and complaints, and orders of products and services. This has helped to increase the speed and effectiveness of handling inquiries and transactions between the company and its customers.

The future with CRM

There is still a need to focus more strategically on CRM initiatives to help the company to grow. Suppliers from other industries such as utilities are selling discounted telephony services. The company could respond by offering to bundle gas, electricity and other utility sales to its huge base of residential and business customers. Other differentiated products and services from other industries could also be offered.

Business intelligence solutions

Company Y's experience has shown the importance of developing CRM initiatives in customer acquisition and retention. Data warehousing and advanced analysis, including data mining, have played an important role in enhancing the effectiveness of its CRM.

COMPANY Z

Key activities

Telecommunications and Internet services.

Market performance

As a new entrant in the telecommunications market after deregulation, this company achieved rapid growth and gained 17 per cent of the residential market. This was achieved through heavy investment in new telecommunications technology; bundled services to drive market penetration; and an annual advertising spend of around £36 million. Its residential customer base reached 3 million customers in seven years. Penetration in the domestic telephone market reached above 50 per cent in its original franchises. It ranks amongst the top five telecommunications companies in the country.

Problems in customer acquisition

The focus on customer acquisition in the rush to increase market penetration caused problems. It could not meet the expectations it raised about its free Internet promise or its service. The huge demand for its free Internet service created long customer queues. Some had to wait for several months for connection. Problems caused by too many people attempting to register at the same time meant that customers had to resort to the company's expensive premium-rated help line. Customer complaints about the difficulties of contacting the company mounted. This led to high customer attrition rates – around 20 per cent annually.

Improvements with CRM

Company Z is moving to a single customer management system. It has invested in creating a company-wide data warehouse to support personnel in managing customers. Improved CRM has helped cut the attrition rate significantly. A national approach to dealing with customer complaints was introduced, involving an e-mail process and e-care systems to deal efficiently with faults and to shorten delays for customers. Examples include shortening waiting times for Internet connections, and cutting call centre response times. Customer retention activity focuses on achieving revenue growth from existing customers and reducing acquisition costs for new customers. Even when basic prices were raised for its combined telephone and Internet service by 50 per cent and connection charges were applied to its previously free local calls, the company's research showed that these had not significantly affected customer loyalty. Most customers accepted the price increases as reasonable.

Strategic directions

Company Z improved customer access by making high-speed digital services and broadband media available on demand. It aggregated its entire range of products and services, simplified pricing structures, and moved to highly competitive rates supported by efficient delivery.

Accessibility for customers for new broadband content and
high-speed digital services.

Increase connectivity and reliability of provision for a whole
range of media and related services.

Company Z as the preferred choice for customers and as
the provider of integrated services for telephone, television,
mobile telephony and the Internet.

Figure 24.1   Company Z strategy

To sustain and enhance the customer experience, the company focused on delivery of
content. Its strategy is summarized in Figure 24.1.

BUILDING THE CRM STRATEGY

Certain key points arise from these case studies. Companies are not alike in their development or in their adoption of CRM practices. Often changes occur in their industries,
such as those from increased competition and the applications of new technologies, and
these lead to problems. The focus on building CRM practices has been a contributory
factor to improvement in the companies. Each company has dealt with its problems and
introduction of CRM practices in a different way and at a different rate. There is also the
realization by the management that customers are increasingly looking towards
improvements, not just in products bought, but also in satisfaction from their service
encounters with their suppliers. So there is no intended prescription for CRM in this
paper. Therefore, the points below show areas where the adoption of CRM could
enhance organizational practices.

Market orientation

There are always new opportunities to implement CRM-based approaches – witness the
growth in the shift from mass marketing to one to one marketing, renewed emphasis on
customer care and service, and changing work practices to reflect customer focus. In a
perfect world in which businesses embrace the marketing concept and customers are
satisfied, it is assumed that both parties will commit to strengthening their bonds. The

reality is that we live in an imperfect world. Different rates of development in economies and markets, in competitors' activities, and in lifestyle changes, plus fickleness in end-users' choices, will ultimately force changes in strategic directions for companies, creating gaps in competitive armour that can be exploited using CRM-based approaches.

Improve collaboration

Find new ways of collaborating with others to build strengths and contacts. From the company intranet to the global Internet, it is possible to draw upon the core of knowledge and expertise that exists across the company and its business partners (suppliers, distributors and so on).

People management and commitment

Human beings and not technologies are the most important assets. In applying the principles of strategy there is a need to rely on the knowledge, skills and expertise of company personnel. So companies need to develop good working environments and incentives for their personnel in order to keep good managers and their staff.

Knowledge acquisition and knowledge management

Knowledge is power, and getting people to share knowledge can be difficult. Standardization for IT protocols, buying systems and processes, and better use of internal communications systems can help to avoid duplication of efforts. Just as customers like the familiarity of brand names that encapsulate notions of quality, so they like the familiarity of company Web sites, ease of access and navigation on and around them.

Data proliferation and data management

The Internet provides cost-cutting opportunities combined with the potential of mass-customization to reach very large numbers of people. A CRM strategy relying on integration of different databases should aim to develop efficiencies in accessing and analysing data. The 'garbage in, garbage out' principle applies, so companies need to avoid being swamped by increasing amounts of information from databases. An efficient and standardized CRM system is necessary in order to provide the guidelines and practices for those involved in sorting out what is crucial and directly relevant when faced with a vast array of information from databases.

Efficiency and effectiveness

The CRM focus is not only on new and more cost-effective ways of keeping customers. There is a need to distinguish between efficiency in day-to-day operations and effectiveness in delivering applications to create benefits in the implementation of CRM strategies. There are compelling reasons for developing new ways of looking at CRM or new CRM business models to improve the customer experience dramatically. New media and channels of delivery can be found for business customers by reducing relationship marketing, transactional and logistical costs via new business applications. Customers also reap real gains from common practices in procurement, such as cheaper prices.

Speedy solutions

Customer satisfaction and company profits are often closely related to the speed of solving problems. A CRM strategy should use the analytical techniques of data mining. Data mining helps to identify trends, patterns and relationships of data, for example prediction of customer value.

Profitability

The revenues from implementing e-CRM systems must be greater than relationship management costs. There is therefore a need to examine closely two major groups of customers. The first consists of those buyers or customers who are relatively undemanding in their relationships with their suppliers for various reasons: for example, where trust has been built up over a number of years or where the immediate costs of switching suppliers are greater. The second consists of other types who are more demanding, requiring their suppliers to reduce prices while at the same time expecting continual innovations to sustain their own competitive positions. Both groups of buyer are essential to the generation of significant revenues for their suppliers. The art of CRM is to keep both groups and to retain their business. A modified CRM strategy to adapt to the needs of both groups is potentially more enriching than one strategy for all. It is important to identify such customers with the possibility of deselecting others who generate poor revenues, add high costs and take up a lot of time.

Organizations in the telecommunications sector must further address the revenue growth and cost reduction benefits to be gained from their chosen CRM strategy before implementing it. At the time of writing, this industry is feeling the fallout from deregulation, shortening product lifecycles and a huge amount of churn as the technological advances mean increased competition and the potential for switching (as discussed above). Figure 24.2 shows the potential benefits to be gained from a complete CRM solution that concentrates on not only the customer contact management aspect that is often the key driver for CRM, but the equally important back-end infrastructure that allows the enormous amounts of data collected to be manipulated and fed back into the system to increase knowledge of the customer. Figure 24.3 goes on to further break out the key areas of cost reduction, revenue growth and the building of a customer community, showing the potential areas of benefit for CRM in this fast-moving sector.

Finally, here are two real-life examples of how CRM can benefit a company in this sector. The first example is BT Cellnet, who have implemented a new complaints resolution system, and the second is Telecom Italia who have recently installed an enterprise data warehouse. These are two very different solutions, showing the importance of both back and front-end systems, and both have brought enormous benefits to the businesses. These case studies are public domain and have been written with the help of the companies involved.

PAPERLESS COMPLAINT RESOLUTION

When a complaint gets escalated to the highest level, the last thing you would expect is for all the paperwork relating to that complaint to be torn up and thrown away. That is

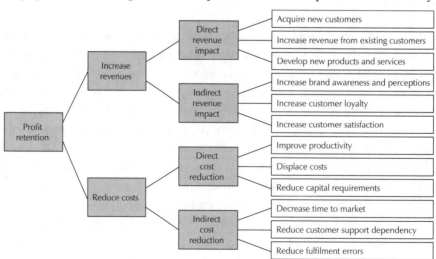

Figure 24.2　Focus of CRM

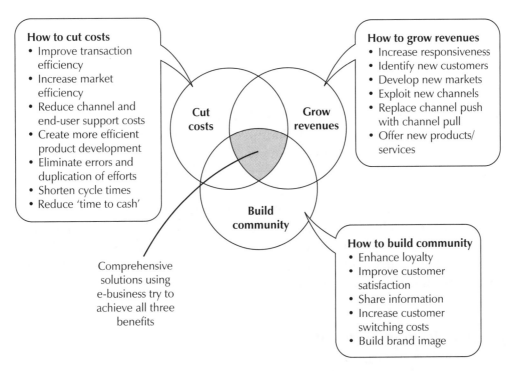

Figure 24.3 Addressing the right issues

exactly what happens at BT Cellnet (now O_2). Being adept at handling customer complaints is a laudable attribute. Being able to identify trends, relay those trends across the enterprise and effectively reduce the number of complaints is nothing short of idyllic. When BT Cellnet embarked upon the introduction of the CHARTER customer management system, they were reaching for just this idyll. All four of the market-leading customer management systems were considered before CHARTER, supplied by Swallow Information Systems, was selected. One of the key criteria that made it the system of choice was its integration capability with the BusinessObjects package. This ensured that the management team in the department was capable of trend analysis: a valuable resource in ultimately identifying the source of most complaints and the erosion of them by proactive reporting.

Through CHARTER, the company can now pull reports on various business segments – marketing, pricing, and so forth – and track any emerging trends. If a trend is identified that shows more complaints are emerging from a marketing activity, the complaint resolution team can pull a report indicating this trend and circulate it across the enterprise. While this in itself does not resolve the individual complaints, it does serve to reduce the creation of a new tranche of complaints from the same source.

E-complainers

BT Cellnet has implemented the new system across all of its complaint resolution teams, who have seen first hand the benefits that the system offers. When a complaint reaches an adviser in the department all paperwork is dispensed with. This action is not as drastic as it sounds. Before discarding all the paperwork it is scanned into the CHARTER system, effectively making the complaint electronic. The immediate benefit of a paperless environment is that all the salient information pertaining to any given client's communication is stored in one file on the computer. Letters, notes of conversations, copies of agreements, guarantees, receipts and insurance documents are all available in the same place at the same time. The confidence that this instils in the agent is beyond measure, but the productivity gains are easily measurable. 'Since we introduced CHARTER we have been able to increase the speed of complaint resolution and decrease the number of FTEs [full time employees] required to solve cases,' said Peter Henderson, Senior Complaint Resolution Manager.

Implementation investment

CHARTER cost BT Cellnet less than expected to install, but it does not work by itself. It needs capable operators, and to this end one of the favourable factors is its user-friendliness. Peter Henderson again:

> Originally a one-day training course for all operators was earmarked. But it is so simple to use that it would take around 35 minutes to become familiar with it. In fact, it would probably only take about 10 minutes to teach someone how to log a complaint. The 'wizard' facility ensures that all required fields are completed and gives on-screen instructions of the next stages.... Because we rely on the CHARTER systems integration with BusinessObjects® for the trend analysis and reporting methods, we make sure that we constantly check on the quality of the input. Our advisers are subject to a 32-point checklist (randomly carried out), which is designed to constantly drive forward quality controls. This gives us a constantly rolling measurement of the level of input, which in turn ensures that the trend analyses are accurate.

Return on investment

The company reached a return on investment within six months of full rollout of the system. This was measured in terms of increased functionality, an overhauling of the workload management, and savings in time for dealing with individual cases and the elimination of duplication:

> Because the system archives each and every case, we want the functionality to be able to 'flag' customers automatically on registration / re-registration. At the moment we have to ask our current version of CHARTER to do this for us, but upgrading to the new version, CHARTER Continuum™ will give us the ability to provide a more complete service to our customers. We will have a full history of their interactions with BT Cellnet and therefore will be able to avoid further conflict. The other benefit will be that we will more easily be able to identify serial complainers who believe that if they complain to the right agent at the right time, they will push the right buttons and get something to which they are not entitled.

The implementation of the system was not all plain sailing. The entire complaint handling processes had to be rewritten to accommodate the required new working practices and the new technology. The groundwork for this had to be carried out from an early stage. To avoid any internal issues a full and open account of the measures being taken had to be explained to everyone that the implementation would directly affect. Planning and training managed it well in advance of the changes taking place. This led to a virtually seamless integration of the new software into the working environment. Team motivation was made easy by the functionality and features of CHARTER. The new technology 'sold itself' to the team by clearly defined benefits being obvious to them – especially when rated against the existing workflow management. Job satisfaction increased because case management was made simpler. The team now feels that the information that it gleans from complaints is valuable data being made available enterprise-wide, shaping decision making in various disparate departments.

Conclusion

The introduction of the automated complaint resolution system has led to an improved complaint handling strategy. It has allowed reporting and feedback to drive through improvements in problem areas on an enterprise-wide basis. It has enabled a faster customer resolution, making the department capable of resolving a greater number of complaints. Choosing the right system has ensured easy expansion and effective use of the technology across other sites and areas of BT Cellnet.

TELECOM ITALIA

Background

The Telecom Italia Group (a US $83 billion company) is the world's fourth largest telecomms group in terms of turnover. The group's core businesses include Telecom Italia (operating parent company, offering fixed telephony products), Telecom Italia Mobile (mobility telephony services), Telespazio (satellite telecommunications), Stet International (international finance company), and Telemedia International or TMI (multinational provider of added value Internet services). A host of other Telecom Italia Group companies delivers such services as cable, satellite pay-per-view digital tele-vision, IT services, networking and installation, frontier technologies and transmission networks. Telecom Italia also is a stakeholder in a number of international telecommunications companies, such as Telecom Argentina and Tele Centro Sul.

Italians like to stay in touch. Colourful public telephones juxtapose ancient land-marks. Cellphones accessorize communicators of all ages. Pagers deliver signals day and night, and Internet connections are now as plentiful as Renaissance art.

To keep pace with this continually evolving telecommunications environment, Telecom Italia needed to understand its customers' behaviours. Today, thanks to a new IBM business intelligence solution, the company's marketing, sales and customer service departments have the actionable information needed to address age-old industry problems such as customer loyalty and competition. The bottom line? The decision to implement the new technology is proving to be a good call.

Insight and communication

Since deregulation, an incredible number of competitors – providers of telephone service as well as suppliers of Internet capabilities – vie for Italian customers' attention. Despite the fact that the Telecom Italia data warehouse has been live only for a matter of months, the company's project team has begun already to use insight generated from the system to combat the ever-increasing field of competition.

Telecom Italia's team plans to continue to gain valuable knowledge to help in the sales, customer care, marketing, special promotions and electronic-commerce areas. What is more, the company will analyse data to gain the insight necessary to increase customer retention, encourage cross-selling, curb customer attrition and build customer loyalty. Telecom's team will study customer behaviour, service types, changes in service, effec-tiveness of promotions and a host of other factors that impact overall customer satis-faction and value.

'Having an in-depth understanding of how our customers use the products and services we offer will help us build very targeted customer loyalty programs,' says

Stefano Trisolini, director of data management/data warehousing. He continues, 'We'll be able to find out about what types of competitor offers entice our good customers to defect and then put plans in place to counter these promotions. It's impossible to place a value on this capability – in today's competitive market, it's essential to have a weapon like this one.'

Trisolini does not expect results overnight. Ultimately, he feels that having actionable information will enable Telecom to measure such things as how much additional revenue specific promotions net the company, or which products and customers are more profitable than others. 'We intend to learn a lot about how to run effective discount campaigns and how to bundle products while retaining customer profitability,' explains Trisolini. He adds, 'Gaining such a competitive advantage is only possible through the use of data warehouses.'

The solution also will help Telecom Italia's team determine specifics about customer service: for example, key facts such as the number of times one customer calls for assistance on the same problem. By determining patterns, changes may be put in place to stop recurring problems.

The data warehouse contains a variety of data about Telecom Italia: products and services, possible configurations of products and services, contracts and usage of 25 million customers. This information helps Trisolini and his team segment customers according to behaviour. Analysing customer segments provides valuable actionable information about when, how, why, how much, where and how often customers interact with their products and services of choice. 'By knowing more about how customers behave, we can determine what they want,' Trisolini contends. 'Armed with insight, we can offer them the right products and services at the most appropriate point in our business relationship.' He adds, 'By providing data-mining capabilities to analysis experts and to a broader base of business users, we are enabling more people in our organization to be customer-centric.'

Constructing the warehouse took six months. Today, the Enterprise Data Warehouse collects data from four data centres; however, Telecom Italia is developing further warehouse content to support customer profiling. It is expected that the warehouse eventually will hold between five and ten terabytes of data. There may be as many as 10,000 people from Telecom Italia and its subsidiary companies who ultimately rely on the warehouse for information.

A key focus for the Telecom Italia team is now CRM. Sales and marketing teams will work to better understand details about the behaviours of the telecom customer base. The company also plans to start a CRM project with IBM Intelligent Miner for Data, a key data mining tool within the solution. 'The plan is to continually develop and refine our capabilities in customer profiling, data mining and general business intelligence,' notes Trisolini. He concludes, 'We are very focused on the benefits business intelligence technology brings us and on becoming more in tune with our customers.'

OVERALL CONCLUSION

This chapter has investigated the general situation facing telecommunications companies as they develop their CRM approach. It shows that because of the sheer size of their operations, in terms of number of customers and complexity of relationships, the handling of the data arising from customer contact is the key to success in deploying CRM.

NOTE

[1] Acknowledgement is given to Ranhua Chen for preliminary research in case material while at Leicester Business School.

25

Business-to-business CRM

Genevieve Findlay, Mark Cerasale and Merlin Stone

INTRODUCTION

In this chapter we discuss just a few of the considerations involved in implementing customer relations management (CRM) in a global business-to-business (B2B) market. CRM in wholesale or B2B business markets is quite different from CRM in consumer or retail markets. In retail markets, companies must consider the interaction with a large number of consumers. Segmentation is the key to marketing decision making and implementation, particularly in any area where establishing customer profitability is important. In wholesale, the dynamics are somewhat different: understanding customers (usually a smaller number of them) is essential, but supply chain management and integration between suppliers and third parties are often intimately connected with CRM.

This chapter examines the changing market context of B2B companies. It then examines the role of the customer in the distribution supply chain, illustrating the complexity often prevalent in B2B CRM. It then examines common problems faced by B2B companies and how CRM techniques can be used to solve them. Finally this chapter considers how best to measure the return on investment for CRM across the supply chain, and different approaches to measuring CRM performance in this complex environment.

B2B MARKET CONTEXT

During the 1990s most companies were able to apply manufacturing techniques such as just in time to squeeze excess fat from their operations. At the same time, attention turned to operational efficiency in design, engineering and enterprise resource planning (ERP). This led to the introduction of new organizational models, new IT systems and business process re-engineering. However, there is still room to use such approaches to achieve further improvement in the manufacturing and service supply chain.

Since the late 1990s, most B2B companies have committed significant resources to transforming the one piece of the value chain that had remained relatively untouched for several decades: sales and service relationships with customers. In most B2B markets, it is well understood that CRM performance is a key differentiator, increasing customer loyalty and improving long-term business performance. To exploit CRM based opportunities fully, collaboration is required with suppliers, customers and third parties and between internal business divisions. This is challenging for many organizations. Integrated end-to-end management, supported by robust processes and systems and well defined controls, is becoming increasingly important, as many markets have moved from supply push to demand pull.

In the late 1990s many companies invested in CRM software and CRM-focused business transformation initiatives. When companies came under economic pressure, there was a strong focus on short-term return on investment (ROI), leading to the cutting back of initiatives. Despite this, the drive to improve CRM performance continues in most B2B markets.

The customer in B2B CRM

In B2B markets, the customer is typically a representative of the immediate buying organization. However, this is changing as many global suppliers try to exert further control and influence along the value chain. Thus, in the European automotive industry, vehicle manufacturers face legislation that threatens to reduce the control they have over retail distributors. As a result, many are increasing their CRM spend, in an attempt to build a direct relationship with final consumers. Technology such as mobile phones, Web sites, kiosks and multi-channel devices is enabling this transformation. The need for greater value chain integration has led many organizations to view their suppliers and business partners as customers. Indeed, the prevalence of supply chain management (SCM) and partner relationship management (PRM) application software now available reflects this.

A new type of customer

In many B2B marketplaces the decision maker is changing. As a result, many suppliers have relationships with their customers at many levels of seniority and in many different business functions. In the IT industry, IT expenditure was controlled by IT and finance managers. As technology has become pervasive at work and home, it is has moved from being an efficiency enabler to a key factor in business performance improvement. Line of-business executives often make buying decisions. They need a business solution to their business challenge. So many B2B suppliers now focus on developing and sustaining relationships with this new breed of 'integrated business solution' customers. They have developed sophisticated techniques for consultative marketing and selling.

Consultative marketing

The aim of consultative marketing is to target key decision makers and influencers and promote the supplier to them as a value-added solution provider. Consultative marketing also supports the creation and communication of thought leadership and value-added content through which the relationship is sustained and developed.

Consultative solution selling

Consultative solution selling focuses not just on the intrinsic value of products and services but on ensuring delivery of value. This requires understanding the customer's business challenges and helping to shape the solution to meet the customer's need. Solution selling also involves being able to articulate the supplier's capabilities and then assessing whether the solution can be provided profitably, before developing it in partnership with the customer and perhaps other relevant parties.

EFFECTIVE ACCOUNT MANAGEMENT, POSSIBLY GLOBAL IN SCALE

The increasing need to anticipate customer requirements and serve customers more effectively on a global scale requires large B2B companies to further develop their customer management capabilities. Technology clearly plays a key role in the sharing of information and orchestrated targeting of accounts, but equally important are:

▌ organization of the ownership of accounts;
▌ refined and clearly understood customer management processes;
▌ an understanding of the profitability of accounts;
▌ an effective incentives scheme.

Organization of the ownership of accounts

In a company that spans geographies and multiple divisions, there is often ambiguity in account ownership. Where there is ambiguity there is confusion, and frequently the customer will be on the receiving end of a seemingly disorganized service, leading to frustration and dissatisfaction on both sides. There needs to be clear coordination of responsibilities for managing accounts. Where such an exercise has been undertaken we have seen the following benefits:

- A common language has been established to categorize different account types and the roles and responsibilities of account owners, thus leading to less internal and external confusion.
- More effective account planning and execution.
- Customer requirements can be forecast and actively provided for.
- Improved focus on target and key clients, leading to higher revenue per account manager.
- Increased opportunities for cross-selling (leading to increased sales per customer).
- Improved management of account management performance, improving the productivity of account managers.
- Improved understanding of account management competencies, ensuring that account managers are more effective, leading to greater customer satisfaction, improved retention rates and increased conversion rates for new business.

Refined and clearly understood customer management processes

Typically, large companies have several different approaches, in product divisions and countries in which they operate, to planning and monitoring account development. Alignment to a common approach assists the development of account strategy and management review, particularly for ensuring continuing contact management across divisions. Processes that must be clearly defined, communicated and implemented across the organization include:

- **Customer profiling and understanding.** This equips customer teams to maximize development opportunities with each customer, using a comprehensive profile for each individual customer. A common profile improves sharing of information amongst account teams and ensures that there is a common view of issues and macro trends affecting the future direction of the organization.
- **Account planning and monitoring.** This uses customer profile information to develop and detail a business plan, including milestones, responsibilities and key

performance indicators. Measurement information is shared across the organization and used in profiling and in refining plans.

- **Relationship and contact management.** This focuses on identification, development and tracking of relationships with customer executives. Typical activities include development of an organization map of the customer, 'pain sheets' and contact planning. The process also incorporates tracking of customer meetings and contacts, to ensure a coordinated approach to managing customers.
- **Opportunity management and execution (including pipeline management and qualification).** This focuses on the different stages any sale should go through (however large or small). Having a common approach to opportunity management provides greater transparency of opportunities for senior management and instils appropriate sales disciplines in account managers.
- **Sales management and leadership.** This focuses on how executive management tracks and reviews account opportunities during the opportunity management process. It covers mechanisms for reviewing the pipeline, and escalating opportunities up the management chain.
- **Customer satisfaction tracking.** This focuses on how customer satisfaction is measured and how it is supported in terms of account management and operational performance. The aim is to strengthen the relationship with customers by identifying and addressing any issues a customer has. It instils a focus on customer satisfaction as a metric.

An understanding of the profitability of accounts

Many companies are now able to report this, at least on an estimated basis. Having this information:

- provides a clear understanding of which customers are high or low-value and which must be retained;
- enables fast decision making, a prerequisite for global account management;
- provides better information to assist in commercial negotiations with customers;
- increases clarity on 'cost of sale' and 'cost to serve' issues;
- highlights differences in profit margin across geographies for the same account;
- highlights the economic value of certain business locations/routes;
- assists in evaluating economic value of particular products or services;
- provides an input to the personal performance measurement of account managers and teams.

An effective incentives scheme

Service differentiation will increasingly be in the selling of integrated solutions, enabling the deepening of the relationship with the customer and a move away from the provision of a commodity service. Some customers demand that their supply chain partners operate globally in terms of both operations coverage and relationship management. This means that account teams must be able to operate across country borders in the provision of integrated solutions. To facilitate the move towards a more collaborative environment, it is very important that customer-facing staff are given the correct incentives to respond to customer requirements at a global level. If the remuneration structure does not sufficiently reward account teams, business outside their domiciled country or division might not be developed, and the selling of integrated solutions at a regional or country/local level will not be promoted. Incentives schemes need to be structured so as to engender the following:

- encourage integrated solution selling;
- promote the identification of opportunities for other areas of the company (eg other products/services and in other geographies);
- support the global account management roles and encourage account managers to act in a way which is consistent with the desired roles and responsibilities as described in the 'ownership' section above.

CUSTOMERS: THE FINAL LINK IN THE SUPPLY CHAIN

Processing a single B2B order can cost suppliers US $100 or more, and sometimes thousands of dollars. Most of the cost is because of the number of different people who are involved in the order before fulfilment. ERP systems were widely adopted in the late 1990s by companies eager to streamline and automate their operations. Since then they have become the core of many corporate technology initiatives. ERP systems were implemented for various reasons, ranging from the reduction of inventory levels to increasing process efficiencies in the supply chain and integrating core business systems.

In much the same way that many B2C organizations have taken to aligning their business processes with CRM systems, ERP systems have frequently dictated B2B corporate procedures. This is because ERP products offer easier information sharing between different departments, such as purchasing, operations or manufacturing, finance and human resources. ERP automated key corporate functions, making general ledger systems and warehouses brimming with filing cabinets full of purchase orders a thing of the past. Key business processes that are automated include:

- inventory management;
- production forecasting;
- distribution and logistics management;
- finance;
- HR processes.

ERP systems allow companies to automate these and other functions and also to link them together. This bringing together of disparate systems and processes enables integrated operations across the enterprise; reason enough in itself for implementation of ERP. Sales teams can access a single system to check inventory, a purchasing agent can look up a supplier's history and product managers can track defects in their products reported by the field service operation. The links between ERP, supply chain management and CRM are stronger than ever. Better knowledge of the customer means better understanding of how to build the relationship with that customer. For instance, a company's accounts receivable staff might choose not to open collections on past-due customers who have in-process trouble tickets. Likewise, CRM business users can use accounting and supply chain information to decide how to treat customers who do not meet provisioning deadlines.

ERP vendors (such as PeopleSoft and SAP) have recognized the connections between tighter, more integrated operations and business customer satisfaction and have released CRM modules that tie their core products, rendering the customer a key link in the supply chain. Figure 25.1 shows the broad range of integrated logistics capabilities that a distribution company needs to be able to deliver in order to assist their customers in optimizing the potential of the supply chain.

Throughout the supply chain, companies are expected to provide their customers, suppliers and partners with more information than ever before. To do that, they need the best databases, holding accurate and current data, and the applications and processes necessary to deliver that data (not to mention an organizational willingness to share data with suppliers and customers). The introduction of the Web as a channel has meant that key processes such as ordering, fulfilment, inventory management, and distribution all have to run at Web speed. The challenge of streamlining the supply chain is compounded by this need for speed. Data is also required internally in order to be able to anticipate demands and work with third parties to realign focus accordingly.

One of the main reasons for the growing requirements for end-to-end integration, better and more visible information, and greater speed of response is the need for some companies to act globally. Global businesses expect a global service, while maintaining the high standards they have become accustomed to at a local level. One of the main aims of B2B companies that operate globally is to anticipate customer demand at a global level while acting upon it locally.

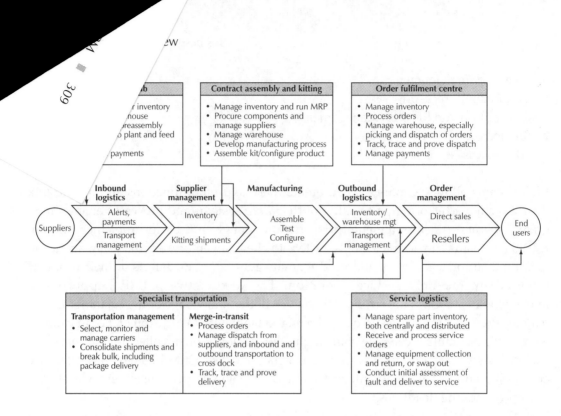

Figure 25.1 The intellectual and systems content required to run a modern supply chain

MEASUREMENT AND CRM METRICS IN B2B

Until now measurement of CRM performance in B2B has been largely determined from a supplier perspective, predominantly revenue oriented: that is, reflecting not what is valued by the customer but rather what is important to the supplier. Despite this, customer satisfaction was measured in B2B companies long before CRM became the buzzword in B2B. Particularly in key account management, the value of customer relationships and loyalty have been long recognized, although it had been very ad hoc until recent years. In most cases, B2B CRM was personalized: account managers had to manage relationships effectively in order to achieve their targets. Today we are seeing that awareness and responsibility at an enterprise level.

The main metrics for key account managers until now have been:

▨ quarter-end revenue;
▨ year-end revenue;
▨ customer satisfaction (mainly based on transactions: whether the goods were delivered on time, and so on).

We are seeing a move towards more appropriate relationship oriented measurement, measuring for example how many senior executives have been contacted in a given time period. Inevitably, revenue metrics (which are supplier oriented) will remain, although they will become more relevant to the customer as risk–reward and profit sharing arrangements become more pervasive. That is to say, the metrics will reflect supplier and customer shareholder value.

The 360-degree feedback approach, in which customers give feedback to their suppliers about the quality of the latter's staff, has been adopted in many global organizations, and appears to be a step in the right direction in terms of understanding the CRM performance of key individuals. The problem here is measurement: few supplier organizations are willing to reward their representatives for anything other than revenue. What is needed is a key set of human relationship metrics for CRM in B2B. In the meantime, a common approach is to ask customers at the beginning of a time period what they value and then measure CRM performance against this. Indeed this is IBM's approach on a project-by-project basis with the pre-consulting engagement 'conditions of satisfaction' assessment, in which IBM asks its customers what five things it needs to do to achieve customer satisfaction on the project.

CONCLUSIONS

The world of B2B marketing changed irrevocably with the advent of ERP. Today, the key to improving CRM in B2B is integration with ERP systems. While ERP systems are usually characterized by use of well-established metrics, this is not so for CRM in B2B. Throughout this book, many aspects of CRM measurement are discussed. Our view is that a necessary condition for the success of B2B CRM is the adoption of metrics that make sense to customers and to staff, and support of these metrics by appropriate incentives.

Part 4

Channels and media

26

Multi-channel customer management

Matt Hobbs, Mahnaz Khaleeli and Merlin Stone

CHANGING TIMES, CHANGING CHANNELS

It all used to be so simple: separate channel managers, separate segments targeted by separate channels, products aligned by channel, customers asked to deal with specific channels, measures of effectiveness purely on business transacted per channel. However, things have changed. Many companies are in a transition in channel management, typically covering the following:

- They are moving away from channels dedicated to restricted tasks and not communicating with each other, but are not certain how far to move towards channels which all work with the same data and to the same objectives.
- They have seen some of the disadvantages of having different and possibly incompatible technology platforms for each channel, but are not certain of the benefits of moving to a single platform.
- They have been through the process of setting up dot.coms as separate Web channels.
- These often had their own objectives, management, staff and systems, usually experienced escalating costs, provided a customer experience which was very different from that of other channels, and in some cases created brand damage and increased customer churn.

They are moving towards the world of multi-channel integration: whatever that is! It is the purpose of this chapter to investigate the meaning of multi-channel customer management, and its benefits and challenges. For example, Forrester reports that 63 per cent of retailers and travel suppliers expect to use three or more channels by 2003.[1] Furthermore, 37 per cent of European consumers are currently using the Internet channel to research products, with 85 per cent of this group buying offline the product they identified online.[2]

The purpose of this chapter is to define multi-channel customer management and to investigate the opportunities and problems created by multi-channel customer management, and to help companies determine what their strategies and tactics in this area are. It does not provide a complete recipe for multi-channel management, as we do not believe that this can be done in just one chapter. A checklist of questions to help companies examining this area is provided at the end of the chapter.

DEFINITION OF MULTI-CHANNEL CUSTOMER MANAGEMENT

In this chapter, we use a broad definition of the term, as follows:

> Multi-channel customer management is the use of more than one channel or medium to manage customers in a way that is consistent and coordinated across all the channels or media used.

Note that we do not say 'the same way', as different channels may be best used for different tasks. For example, in a complex, technical, business-to-business environment, a salesperson might be best for explaining the product, meeting objections and dealing with queries, and setting up initial contacts, while the Web or call centre might be used for reordering or checking progress with delivery. Also, it might be that channels are used in a differentiated manner, for example, if you want to buy tickets for last minute cancellations by other customers (anything from flights to equipment orders), you are referred to an auction Web site, as other channels cannot support this kind of interaction cost-effectively.

Note too that for the purposes of this chapter we include both distribution channels (the mechanism by which products or services reach customers from suppliers, including transfer of title) and communication channels (the mechanism by which customers and suppliers communicate with each other before, during and after distribution channels do their work).

A multi-channel strategy is one that provides numerous customer touch points – the points at which products and services are purchased or serviced – across several distribution channels, such as:

▌ direct channels, for example, telephone, Internet, mobile telephone (voice, SMS and eventually WAP) and interactive television (iTV);
▌ counter and kiosk service in branch networks or retail outlets;
▌ partnerships and alliances;
▌ sales force;
▌ service force.

In some cases, these may be supported by broadcast media, in which the customer is not necessarily identified, for example, television, radio, press and some Web applications.

WHY MULTI-CHANNEL CUSTOMER MANAGEMENT IS IMPORTANT NOW

There are two main reasons for this: first, developments in new channel technology: the increasing reliability and speed of storage and telecommunications technology, convergence of voice, video and data; and second, customer requirements and expectations: some (not all) customers expect technology and processes to be used to manage them more consistently across channels.

Although it is now easier to ensure that every channel dealing directly with a given customer has the latest data on the state of interaction between supplier and customer, and follows related, connected processes, this is not without cost or without technical problems. In particular, it should be noted that the companies for whom it is suggested that multi-channel customer management will yield the most benefits are those for whom achieving it is most problematic. They have the largest customer bases, the most complex lines, and the longest history of systems development, with many business-critical systems that support the process of customer management being quite old. This applies, for example, to many companies in financial services, logistics and manufacturing companies.

THE BENEFITS

However, the benefits are numerous. These include ones that work through customers, ones that work for customers and ones that work through efficiency, as follows:

Benefits that work through customers

▌ The identification and capture of opportunities for increasing value per customer.

▓ Giving customers increased convenience and an improved experience, reducing customer churn rates and increasing their motivation to buy more from the supplier.
▓ The ability to leverage an established brand, creating positive impacts on brand perception and mitigating the risk of brand damage, increasing the incentive for customers to stay and buy more.

Efficiency benefits

▓ Increased efficiency through the sharing of processes, technology and information.
▓ Increased organizational flexibility.
▓ Increased efficiency in dealing with business partners, so they can reduce their costs.
▓ Increased efficiency in exploiting customer data to identify customer needs, possibly indicating new paths for growth.

Benefits for customers

▓ Increased choice in the way they can interact.
▓ The ability to switch easily between the various channels, when it suits them and wherever they want to, depending on their preference and the type of interaction, whether it be the exploration or purchase of a product or service.

For the supplier, channel integration helps the sharing of customer data across channels to create a more complete customer profile helping to maximize cross-selling opportunities.

THE CHALLENGES

Multi-channel integration does not come without its challenges. Problems experienced by companies include:

▓ Heavy investments in unconvincing multi-channel strategies and technologies that result in a poor return on investment (ROI).
▓ Problems in bringing together and standardizing data about customers or resulting from interactions with them.
▓ Problems unifying different systems which may have very different data models.
▓ Difficulties in reducing or abolishing organizational boundaries.

For example, a recent survey of 50 retailers in the United States revealed that 48 per cent had learned nothing about their cross-channel customers and the number one problem they faced was their inability to recognize known customers across all touch points.[3] Research to identify how far financial institutions have moved towards integrating customer touch points was conducted by Forrester.[4] It interviewed 50 IT executives at banks, brokerages, and insurance firms and found that for 52 per cent of the interviewees, channel integration projects were only just commencing, and for 54 per cent, less than half their products are integrated across channels.

Examples of organizations that have already gone some way towards integrating their channels include Allstate, Gateway and E*Trade; all of whom have invested hundreds of millions of dollars to build and integrate field, phone and Internet sales and service.

SEVEN FACTORS DRIVING CHANGE

Seven factors are causing companies to focus on multi-channel management, as follows:

1. Customer demand.
2. Channel costs.
3. Strategic competitive advantage and differentiation.
4. Allowing customers to manage relationships.
5. Convergence of channel roles.
6. Increased variety in customers' channel use patterns.
7. Regulatory pressure.

Customer demand

Customers' desire for convenience has partly fuelled the increasing requirement for multi-channel integration. Increased customer expectations translate to a demand for 24/7 high-speed access and choice in how they interact with a company. Customers often have strong preferences for using a specific channel for particular kinds of interaction: for example, they might use the in-store channel to commit to a buying decision, while using the often more convenient online channel for exploring options. Forrester research identified that 46 per cent of online buyers research online to purchase offline, while 27 per cent research offline to buy online, and 17 per cent do both.[5] The focus should be on not providing all things in all channels, but instead providing the expected level of service for the target user group of that channel.

Channel costs

Maintaining channels (including marketing, advertising and managing the channels themselves) can typically account for around 40 per cent of a company's costs. Channels tend to be managed and maintained in silos with multiple infrastructures, management teams, technology and possibly different marketing strategies. However, the potential sharing and reuse of people, process and technology that can be achieved through an integrated channel strategy can help improve an organization's channel cost structure. Furthermore, the mapping of high-value customer usage and preferences can help identify channel areas of over-investment and channels that are not providing their optimum ROI, and consequently identify channels that require some form of disinvestments and asset reallocation.

Strategic competitive advantage and differentiation

Products can be copied within days (H&M, the fashion retailer, can copy a design from the catwalk and get it on the high street within 72 hours). Pricing can be undercut within minutes. Apart from branding, multi-channel management is one of the few customer-facing differentiators that can deliver true sustainable competitive advantage.

Allowing customers to manage relationships

Badly executed CRM (as sadly many CRM implementations are) can result in the organization trying to control customers almost against their will through specific channels at specific times in the buying cycle. Customers can end up being made to feel like cattle being herded. Customer satisfaction and sales plummet. The term 'customer-managed relationships' (CMR) recognizes the possibility of the customer being in control (haven't they always wanted to be?) and the idea that it is the supplier's job to nurture and service the relationship.

Convergence of channel roles

Traditionally channels were usually silos, with most, if not all, of the functions required in the customer buying cycle being fulfilled through one channel. Now in many companies, several channels are used during each customer buying cycle, and they need to be designed, maintained and measured appropriately.

Increased variety in customers' channel use patterns

Those who synchronize their distribution channels will preserve or gain market share. Research has shown that multi-channel shoppers in the financial services and retail sectors represent an increasingly large proportion of the attractive buying population. Furthermore, in the retail banking sector, multi-channel customers can be 25 to 50 per cent more profitable than those using one channel, while retail shoppers who use multi-channel purchasing spend two to four times more than those who purchase through a single channel. This is reinforced by the Boston Consulting Group whose research revealed that European retailers who have an offline presence and manage an integrated Internet channel enjoy a disproportionate market-share, and online satisfied customers spend 71 per cent more and transact two and a half times more than dissatisfied ones.[6] Providing the target high-value multi-channel customer segment with increased convenience through integrated channel management therefore not only encourages customer lock-on and brand loyalty, but results in improved customer lifetime value.

Regulatory pressure

In some sectors (for instance, financial services, public sector), government has a strong interest in the cost-effectiveness and quality of channel use, particularly where high channel costs lead to customers apparently getting poor value or even to customers being excluded or disenfranchised.

DETERMINING CHANNEL FUNCTIONALITY

Careful thought needs to be paid to the use of each channel in multi-channel programmes: 'one channel fits all' is not the case anymore. Car buyers no longer just visit their local dealer, and television buyers no longer just go down to their local electrical store. Research shows that many customers use multiple channels throughout the buying cycle; some channels are used to research while others are used to purchase or service.

If a company decides to adopt a multi-channel strategy, it must consider whether all its channels should offer the same range of products and services, and whether all channels should support all functionality areas. If necessary, one channel can perform all three functions, online retailers or bricks and mortar retail outlets, for example. It is essential to define the role of the various channels and how they interact. This helps identify and clarify the target customer usage and preferences.

CUSTOMER EXPERIENCE MUST BE THE START POINT

Customer experience should be the starting point for defining required channel functionality. Here are some suggestions as to how to build on it.

Experiment with scenario planning

It is vital to understand customers' channel preferences and usage. Customers not only want to buy, but may also need information and advisory tools. So scenario planning can be used to understand which channels customers want to use for each part of the interaction process. Customer scenario planning is a powerful tool. It helps at all stages, from articulating the vision, determining processes and selecting technology. Thus, for expensive products customers may prefer to pre-shop online and then visit the store to look at the product and buy. For example, Charles Schwab, the financial services company, not only provides online, phone and in-person trading but also actionable information and advice through their online Learning Centre investment courses, online Portfolio Consultation and offline interactions.

Consistency

Suppliers should plan for consistency of their brand, customer information and the customer experience across different channels. Scenario planning is also useful here. Channel synchronization may be used to deliver a consistent customer experience. Consumers can become frustrated when suppliers' online channels only sell a selection of their offline products or services, or altogether different products or services. However, many suppliers currently offer either the same or fewer product categories online as in other channels, and 58 per cent say that their sites offer a narrower assortment within those categories.[7] However, there might be very sound commercial reasons for this: for example, delivery costs and risk of customers making poor choices, leading to high returns ratios. We suggest that to improve consistency in the product/services offering, suppliers should stage online product roll-outs, first focusing on depth in their core product/services categories, then add breadth through new complementary products, and finally, once the depth and breadth of products online reach critical mass, suppliers should introduce not-so-obvious categories and services both online and offline. Alternatively, the online and offline channels should be clearly positioned as different.

Consistency in customer service and promotions

Services and promotions can be integrated across channels. Companies can use various strategies to achieve this: merge mailing lists, to better target e-mail and catalogue promotions; launch cross-channel loyalty programmes to increase customer retention; reward customers for whichever channel they complete their transaction within; and use of bricks and mortar stores to provide local services to improve customer convenience for online shoppers. Examples of the latter include accepting returns in-store from online shoppers, and offering in-store pick-up to get online shoppers to favour them.[8] Where companies fail to integrate services and promotions across channels, this will shift the balance of business elsewhere, as customers' expectations are not met.

Pricing

In making the transition from single channel to multi-channel, companies face the challenge of pricing issues: that is, can they charge different prices to their customers for the same product online and offline? Many believe that different prices for the same product from the same company are not feasible; customers expect to be charged the same price whether purchasing online or offline, whether or not it is more cost-effective for a suppliers to sell online. The argument of suppliers is that a universal pricing strategy is not realistic, as offline customers must inevitably pay a premium for the added satisfaction of the in-store shopping experience.[9]

Research has been conducted into pricing efficiency between online branches of multi-channel retailers and their Internet pure-play counterparts, to establish whether online pricing efficiency will weaken because of the presence of multi-channel retailers. In the DVD market, online branches of multi-channel DVD retailers sell at higher prices than their online-only rivals, while in the car market online consumers paid slightly less than offline consumers. Therefore, in developing their channel strategy, companies must give consideration to the very real consumer pricing expectations: consumers expect prices to be competitive, whichever Web site they purchase from, regardless of whether the site is a pure Internet operation or an online channel as part of a wider multi-channel operation.

OVERCOMING TECHNOLOGY COMPLEXITY

Technology is not the be-all and end-all, but it is key. Implementation of IT packages for multi-channel integration projects can not only mitigate risk but also enforce best practice. Forrester asked 50 financial services organizations what technologies they were using for channel integration. Most said that they relied on 'off the shelf' tools from 36 different vendors and consultants, with IBM's technology leading with 32 per cent of this vote.[10] An example of this is Cahoot, the online bank owned by Abbey National.

The aim is to implement an integration solution that will reduce the need to build custom interfaces and speed up application integration and deployment. Organizations need to employ technologies that connect customer-facing systems by uniting application and integration servers, as well as embed process tools to codify and manage business processes. Technology is key to implementing an integrated channel strategy, but channel innovators may find packages are not sufficiently mature to meet their needs. The 'one application fits all' approach might not be the best strategy. An organization might have to use a mix of available tools to address particular needs, using best of breed by channel and using efficient systems integration to work with channels that have established systems.

Technology can hinder a channel integration programme. No technologies are capable of everything. It is essential to involve the technical team early on, and pay careful attention to the parameters of selected technology, to avoid costly redesign of processes. However, do not allow the technology totally to dictate the customer experience.

ORGANIZATIONAL ISSUES

Multi-channel integration requires a new organizational model: one that adapts people, processes and technology to meet this coordinated approach to channel management. Redefining the organization, and processes and technology that support it, to meet the multi-channel challenge, requires strong support of the CEO and his or her management team. They need a clear vision of how channel integration will generate business value for the organization and where the main changes need to be in the organization. Decisions will need to be taken on the size of team and skills to ensure the necessary resources and flexibility. Employees must have the right skills to understand increasingly sophisticated customers, analyse customer preferences, and create value from these customer relationships, while organizations must train their employees to develop the right skills. Organizational processes must be redefined to overcome organizational barriers, reduce operational costs, increase efficiency and improve the cross-channel customer's experience.

Organizational structures can be a barrier to multi-channel integration when a company is product or function-focused rather than customer-focused, so organizations need to consider whether to establish a separate company to exploit a new channel. This may be suitable where a single-channel strategy is appropriate to one or more customer segments, but a hybrid organizational strategy might be appropriate to meet the different channel needs of the company's target customer groups.

While developing a new organizational model for multi-channel integration, organizations should consider cross-channel opportunities generated through channel cooperation: 'Retailer-manufacturer relationships based on shared data, technology, and investments ... to create coordinated efforts that leverage discrete assets to better focus on the customer'.[11] Thus, research showed that online cooperation of retailers with their manufacturers could enhance sales through referrals. Fifty per cent of retailers and manufactures surveyed by Forrester said that their online sales increased by collaborating, for some by as much as 25 per cent. While online cooperation between retailers and manufacturers allows channel-hopping Internet customers a fuller product selection, it also minimizes channel conflict between retailers and manufacturers. Both the manufacturer and the retailer benefit, as they give each other the opportunity to increase online and offline sales by providing each other with customer referrals. 'Manufacturers will close US $50 billion in online sales ... but influence US $235 billion in other sales. The power of manufacturers online lies in their ability to affect retailers' sales, both online and offline. Consumers will take what they've learned while visiting manufacturer sites and spend almost US $90 billion online and US $147 billion in brick and mortar stores and catalogues.'[12]

MEASUREMENT

An organization is unlikely to get it right first time, so it is vital to measure, monitor and review your channel integration programme. Financial measures are important, but are a blunt instrument in a multi-channel world where not all channels are used to fulfil or 'close the deal'. Instead a balanced scorecard approach is needed, in which a mixture of relevant strategic and operational measures are applied. These include customer-focused measures, innovation and learning measures and process measures, all of which drive the financial and value measures. Profit rather than sales targeting should be used: sales targeting focuses on promoting volume at the expense of profits and the quality of the customer base, while profit targeting focuses on contribution rather than volume, and provides a basis for prioritizing multi-channel offers.

Consideration should be given to how employees are measured. Are Web and call centre staff going to cooperate or compete if they are given independent targets? Employees should be measured on customer profitability (present or ideally estimated future), as opposed to rewards being tied to a particular channel, as this can lead to focus on maximizing returns from that channel. Bricks and mortar employees are unlikely to divert customers to a low-cost Web channel if this reduces their bonus; so single-channel metrics should be replaced with cross-channel metrics. This may include crediting one channel for purchases through another channel, or rewarding different customer service representatives for their shared involvement in resolving a customer inquiry.

THE ECONOMICS OF MULTI-CHANNEL INTEGRATION

Managing channels separately might not damage customer relationships but also increase costs unnecessarily. The costs of running separate order-tracking and customer service operations, operating multiple warehouses and fulfilment systems, employing buyers and merchandisers with overlapping skills, and building multiple brands is high.[13] Given the potential of significant operational cost savings, the economic argument for consolidating infrastructures, management functions and technology through multi-channel integration is strong. Efficiency savings will directly affect the bottom line. Integration can improve service levels but also lower cost to serve. However, such cost savings may require high initial investment: Forrester research into 50 financial services organizations, to determine the cost of channel synchronization, revealed that 58 per cent of these firms believed that implementation of such an integration strategy would cost at least US $1 million per year, with 16 per cent spending more than US $20 million per year.[14] So failure to plan properly may result in no cost benefit, or at worst actually significantly increase costs. For example, a move to self-service over the Internet may increase call centre load and reduce profits temporarily. Consideration must be given to the costs of integrating new e-channels with 'legacy processes and systems, new fulfilment processes, origination and management of the online catalogue and supporting text and pictures and customer-service staff'.[15]

So companies need to ensure suitable ROI from their multi-channel investments. Scenario analysis should be combined with testing and piloting where possible to develop a business cases to ensure an adequate return on investment. Ultimately channels must be used selectively, according to their strengths and customer preferences. A balance must be struck between growth, effectiveness, cost control, and centralization and channel autonomy on the other.

RECOMMENDATIONS

Our main recommendations are:

- **Look at what you've got, you might be pleasantly surprised.** Rarely, if ever can we all start with a blank sheet of paper so we must build, adapt and add to what we've got.
- **Build a roadmap for change, not an unachievable vision.** Search for quick wins and prepare to be pragmatic: multi-channel integration projects by their very nature are enterprise-wide and very hard to get right.
- **Start with rapid ROI and build.** Process redesign and a channel function review are good places to start, and this will often deliver significant ROI within a short time period.

Flint and Spieler[16] detail a four-stage process, which should be followed to create a successful multi-channel enterprise:

1. Create a customized multi-channel strategy.
2. Determine the relative positioning and priority for the channels.
3. Organize for multi-channel operation: reconcile the need for central control over branding and service standards with the need for local autonomy in managing individual channels.
4. Adopt best practices for integrating the new with the old.

A starting point could be to transform yesterday's cost-intensive call centre into today's multi-channel CIC (customer interaction centre). The CIC is the first line of communication with your customers, and its 'hub like' quality means that all customer touch points and departments connect to it. The solution can include call recording on a sampling basis, searchable tagging to route customer intelligence to where it is needed most, and the ability to monitor any call at any time from any location. Another advantage is the ability to build and maintain a data-rich, 360-degree profile of each customer, such that even if a customer leaves and returns, the company is able to view and maintain a complete record of the relationship.

Although many channel integration projects are currently still in their infancy, with an expectation that such strategies are a long-term play, failure to act swiftly might mean that companies are left behind by the competition and exposed to the risks of inconsistent customer expectations and channel disconnect, which in turn might affect revenue and efficiency. Consumers are becoming ever more multi-channel in behaviour, using specific channels at various stages of the interaction process. Consequently, companies must understand their customers' expectations, in particular their customers' interaction preferences and patterns of behaviour across different channels, particularly for those segments that are critical for the company's future. They must improve channel performance for these segments, rather than try to be all things to all customers.

Companies will find it hard to implement a fully synchronized multi-channel strategy. They therefore need to undertake staged rollouts of their multi-channel strategy, while ensuring that any multi-channel investments are prioritized and backed by a sound business case. Ultimately the organization needs to balance the goals of growth and reduced costs, and centralization and channel autonomy.

CHECKLIST

Strategy

▮ What do we mean by integrated channels?

▮ What would they look like from the point of view of supplier, partner and customer?

▮ How should how you manage your channels vary between transactional products (where customers are in regular contact) and lifecycle products (where customers might make a decision infrequently)? What about the middle ground?

▮ What could be the benefits and costs of integration – for supplier, partner and customer? What are the risks of not doing it well?

▮ Where is your business on the evolutionary path? Who is doing it well in your industry and what results are they getting? Are they focusing their attention on particular combinations of channels, particular products, particular market segments?

▮ What channels do you use? Are some more important than others, and if so, why? Are any strategically more important than others?

▮ How many of your channels are integrated – partially or completely, and across different episodes in the customer buying cycle?

▮ Do you have a multi-channel strategy? Have you tried to implement one before? How far did you get? If you failed, why was it?

▮ If a competitor introduced a brilliant new product, would it need to use an integrated channel approach, or would it use a variety of business partners to achieve communication and distribution?

▮ Have you experimented with x-channel scenarios yet?

▮ Are you fully using your channel functions?

▮ Do your existing products work across multiple channels? Could they?

Understanding customer behaviour and needs

▮ Who are your best customers? Use strong data mining tools to identify the 20 per cent of customers who use those multi-touch points and generate high value for the company, and whose preferences will satisfy 80 per cent of the customer base.

▮ What channels do each of your customer segments use? Is there a clear pattern? Why do they do it?

▮ Do you fully understand your customers' needs and preferences?

▮ How confident are you of your current segmentation?

▮ Does your current segmentation reflect failure to achieve multi-channel integration?

▮ Does your company precisely understand your target multi-channel customers' preferences?

Channel costs

▮ Do you know how much each of your channels costs, overall, for different kinds of transaction and for different types of customer?

▮ How cost-effective are your channels? Do they meet regulatory requirements in terms of cost-effectiveness and quality?

▮ Are you using your channels economically?

Implementation

▮ How can customer information be better used to improve the cross-channel customer experience?

▮ What is the relative importance in achieving channel integration of technology, versus people and processes?

▮ How important is data integration, and is it possible?

▮ Are you optimally organized for multi-channel?

People and organization

▮ Are your staff paid on performance only in the channel they work in (multi-channel unfriendly targets)?

▮ Do you have cross-organizational support for cross-channel scorecards and compensation?

▮ How can you allow for flexibility we might need today (for situations you have not expected) or tomorrow (for example, future mergers and acquisitions)?

▮ Is your organizational structure optimizing the benefits of channel cooperation?

Measurement

▮ What would a balanced multi-channel scorecard look like in your organization? How would it work?

▮ How should customer-facing staff work with it? What about managers with accountability for different products or channels? How do your processes support use of such a scorecard?

▮ How are you measuring multi-channel effectiveness?

▓ How accurate is your multi-channel performance data analysis?
▓ Do your channel measures support the corporate strategy?

Business case and roadmap

▓ What is the case for change?
▓ Do you have a business case for your multi-channel programme?
▓ What evidence do you possess to prove your business case, and what evidence do you need?
▓ What is your multi-channel vision?
▓ What is your roadmap?
▓ What are the risks?
▓ How long will it take?
▓ Can it be phased?
▓ How are you going to achieve quick wins?
▓ If multi-channel turns out to be infeasible or too expensive for all or part of your business, what are the options?

NOTES

[1] Forrester Research (2001) Implementing customer heuristics, *Forrester Report* (April), Forrester Research.
[2] Boston Consulting Group (2001) *The Multi-channel Consumer*, Boston Consulting Group, (July).
[3] Forrester Research (2001) Turning Web traffic into store sales, *Forrester Report* (August).
[4] Yates, S, Shevlin, R, Watson, T and Sweeney, J (2001) Integrating financial channels, *Forrester Report* (August), Forrester Research.
[5] Forrester Research (2001) Retail and media data overview, *Forrester Data Overview*, Forrester Research.
[6] Boston Consulting Group (2001) *The Multi-channel Consumer*, Boston Consulting Group (July).
[7] Williams, S (1999) Synchronize channels or bust, *Forrester Report* (April), Forrester Research.
[8] Ibid.
[9] Ibid.
[10] Yates, S, Shevlin, R, Watson, T and Sweeney, J (2001) Integrating financial channels, *Forrester Report* (August), Forrester Research.
[11] Forrester Research (2000) Retail e-business networks emerge, *Forrester Brief* (September 7), Forrester Research.
[12] Channel cooperation pays off, *Forrester Report* (May), Forrester Research.

13 Flint, D and Spieler, G (2001) *Multi-channel Retailing: Bringing the new into the old*, Gartner (5 July).

14 Yates, S, Shevlin, R, Watson, T and Sweeney, J (2001) Integrating financial channels, *Forrester Report* (August), Forrester Research.

15 Flint, D (2002) *Questioning Your Multi-channel Strategy,* Gartner (28 June).

16 Flint, D and Spieler, G (2001) *Multi-channel Retailing: Bringing the new into the old*, Gartner (5 July).

27

Permission-based e-mail

Teresa Waring and Antoine Martinez

INTRODUCTION

Direct marketing via the Internet has been growing at a phenomenal rate over the last five years as more customers in both the United States and Europe begin to go online. Historically organizations have usually communicated with their customers through various media that follow a passive one-to-many communication model. This model has allowed those organizations to reach many current and potential customers, segmented or not, through marketing efforts that permit only limited forms of feedback from the customers.

One of the defining qualities of marketer–customer interaction over the Internet is the ability to develop relationships with customers. Marketers can use this unique medium to collect market data, to question, listen to and respond to customers in ways that had never been previously possible. However, there have been examples of bad practice that have angered many of the Internet community and made potential customers highly suspicious of any attempts to foster customer relationships. A number of organizations are now becoming increasingly aware that they need to proceed more cautiously and take a more ethical approach towards marketing their products and services.

This chapter examines one specific development in building more ethical customer relationships: permission-based e-mail marketing. The aims of the chapter are first to explore the concept of ethical behaviour and how it relates to the Internet. Second, it examines the literature on how permission-based e-mail marketing arose and what is considered to be good practice. Third, it presents primary research conducted over a six-month period that investigated how permission-based e-mail marketing is carried out by a sample of organizations in both the United States and France, and examined two e-mail marketing service bureaux that offered a complete outsourced solution for companies in Europe. Finally the chapter discusses the success of permission-based e-mail marketing for the organizations investigated, and how other companies could learn from their experience of adopting a more ethical practice.

ETHICAL ISSUES AND THE INTERNET

Ethics is a branch of philosophy that deals with what is considered to be right and wrong. Ethics is highly contextual, and with the passage of time society is continually updating its ethical guidelines. However, what is unethical is not necessarily illegal, and in many instances individuals are faced with ethical decisions that do not fall into the illegal bracket of law breaking.

Communications technology and the Internet are facilitating easy access to people in their homes and at work across the world, and through this we are developing new perspectives on what is right and wrong in the global society.

Much of what takes place on the Internet is highly unstructured, and more recent e-business is so new that the legal, ethical, and other public policy issues that are necessary for its existence are still evolving. The spread of e-business has created many new ethical situations: for example, putting 'cookies' on customers' PCs, or monitoring staff e-mail. Whether these actions are considered unethical depends upon the organization, country, culture, value systems and so on.

In the globalized economy, companies operate under increasing environmental pressures. These pressures are not new but with the introduction of the Internet as a new, and some would say better, distribution channel that can compete against traditional ones, the need to attract and keep customers online is essential. In their race for customer acquisition many companies have developed practices that raise ethical issues, and these ethical issues are not necessarily the same throughout the world. An attempt to organize IT ethical issues into a framework can be seen in the work of Mason et al[1], who categorized ethical issues into privacy, accuracy, property and accessibility.

- **Privacy.** The collection, storage and dissemination of information about individuals.
- **Accuracy.** The authenticity, fidelity and accuracy of information collected and processed.
- **Property.** The ownership and value of information and intellectual property.
- **Accessibility.** The right to access information and payment of fees to access it.

Ethics has assumed a new dimension of importance as e-business opens up a new spectrum of unregulated activities, and one major area for concern has been in marketing on the Internet.

PERMISSION-BASED E-MAIL MARKETING

E- mail has been available since the Internet began, and is 'not subject to some of the technical changes that might force people to update their Web browsers every three months.[2] As a result, e-mail can be considered as both stable and reliable. For many people e-mail is their main reason for being on the Internet, as it is cheap and convenient, and companies have come to recognize it. The commercial e-mail market is predicted by Jupiter to rise to an estimated US $7.3 billion in 2005, cannibalizing direct mail revenues by 13 per cent.[3] Numerous companies have been impressed by the high rate of response obtained when sending e-mails, and a recent Forrester report found that 10 per cent of e-mail recipients click through to the sender's Web page, and about 2.5 per cent of those recipients make a purchase during the visit.[4] However, not all e-mails are equally effective.

Forrester stresses the important role of e-mail in opening a dialogue with customers and gradually building a relationship that will eventually allow more personal information to be gained. However, many organizations are using it indiscriminately to aggressively market products and bombard consumers with unsolicited e-mails. The potential to develop better customer relationships is being eroded by unreflective practice. Consumers are discerning and have experienced aggressive direct marketing through unsolicited 'snail mail' and telemarketing, and they are not prepared to accept 'spamming' on the Internet. Organizations need to adopt better practice if they are to acquire and retain customers, and one way could be through permission-based e-mail marketing. Meta Group defines a permission e-mail as 'A promotional e-mail whose recipients consent to receive commercial messages from the sender, typically by signing up at the company's Web site'.[5]

This new form of direct marketing is well established in the United States and is beginning to develop in Europe. It enables companies to achieve higher response rates because consumers give their own details freely. In this respect, e-mail marketing uses what is called 'push technology' in order to deliver targeted messages, and it is consumers who define what interests them (often by filling out online questionnaires) and as a result are only sent relevant information or messages. Compared with other online marketing vehicles, such as Web banner ads, permission e-mail marketing delivers superior performance and more measurable business impact and when approached responsibly and in an ethical manner can achieve good results. Unlike Web banners, permission-based e-mail puts the marketer back in control of what messages consumers receive and when they receive them. In addition, cost per message sent for permission e-mail allows marketers to improve their marketing economies by five times or more compared with direct mail, and by as much as 20 times compared with Web banners.

As more marketing is done on the Internet and e-mail marketing is studied further, it is possible to understand more about the buying behaviour of the consumers who respond to e-mail offers. For example, Cross and Nassef[6] have identified two specific categories. The first are the 'hot clickers' who are quick responders and usually act on an e-mail promotion within 24 hours. If they like the offer, they will even act as advocates, forwarding the message to friends and relatives who might also be interested in the offer. However, such behaviour is difficult to predict and there is no consistent buying pattern.

The 'warm clickers' will think about a specific offer they receive, often taking up to three days to respond. They also like to receive more information about products and services before making commitments. However, these buyers make up for their slower response time by being predictable long-term performers, and it is possible to predict their annual buying patterns within 5 per cent.

Permission-based e-mail marketing is a relatively recent phenomenon, and much of the literature on the subject and considered best practice has emerged from the United States. However, practice from the United States does not necessarily translate directly into Europe, and it is the purpose of the next section to compare a sample of US companies using permission-based e-mail marketing with a sample from France, and examine whether there is any notable difference in their approach, and how this contributes to our understanding of ethical best practice in a European context.

RESEARCH METHODOLOGY

E-business is growing at a phenomenal rate, and any research done in the subject area is likely to be outdated in a relatively short period of time. The research discussed in this chapter was carried out over a six-month period between March and September 2001. We adopted two approaches to data collection.

In-depth interviews

We contacted six companies in France to request interviews about their approach to permission-based e-mail marketing. Two companies out of six approached who used permission-based e-mail agreed to be interviewed with respect to their practice. The companies were relatively new marketing service bureaux offering a complete outsourced solution for companies who needed assistance with their customer relationship management through permission e-mail marketing campaigns. The in-depth interviews with the CEO of E-mail Vision (Paris) and the PR manager of Cabestan (Paris) lasted for 90 minutes and gave insight into how these companies approached and implemented permission-based e-mail marketing. The companies that refused to be interviewed gave reasons of confidentiality. Our analysis of these interviews used the criteria of good practice and ethical practice along with efficiency and effectiveness of the marketing approach.

Online e-mail data collection

Online data collection was carried out between June and August 2001. This involved one of the authors setting up a specific e-mail address and then registering online for a company newsletter and other information related to specific consumer interests with 20 companies, 10 from the United States and 10 from France. Although a particular sector was not chosen, the focus was mainly on business-to-consumer Web sites, as shown in Table 27.1. Over the three-month period e-mails were collected from the companies and then analysed using the best-practice criteria synthesized from the literature. We do recognize that the samples used are quite small, but it must be recognized that the research was exploratory, and if there had been more time a much larger sample could have been used. However, we believe that our results do give some insight into practice within a European context.

RESULTS

The in-depth interviews

From the point of view of the PR manager at Cabestan, permission-based e-mails must be highly personalized, not only addressing the customer by his or her name, but with content that reflects his or her particular needs. He viewed permission e-mails as a major customer relationship tool that completes the company Web site. In fact one of the main reasons customers visit a site is because of effective permission e-mail marketing. The CEO of E-mail Vision supported this and added, 'E-mail marketing maximizes each customer's value over time by building long-term relationships and loyalty.' To an online company, customer loyalty is extremely important.

The companies using permission-based e-mail marketing while working with an ASP are generally charged on a cost-per-message delivered basis and this can be very low. The CEO of E-mail Vision estimated that these costs are 80 per cent lower than those connected with postal direct marketing. The standard cost of an e-mail managed by E-mail Vision is about 0.03 euros. Also, companies using e-mail will probably only need the service of a Web graphic designer rather than a specialized advertising agency to set up their campaigns.

Table 27.1 French and US companies investigated in the study

French companies	US companies
Business-to-consumer sector	**Business-to-consumer sector**
La Fnac (CDs, books, DVDs/videos, hi-fi etc)	Amazon.com (CDs, books, DVDs/videos etc)
Chapitre.com (books)	CD Now (CDs, DVDs etc)
Digitall.fr (CDs, DVDs, video games etc)	Dell (computers)
Yves Rocher (cosmetics, fragrances)	Columbia Records-Sony Music (information concerning musical events)
Lancome France (cosmetics, fragrances)	Victoria's Secret (women's clothing, underwear, fragrances etc)
Le Club des créateurs de beauté (CCB-Paris) (cosmetics, fragrances)	Petco.com (products and food for all sorts of pets)
Decathlon (sports articles)	
Le Club Med (Travel and travel goods)	
Business-to-business sector	**Business-to-business sector**
UpDesk.net (Web site dedicated to the new economy and supplying information about this subject)	IBM (provides news and updates related to the activities in which IBM has an interest)
	Ziff-Davis: The Best of ZDNet (product reviews, downloads, shopping deals, special reports on new technologies)
	Ziff-Davis: Anchordesk (computing news and trends with concise summaries and expert analysis)
Non-governmental organizations	**Non-governmental organizations**
Médecins Sans Frontières (NGO acting against war, poverty and injustice around the world)	Greenpeace (NGO promoting the protection of the environment through active campaigns against organizations and governments)

The CEO of E-mail Vision believed that permission e-mail marketing is highly effective and produces a good return on investment (ROI), and figures given to us by the interviewees are similar to those within the literature. The CEO of Cabestan pointed to companies that they deal with such as Bayard Press Publishers, France Loisirs and La Redoute, which have all benefited from a permission-based e-mail campaign that has not only shown a good ROI but has developed a good base for better customer relationships.

Neither interviewee expressed any doubts about the need to 'spy' on their customers while they are online. They saw this as a vital aspect of Internet marketing and believed there was the need for expertise in this area. They both argued that e-mail service providers can help in this by providing powerful hardware and software to track customers, and by outsourcing marketing campaigns to these specialist organizations businesses can take advantage of skills and infrastructure that they do not possess in-house.

Cabestan explained its approach to permission e-mail marketing through the 'e-mail customer contact cycle' as shown in Figure 27.1.

The customer acquisition phase constitutes the starting point where the company hunts and gathers new online customers by identifying its market, creating the best offers for the business and promoting to its potential target audience. The company might already have a mailing list but might need help in building this further. It might turn to an ASP such as a brokerage service for an 'opt-in' list. The testing phase works on the principle that by testing the past offers and their outcomes, the company will acquire a better understanding of what customers expect and therefore improve its e-mail marketing campaigns. The company then enters the profit-making stage: customer retention. As the PR manager of Cabestan says, this is where the company 'needs to build genuine relationships with its customers by marketing to them individually, personalizing the messages and offering products that fit exclusively their wants and needs'. The customer service phase completes this cycle, and consists of keeping customers happy with timely responses to their messages and actions.

From a company's perspective both interviewees believed that permission e-mail has improved the performance of the direct marketing function. The PR manager of

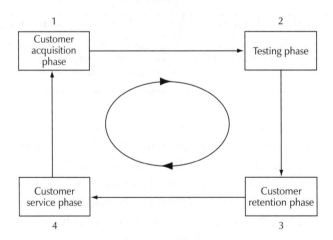

Figure 27.1 The e-mail customer contact cycle

Cabestan said that, 'the amount of time related to the technical implementation of an e-mail campaign is ridiculously small: as soon as the customer database is available, only a few hours are required for the compulsory testing phase and, by the next day, 50,000 e-mails per hour can be sent.'

This compares with several weeks or months in other traditional direct marketing methods such as catalogue marketing. The CEO of E-mail Vision suggested that an entire e-mail campaign could be designed and executed within one single week, as the technology provided by an ASP enables companies to start collecting 'opt-in' names within 48 hours, and test results can be tracked in real time and conclusions delivered within 72 hours. Companies can even monitor customer reactions to e-mail campaigns by integrating customer satisfaction surveys into the message, to interrogate the readers' perceptions of ergonomics and content, and ask what else they might want.

The ability to measure the effectiveness of an e-mail campaign is an aspect of this approach that is potentially seductive to companies. Traditional approaches to direct marketing have required analysis of results over weeks or months after the campaign is finished, but e-mail campaigns can be analysed instantly using software tools at any point in the campaign through a Web browser.

Neither interviewee believed that permission-based e-mail marketing will replace traditional approaches, and both view it as a complementary addition to any company's marketing strategy. It is their belief that paper-based advertising media have a much better visual impact at present, and not everyone has access to computers.

Online e-mail data collection

A vast amount of data was collected online through the e-mails received, and a summary is presented in Table 27.2. The e-mails were analysed using criteria that we understood to be significant in relation to an ethical approach as well as best practice.

All organizations request information at the registration point, but some request much more than others. Here is a definition of some of the terms in the table:

■ **Basic**: Name, address, phone number, e-mail address.
■ **Fairly detailed**: As above and age, gender, job, company name, size, address of company.
■ **Detailed**: As above and details about interests, purchase details and so on.
■ **Basic personalization**: E-mail that starts 'Dear [Name of Customer]'.
■ **Content of e-mails**: Where personal details were supplied, whether they were used to target the customer.

Table 27.2 The performances of the French and US companies involved in the study

French companies

	La Fnac	Chapitre	Digitall	Yves Rocher	Lancome	CCB-Paris	Decathlon	Le Club Med	UpDesk	MSF
Requested information for registration	Detailed	Detailed	E-mail address only	Basic	Basic	E-mail address only	Detailed	Detailed	Basic	Basic
Basic personalization	Yes	No	No	Yes	No	No	No	No	No	No
Frequency of messages	6 e-mails	4 e-mails	1 e-mail	6 e-mails	1 e-mail	3 e-mails	1 e-mail	4 e-mails	2 e-mails	4 e-mails
Text/HTML	Both	HTML only	HTML only	HTML only	Both	Both	Both	Both	Both	Both
Content and objectives of e-mails	Specific to customer	Specific to customer	N/A	Only promotions and savings	N/A	Only promotions and savings	N/A	Advertises services	Not specific	Information and invitation to subscribe
Opt-out?	Yes	Yes	Yes	Yes	Yes	Yes	Yes	Yes	Yes	Yes
Tracking and reporting?	Use of cookies	Use of cookies	Use of cookies	Use of cookies	Use of cookies	Use of cookies	Use of cookies	Use of cookies	No	Use of cookies

Table 27.2 (cont)

US Companies

	Amazon	CD Now	Dell	Columbia Records	Victoria's Secret	Petco	IBM	Best of ZDNet	Anchordesk	Greenpeace
Requested information for registration	Detailed	Detailed	Detailed	Detailed	Detailed	Detailed and includes pets' details	Detailed	Fairly detailed	Fairly detailed	Basic
Basic personalization	No	Yes	Yes	No	Yes	Yes	No	No	No	No
Frequency of messages	7 e-mails	12 e-mails	6 e-mails	30 e-mails	7 e-mails	Customer chooses	30 e-mails	9 e-mails	44 e-mails	3 e-mails
Text/HTML	Both	Both	HTML only	Both	Both	HTML	Both	Both	Both	Both
Content and objectives of e-mails	Specific to customer	Specific to customer	Specific to customer	Specific to customer	Specific to customer	Specific to customer and pet	Specific to customer	Specific to customer	Specific to customer	Information and invitation to subscribe and take action
Opt-out?	Yes	Yes	Yes	Yes	Yes	Yes	Yes	Yes	Yes	Yes
Tracking and reporting?	Use of cookies	Use of cookies	Use of cookies	Use of cookies	Use of cookies	Use of cookies	Use of cookies	Use of cookies	Use of cookies	Use of cookies

All organizations that intend to do business on the Internet must recognize that developing customer relationships that respond to the needs of the consumer are essential. Rarely do online vendors meet their customers, and therefore developing trust and confidence has to be of the uppermost importance if there is to be retention of their business. This is something that cannot be done overnight, and requires respect for the individuals engaging in transactions. Many companies online do not have the expertise or hardware and software to develop good customer relationships.

In the United States there are at least 20 new companies providing specialist e-mail marketing services for businesses online. In France, Cabestan and E-mail Vision have emerged as new companies (ASPs) that are providing a service for other companies who need to progress their marketing strategy into e-mail marketing. They have recognized and applied much of the good practice identified in the literature, and through the use of sophisticated software have been able to assist their clients in targeting specific sectors of markets and competing better with rivals. However, the ethical framework within which they work is not explicit, and they are focused on maximizing profits for their clients.

It is fair to say that both Cabestan and E-Mail Vision rely heavily on technology to support the customer relationship marketing strategy, and companies who use their services do not need to concern themselves with logistics of their marketing campaigns. Both companies appear to use e-mail lists acquired in an ethical manner, though for reasons of confidentiality we were unable to verify this. However, they see one of their roles as monitors of individuals on those lists when they go online. This raises an ethical issue alluded to earlier: the issue of spying on customers and the placing of 'cookies' on their computers. From a company perspective, the more detail they have on customers, the better they can target products and promotions and understand what it is that motivates the customer to buy. Cookies can raise greater concern than self-registration, because cookies allow Web sites to collect private information that includes surfing patterns of users. Furthermore, personal profiles created by cookies are more accurate than self-registration on Web sites, because it is known that over 40 per cent of all users falsify information when registering online.[7] The potential for abuse of cookies has been recognized by a number of governments, and in Europe the updated Data Protection Act 1998 came into effect on 1 March 2002. This will enable individuals to take legal action against those who process data about them without their active consent. The latest data protection legislation makes cookie technology illegal unless users are clearly told how the information is being used. This is a highly controversial move that companies feel will destroy their competitive advantage across the world, as competitors in non-EU countries will continue to use cookies indiscriminately. It might mean inevitably that companies will move their business out of the EU in order to bypass the law and individuals' rights to privacy.

If we now look at the companies in the United States and France we registered with then, it can be seen that the US companies appear to have adopted an approach that is customer-focused and on the surface has an ethical dimension to it. They all collect registration information in various quantities, and go on to target the content of their e-mails at the customer. This would suggest that they are actually using the registration information in a responsible manner. We did not receive similar e-mails from other companies within the time frame, so this might indicate that our details were not passed on. It is surprising, however, to note that 5 of the 10 did not personalize those e-mails and three, IBM, Columbia and Anchordesk, sent high volumes of general information, although they all have 'opt-out' if the customer wants to stop the e-mails. All of the US companies use cookies, and this reflects the lack of legislation there. It is not seen as unethical to use cookies, and is in fact regarded as an essential part of Internet business.

Of the French companies investigated, it appears that practice is varied, and six of the companies only collect what would be considered to be a minimum amount of information from consumers. This lack of detailed information results in e-mails that lack personalized information and content. They all contained 'opt-out' to end the e-mails. It was also noted that the French firms on the whole contacted us less frequently than the US companies, and therefore were less likely to establish any type of customer relationship. However, in 2001 they were all using cookies to track customers. Obviously since March 2002 European companies have had to rethink the cookie issue. Many are now informing consumers of what they intend to do, and that the alternative is re-registration each time the customer visits the Web site. Many consumers would prefer that to having their privacy invaded.

It appears that the French companies studied here have adopted much of the practice from the United States but are still developing their approach. Companies such as Yves Rocher and Lancôme, who have a strong presence in traditional markets, may feel that the Internet is complementary to their other distribution channels, and hence do not need to develop online customer relationships to the degree that Amazon and CD Now do. There is also a cultural difference between France and the United States. In the United States, chasing business and customers aggressively is not seen as out of the ordinary. However, in France aggressive marketing as typified by US companies is practised less. This could explain the difference in frequency of messages we received from the companies in the two countries.

CONCLUSION

Permission-based e-mail marketing is a phenomenon that still has to develop in France, and it is uncertain whether it will grow as rapidly as it has in the United States. Although they have adopted some US ideas such as Disneyland and McDonald's, the French have not embraced them wholeheartedly, and many would argue that the concepts are at odds with the French culture and psyche. If Internet marketing is not developed in a specifically French manner, then companies will feel uneasy with the process and potential customers will be lost. It is important for all companies to learn from US experience, but to think very carefully about customers in their own specific markets. Culture and tradition play a major role in the adoption of new methods of communication, and permission-based e-mail marketing will only be ethical if practice takes account of this.

NOTES

[1] Mason, RO, Mason, FM and Culnan, MJ (1995) *Ethics of Information Management*, Sage Publications, Thousand Oaks, Calif.

[2] Ibid.

[3] Jupiter Communications [accessed 7 July 2001] [Online] http://www.jmm.com.

[4] Forrester Research [accessed 17 July 2001] [Online] http://www.forrester.com/home/0,3257,1,FF.html.

[5] META Group & IMT Strategies(2000) [accessed 27 April 2001] *Permission E-mail: The future of direct marketing* [Online] http://www.metagroup.com/cgi-bin/inetcgi/search/disply/Article.jsp?oid=16246].

[6] Cross, R and Nassef, A (1999) E-mail direct marketing comes of age, *Direct Marketing*, **62** (6) (October), pp 44–45.

[7] GVU (1998) *Graphics, Visualisation and Usability Centre at Georgia Tech University* [Online] http://cc.gatech.edu/gv/user_surveys.

28

The data lessons of e-mail in CRM

Jane McCarthy and Merlin Stone

In some ways, e-mail today is like direct mail in the 1980s and inbound call centres in the late 1980s and early 1990s. The problems of handling huge volumes and immense variety were resolved by testing to establish likely volumes, coding of campaigns so that responses to particular campaigns went to particular addresses or telephone numbers, learning which kinds of response vehicles and scripts worked to trigger the next appropriate action more quickly and efficiently, and eventually by improved targeting and media selection based on campaign learning, so that the right people were addressed by outbound communication, making their inbound responses easier to process. These different kinds of progress were of course facilitated by a supply-side response, whether through the offer of much higher quality outsourcing capabilities for response handling, or through the provision of systems, software and external data for clients to improve their entire direct marketing process.

In the e-world, we are nowhere near the maturity of classic direct marketing media such as mail and telephone (though here there is still plenty of room for improvement). Good inbound and outbound e-mail management systems are now available. Where e-mails are stimulated by Web browsing, click-stream analysis can give us better understanding of how customers behave, and for advanced users they act as predictors of the likely volume of inbound contacts. The use of Web forms is now widespread, so for more mature users the era of unstructured e-mails is coming to an end. Finally, users of the most advanced software that integrates Web and telephony can see an end to the problems caused when customers are having problems approaching them via the Web, and need to move to the telephone.

However, it has taken around 20 years for most companies to get to grips with mail and telephone. Even the most advanced practitioners readily admit that they still experience problems that have their origin in data. Deduplication may no longer be as difficult as it was, but in sectors experiencing rapid changes to their customer base (usually because of mergers and acquisitions, or because of frequent entry into new products and/or new markets), problems still abound. In the e-world, deduplication is made harder by use of multiple addresses, possibly unconnected to physical addresses. However, these problems can be resolved by the same direct marketing techniques: the development of data sources with declared quality standards applying to particular fields (from names and addresses to interests and media preferences). We do not know what the likely relative balance between external and internal data sources will be. Certainly, companies that ask their own customers to state e-mail preferences (frequency of contact, subject matter and so on) are getting good results, typically increasing response and sales rates many times over. External data providers are providing opt-in services which product good results. However, bad money may still drive out good. Ask anyone who has not logged into one of their (usually several) Web-based e-mail addresses for a few weeks how many unsolicited e-mails they received (often from far-off countries offering strange products and services), and whether they responded by wholesale deletion of all e-mails from unrecognized addresses. Could this lead to a situation where ISPs start to control access to their customers? On privacy grounds alone such a move might be sensible.

E-mail has a clear edge over direct mail both in terms of cost and response rates, so it has an immediate appeal to marketers. Traditional direct mail costs between 20 and 40 times as much as e-mail per item. Response rates for direct e-mail campaigns targeted to permission-based audiences generate between 3 and 10 times more responses than traditional direct mail. Properly profiled e-mail to existing customers typically can get three times the response of e-mails to rented lists, and permission-based e-mail campaigns focused on existing customers are 10 times more effective than direct mail campaigns. This makes e-mail a highly effective way to communicate with customers. It is also easy to track results, so the return on investment is demonstrable.

However, e-mail marketing puts the spotlight on data management. Effective e-mail marketing is as much about data as it is about transmission and good creative. The challenges of planning, managing, and tracking multiple high volume consumer campaigns are intensified via e-mail. Companies may think it is a simple task to send out an e-mail campaign, but there are many complex technical issues that need to be managed as part of a successful e-mail campaign. Many companies, for example, lack the technical infrastructure or software to track results effectively and ask:

▌ How many people opened the e-mail?
▌ Which links did they click on, and if there were different creative treatments for the same link, which one was more effective?
▌ Can the responses be acted on quickly enough, and fed through to other sales/marketing/service channels?

Companies' failure to respond to customer e-mails can have a very negative effect on customer attitudes to the company and their propensity to buy. An e-mail campaign to existing customers is likely to generate up to 2 per cent direct replies to the e-mail, so in a mailing to 100,000 there might be 2,000 replies to handle over a very short period of time. People expect e-mail to be a very immediate channel, so a delayed response, or no response at all is unacceptable. At the very least they should receive an auto-response, and even better would be a personalized, relevant response, but this takes a sophisticated e-mail data management system with infrastructures optimized to handle high volume campaigns. Some of the other technical issues that need to be addressed are:

▮ Being able to manage bounces effectively (by using the information to clean the database).
▮ Being able to send out multi-part e-mails (combining HTML with plain text so that the recipient's browser can display the message appropriately).
▮ Including an automated and customer-friendly unsubscribe option which you are able to act on quickly.
▮ Re-routing responses to relevant departments for action.

One reason why outsourcing is a favoured option is that the cost to an individual company of setting up this kind of infrastructure may be prohibitive, and there are a number of specialist suppliers that offer very competitive rates for an outsourced service. As this is a relatively new medium, companies would be wise to draw on external expertise to get started and gain an understanding of what is involved.

A number of e-mail marketing suppliers can deliver sophisticated personalization (including rich media), narrow-casting and tracking technology, and will have an existing large-scale technical infrastructure optimized for e-mail (which would probably take a minimum of three months to set up.) Combining this kind of expertise with traditional skills in direct mail campaign planning and data management can produce excellent results. Companies gain the ability to send high volumes of e-mails, multiple waves/segments and track responses, and to send messages in multiple character sets for regional or global campaigns. The most effective solutions will include a separate e-mail marketing data-mart or e-CRM database that is specially configured to handle e-mail campaigns, while at the same time being able to exchange data with the central marketing database or data warehouse.

Suppliers have some catching up to do too, though. The cycle of updates from operational systems to an e-CRM database is faster because of the generally higher frequency of e-mail contact compared with contact via direct mail and telemarketing. If the e-CRM database is not up to date, customers might lose confidence. Most users of e-mail marketing market via e-mail at least monthly. This means that database bureaux oriented to dealing with physical mail may not be able to cope with the pace of change. However, as their clients increasingly want to include an e-mail element in their marketing campaigns, they will either have to build the expertise internally or partner with specialists.

In some companies, even today, it can still take between one and three months to get a traditional direct mail campaign out of the door, and some marketing databases are still only updated on a monthly or weekly basis. This is far too slow in the online world. The power of e-mail is that it is theoretically possible to get feedback on a campaign instantly, and refine the message and the creative treatment in a matter of hours. Subsequent waves might be going out the next day, or the next week, so it is important to close the loop on unsubscribe/opt-out requests before the next one goes out.

In-house marketers are keen to exploit this new channel, but many of today's e-mail programmes are not sophisticated enough to meet the needs and preferences of the rapidly evolving online customer. In many cases they do not even have classic direct mail disciplines applied to them. Sometimes, this is because it is almost too easy to send out an e-mail campaign, so multiple departments, or regional offices within an organization, might be sending out e-mails with little central control over branding and contact strategy. As this is all still fairly new, companies have few rules and processes covering how both outbound and inbound e-mail should be handled, and even fewer have a data strategy in place to handle the additional data generated. In many cases existing marketing databases are not set up to even hold e-mail addresses, and while they might hold opt-in/opt-out data for customers, are unable to differentiate by channel: that is, offer the customer the option to be contacted by e-mail, but not by mail or phone.

E-mail data management issues are more complex than with classic direct mail. The e-CRM database needs to manage individual customer-based opt-ins and stated preference codes in real time. These opt-in/outs and preferences can change much more frequently than in the offline world.

A key question is whether to put customers in control of their own preference management, that is, allowing them to change it themselves online. As maintaining preferences online means that customers will be able to view some or all of the data, customers will be more aware of the quality of data held about them. With the flexibility of the medium, it is worthwhile considering making preference choices more granular: that is, not just asking customers to opt in or opt out, but consulting them about what kinds of products/services/content they are interested in receiving information about, how often they would like to be contacted and so on.

This approach is not without its pitfalls, however. If individuals transact through different sites or divisions belonging to the same company, it will be evident to them if data about them is not coordinated across different access routes and channels, so a single view of customer preferences across brands and channels becomes even more important. Customers may keep their preferences under review, switching them on and off for different purposes, so there is increased complexity in terms of managing the opt-in/opt-out data. The reason it is worth taking on these challenges, however, is that online preference management has the potential to improve targeting and minimize opt-outs. As customers can choose the kinds of product or content areas they are interested in, and even how often they want to be contacted, they feel in control and consequently more receptive to receiving further e-mail communications.

Companies not moving up the e-mail learning curve fast enough and offering more sophisticated preference options will find that more and more recipients just opt out completely. We have already seen this in the United States, where companies inundated consumer in-boxes with little differentiation or preference management. The result was a significant drop in response, and many users have cancelled their registration for e-mail lists they previously joined. Over-use not only leads to diminishing returns but also damages the brand.

Personalization is also a key element in minimizing opt-outs. Here again, some of the specialist providers can help you get this right from the outset. They achieve this by using rules-based engines to allow marketers to personalize e-mail message content for each customer. Message content, including images, paragraphs, words and links, can be assembled based on, for example, customer attributes in the data file (for instance, age group, past purchases) and data returned at run time from an external application (for instance, account status or credit status). In principle this is not difficult to achieve – the technology certainly exists – but it might be difficult for internal marketing departments to coordinate their agency, data bureaux and internal systems providers to bring together the various sources of data to be able to make it happen.

The fact is, though, that whether through improved systems integration, content personalization, data management or rich media personalized e-mail microsites, personalization is essential to protect the medium for the company and for marketers in general. If every message is relevant and different, if consumers only receive messages they are interested in, or special offers just for them, then they will open the message and read on. If these offers are exclusive to the medium, for example, special rates or fares not available over other channels, then opt-out rates are typically very low.

With careful planning and some external expertise, e-mail personalization can be used to impressive effect. Thus, an office supplies company might wish to send out an e-mail with its top five special offers. These offers can be selected on the basis of each customer's previous product category purchase transactions. A bank might want to send an e-mail to current account customers promoting a share broking service and inviting the customer to drop into the nearest branch. The system could calculate the nearest branch to home or office and embed the address, directions and map. For any company, newsletter content can be assembled based on the transaction patterns, registered preferences and socio-demographics of the customer.

Most customers will respond positively to receiving e-mails if they are asked permission, and feel favourably about the brand. In fact, consumers are generally enthusiastic about the medium as a convenient way to exchange information with the companies they deal with, but this enthusiasm may be short-lived. This is an opportunity to redress some of the excesses of direct mail that have alienated many customers. E-mail can easily be abused, but if used only with permission, and if the technology and data is managed effectively to create timely, relevant communications, then most consumers will welcome it, and response rates will remain high.

With the uptake of broadband services gathering pace in the UK, it is likely that customers will increasingly demand richer media. Consumers are becoming more sophisticated and more discerning, making it harder to get and retain their attention. Two years ago 95 per cent of e-mails sent were pure text. This severely limited their impact. In 2001, 72 per cent of consumers said they enjoyed rich media e-mails. Forrester shows that only 9 per cent of companies are currently trying rich media, but 30 per cent will use it in 2003. This adds further complexity, but is an excellent opportunity to maintain high response levels and opt-in rates. In order to be able to deliver and track audio and video elements in e-mails, you need an even more powerful infrastructure and it is probably not going to be cost-effective for an individual company to make the kind of investment required themselves unless it is core to their business. With access to the right technology, however, you can achieve high levels of rich media personalization even when accessed by large numbers at peak click-through times, and can track consumers' interaction with these rich media components whether they are sent as attachments in the e-mail or as links.

So, for many companies, some form of external support is required. External suppliers take many forms, however, and it is important to choose the ones that can provide the right kind of service. Among the contenders are the creative agencies, but a good creative solution will fail if the agency does not have sufficient technical experience in this area. Then there are the new media agencies that understand the technology, but may not be skilled enough in direct marketing and data management to carry out effective end-to-end campaigns. They will also typically operate in isolation and will not connect up the e-mail activities with other customer contact channels.

E-mail activity must be incorporated into the overall customer communication strategy from both marketing and technical perspectives. Traditional database marketing bureaux have the marketing skills required, but not all of them have invested in the necessary Internet-based skills and technology to manage the process effectively, and they may struggle to cope with the real-time data exchanges required.

Our recommendation is to look for a company that has a good combination of specialist e-mail expertise and direct marketing/data management experience, typically with roots in database marketing, offering both specialist outsourced e-mail and data management services, plus an ASP model for those who want to maintain direct control over their e-mail campaigns. It might be sensible to use a bespoke communications agency with a good track record in contact management, especially if they have an ASP solution combined with professional data management and integration services.

The conclusion is that in this brave new world, marketers should not miss this opportunity for precision targeting and personalized communication with customers. However, traditional direct marketing disciplines must be applied to e-mail marketing programmes, and one should not under-estimate the complexity of some of the data management and technology issues involved. In the short term at least, using an external supplier can help meet the challenge and get best results from the medium. To enhance rather than damage the brand, you need the process and the technology to handle responses efficiently and see them through to fulfilment.

29

Measuring and improving the usability of new media

Vanessa Donnelly, Emma Reeves and Lada Gorlenko

INTRODUCTION

The new media, particularly the Web and wireless, are more customer-controlled by customers than older media such as mail and telephone. In this chapter, we examine some of the problems and solutions, and consider the case study of government.

Ensuring that new media can be used by customers to buy means more than having a team of good Web developers, maybe a database expert, and some graphic and creative skills to deliver a professional-looking interface to produce an outcome that meets a company's marketing needs.

There might seem to be little need to involve the marketing team. Many Web site projects are conceived, designed and delivered totally independently from the marketing arm of the business and without gaining any customer validation of what is being designed. However, losing customers, damaging the brand and recording very low customer satisfaction ratings are some of the symptoms that things are not right in the world of transactional Web site design. Just imagine a department store where 62 per cent of the customers get lost, or a coffee shop that makes a customer queue three times to buy a drink. This may sound ridiculous, but many Web sites are like this. The usability of computer systems might be so poor that it hampers e-business growth.

IMPROVING USABILITY

To improve usability, it is not enough for the development culture to change. In most cases the underlying business processes need to be changed as well. This means understanding the different ways customers come into contact with the company and whether that experience is positive or negative. For example, customers might find products and compare prices on the Web, but may prefer to talk to someone on the phone before buying. In this case, it does not matter how usable the Web site is. If someone on the end of the phone is unhelpful, has poor systems to look up information, or worse, provides the wrong information to the customer, the perception of the company by that customer is negative and the total customer experience unsatisfactory. Unfortunately, it is very difficult to measure this poor experience using metrics, and even if it were possible, metrics still do not tell you why it is happening.

This is where user-centred design techniques can help. This involves testing with customers, collecting their comments and making recommendations based on these tests. User-centred design needs to be integrated into the development culture and used to help simplify the business processes. This requires involving customers in design work. This might seem to make the process longer and more expensive, but it enables poor design decisions to be eliminated very early on in the process.

If a company decides to follow a user-centred design approach to improve its customer experience, the role of the marketing professional becomes pivotal. User-centred design requires using a multi-disciplinary team to design customer solutions, and requires the participation of customers, both in the design and evaluation stages. Traditionally, Web sites have been owned by IT departments and run by developers, and any real usability work gets pushed out as a result of time and cost constraints. By setting up a team that includes marketing and usability professionals the importance of the customer experience remains high on the agenda, with the marketing representative able to lead target audience definitions and customer recruitment and (by working closely with the usability professional) measure customer satisfaction and attitude through user testing.

Of course, working as part of a multi-disciplinary team can be difficult, but it usually produces the best results. In many cases Web site projects have not been run with the right mix of people, often failing to involve the very skills that will make the project a success. Customers need to be involved in the process, and their satisfaction and attitude measured along the way. Executives need to understand that the business justification for doing this is exactly the same as testing different advertisements with a representative sample and measuring the effects and success of an advertising campaign. Why is a Web site any different? Management needs to know that the money being spent on the Web site will create a satisfying and positive customer experience.

WHY PEOPLE DO NOT BUY FROM WEB SITES

Trying to answer this fundamental question has prompted much research in academic and business circles. Poor e-commerce sites can lose up to half of their potential sales and 40 per cent of their return visitors if customers experience difficulties finding products. Two problems are that customers are being asked to fill in too much information, and they cannot find the products they are looking for. It might require too many clicks to get to the information they want: up to 80 per cent of customers leave a site without buying for this reason. Therefore, easy navigation and ease of use are often the most important features of a Web site.

It is not the technology that gets in the way of progress, but complicated and difficult to use designs that are stopping businesses realize the full return on investment from their Web sites. This might be happening not because of the computer systems that are being used, but because people are trying to use designs that they either do not feel comfortable with, or in many cases do not understand. One of the main problems is that the people who design these sites are too close to the business and have forgotten what it is like to be a novice. When customers come to a Web site they do not understand the business, they do not know the product catalogue, but they do come for a reason, and many companies do not design their sites to support what users are trying to do. In addition it seems that the language that is being used can be complicated, contradictory or simply missing, leaving the user unsure how to proceed. So even if customers find something they want to buy, they still will not buy it because the information is not there to make them feel comfortable enough to hand over their credit card number.

Trust is a real issue. There are many factors that can build and break down consumer trust. A strong brand can be very useful in bringing to the site people with a positive mindset, but this mindset can easily be broken if a Web site behaves in an unexpected manner. The model for buying on the Web in the customer's mind is very similar to buying in a normal shop. If a shop assistant starts asking for personal details before the customer is ready to buy, the customer would be very surprised, probably feel uncomfortable and more than likely walk out of the shop. Another 'trustbuster' is where sites try to conceal information and 'opt-ins' from the customer. A common 'opt-in' is where customers are required to click a box to ensure they are not placed on a mailing list. This kind of thing might seem a clever ploy to increase the chance of selling more products, but it is definitely seen as trickery by users and causes all sorts of brand damage.

THE SOLUTION

So what can companies do to increase their Web sales? Make the sites easier to use is the obvious answer, but how? How can one predict what customers want to do on one's Web site and more importantly, how they will try to do it? The best way to design a Web site is to involve people who will eventually be trying to use it. They say what they want to do, how they want to do it, what words they will be looking for and what will stop them buying. When one has an idea of the concepts involved, one can quickly and cheaply create a design on paper and test it out with them. Only when a company is happy that it has something that its customers will understand should it go to the expense of developing it. This is where many companies go wrong. They rush into expensive screen layouts and coded prototypes without making sure they have understood the fundamentals of the design. Then when they find out they have problems, they become too expensive to fix.

So if it is that easy, why do companies not do it? One reason is that the marketing research part of a company has become completely detached from IT departments. Market research has the remit to define and understand target markets for advertising, and regularly tests customer attitudes, but the equivalent usability skill has not been integrated properly into the Web site design process. Therefore, capturing customer requirements and integrating them into a design needs to be planned in from the start. This also applies to testing customer attitudes, and customers' success as they try to use the Web site, to ensure that the brand is protected and strengthened through a good user experience.

THE BENEFITS

Customers will vote with their mouse. Sites that are difficult to use will be avoided as customers find alternatives that are easier to use. This will cause many businesses to examine what they are offering to their customers and how they can improve their customer experience. As soon as businesses see usability as a key differentiator they will start to invest in better designs, which will be good news for the user. The message is clear: make it easier or lose customers to the competition.

WHAT TO DO ABOUT IT

For companies that have an e-commerce Web site, the most sensible thing to do is run a usability test with customers to see whether they can find the company's products and buy them, and what they think about the company's site. Decisions on any redesign work can then be based on customer needs rather than guesswork. Table 29.1 shows measures for assessing usability.

Table 29.1 Measures used in user-centred design

Measure	Description	Purpose	Technique	Units	Collection stages
Satisfaction: performance	A subjective measure of users' satisfaction with the speed with which the offering responds to their requests. Performance encompasses every aspect of the way the offering responds to interactions. This includes any start-up time, general operation, critical situations and assistance.	Establish the degree of user acceptance of the performance of the offering	Mean user ratings expressed as a per cent	%	Understanding users Initial design Development Deployment Lifecycle
Satisfaction: reliability	A subjective measure of users' satisfaction with the reliability/availability of the offering. Reliability encompasses the dependability of the offering. It includes its availability, robustness, durability and users' overall confidence in the offering to stand up to their demands.	Establish the degree of user acceptance of the reliability of the offering	Mean user ratings expressed as a per cent	%	Understanding users Initial design Development Deployment Lifecycle
Task: assists	When participants cannot proceed on a task, the test administrator sometimes gives direct procedural help in order to allow the test to proceed.	Determine the level of assistance required in completing tasks	The average number of assists provided during a test	Number	Understanding users Initial design Development Deployment
Task: completion rate	The completion rate is the percentage of participants who completely and correctly achieve each task goal.	Determine the completion rate for performing tasks	The per cent of users who correctly completed each task goal	%	Understanding users Initial design Development Deployment
Task: error rate	Errors are instances where test participants did not complete the task successfully, or had to attempt portions of the task more than once.	Determine the level of errors made in completing tasks	The average number of errors made in performing a task	Number	Understanding users Initial design Development Deployment
Task: time	The mean time taken to complete each task, together with the range and standard deviation of times across participants	Determine the time taken in completing tasks	The mean time taken to complete each task	Time	Understanding users Initial design Development Deployment

CASE STUDY: PUTTING CITIZENS FIRST, ESTABLISHING USABLE E-GOVERNMENT

The UK initiative for all government services to be electronically available by 2005 presents a major challenge. However, the act of simply making services available online will guarantee neither that they will be easy to use and inclusive, nor that the overall investment into such services will be long-lasting.

Putting the citizen at the heart of the design process and adopting a user-centred design strategy will ensure that e-government services take into account the citizens' previous experience and requirements, the language and concepts they are familiar with, and the processes they expect to go through. This will ensure the much sought-after social inclusion and usability of the system and high customer satisfaction.

Excluding citizens at the analysis and design stage will result in delivering services that are based on opinions and assumptions about what people want, how they think and how they perform tasks. This is a very risky strategy, and one that is likely to lead to low adoption. For local government, if the design of online services does not provide adequately for the needs of local people, the consequences will be far-reaching. In addition, services will prove to be unintuitive and unfamiliar, if the words, concepts, and processes do not match local people's expectations. As a result, users of these online services will take longer to complete their tasks – if they complete them at all – and will have limited confidence when using the system. Certain groups may feel excluded or alienated, if the services are first, not presented in a way that is meaningful to them; second, do not address their specific needs or abilities; or third, do not adequately consider the interaction devices they are using (text readers, small screen devices, non-keyboard input).

This goes against the principle of an inclusive, accountable, open council, working against the digital divide; it contravenes the ethos of improved customer service and high success rate for all those who visit the site. Such consequences would adversely affect the public perception of the council's online presence, and also the government generally.

If citizens find an online service difficult to use, or if it does not adequately address their needs, they might persevere and try to use it, but are more likely to revert back to more traditional means of communications with their council. Consequently, money will have been spent on a service that does not deliver, that is not used to its full capacity and actually increases costs with no change in the use of traditional methods.

The goal to make all e-government services available by 2005 is laudable, but if the usability is poor, citizens will be frustrated by being unable to complete the tasks they have started, or they might not be able to find the facility they require, in which case the electronic service is worthless. This makes user-centred design a strong selling point when bidding for resources, as it maximizes the benefit of any money spent, and minimizes the potential for costly future redesigns, securing a longer-term return on investment.

Many projects do include users in the project lifecycle at some stage. However all too often they are introduced in the latter phases, once a significant amount of design and development has already occurred. There are several drawbacks to this approach. Fewer problems are highlighted, as users who are asked to 'test' the system in the final stages are less likely to criticize, as the system appears to be more finished. Also, there is more emotional buy-in to the work that has already been carried out, which is likely to cause both the development team and the commissioning organization to curb any suggestion of change. Furthermore, there is often a reluctance to scrap any development that has already cost time and money.

Resistance to change is exacerbated in the latter stages of the project cycle, as any usability problems found at this time will result in expensive and time-consuming redevelopment. The alternative is an unusable product release, with consequential impact on the public perception of the e-government initiative. In relation to the 2005 objective, this would mean that the systems were up and running but the longevity of any investment was minimal, resulting in more money being required soon after the initial outlay. It is important, therefore, to separate the design phase from the development phase, as this ensures that less time and money is spent every time a usability problem is found.

The inclusion of the intended user group early in the design process provides many benefits. User-centred design involves users at every stage of design from initial requirements gathering through to evaluating mock-up prototypes and beyond, so there is immediately some buy-in by users to the process at hand. This stimulates interest in the project and provides a positive light for the government as it is seen to be listening to its customers. This increases the likelihood of acceptance of the final version of the online services.

Similarly, if the intended audience is included in the initial requirements gathering, it is possible to establish its primary requirements, which can aid in planning and prioritization of development.

It is also possible to ascertain the fears or barriers the intended users have with regard to using the system – for example, fear of fraud – what factors contribute to these fears, and what could be implemented to remove or reduce these barriers, thus improving citizen confidence, and consequently increasing site usage. If users are fearful because they do not understand the security features of the online service, then this information needs to be made clear and easily accessible in order for the citizen to feel secure, regardless of how secure the site actually is.

Equally, it is possible to establish features that might encourage citizens to use the online services, and to promote repeated online usage. This would be especially beneficial for identifying the needs of users who have been highlighted as less likely to use the

Internet – older people, lower income people, young unemployed and the disabled – to encourage a narrowing of the digital divide.

To conclude, it is never too late to incorporate usability into the development process. Early involvement of users can reduce the likelihood of money being spent on designs that are based on assumptions and opinions, which often turn out to miss important user requirements and to introduce usability problems. User-centred design thus minimizes the need for future reinvestment, providing easy to use solutions at launch.

Part 5

Implementation and the future

30

Customer and employee loyalty

Colin Livingstone and Julie Abbott

So much is written about customer loyalty that one sometimes wonders what it all means. Similarly, one wonders where loyal employees fit, if anywhere. Do not loyal employees deliver the service that ensures customer loyalty? 'Experts' say that loyal employees are critical to successful organizations and that their contribution is recognized.

Some organizations rarely or never think about their customers, some organizations would find it difficult to define who their customers are, let alone estimate their value, and some believe they do not have time to think about such things. Senior managers sometimes discuss employees as assets that can be removed quickly to protect the bottom line. What price employee loyalty in such organizations? How does such an organization present itself to its customers and how does it ensure customer loyalty?

The authors believe that employee morale is a very important determinant of customer satisfaction. Satisfied employees have such positive energy and willingness to give good service that customers at least perceive they are getting a better product or service, and in turn become much more satisfied and loyal to the company. 'There is considerable evidence demonstrating that customer loyalty is a leading predictor of financial results, and employee satisfaction is predictive of customer loyalty.'[1]

People are an integral part of CRM. However, unless the employee is trained and empowered to manage customers within an organizational structure that is customer focused and flexible, CRM implementation will suffer. Employees need to work at the levels of their abilities and have responsibilities commensurate with these if they are not to feel under-utilized, which can lead to dissatisfaction. 'Staff members who manage customers are usually capable of much more than they are asked to do. That is why policies that empower your staff to manage customers better work so well.'[2]

Satisfied employees tend to stay with the company longer and so give a higher return on the investment the company makes in them (for example via training and benefits). Employees with morale problems tend to be inwardly focused and more concerned with internal company processes and procedures (and issues) than the customer. This can lead to a vicious circle of reduced customer satisfaction and profits, further reducing morale amongst employees, as this leads to increased probability of redundancy. Fear of redundancy can by itself lead to higher employee attrition. Reichheld states that his studies 'show quite clearly that keeping good people longer can have a substantial economic impact on the firm', and 'a layoff rarely exhilarates employees. What it does do is stifle creativity, discourage risk-taking, and destroy loyalty. The fear that goes with a layoff soaks up energy and draws people's attention to their own safety and careers, away from the success of the enterprise.'[3]

Defining business vision (what the organization should look like in three to five years' time), and creating goals and critical success factors (the things the organization must do this year) that will help achieve the vision, are fundamental to developing loyalty. Capturing the voice of the customer is also critical. Unless these actions are done and communicated to employees, the organization will have an uphill struggle to retain loyal customers and employees. Many organizations have vision statements, but employees do not have a clue what they mean. No one has taken the trouble to explain the vision statement to them.

A solid approach to managing loyalty of staff and customers requires an understanding of:

▌ the need for a business vision with the voice of the customer aligned;
▌ who customers are;
▌ which are high and low-value customers;
▌ the target markets the organization wishes to serve;
▌ customers' basic requirements from the organization as a supplier;
▌ the things customers value;
▌ how that value can be made a reality (ideal value) that will keep them loyal;
▌ the things that the organization does well and the things it could do better;
▌ who does it better than the organization;
▌ how it could attract new customers.

If an organization does not know who its customers are or has done little in the way of segmentation, then it has little chance of finding out the basic requirements of its customers. If this work is done and customers are prioritized, then the organization can create the capabilities, processes and enabling infrastructure to ensure it delivers basic requirements for customers. Why is segmentation so important? Without segmentation, differences in customer needs might never be recognized. One runs the risk of guessing and getting it wrong.

Customer loyalty often results from how the customer is treated in a given situation, that is, 'moments of truth'. A simple rule is always to treat others as you would want to be treated yourself, or 'good manners'. It is through this principle that people who are empowered to act can generate customer loyalty and reinforce their own sense of being valued, as well as reinforcing their loyalty to their own organization. Each 'moment of truth' is an opportunity for a supplier to add value to the interaction between customer and supplier or to create a 'point of pain'. If that 'point of pain' relates to a basic need of the customer, then the chances are that he or she will leave and go elsewhere, which is why it is important to understand the 'moments of truth' between customer and supplier and then test these with the target customers to understand their wants and needs at that moment.

Listening skills, telephone techniques, negotiation skills, problem solving and so on, are all important in keeping customers satisfied. Over the past decade or so, many companies have cut their workforces (using technology where they can to bridge the gaps) and have expected the remaining employees to make up the shortfall. People are working longer hours, often with little or no recompense or appreciation, motivated perhaps by fear of being a casualty of the next recession.

Many of those who work longer hours just to get through their workload are experiencing the breakdown of family life. Many of the workers are white collar/management, and also a growing percentage of women are among them. This trend is visible in many public sector organizations and call centres, which is ironic as CRM uses such call centres to get closer to the customer. According to one call centre worker, 'you take call, after call, after call for seven hours or more. You can get very tired at the end of a shift, uncomfortably tired.... It can be very stressful – dealing with customers who aren't very happy … companies should spend as much as they can to make sure they have happy, productive call centre staff.'[4] Problems such as these are likely to have an adverse effect on the customers the staff are dealing with.

Employees need to be shown that their organization values them and their contribution to customer loyalty. If customer loyalty is important to an organization then it must be made important for employees. Some organizations are product-driven, measuring customer satisfaction once a year, offering no specific customer training to their employees, and then telling shareholders that they are 'customer driven'! Good customer-focused organizations motivate employees to offer good service, perhaps having a reward programme to recognize good service. They ensure that customer service and satisfaction are part of their appraisal system. Complaints will be seen as an opportunity to improve customer satisfaction and add value. Customer comments will be communicated to staff regularly. There will be a process to survey customers often and also to understand the wants and needs of customers. Education and training will focus on customer service.

Many organizations today employ third parties to handle their call centres, reception and security: the three most critical areas of entry into an organization by a customer or prospective customer. How many of these people are trained by the company they are contracted to about the organization's customer service needs? A service-level agreement is simply not good enough to ensure quality. When customers call or turn up at reception looking for someone, they expect professional assistance. They do not differentiate between the company they are calling and the third-party supplier of the telephonist or receptionist. As far as customers are concerned, they have basic needs. If these are not fulfilled, they will go elsewhere.

Once the organization understands its customers' wants and needs, it can decide whether or not the vision needs to be realigned. Having understood the 'ideal value' customers require, the organization can then develop a set of capabilities: the things it must do to achieve the ideal state. Then it must determine the enabling infrastructure that will achieve the capabilities. This is where employees come into their own. The customers will determine the ideal state, but employees determine the capabilities and enablers. Projects in areas such as process, organization, technology and communication are likely to feature highly. These enablers will address the basic requirements and the ideal-value requirements. Having completed this, the organization can then complete a gap analysis to determine which areas most urgently need change.

Organizations that take no account of their customers' needs and wants and that think they know best, will fail. The organization that takes the 'outside-in view' – the customer view – and bases its business decisions on it, will succeed, if it harnesses the collective energies of its employees. Organizational change and cultural change take time, and employee buy-in is critical.

Here are some examples of success.

▓ Sears implemented a set of total performance indicators using the 'soft' measures of employee satisfaction and customer loyalty to create a linkage that makes it possible to estimate their impact on the company's financial performance and set targets for employee and customer satisfaction. 'Every five point increase in [employee] satisfaction is related to a 1.7 per cent increase in customer loyalty which in turn is associated with a 3.4 per cent increase in earnings'.[5]

▓ Southwest Airlines in the United States has carved a successful niche as a low-cost, no-frills airline, taking pride in giving customers what they want. Similarly it has a commitment to its employees as it 'believe[s] that relaxed and secure employees will act on their own to take good care of customers'. This resulted in the lowest employee turnover in the industry and a consistent return on investment of 15 per cent over 27 years. (These figures were issued before increased competition in the low cost airline industry and also the atrocities of 11 September 2001.)[6]

HAPPY EMPLOYEES, HAPPY CUSTOMERS, HIGH PROFITS?

We carried out some research on a small but representative sample of UK business-to-business companies from three industries (IT, process and business banking), by e-mail questionnaire. The results give an indication as to the state of employee morale and how it affects the companies' profit margins. The trends correlated well with those of another recent study, this time in the retail industry, by MA students from Bristol Business School.[7]

Of the respondents, there were six IT companies, ranging in age from start-up to well established (over 25 years) and ranging from fewer than 100 employees to many thousands of employees. Business reach varied, with one working only in UK markets, one a European company and the others being more international. Most were large multinationals that were well established but two were younger, with a smaller reach and smaller number of employees. The majority of respondents were directors, managers or career professionals.

Employee satisfaction

Regardless of industry and status within a company, morale was low. There were two exceptions. The first was a director of a young IT company (established less than five years) that had global reach but was not making a profit. This company had family-friendly policies and appreciated the long hours worked by its employees. The second was from a senior stores worker in the process industry who worked shorter hours than anyone else in the survey and also had a good work/life balance, but was not able to answer many of the general questions about the company.

The overall impression was that everyone thought everyone else had a higher morale (for instance, marketing respondents cited sales, others working in sales cited service delivery, and so on). Interestingly one career professional who managed key customers believed that management levels and above had the highest morale, whereas of the respondents in the survey it was typically the higher levels that had the lowest morale. The closer to the top, the lower the morale (and incidentally, often the longest hours), especially those from the larger corporations.

Morale and job satisfaction were not completely correlated, but the main factors affecting both were disillusionment about management, long hours and work/life balance. Almost all respondents worked more than 40 hours a week, although they were contracted for much shorter working weeks, and the reason most often cited was workload or culture, 'you have to be seen to be there' (survey respondent), although travel also played a large part. People were under stress but could not cut back the hours because of a backlog of work and low resource levels. This combined to make people feel that the company did not care. More personally, they felt that their management either had no time (because of their own high workload) or inclination to listen to them. Another problem was that people *expected* to be empowered in their jobs but in reality it tended not to happen. In the finance industry this was because of a risk-adverse culture and in the other industries owing to budget issues – the effect of different levels of authorization. Those in smaller, younger companies had the most autonomy, especially those with account responsibility.

Lack of budgets was also often cited among marketers for low job satisfaction. They were unable to do their jobs properly and felt that their training (often to high levels) was wasted. Education helped raise morale, as it showed that the company cared enough to invest time and money in improving their employees, and gave those affected more insight into their company, making them feel more involved and raising their satisfaction levels. However, it lowered the morale of those who had been through high levels of training (such as an MA or MBA) with the company and then did not have the empowerment and decision-making capabilities relative to their higher academic qualifications.

Salary was not a large factor in the low morale, as most of the respondents felt that their overall package was in line with others in their industry. It was noted by a minority that the hours worked actually made their remuneration per hour very low.

Customer focus

Most of the companies had embraced the ideas of CRM, though this did not always take employees close to customers. One respondent from a company that was less keen on CRM said, 'Seeing a customer helped by my work makes it all worthwhile, there is no point otherwise'. This confirms that individuals within a company can adopt the CRM practice and customer focus even if their company does not officially embrace them via the use of technology.

Of the companies that have embraced CRM, all measured customer satisfaction, and all the respondents saw the measures and their work affected in different ways. One received a bonus on attaining a certain level, one was adversely affected when levels dropped, and others used it as a way of balancing the customer and company needs and ensuring that both gained benefit. There was no correlation between implementing CRM and employee job satisfaction and morale, although it was noted that those with a very low morale made cynical comments about their company's implementation. For example: 'Apparently, more in the term than the practice', 'Company would say yes', and 'Not really. Systems installed, but because they are in vogue.'

Customer satisfaction

Ten of the 13 companies actually monitored customer satisfaction levels. Of these, only four saw a correlation between job satisfaction, morale and customer satisfaction ratings. Of those that did monitor customer satisfaction, the levels were mainly improving, apart from in the finance industry where levels were mainly dropping slowly or flat. There was a correlation (as expected) between customer satisfaction levels and growth of the customer base. This was interesting for one process company, where because of improved portfolio realignment and CRM practices, the customer satisfaction ratings had improved but the number of customers had been reduced. Three out of four finance companies tracked customer satisfaction over the Web (these were all large banks); only one process company (a large multinational) and two of the six technology companies also did this.

Profitability

Over three-quarters of the companies studied were making a profit (one bank was making 'obscene amounts' according to the employee who responded), and of the three that were not, two were young (one was the result of a merger). There were very strong direct relationships between employee morale, job satisfaction, employee satisfaction and profits, but there were also very strong inverse relationships between the same factors, especially in the IT industry. Further research is needed to understand this properly. Most companies researched had just one respondent, however there were a number of responses from one large business that was in profit, and of these 57 per cent showed an inverse relationship between all of the factors. (Fourteen per cent had a direct correlation and the remaining 29 per cent were borderline inverse.) The process companies showed more direct relationships than the other industries.

Commodity or value add?

The inverse relationship between employee satisfaction, customer satisfaction and profitability shown in both studies is directly opposite to that cited in much literature today: 'employee loyalty and customer loyalty reinforce each other, making jobs more satisfying and further increasing the potential for superior customer value'.[8] 'In a nutshell, if employees are more satisfied then so are customers.'[9] However, 'fifty percent of people in business refuse to accept the strong evidence that good people management practices lead to higher profits in the long term'.[10]

The respondents from this study certainly individually embraced the values of CRM by making sure that they focused on customer needs, regardless of whether these were primarily internal or external customers. It was often the customer interaction, and the satisfaction of doing a job that customers appreciated, that kept job satisfaction and morale as high as it was shown to be. However, in contrast, the same respondents were often cynical about the company's attitude to CRM and also were unhappy about the way they were treated.

One thing that became clear was that generally morale is lower than it used to be because of lack of resource, budget and managerial concerns. Further research is needed to discover why this is, but certainly working practices have changed radically in many industries over the last two decades. Strong-knit communities have been replaced by virtual teams, remote working and communication via e-mail, Web and telephone rather than mainly face-to-face. Efficiency has been improved enormously, to the point that many people have become superfluous and have been let go by companies during lean times but not replaced when economies have strengthened again.

Remaining employees (including the managerial levels) pick up the extra work, drop the least important and work longer hours. This reduces effectiveness, and more technology is brought in to try to fix this (for example call centres, sales force automation, Web sites and mobile working). Many customers adapt to the new way (some even force this way of doing business via their supply chain systems) but not all. Amazingly in all of this, companies remain in profit in the majority of cases. (There were of course pockets of higher satisfaction, as noted in the main body of the paper, but they were in the minority.)

Another research question to come out of this study is, 'Are employees becoming commoditized?' Reichheld discussed the economic models of why long-term employees create value to a company and how layoffs have a destructive effect on employee loyalty.[11] According to this survey, the effect of investing in employees (via education and good packages) to encourage retention and loyalty was not the positive one that Reichheld argues; because the employees were not using their training, it negated feelings of being valued by the company, thus reducing morale. Combine this with the fear of redundancy and high workloads, and employees feel as if they are a commodity rather than a high-value part of the business.

NOTES

1 Norquist, M *et al*, A great place to shop, work and invest: measuring and managing the service profit chain at Sears Canada, *Journal of Interactive Marketing* 3 (3), pp 255–61.

2 Stone, M, Woodcock, N and Machtynger, E (2000) *Customer Relationship Marketing*, Kogan Page, London, p 142.

3 Reichheld, FF (1996) *The Loyalty Effect*, Harvard Business School Press, p 103 and p 95.

4 BBC, *Long Hours Hitting Productivity* (accessed 5 February 2002) [Online] www.bbc.co.uk/business; and *Call Centre Confidentiality* (accessed 21 February 2002) [Online] www.bbc.co.uk/business.

5 Norquist, ? *et al*, A great place to shop, work and invest: measuring and managing the service profit chain at Sears Canada, *Journal of Interactive Marketing* 3 (3), pp 255–61.

6 Anon (1998) South West Airlines redefining relationships with customers, *The Antidote*, **15**, CSBS, pp 38–39.

7 Pai, R, Pudlo, Z and Slaich, A (2002) *Does Job Satisfaction of the Staff at Debenhams Affect Customer Satisfaction?*, unpublished dissertation for MA in marketing, Bristol Business School.

8 Reichheld, FF (1996) *The Loyalty Effect*, Harvard Business School Press, p 303.

9   Peck, H, Payne, A, Christopher, M and Clark, M (1999) *Relationship Marketing: Strategy and implementation, text and cases*, Butterworth Heinemann, cited in *The Antidote*, **18** (1998), CSBS, p 24.

10   Pfeffer, J (1998) *The Human Equation: Building profits by putting people first*, Harvard Business School Press, cited in *The Antidote*, **18** (1998), CSBS, p 14.

11   Reichheld, FF (1996) *The Loyalty Effect*, Harvard Business School Press, pp 91–116.

31

Declining UK customer service standards

Alison Bond and Merlin Stone

If we are to believe the headlines, we live in a customer-focused society. The high streets of predominantly service-based economies are dominated by organizations that profess to put customers first. Newspapers, trade magazines, the professional and academic press and the broadcast media are full of case studies of 'service excellence'. Airport bookshelves are stacked with books exhorting managers to transform their service or to deliver the ultimate customer service experience. The UK government is committing big budgets to e-enabling UK society, with the aim of achieving the magic combination of better service to citizens, at lower cost.

The high level of expenditure on customer relationship management (CRM) programmes and systems is testimony to the fact that private sector companies have focused on this as an area of potential competitive advantage. Sadly, the reality is very different. For all the rhetoric and investment, consumers are feeling baffled, berated and betrayed. Customer service is gradually slipping into customer lip service. This chapter shows how bad the situation is. We now know why. What customers are saying reflects the chaos that exists in many companies. Evidence from the first part of this book indicates that many companies that have invested in CRM programmes are going off the rails and wasting money because they are not managing their programmes well. Another recent study in the financial services industry shows that one of the major problems is that the processes companies have for handling customer feedback are often weak and fragmented and are not supported by systems.[1]

If companies really want to put their customers first and deliver the service that they profess purchasers deserve, this chapter shows that they need to:

- Understand what it is like to be a customer at the receiving end of service, and use all the tools at their disposal to identify what the problems are and when service is not working.
- Learn to deliver what they promise, without over-promising. This means being much smarter at marshalling their people and systems to deliver service and tightening up on their processes.
- Help employees deliver it. This means investing in improved training and empowering them. It means valuing them.
- Educate customers about how they can help themselves: where information is easiest to obtain, and how to complain.
- Manage anger at their peril – customers are not stupid. They cannot be treated like children. They know when they are speaking to a call centre, not least because many have friends or family who work in call centres, or they may do so themselves.
- Start to treat customer complaints as important matters that need to be settled and avoided in future, not frustrations to be dispensed with.

METHODOLOGY

The research took two forms, qualitative and quantitative.

Qualitative research

A series of in-depth focus groups was conducted in London, Manchester and Glasgow. Participants from a variety of socio-economic backgrounds were asked their views on customer service in Britain and about their personal experiences, both good and bad. Comments arising at the focus group sessions are indicated in italics throughout this chapter. The groups were a random sample of age, socio-economic groups and buying habits.

The groups were:

Glasgow

1.   40–65 years, mixed socio groups from C2, C1 and Bs.
2.   25–45 years, C2 and C1s.

Manchester

3.   35–65 years, C1 and Bs.
4.   25 –45 years, mixed socio groups from C2, C1 and Bs.

London

5.   30–55 years, C1, B and one A.

Quantitative research

To test some of the key focus group findings, telephone-based quantitative research was carried out among 1,007 UK adults aged 16 and over during July 2001.

CUSTOMER SERVICE: BUSINESS FASHION OR WORTHWHILE INVESTMENT?

Good customer service is often thought to be apple pie and motherhood. Every organization professes to give it. Every consumer wants to get it. So why is not it happening? This chapter shows that perceived levels of service are declining: and from a pretty low starting point.

Commercial and public services organizations are increasingly working to the mantra that the 'customer is king', but too often they do not live up even to their own platitudes, and attitudes to service differ depending on whether you are on the serving or receiving end.

For consumers, the concept of service is based on their individual expectations, which differ according to a range of circumstances. Until something is outside the norm, there is little appreciation of a service being delivered, merely a product. Where service expectations exist, they tend to be neutral. Service only seems to begin once something has gone wrong or there is need for special advice or help. Yet despite the emphasis on consumer power in today's society, consumers are not getting what they want or deserve.

This is surprising for two reasons. The first is that companies are spending millions on customer relationship management (CRM), so their offerings and advertising should be better targeted to those who will be receptive. Data systems can now retrieve a host of relevant customer information in seconds: and people hate them.

The second is that in a world of bewildering product choice, where previously exotic goods are increasingly sold as commodities, what is left to differentiate an organization but service? However, in spite of the enormous sums spent and the competitive imperative, this report indicates that companies are alienating the very individuals they should be having a 'relationship' with.

Technology is coming between the customer and good service. Or rather, technology is being used as a substitute for good service. There is no point in a current account holder calling his or her telephone bank and speaking to a clerk with all relevant data at his/her fingertips, if the operative is not trained well or empowered to solve the customer's problem.

Call centres ('the new sweatshops') are cheaper to run than regional branches and IVR (interactive voice recognition) systems cost less than switchboards; but the public feel that service is being sacrificed to these economies. They are marshalled in never-ending queues, given push-button options that do not fit their needs, and finally they speak to a 'human' who cannot or will not help, and who appears to have been told to fob them off with platitudes.

Customers on the telephone hate listening to 'hold music' even when the call is free. They want to know where they are in the queue and how long it will take. Selecting options via the keypad is unhelpful, as the options are tailored for the company but not the caller.

Our research showed that despite the huge investment in technology that, in theory, has been implemented to improve customer service, 82 per cent of UK adults agree that too often customer service is worse because companies use automated telephone systems rather than human beings. It is a sad indictment of customer service that many consumers would prefer to take time in their lunch hour to stand in queues at the bank, because, being *in situ*, they feel they have a much greater chance of resolving their issues.

'Computers should be doing the donkey work and the people should be the icing on the cake, but it doesn't seem to be happening in call centres.'

Nevertheless, there is widespread sympathy for those working in call centres, especially those who are clearly working to a script. Too often, customers can see through this, and when a script is obvious, it is not delivering service. For such centres to work better, investment in both the scripting and staff training is vital, not just at launch, but also as part of a continuous programme of training and development. Such programmes would help, but the difficulty in 'asking to see the manager' over the telephone will always leave customers feeling weak, relative to being able to use their physical presence in a retail environment.

Another potential issue is that of 'covert vetting', whereby companies decide what level of attention a customer is worth depending on their level of spend, for example. Less-valued clients will receive more automated push-button menus or be directed to customer care Web sites. It might be argued that this makes commercial sense when looking at a management spreadsheet, but it overlooks one harsh reality of human and commercial behaviour: people talk to each other, and when they have a gripe they advertise it. It is a short-sighted policy, as those who get 'good' service do not realize it, and those who do will never improve their feelings towards the organization. While covert vetting might be designed to reward high-value customers with a 'premium' service, all too often it simply condemns 'lower-value' customers to a spiral of discontent.

So has the money that has been poured into CRM technologies in recent years achieved the end result desired: better customer service and lower costs? Our research suggests not. Sixty per cent of those questioned felt that customer service had got worse over the past five years.

BENCHMARKING BEST PRACTICE CUSTOMER SERVICE

So who does it well? The quantitative study in this chapter shows that corner shops are perceived consistently to provide the best customer service in the UK. Given the commercial importance and level of corporate investment that is committed to providing good customer service, this might be surprising. Nevertheless, the traditional, low-tech corner shop illustrates a number of customer service lessons that many larger corporates would do well to learn:

- **Face-to-face service**: often knowing their best customers very well. (No covert vetting here: customers are either regular or not.)
- **Open for long hours**: providing their services at times that suit their customers rather than themselves.
- **Clarity of offer**: usually a limited stock of basic essentials – a significant finding. People want a basic selection of decent goods, well explained, available stress-free for a reasonable price: less is more.
- **Tailored and relevant**: working from the basis of providing core essentials, stock is based on the local (or target) market.
- **Premium priced**: customers know they pay over the odds, but are generally happy to do so for the service they get and for the convenience. For many customers (students, older people), the corner shop fits brilliantly with their lifestyle, particularly if they do not have their own transport.

It seems the corporate retailers have learnt this lesson, judging by their commitment to the city centre and suburban convenience format.

Consumers did not see that the huge amount of choice available today via different distribution channels constituted some kind of improved service. Service equals problems, and problems have to be sorted face-to-face. In the corner shop, they care about your custom. What is the point of having enormous choice if service is poor?

We asked consumers their opinion of who provided the best service.

The customer service league table (high scores for service at the top)

1. Corner shops.
2. Supermarket chains.
3. Restaurants.
4. National Health Service / general practitioners.
5. Travel agents.
6. Banks and building societies.
7. Department stores.
8. Telephone companies.
9. Electricity companies.
10. Gas companies.
11. Water companies.
12. Solicitors.
13. Electrical goods retailers.
14. Insurance companies.
15. Estate agents.

The customer service league table shows that the supermarkets have perhaps made the most ground in replicating the service offered by their smaller counterparts. Increasingly, their stock will adapt to the local market, the proliferation of deli counters provides an element of tailored services, extended opening hours make them ever more accessible, and customers understand the offer.

Conversely, the lack of face-to-face or immediate experience, except in the direst circumstances, helps explain why utility companies, for example, appear mid to low down in the table. The only contact customers have with them tends to be over the phone and often for potentially calamitous problems. Utilities are remote until an engineer is needed – and he or she had better come quickly – or until bills are questioned, itself a time of frustration.

In many cases consumer attitudes are coloured by the issue of discretionary spending. In corner shops, supermarkets and restaurants, purchasers choose to buy or not to buy: and expectations for service levels vary according to these choices. Expectations of the service in a fast-food pizza parlour will differ from those in a glamorous city venue. In contrast, with many insurances and water supply there are supplier choices (a bewildering number, said the research) but customers cannot opt out.

In the cases of solicitors and estate agents, these may be seen as irritating but inescapable intruders into already stressful processes. Thus being forced to spend money on a service predisposes the customer to feel negatively about it. Unless the service provider is sympathetic to this and is determined to compensate for it, then the net effect is for the predisposition to be confirmed.

Comparing similar operations, it would appear that department stores could learn lessons from supermarkets, while electrical retailers obviously have far to go. Here, the crucial element is the familiarity of sales staff with the products that they sell and the availability of goods. Customers at department stores and electrical retailers typically spend several hundred pounds on occasional purchases and must choose between products with only subtle, though important, differences in functionality. They do not buy them often and are rarely experts about the product, hence they have to rely on the expertise of salespeople, who do not always have the knowledge the customer requires and often appear uninterested, uncaring and unqualified to explain what they are selling.

This frequently gives the impression that the department store or electrical retailer has decided against investing in staff training and therefore is not concerned about the level of service that it offers.

The core component of good customer service can be characterized as the willingness, ability and licence of customer-facing staff to take personal responsibility. Though they may not always be able to solve a problem or provide an answer, their preparedness to tackle an issue, thus relieving a customer of the burden, is crucial. Compare 'You learn to say, "Sorry, and I will sort it out," even if it has nothing to do with you' with 'The man at [well-known department store] said he was going to make a mission of finding a machine with this function. Well, it's been his mission for nearly four weeks and I still haven't heard from him.'

When service works well, particularly if it is unexpected, it can revolutionize a customer's attitude to an organization. 'The service at [large retail chemist] was extraordinary, it was so good. I was amazed.' Conversely, where the burden of problem solving is not removed, the effects on consumers can be startling: 'When you mentioned [utility company], I felt physically sick. The service was so awful I did actually have to write to a television consumer programme.'

UK COMPANIES ARE SITTING ON A CUSTOMER SERVICE TIME BOMB

Customers are not happy, but most of them do not do anything about it. When they do, it is likely to involve a mental shift towards a US-style litigation culture, rather than simply being more assertive. British reserve is not helping here. Consumers feel that complaining instantly and publicly to get improved service is rather 'American', and they would not necessarily be liked for doing so. Far more British not to make a fuss, grind your teeth and plan a stinging letter to the MD: a letter that probably never gets sent.

But when the worm turns: watch out! When ultimately riled, the Brits write letters to newspapers, demand high levels of compensation and make it their life's work to denigrate the organization in question. However, even if such efforts are successful, have they struck a blow for improved service or merely added grey hairs and enhanced solicitors' bank balances? At present, poor customer service is choking UK enterprise because most people take the 'better the devil you know' approach. Thus, customers stay with bad organizations, and good ones find it very hard to dislodge customers (for example, changing bank current accounts).

A frequent obstacle to improving customers' perceptions of service is the deployment of 'anger management techniques' by service providers. Companies train their – often call-centre based – staff to defuse angry callers by sounding gentle and sympathetic, letting them get things 'off their chest', but the clerk is not actually able or empowered to solve the problem. Thus customers are 'handled' but make no progress, enhancing the opinion that they are being endured and managed, rather than listened to.

Forty-seven per cent of respondents noted that customer service staff sometimes seemed to be trained to 'calm me down and make me go away', rather than solve the problem. Fifty-five per cent were aware that staff were using 'scripted' answers to enquiries. 'If someone is prepared to argue with you over the phone you feel more fulfilled. Especially if you get them to see your point of view and they do something about it.'

No doubt, when this containment works well, it works very well indeed: the customer is satisfied and the company does not have to pay for a problem to be solved. But when customers realize that they are being 'managed' in this way, it only serves to compound the initial problem. Anger management is often recognized for what it is: a deliberate decision to invest valuable resources in frustrating customers into submission, rather than solving their problem and preventing it from happening again.

The economics for the service provider are clear: a small investment in staff training will save far larger significant sums in after-sales care and product repairs or returns, all of which would deliver real customer satisfaction. Our research shows that, in spite of their statutory rights, 44 per cent of consumers have been refused their request for a refund on faulty goods and offered a repair or credit note instead. Frustrations faced trying to enforce these rights have been so severe that one in four (25 per cent) have simply given up trying to get a refund.

Overall, half the respondents agreed that customer service had got worse in the last five years, an opinion held most strongly by those aged between 45 and 54. A massive three-fifths (62 per cent) thought that companies give the impression that they would rather get customers off the phone than solve the problem. Interestingly men and those with children were more likely to take this view.

But the ultimate indication of the failure of customer service expenditure to improve customers' experiences is that 82 per cent agreed that automated telephone systems are a cause of inferior service. Again, those aged over 45 felt this most strongly. 'It costs you more money on your phone bill and the last option is usually "Please hold for further assistance"!'

A third of us dread picking up the phone to complain, and a similar proportion put it off to avoid confrontation: no wonder we often do not do it at all. More worryingly for the future, 16 to 24 year olds were the most likely age group to shy away from making a stand.

Unfortunately, poor service is so endemic now that people do not complain when they receive it and, for many, it is a very stressful business:

- 52 per cent admitted that complaining and dealing with customer service failure was very stressful.
- 59 per cent feel that the stress of making a complaint is often more trouble than it is worth.
- 33 per cent dread picking up the phone or going into the shop to complain.
- 31 per cent put off complaining because they do not like confrontation.

Should these latent frustrations boil over, and customers wake up to their rights, it could spell trouble for service providers. Not only would they start to sink or swim on their ability to turn platitudes into action, but also they could be at a very real risk of finding themselves at the sharp end of increased litigation.

At present, for hardened complainers the process is not only stressful but often requires the planning and preparation of a military operation. Nine out of ten (87 per cent) sit down and get all the facts straight before going into battle with customer services departments. A minority are so accustomed to questioning the service they receive that they have prepared rituals for doing so. These range from the informal 'you ring off peak, you flirt, you chat and generally cajole your way round the operators' to the more tenacious and canny.

Anecdotally, men spoke about their preparations: putting the paperwork in order, having every conceivable answer ready, and then psyching themselves up in the store toilet before a confrontation. This is primitive fight-or-flight conflict behaviour. The popular alternative was to get their wives to do it! 'Every step closer to the shop I could feel myself girding myself up for the confrontation. When it didn't happen I felt a bit let down really.'

THE EFFECTS OF POOR SERVICE

Clearly, the public's perception of the quality of customer service is very low, and this has produced an attitude that complaining simply is not worth the effort. The result is that not only does service not improve (as consumers are not voting with their feet and going to the better companies) but customers also lose financially. Twenty-eight per cent say the fear of poor customer service puts them off switching financial service providers, despite that fact that 74 per cent claim that terrible service would make them change. The loyalty prize is there for the providers who get it right: 77 per cent of people think that customer service is a very important factor in staying with their current bank or building society. Despite the millions financial service companies have thrown at 'improving' customer service, under half (48 per cent) of those questioned felt that the companies they dealt with offered really good service.

The fear of poor service elsewhere prevents 3 in 10 of financial services customers changing supplier (see Table 31.1). Nearly 20 per cent say such organizations generally offer 'terrible' service.

'I had offers from [three competitors] asking if I would like to change. I was so confused I stayed with the one I was with. I don't know if they were the cheapest.'

Many organizations – especially those in financial services – rely on inertia for their profits. However, staying with an insurer or bank, for example, because 'they're all the same' could prove very costly. Few customers seem to move because of bad service. A respondent from a focus group in Glasgow talked at length about the terrible service from her bank but, months later, had not got round to changing supplier.

The economics of making sure customers are satisfied with the service they get are difficult to dispute. For every disenchanted customer that ends their relationship with the company, the high costs of winning them back drives the economics in the opposite direction. This must be a huge incentive for businesses to get customer service right. However, businesses face many challenges if they try to provide good customer service for all:

▌ They must either empower their employees to deal with problems or elevate complainers immediately to the right level or department to ensure swift resolution.
▌ This requires more training and fluidity between business divisions, as well as a more experimental approach: it is not always clear what works and adds value.
▌ They must invest in the right systems.
▌ They must create the right processes.

Ultimately, companies that get it right will enjoy a competitive advantage and the chance to differentiate their otherwise commodity offers on a service proposition.

CONCLUSION

Companies are beginning to realize that customer service is the key to keeping good customers and doing more business with them. Yet it still seems as if customer service works more effectively to deter customers or make them feel bad about doing business with companies. Customers do not usually have a mechanism to express to big companies 'what it was like for them'.

Poor service happens in every sector and in all areas of the country. On the whole people do not expect good service, and this means that they tend to be on the defensive when requesting service or having to make a complaint. This has a negative effect on both the supplier and the customer. Neither side has any incentive or even the possibility of talking to each other about how the whole process is working. A customer telephones to buy or to complain, the purchase takes place or the complaint is registered, and that is that.

Few customers have the opportunity to have a chat with the service team. While there is sympathy for those who work in call centres, we saw no evidence of customers wanting to have conversations with those working in the centres. Perhaps they thought that it was not worth bothering because they were not empowered to help?

To get good customer service takes time, and time seems to run in short supply. On the other hand, poor customer service wastes time – for the supplier and the customer. Many companies think they have 'sorted' customer service. They are nearly all wrong. But as service costs money, companies must look harder at which customers are least happy, and in particular which customers who have money to spend would spend more of it with them if service were better.

However, the reality is that they also need to give better service to all customers. Who is to say that a customer who is lower value today will remain so tomorrow? Who is to say that these customers do not have friends with whom they talk about service and who want to do business with the company?

This means that while some companies are having delusions of grandeur in terms of how they want to use CRM, many need to get back to basics in terms of using it to serve customers well and cost-effectively to yield better business returns. Here the answer probably lies in more, but much friendlier, technology and smarter processes.

This chapter shows that until businesses improve customer service, reduce complaints and win the confidence of the British public, consumers will, by default, adopt an attitude of 'better the devil you know'. Our research clearly indicates that people are discouraged from switching providers, financial services or otherwise, because they are fearful of the treatment they will get elsewhere. This is seriously stifling competition.

Companies are getting away with the type of servicing they offer customers because most companies are doing it. Customers do not like it, and one can only assume that eventually the moaning will stop, the worm will turn, and some companies will find themselves very short of business.

Table 31.1 Why customers do not switch after bad service

		Sex %		Age %					
	Total	Male	Female	16–24	25–34	35–44	45–54	55–64	65+
The fear of poor customer service puts me off switching financial service providers	28	31	24	26	26	25	30	32	28
Good customer service is a very important factor in staying with my current bank/ building society	77	77	77	76	77	79	78	81	72
Terrible service would make me change my bank/ building society	74	73	74	77	72	77	75	76	69
Few of the financial service companies I deal with offer really good service	48	47	49	57	53	47	40	54	38
Financial services companies offer terrible customer service	18	22	14	16	22	18	15	27	11
I am not happy, but can't be bothered to change providers because I don't believe it will be better elsewhere	28	32	23	26	23	30	36	31	24
None of these	9	9	9	9	5	7	9	6	16

NOTE

[1] Stone, M *et al* (2002) Customer service, complaints management and regulatory compliance, *Journal of Financial Regulation & Compliance*, **10** (1) pp 37–54; and Stone, M, Cox, D and Wiltshire, G (2002) Complaints management in financial services, *International Journal of Customer Relationship Management*, **5** (1) pp 49–58.

32

Governance and executive sponsorship in CRM programmes

Peter Floyd and Bryan Foss

INTRODUCTION

This chapter discusses two critical areas for successful customer relations management (CRM) programmes. The first is the subject of programme governance and the second is the role and function of executive sponsorship. Programme governance is critical to programme success. Businesses with strong governance succeed. Any good organization undertaking a long-term business transformation knows that strong governance is required for successful change. Our research and experience proves that return on investment is limited, or even nonexistent, where no governance structure is in place, or where dependencies are not managed effectively. It is far easier to build business cases and to spend on additional organization and systems than it is to ensure the market and internal dependencies are sufficiently controlled to deliver the required revenue returns.

A critical component of programme governance is strong executive sponsorship. Personal sponsorship is required from the highest levels; this must be as an involved champion of change. In IBM's global CRM programme this was the chief executive personally, Lou Gerstner. The sponsor needs to do more than 'wear the T shirt', becoming personally involved and providing direction to the executive board. 'Walking the talk' and leading by example is key to pre-empting and removing barriers to change. In one global financial services company, where the CRM programme director was also the managing director of a subsidiary bank, the executive measurement and pay system was changed by the chief executive officer (CEO) to pay each executive 75 per cent on team transformation results, leaving 25 per cent payment for his or her personal ownership of subsidiary revenue and profit success. Of course the CEO was not expecting any executive to neglect his or her personal business targets, but at the same time he was emphasizing the importance of change across the enterprise, and his expectation of achieving this through enterprise and executive teaming.

This brings into focus a highly relevant but less well-known area, critical to executive sponsors of CRM programmes, that of 'symbolic action', where the ability to play an acting role becomes critical in managing the various audiences involved. The role of an executive sponsor can be summed up in the following short analogy. Imagine the scenario: you are a movie producer and one day you get a call from a studio, 'We've got a great idea for a movie and we want you to produce it for us, oh and there's a small acting part in it for you as well. Here's the brief, now go and make it happen.' It is a low-budget production so you need to do a bit of scriptwriting and directing as well. Throughout this chapter we will be comparing the parallels between the role of executive sponsor and the multiple roles associated with the making of a movie: producer, scriptwriter, casting director and actor, focusing primarily on the actor role.

There are two main differences between the world of movie production and that of change leadership in organizations. First, movie production is a totally project-based operation, whereas change in organizations entails a project operation being overlaid on existing organizational structures. This creates a significant set of discrete challenges that are not faced in movie production. In fact the governance and change project aims to provide the continuity through various organization stages, selecting the most appropriate structure at any one time, and planning the level of change that can be absorbed and the emphasis that needs to be made (for example innovation or roll-out).

Second, in the movie business there is a final result: the creation of the film, at which point the team disbands. Contrast this with an organizational change, where there are major effects on all aspects of an organization, which need to be sustained for further periods in the organization's evolution. Some might suggest this is the largest obstacle and success factor of programmes within an organization.

In this chapter, the term 'executive sponsor' refers to a senior person within an organization who is given the 'responsibility' for the implementation of a change programme. The term should not be confused with terms such as 'programme sponsorship', which refer to funding arrangements for commercial sponsorship of events. The word 'responsibility' is important because the specific role and responsibilities, or authority, for an executive sponsor are rarely defined or clear and are generally left to the individual who has such an honour bestowed – which is an issue in itself. In CRM programmes there are many issues faced by the programme sponsor, depending on the specifics of the situation. Ideally the programme sponsor of any CRM programme is the CEO or managing director, who has the remit and power to address the complex 're-engineering' that is required for any successful CRM programme. Many issues are faced in implementing successful CRM, including changing the mindsets of those involved, making the sometimes difficult transition to a more integrated and customer-focused approach to an organization's operations. Another is addressing the 'functional silos' that exist within organizations and have a strong influence on group behaviour, particularly at senior levels. One of the biggest challenges for CRM implementations is making the organizational structure match the organization's new alignment. Any CRM implementation will affect all functions – sales, marketing, customer support – and all business processes – customer attraction, the sales process and so on. This can be a political minefield for senior executives in organizations, including the sponsor.

Too often the sponsor has never made such an extensive and enterprise-wide transformation journey, yet is expected to lead by example, cascading clear objectives and roles to the executive and management team. In the early stages it can be very valuable to develop links with external mentors who have been in such a role and can relate the critical success factors to the new sponsor. The most active sponsors will research the role and learn quickly, while others will simply pass the problem down to the executive team without clear direction.

This chapter discusses the role(s) of the executive sponsor and the specific actions and behaviours that should be adopted to ensure the success of the programme, particularly within the crucial initial stages of a programme. The chapter focuses on the significance of 'symbolic action' for sponsors, whose appointment can be viewed as a largely symbolic one anyway.

Symbolic action is different from more substantive action because symbolic action has no explicit, direct intention for the audience, but is more suggestive and symbolic. It is not driven by pure logic but rather has its value in the meaning that people attach to it. Examples are the use of a metaphor, the type of language used, and actions that surprise or are not expected.

Any new programme faces a range of resistance and barriers. The typical response of leaders is to present very logical and rational arguments for the programme. This helps in many respects but invariably does not either win over all people or does not provide a totally compelling case for people.

This chapter argues that, in order to gain commitment and win the hearts and minds of all stakeholders, attention must also be given to more emotive levers. Hence leaders and particularly sponsors of new programmes should give consideration to symbolic action as well as the more substantive actions. Here we discuss what these actions might be, then go on to discuss some of the implications of these ideas for management. But first, programme governance.

PROGRAMME GOVERNANCE

Effective programme governance comprises a number of key roles and activities. These are outlined below.

Programme manager

The programme manager needs to be of a sufficient level and capability that the stakeholders view him or her as an equal and have confidence in his or her ability to succeed. The sponsor needs to personally appoint the programme manager, and champion change through identifying and resolving issues very rapidly – even in advance!

Programme board and team

The best skills are always in demand to run business operations. However these same people are required to manage change. It may be a tough decision but it is essential for success that key people are selected to join the programme team. These people represent the stakeholders at a working level. They may be allocated to the team for short periods, to achieve specific objectives, and then released back to roles, which will take advantage of their new skills and knowledge.

Architecture board

The leader of the architecture board is normally a member of the full programme board. The role of the architecture board is to achieve a level of consistency and synergy across the enterprise systems and data structures. This is essential for achieving enterprise cost reduction and operational resilience.

Project budgets are more usually allocated to the business today, which can create a tendency towards isolated quick wins at the expense of increased ROI from shared infrastructure and leveraged successes.

Figure 32.1 shows a typical governance structure for programme management.

Where are we starting? What do we do next?

CMAT provides the required evidence-based diagnosis of intention versus reality and effect. Based on this diagnosis and external benchmarks, a stakeholders' workshop should develop and decide the priorities, responsibilities and potential return on investment (ROI) of efforts. With special attention during deployment, the CMAT exercise can also provide the basis for a cascade of new and appropriate transformation objectives and measures of control and success.

Business cases

Business cases should be developed using the evidence resulting from the CMAT assessment or subsequent detailed analysis of priority project areas. Cases must be

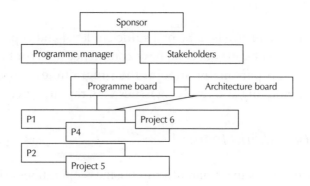

Figure 32.1 Programme governance structure

sufficiently realistic to be achievable, formed as a plan of activities, expenditure and dependencies for ROI. Many companies now use standard modelling techniques and hurdle rates for comparative business cases. However, business cases have become more difficult to substantiate as the focus has moved from efficiencies and cost reduction to effectiveness and customer retention, development and appropriate acquisition.

Objectives and measures

The new objectives (both operational and transformation-related) are developed and cascaded through the same design process. It is important that these objectives and measures reflect the organizational and project dependencies required for success. Too often projects adopt standard or 'best practice' measures which are inappropriate and which work against cooperation and enterprise success. For example call centres may still be focused on elapsed call-time reduction, when the objectives have changed to encourage the call centre to move to an active role in customer development, through achieving retention, cross-sell and up-sell objectives. Poorly formed measures can easily work against change objectives. Strategic or balanced scorecards can be developed for regular measurement and management of change, not only identifying revenue and profit success, but also providing a hierarchy of success criteria that can be used to identify and control business pipelines and customer management activities.

Risk management plans

The overall programme and each subsidiary project require a risk management plan, with prioritization of risks by probability and potential impact. The risk management plan must be active, focused on identifying and mitigating selected risks. These plans are developed in the traditional manner, but with special focus on the external and internal dependencies of ROI achievement for each project and across the programme as a whole.

Setting up and managing sub-projects within the programme

A traditional project office can provide the supporting and administrative role required to release substantial productive time for the programme manager and boards. There are well-developed models for good practice of traditional project office operations. Programme management is more complex than the management of a single project, requiring the project office to manage multiple projects and their interdependencies concurrently.

Managing process and application change

When a new application suite is purchased, or applications are integrated to create parts of the new business process, there can be a desire to over-customize applications to fit existing operations. It is important to identify and close only the essential modification 'gap' in the first stages of deployment, allowing more rapid rollout and early achievement of ROI from breadth of implementation deployment. Once the 'new world' processes and application set have been introduced and experienced, it is far easier to identify the essential changes required for business success in this world. This ensures that focus remains on the development of change for future value, rather than for compromise to existing norms.

Ensuring ROI

This is a more significant part of most projects and programmes than is normally allowed for. It requires the programme team and the stakeholders to act together in an integrated plan, releasing previous costs through commitments to implement timely migration and delivering on identified dependencies to ensure ROI. Having achieved isolated project steps, often delivering their own (limited) ROI, it is often more effective to replicate or integrate business operations to achieve much more substantial ROI, than to embark on the implementation of another separate project step. This would normally have been identified in the prioritization process, but can be revalidated as the measures of success become apparent.

THE HISTORIC VIEW OF ORGANIZATIONS AND CHANGE

The traditional view of organizations, particularly within academic literature, has been that they are places of great rationality, where matters are discussed openly, impartially and objectively, and decisions are made in a similar manner. This was also true for organizational change. The process of change has been viewed as a highly rational, logical and systematic process. Executives leading change initiatives also adopted a highly logical and rational approach. This manifested itself in many ways, ranging from the justification and rationale for the change through to the process by which the change was managed. The other main lever adopted was the use of formal power to drive the change through, which meant that all parties 'fell in line' most of the time.

A number of developments have led to this rather simplistic model of both organizations and change being radically rethought. As organizations have become larger, and the complexities exponentially increased, the sole use of formal power to drive changes through has not worked. A single power source in the new matrix organizations was not enough. Second, the articulated rationale and logic for change was not acceptable to many of the stakeholders who saw things rather differently. Third, change programmes had an abysmal success rate, with over 70 per cent of programmes not living up to expectations or being cancelled prematurely. Many academics working in the field also developed new thinking and ideas to capture these new, more sophisticated models, based on a broader understanding of 'organizational behaviour'. Their thinking evolved to see organizations from a range of viewpoints: cognitive, cultural and political. Writers invented wonderful phrases to articulate this more diverse approach to organizations, change and the issues, including terms such as 'bounded rationality, pluralistic competition, muddling through, co-optation, resource dependency, garbage can decision processes and loose couplings'.[1]

THE PROCESS AND STYLE OF CHANGE

Many writers and academics portray change as a process. Several authors developed more sophisticated models of the change process based on the new, broader view of organizations and change. Beer, Eisenstat and Spector developed a good model for the process of change with clear implications for the executive sponsor role.[2] This model defined six steps:

1. Mobilize commitment to change through joint diagnosis of problems.
2. Develop a shared vision of how to organize.
3. Foster consensus for the new vision.
4. Spread re-vitalization to all departments.

5. Institutionalize revitalization.
6 Monitor and adjust strategies.

The words used to summarize each of these steps are key, and a close reading of each, or indeed the article itself, is recommended.

These six steps represent one relatively consensual approach to change. This is the approach that the authors believe produces the best results. However, a wide spectrum of change approaches is documented, ranging from the 'totally autocratic' through to those of the OD (organizational development) movement such as Beer's. This subject is also influenced by the question of leadership style. One of the very early models for leadership style was Tannenbaum and Schmidt's[3] continuum of leadership styles, which ranged from the 'tell' approach through to the approach of 'giving the problem to the group'. Each style has of course differing benefits and issues or risks associated with it. Some of the factors that determine the defined approach or steps to a change include:

▮ the organizational culture, and the context in which the change is taking place;
▮ the context or change itself, potentially either a difficult change or one that needs to be implemented fast, so could/should have less of a consensual style and more of an autocratic style; the start point of any change is often unclear, and is open to interpretation. It could be defined as:

▮ when an issue gets air-time at senior levels (issue is surfaced);
▮ when some action is taken (a start is made);
▮ when a proposal, recommendation, or solution is proposed (a solution is defined);
▮ when goals are defined, scope is agreed, resources are allocated, a sponsor is found, a workshop is held, a team formed, and a plan devised.

The process for the early stages, and when the team responsible for it should get involved, are both important. The early stages of the change are crucial for two main reasons, first and most importantly for the success and lasting adoption of the programme, and second for portraying the style of change that will be used, and therefore defining the ground rules for the process and participation in it. Both these points are key and are developed further in the chapter.

THE CHALLENGE OF CHANGE

Whatever style is selected, there will always be many challenges faced by those involved in driving the programme, including the executive sponsor. The literature highlights many issues inherent in any change programme. These include resistance to the change, the dynamics of power and political battles around it, and sustaining the change. These barriers can at worst derail any change, or at best delay and slow it. For programmes that cut across existing functional boundaries, especially successful CRM, one of the biggest issues and challenges for the programme (and key activity for the sponsor) is ensuring commitment and consensus from key players across the organization.

Typically, at the more senior levels of the organization, politics plays a key part in the change and its implementation. The word 'politics' itself arouses strong emotions with executives, and is often ignored or buried. This is manifestly wrong because differing views on the multitude of issues associated with any change need managing. These might include the reasons for the change, the chosen solution to the problem or opportunity, and the way in which the implementation is planned.

IBM uses a straightforward model at the macro level for managing complex change programmes. This divides the work into one of four components: organization, processes, people and IT. The 'people factor' is by far the most interesting, complex, challenging and absolutely crucial to successful change, as the next section will demonstrate. This is an area that has little relevance to the old traditional or rational approach.

THE RISE OF PEOPLE, OR STAKEHOLDER, POWER

The word 'organization' presents a rather depersonalized and abstract view of an entity, almost hiding the fact that its key constituents are its people or employees. An organization's key assets – its people – are both its biggest strength and its biggest weakness. The drivers of individual and collective behaviour are complex. There are almost as many theories on the matter as there are variations in individual personalities and styles. Personal attitudes, beliefs and motivation manifest themselves in a range of behaviours. It is useful to consider the world of politics through the lens of individual self-interest, particularly around change where there are inevitably clear winners and losers.

This is a complex and dynamic organizational world where people are driven by self-interest and organizations are driven by multiple goals in a political context; therefore the challenge for executive sponsors is sharply put into focus. It is within this environment that the key role and activities of the sponsor supporting the programme are required. Thus the focus of the sponsor on generating understanding and gaining commitment to a goal and course of action from a broad range of stakeholders and interested parties is paramount.

In the movie analogy, an interesting parallel can be drawn with some of the issues around managing actors and movie stars. Typically these people are driven far more by emotions and egos than any logical or rational element. Consequently they have to be influenced and managed in very different ways from that typically experienced in more 'rational' organizations. In CRM implementations the most critical stakeholder issue is the 'joining of minds' of the senior functional business leaders, those representing marketing, sales, operations and IT. Whereas before the functional silos were clearly delineated, a CRM strategy forces an organization to rethink its functions, the roles, the performance metrics, and most importantly emphasizes the interdependencies between functions and people. For people at all levels across the organization this change can be perceived as an opportunity but also a possible threat, and possible overt, or worse covert, operations can begin to sabotage the change.

A RANGE OF ROLES AND TYPES OF LEADERSHIP

Conventional wisdom suggests that good, effective leadership is core to any successful change. However it is also true that there are a multitude of theories on leadership and on the variety of roles of leadership. With such little literature available on sponsorship, there are few models or theories that relate closely to the role of executive sponsor. Nadler and Tushman[4] devised an excellent model considering the core capabilities of a leader, which suit that of the executive sponsor. Their model defined three forms of leadership:

▌ visioning;
▌ institutionalizing;
▌ developing.

The typical view is that the CEO is the 'visionary leader', and people selected for executive sponsor positions are seen more as the implementers, doers or 'institutionalizers' to use Nadler and Tushman's phrase. Nadler and Tushman define this role as comprising three main components:

▌ leveraging the senior team;
▌ broadening senior management;
▌ developing leadership in the organization.

Of course the other view is that sponsors are chosen primarily because of their credibility with 'the business', and their leadership skills, and possibly for their political 'noses' for getting things done. The core of this chapter is the role of the executive sponsor in driving and managing the change.

THE EXECUTIVE SPONSOR ROLE: DIRECTOR, SCRIPTWRITER AND PRODUCER

Much of the practitioner literature stresses the importance of top management support for any programme. This is often recognized by organizations and theoretically solved by the creation of an 'executive sponsor' role and corresponding person to take that role for a programme. However, the authors' research has shown that often there is little in the way of 'job spec' for such a role, and little guidance or definition as to either what is expected or what is required. There are a broad number of potential labels for such a role, in addition to that of executive sponsor:

▌ change agent;
▌ champion;
▌ owner;
▌ advocate.

The problem with these labels is that they are broad and ill-defined, and in some instances clearly wrong. This highlights the lack of academic research and rigour that is currently associated with this area. These do not clearly define the role, its tasks and activities. Much research has highlighted the importance of the executive sponsor role, but little has been said about what exactly is the sponsor's role: what it specifically entails, and what responsibilities and accountabilities the sponsor has, particularly in the initial stages. Many people involved in such programmes place the 'final' resolution of all these problems and challenges at the door of the programme sponsor: the supposed 'super-hero' or Mr Fixit of the programme. Initial research by the authors shows that the role of the sponsor, and in particular the types of issue and action that successful sponsors undertake, differ across the various phases. The most important phase is certainly the initial phase, which is discussed below. The movie theme fits this with a range of unique roles, all of which are required to make a successful movie, from the director, producer and scriptwriter down to the 'best boy'.

EXECUTIVE SPONSORSHIP IN THE INITIAL PHASE

The biggest challenge for sponsors in the initial phase is that of gaining understanding, consensus, commitment and the required action to the programme and its goals, expressed by Floyd.[5] Each of these is of course very different but one does lead to the next.

This has to be achieved against the backdrop of a broad range of stakeholders, or more importantly audiences, each having very differing perceptions of the change and its possible implications. This process of gaining understanding, support and commitment is achieved in a number of ways. First, as was mentioned earlier, organizations attempt to achieve this in very logical or rational ways. The 'why, what and how' are communicated, including the rationale, information on the business cases, goals, and approach. Another view of the role the sponsor should play in this initial stage is provided by Gioia and Chittipeddi[6] who developed the phrase 'sense-making and sense- giving' to define a key requirement for the leader of any change. One other concept that is useful is that of managing meaning. These latter ones straddle both the logical and emotional levels.

Again, this is not enough for change to succeed. The human and emotional needs and aspects of people's response to change have to be addressed. This can be achieved in a number of ways. The first is by the choosing a good leader as the sponsor, establishing a credible source of power to the programme. Having joined the programme, successful sponsors can influence the more emotional needs in many ways, such as the words, actions, and behaviours of the key people. Many of these are substantive in that they have an explicit and specific purpose or intended outcome. However all actions can be viewed as partly symbolic, some primarily symbolic rather than substantive, while others have dual roles.

ACHIEVING COMMITMENT VIA 'SYMBOLIC ACTION': THE PART-TIME ACTING ROLE

Symbolic action is defined as 'people's interaction and communication in the course of which they generate, convey, and infer meanings and significance'.[7] Pfeffer[8] states, 'it is the symbolic identification with organizations or decisions, as much as real choice and participation, that produces commitment and action'. The value of symbolic action is that it almost defies rationality; the significance of symbolic action is in its power to convey far more than words can. It cuts across the rational level, working strongly at the emotional level.

Tom Peters, in an early article on symbolic action,[9] categorized the types of action under several headings:

- calendars;
- reports;
- agenda;
- physical settings;
- public statements;
- staff organization.

Symbolic actions are here categorized into two areas. The first is those actions that are 'one-offs'. These include firing or hiring people; giving presentations; setting new directions and goals; defining requirements for new or different information; and selecting which battles to fight and which not to fight. The second are ongoing actions. These include new behaviour, role modelling, where one invests time and energy, who one spends time with and listens to, and meetings attended.

Shakespeare's 'All the world's a stage, and all the men and women merely players' applies equally to the world of organizations as it does to social or theatrical life. Using the movie analogy, specific actions for any actor or actress to convey meaning include the whole gamut of facial expressions such as the lift of an eyebrow, body movement or language, and clothes worn. Each of these in a movie can have a very profound impact on the viewer or audience. Significantly, this is the sole purpose of actors' roles and what they are paid to do, and differentiates between bad, average and great actors.

CONCLUSIONS AND IMPLICATIONS FOR MANAGEMENT

This chapter has proposed a new definition of the executive sponsor role for large and complex programmes that cut across traditional functional silos, that of managing strategic consensus for the programme through symbolic action. A strong governance structure, based on considerable experience of successful yet complex projects, has also been proposed to support achievement of the sponsor's goals. The sponsor's primary role is portrayed as managing, consensus, commitment and action towards the programme's goals through understanding the importance of meaning, and to this end engaging in both substantive and symbolic action to influence and manage the meaning people attach to the programme and its goals. For CRM programmes this is particularly important where senior executives and middle management can perceive these programmes and their impact as a threat of personal loss of power, or a fear of the 'brave new world'.

The implications of these ideas for management are clear.

▌ The initial 'launch' phase of the programme is of paramount importance for the overall success of the programme.

▌ Executive programme sponsors play an absolutely vital role in these areas; their actions and demonstrated commitment to the programme is also an important success factor.

▌ Sponsors must understand the important symbolic nature of their role.

▌ Sponsors must seek to clarify and define their expected role and contribution within the programme, particularly with respect to the core programme team, which includes the programme manager, and with the other members of the organization's executive within a single governance structure for change.

▮ Sponsors should recognize the important role and contribution that symbolic action plays in providing meaning and legitimacy for the programme across the range of stakeholders involved, and how this can provide a powerful emotive influence on their belief in and commitment to the programme.

▮ Sponsors should re-examine how they spend their time and what actions they take in their roles, recognizing the potential impact of viewing their roles through a symbolic lens.

So, at the end of the movie, when the titles and credits role by, it is probably no understatement that the person performing the executive sponsorship role has figured in a number of other lead and supporting roles, both on and off camera. It might also be the case that s/he appears in one or many of the currently fashionable out-takes included at the end of the movie featuring those acting slips. However, remember: the Oscar is just around the corner!

NOTES

[1] March, J (1997) Administrative practice, organisation theory, and political philosophy: ruminations on the reflections of John M Gaus, *Political Science and Politics*, pp 689–98.

[2] Beer, M, Eisenstat, R A and Spector, B (1990) Why change programmes don't produce results, *Harvard Business Review* (Nov–Dec), pp 158–66.

[3] Tannenbaum, R and Schmidt, W (1958) How to choose a leadership pattern, *Harvard Business Review* (March–April), pp 95–101.

[4] Nadler, D and Tushman, M (1990) Beyond the charismatic leader: leadership and organizational change, *California Management Review* (Winter), pp 77–97.

[5] Floyd, S (1992) Managing strategic consensus: the foundation of effective implementation, *Academy of Management Executive*, **6** (4), pp 27–38.

[6] Gioia, D and Chittipeddi, K (1991) Sense-making and sense-giving in strategic change initiation, *Strategic Management Journal*, 12, pp 433–48.

[7] Jones, M (1996) *Studying Organizational Symbolism*, Sage, Thousand Oaks, Calif.

[8] Pfeffer, J (1981) Management as symbolic action, in *Research in Organizational Behaviour*, Vol 3, ed L L Cummings and B M Straw, pp 1–52, JAI Press, Greenwich, Conn.

[9] Peters, T (1978) Symbols, patterns and settings, *Organizational Dynamics* (Autumn), pp 3–23.

Managing customers: challenges for the future

Merlin Stone and Bryan Foss

For many of the authors who have contributed to this book, its contents can be viewed as the culmination of twenty or even more years of work in the disciplines than have been renamed as CRM. These twenty years have been years of success and years of frustration. The lasting gain from these twenty years has been a wealth of experience in all aspects of CRM, from defining it to implementing it. It is not uncommon to end books that document the state of play with a chapter that summarizes the main issues facing readers in the future, so we continue with this time-honoured tradition.

BRANDING IN AN ERA OF CRM

In the market for CRM and related ideas, supply exceeds demand. Dot-coms have collapsed. The mobile telephony companies are much less bullish. Many large consultancies and marketing service agencies were at the time of writing 'letting go' many of their staff. Analysts were busy publishing reports showing by how much systems suppliers and consultancies over-estimated returns and underestimated implementation difficulties in their attempts to push up the price and desirability of their services – as if the analysts themselves were not heavily tarred with the same brush. As the salesmen of these new ideas retire to lick their wounds, what are marketers left with? Can marketers continue to practise and teach marketing and selling as they always did? Have the central ideas of marketing, such as branding, been completely unaffected by the temporary intoxication of senior marketing management with CRM and e-business ideas?

At a recent conference, one of the authors had the good fortune to be a member of the audience at one of the most honest presentations he had ever seen (and honest presentations are rare). A senior manager showed the slides that had been used by one of the major management consultancies to persuade his board that they had no choice but to rush into all sorts of e-based CRM initiatives. The company had ended up with scores of these initiatives, costing an enormous amount. The presenter now had the task of closing down all the stand-alone businesses and integrating the approach into the company's mainstream activities. Putting it another way, much of the way the company managed its customers would now change forever, because customers for every product would now have an option of dealing with the company through e-channels. Managers of every product and every channel would now be able to contact and manage their customers in a number of different ways, and their customers will be able to do the same to them.

However, the lesson of the market collapse referred to above is that change takes time. In particular, changing the way companies and customers relate to each other takes time because there are the two parties to the change – the company and the customer, and customers take a long time to change. One of the reasons for this – well understood by branding experts – is that one of the main determinants of customers' behaviour towards their suppliers is customers' perceptions of their brand perceptions. These are determined not just by advertising, but by all the customers' experiences of the brand – whether in buying, receiving marketing communications or experiencing after-sales service.

Changing these experiences takes time. Here's an example. A UK company has been involved in a CRM programme for many years. Much of the work has been internal and/or infrastructural– sorting out its customer database, analysing its customers, establishing and testing direct mail programmes, and so on. After several years, the company is now in the happy position of being able to offer its customers relevant products at the right time. The value it obtains from each customer is rising steadily, to where it is one of the best in the industry. It is so good that the company is reducing its efforts to recruit new customers. It no longer recruits too many customers whose later value turns out to be suspect, because it is confident that it is already obtaining a higher share of wallet from its existing customers and that it will keep them longer.

Most important of all, this company's higher value customers have noticed that the way it approaches them is more relevant (right offer at the right time), that it uses information about them that they know the company holds, and that it is servicing them better (because it is no longer wasting too much of its service resource on customers of doubtful value). This is clearly a branding change. The company is not seen as 'just another of those big companies that is out to get as much business from me as possible, no matter how much it annoys me in the process', but as a company which is working hard to meet its customers needs and earning the right to get more of their budget.

So CRM (and for that matter, e-business, m-commerce, multi-channel marketing or any other bright idea) can have a really positive effect on branding. In many markets, it can open up new dimensions to branding, eg responsiveness, relevance, allowing control. However, these ideas can also be destructive if used too quickly, at the wrong time or on the wrong customers. It is also easy to break the law or regulations through abuse – in areas such as data protection or in some industries (eg financial services, utilities) specific regulations about the conduct of business. All the more reason, therefore, why these ideas should be deployed slowly, and why companies should be careful about how they deploy them. For example, it is not wise to charge headlong into developing a massive customer database if data quality is very poor, if people who work with customers or their information have a weak data quality culture, or if front-line staff's skills in managing customers using data are weak.

In all our research work, we have found that balanced progress, along a broad front consisting of steady changes in strategy, planning, people, data, systems, measurement and processes, always works better than the big bang approach, as the first example in this chapter discovered. We have found that the best way for a company to improve how it manages its customers is to improve how it manages its people who manage customers. It is through them that the brand is securely established – and this applies as much when its people are designing Web sites or direct mail programmes as when they are talking directly to customers in the store, over the counter or in the call centre. Improving systems and data just helps them to do it better. So despite the technological obsession of recent years, the oldest branding lesson of all has been reconfirmed – branding = people.

BUILDING LOYALTY AND RELATIONSHIPS INTO PRODUCTS

One of the authors of this book is well known for his researches into 'wealth management'. The research showed that the conventional approach to wealth management was to identify a customer's various investment attitudes and needs (eg long term asset growth, risk, short term cash). The company then meets these needs by selling the customer a portfolio of investment, pension and insurance products. A financial adviser normally carries out the diagnostic and matching process. The various products (eg investment bonds, endowment policies) are based on combinations of various underlying financial instruments (shares, bonds, cash, pure life and health insurance). The research also showed that some 'new breed' providers take a different approach. Instead of trying to sell a variety of different investment and insurance products to their customers, they concentrate on a more comprehensive diagnosis of the customer's attitudes to risk and of their needs for returns and cash. They then help the customer understand the nature of risk in financial markets. This includes understanding the positive correlation between level of risk and return, and how investments perform when held over particular terms. They then invest directly in the underlying assets, in proportions that are expected to yield the right risk/return profile. The assets are held in nominee, accounts, ie in the customer's name. These companies charge around half the fees and commissions of the conventional approach. Once diagnosis is complete, review is only necessary if the customer's need has changed. Additional investments by the customer do not require the purchase of additional products. Instead, more underlying assets are bought. Similarly, if the customer wants to withdraw money, underlying assets are sold. Put simply, the company's need to obtain increased value from the relationship by selling additional products (cross-selling) is replaced by a product that incorporates much of the relationship within it. The customer benefits, because the offer is appropriate and valuable, and reduced costs result from the relationship being 50 per cent cheaper to manage.

This research led to a more general conclusion – that relationships and products are intimately related. They are both ways of meeting customers' needs, and they both cost money to deliver to customers. As the dot.coms learnt, they are related in another way. If product profitability is not sufficient to sustain the costs of acquiring and maintaining customers in a relationship, then the whole company may collapse. There are also markets where if products are poorly managed, losses can destroy any attempt to develop better relationships. Take the example of automotive insurance, where risks are increased significantly if the company takes its eye off product profitability. For such companies, within-product CRM (cost-effective acquisition and retention of customers for each of their main products) is more important than cross-selling. The latter can add profit, but may be dangerous if decisions are taken which compromise individual product profitability because of supposed long-term relationship gains. An example would be accepting customers for one product who are certainly riskier, but who might be valuable in the longer term if they buy additional products. This should only be done, if the probability of further value is well understood, and if this is true net value (eg these customers don't turn out to be riskier for other products too!).

A key variable is cost to serve. The greater the variance in cost to serve between individual customers, the more we need to understand whether cost to serve on product A is related to cost to serve on product B. The company also needs to understand what happens to cost to serve when it can choose between a strategy of cross-selling or one of combining products. For example, if a customer insures both home and home contents with one company, claims management costs are reduced – the same kind of investigation is required in the case of, say fire or flood, which destroys home and contents. The same argument applies to any product or service where there are associated services, before or after the sale. The more that a relationship can be productized (subject to it meeting customer needs); the more profitable it is likely to be. Of course, no matter how much relationship or service is built into a product, there is always the opportunity for differentiation through a customized relationship. Still, technological progress seems to be making it easier and easier to allow customers to adapt products, services and relationships to their own needs, with the supplier productizing the relationship for self-management. While the tussle between a strong but complex relationship and a brilliant product customizable by customers is often evenly balanced in the short term, in the longer term the odds are probably on the product.

CRM: JUST LIKE THE CORNER SHOP?

It's not unusual to hear senior managers claiming that their company is aiming to recreate the 'customer intimacy' that was characteristic of the corner shop in earlier generations. Of course, most corner shops sold to poor consumers at very high margins, and in some cases used credit as an insidious loyalty device to ensure that the customer's business did not go elsewhere. In the distant past, for some workers the only shops that would trade with them were company shops, working on terms that were severe enough to trigger the foundation of the co-operative movement. Such analogies can be misleading because they do not ask whether a giant telecommunications company, bank or a retailer should even be aspiring to such 'intimacy'. Today's self-service era has cut out 'unnecessary' human intervention, allowing big companies to supply vast numbers of individuals with products and services that are far cheaper in real terms than those bought by our supposedly 'lucky' forebears, while for those of us who like privacy, the absence of human intervention is a blessing.

This raises some interesting questions. Are large companies going too far in trying to match their offer to individuals? Are CRM initiatives that aim to recreate customer intimacy for very large companies doomed to failure because they aim too high or because they aim to do it too fast? Do those large companies that succeed in creating customer intimacy do so only by adopting an unprofitable business model? Do most customers prefer to avoid intimacy, now that they have discovered that they can get much of what they want from large companies without getting too involved?

The answer to all of these questions is 'possibly, yes, in most cases'. Most analysts agree about the relatively high rate of CRM programme failure and how it is induced by trying to do too much too soon. The American Customer Satisfaction Index is in decline, stimulated by exaggerated expectations and/or declining performance, in which call centres' customer service role has been usurped by inappropriate attempts to cross-sell. Our own study of customer service in the UK (see Chapter 31) indicates rising scepticism by consumers concerning attempts by large companies to manage them. As the first part of this book shows, the scores from QCi's Customer Management Assessment Tool are also in decline, not just in the UK, indicating that many companies are not following basic good practice in customer management. In some industries, such as financial services and utilities globally and the rail industry in the UK, it is also clear that poor quality, inconsistent and unstable regulation is hampering companies' attempts to follow good practice in customer management.

However, the story is not all doom and gloom. In fact, many of the larger companies that are succeeding (by their business measures and by measures of customer satisfaction) in customer management are doing so almost by stealth, over a period of years. In these companies, we see a steady rise in value per customer, declining recruitment of low or negative value customers, better customer retention, and increasing cost-effectiveness of customer management (largely driven by propositions which make it easy for customers to get what they want by using lower cost channels and by their taking on themselves some of the costs of being managed). In these large companies, we find programme management disciplines being observed, by teams which combine marketing, customer service and systems people, working to common objectives and with a clear mandate from senior management to take time to improve customer management, on the condition that returns to customer management are achieved not too long after the investment, and that the benefits of improved customer management are visible in cost savings (eg use of lower cost channels of communication and distribution) as well as in revenue gains (which usually take longer).

Most noticeable of all in these companies is the relatively high proportion of internal input (relative to consultancy input) at the beginning of the journey, with most of the external spend being later, on implementation rather than on reconsidering directions. Putting it another way, big companies cannot do CRM through consultants – they must have critical mass of people in areas such as marketing, IT, customer service and operations who are committed to improving customer management, who have the knowledge and skills required to do so, who are committed to staying with their company to see it through, and perhaps most importantly of all, are wise enough to see through the nice CRM phrases into a more realistic world where it is understood that managing customers is mostly about managing people who manage customers (and only rarely about doing it entirely through computers, as on the Web).

So, size matters in a strange way in CRM. It does make succeeding in CRM more difficult, and makes it take longer. But it probably also means that when you have 'got CRM going', and when you are measuring your progress carefully, with metrics that include not just what customers are doing (hopefully buying more, more often, additional products etc) or thinking (hopefully more satisfied) but also your internal process metrics (fewer leads lost, faster reactions to customers, better targeting), it becomes self-sustaining, partly because success breeds success. Customers like it when companies get the basics right, and so do staff.

A SINGLE VISION OF CRM, A SINGLE CUSTOMER VIEW?

When companies started to realize that they might have been just a little misled about the costs and benefits of CRM, one of our authors renamed it 'Clever Repackaging

Mechanism'. This was because he believed that CRM was just a combination of some very simple (but hard to implement) classic business disciplines, such as database marketing, key account management, people management, quality, supply chain management, change management, risk management, customer service and latterly e-business, combined to create a rather complex but often not very well articulated, planned or managed business change programme. When the first CRM disasters began to occur, the same author referred to 'Client Rip-off Menu', because in retrospect many more consultancies than clients seemed to have made money out of CRM! One way consultancies achieved this was through a sustained campaign of hype, consisting of a combination of almost 'self-evident' requirements, such as 'a single customer view', justified by different 'burning platforms' such as, for example, severe customer attrition, escalating costs of customer recruitment, the need to reduce the costs of customer management radically and quickly, and of course that all-purpose justifier, competitive advantage and so forth.

As much of our research has shown, most CRM programmes are barely worth the name, particularly when a vision of CRM has been foisted on the client by a high-powered consultancy or firm of analysts. Before we explore the perniciousness of this, let us explain why so many companies were (and still are) vulnerable. It is because the quality of what we call 'business discourse' has plumbed depths usually only plumbed by poor first year students of management at third-rate universities. One reason for this is Powerpoint culture, which makes managers decreasingly able to produce connected arguments.

This low quality discourse occurs in a less detectable and possibly more pernicious form within CRM. This version of the disease is called 'personification'. For grammarians, personification means treating something (anything from a car or a company to a country) as if it were a single person. This is harmless in daily life, but potentially catastrophic in management. Why? Well, consider the phrase, 'Company X does Y, or believes Y'. While a small company might be so in control of its actions or thoughts to achieve this degree of consistency, the large companies who constitute the suppliers and clients in the world of CRM are rarely in this situation. Take the suppliers of CRM systems. They can be divided into suppliers of CRM software and services (including implementation and outsourcing), with many companies straddling the two.

While suppliers of single software packages might be capable of maintaining a relatively simple vision of what CRM is and how information technology supports it (indeed, this vision may be their prime differentiator), the implementers – particularly those who serve very large clients – are in a very different situation. The largest implementers are giant companies, usually global in scale. They are typically involved in helping giant clients, themselves often global in scale, change the way they manage their customers. Neither supplier not client can in these situations ever be personified as described above. Our experience is that successful suppliers succeed because they work closely with their clients, whose view of where they want to go in CRM is often fragmented. For example, a big insurance company may in each country in which it operates have different visions of where it wants to go in CRM in its direct division, its life and pensions division, its broker division, and so on. Many such companies have tried to bring their different visions together, and failed. Some have turned to consultancies that have produced simple templates representing visions and implementation plans, and tried to use these templates to impose change upon the organization – and failed. This is because of big differences in the skills and capabilities possessed by the different divisions, and of course differences on the buy side – different competitive pressures, channels of distribution, and of course customer needs.

The lesson – the bigger the company, the less relevant and the more ludicrous the idea that a single vision is needed. In many cases a portfolio approach could be more relevant. The idea that a very large supplier should or even could have a single vision is similarly stupid – many large suppliers succeed by having the skills and flexibility to work with different business partners (eg software suppliers) to develop and deliver very different visions of CRM to their clients. This is, by the way, true in nearly all areas of systems. Of course, there are massive economies of scale to be gained by standardizing on systems, but as our research has shown again and again, brilliant systems are neither a necessary nor a sufficient condition for success in CRM. That is why the more discerning clients do not want a vision, but pragmatic advice and results, taking into account the variety and possible inconsistency that exists in their own situation.

SEGMENTATION, NOT STEREOTYPING

At the heart of most CRM programmes is a segmentation exercise – classifying customers so that they can be managed better. However, on a recent project, we started to discover some of the risks of segmentation. The project concerned wine marketing, and there was a question about how to manage relationships with the post-war bulge generation (often now bulging physically as well as demographically). The wine marketers' answer is to encourage us to drink our merry way towards our end, with the added benefit that it may accelerate the demise while anaesthetizing us to the various ailments that usually precede the end. At the other extreme is a political answer – encourage us to retire later and save more. This is because this generation's pensions are going to be much lower than they thought they would be, due to declining stock market values, higher taxation of pension funds in the UK and in several countries higher income taxation, the apparent inability of companies holding pension funds to control their costs, and (for the younger), the reduced likelihood of a pension based on final salary and/or with linking to inflation. Don't rely too much on the recently inflated value of your property, say the Jeremiahs, because that won't last long. Please also be aware that if you do survive the wine, you are likely to live much longer than your parents did, so the problem will be worse.

Not all is doom and gloom, however. Marketers are aware that a new group of customers has emerged – the young old. These are the people who happily work up to the age of 70 or beyond, and consider themselves middle-aged until they are well past 65. Because they feel young, their purchasing patterns are young too – except that they are beyond the period of accumulation of physical assets. If they are lucky, their children will be married or in stable relationships, and beyond the period when they rely on their parents (though children do seem to have a habit of extending this period of dependence). They enjoy eating out, holidays, perhaps entertaining, the less strenuous forms of sport including just watching, and so on). They are also (because they qualify) often formally within the group that the state defines as needing help (eg public transport concessions, state pensions, access to day centres). In some cases, they provide the backbone of a voluntary force helping even older people.

The number of such people is about to surge, as the post-war bulge (which started in 1946) turns 60. However, we are not sure that most marketers have realized what this implies. Take advertising, for example. With the exception of funeral plans, hair colouring and a few other products that must recognize the age of their customers, most products and services seem to be aimed at people much younger than the typical consumer. Is this because all people want to feel young? Or is it because marketers don't realize the strength of the 'cohort effect' – what happens when people pass through different age groups. This is why the CRM approach can be so valuable for marketers, because segmentation in CRM does not (and should not) mean dividing the market up into large broadly similar groups, but rather finding out what people are like, now, and what they want to do, and allowing them to do it.

COMPETING FOR SHARE OF WALLET

Getting customers to shift their value between suppliers is particularly difficult when the service is binary – when customers either have to be 100 per cent with one supplier or another. This is one reason why customers have not moved between power suppliers after deregulation as much as was first thought. In many markets, higher value customers are often harder to shift, even if they seem the most likely to profit by it. One reason for this may be that any saving is less significant in relative terms – the well-off individual who can save $100–200 a year on electricity may not find the game worth the candle, compared to the poorer user who might switch for a $40 saving.

However, for products and services where share of wallet can be shifted, such as telecommunications or financial services, the story can be very different. If switching is easy, customers will often shift those bits of their business where they feel they are getting worst value. This leaves the incumbent supplier with those bits of business where customers believe they are getting the best deal – and of course these can be rather poor business for the suppliers. So, many telephony customers have switched their long distance calls, calls to mobiles and international calls to low cost suppliers, leaving their local telephone company with unprofitable local calls. The same risk applies to postal businesses. This is why cross-subsidy is so dangerous for suppliers whose monopolies have been opened up to competition.

An interesting version of this problem is where individual customer value grows over time – typically because income rises with age and so customers buy higher value products. This applies in many areas – for example cars, financial services, travel and telecommunications. Here, the question for the attacking company is whether it can get a good share of the higher value business without having the customer from the beginning. The answer to this is – yes. Indeed, banks have discovered to their cost that having lots of loss-making student customers is not much use if they switch suppliers as soon as they become valuable. For the attacking company, the switching proposition is usually based on excellent value for money, because the incumbents can't give such good value because of the cross-subsidies required to sustain the loss-making early-stage customers.

The defence strategy in this case is to be so good at retaining value as customers become more valuable that there is no need to recruit as many customers at the loss-making or low value stage. More selective early-stage customer recruitment, combined with better prediction of which customers have more value available, and when they will have it available, is now becoming the central plank of many companies' customer management strategy. This requires predictive modelling, usually based on events and transactions, as it is the latter that indicate rising value. Of course, it is also important to make sure that the company's products and services, people, processes and systems are attuned to managing this value towards it.

MANAGING BRANCH CUSTOMERS: THE LOCAL VIEW OF CRM

Many banks are now focusing on achieving CRM objectives in branches. The objectives are classic – up-sell, cross-sell, retention, with a strong focus on efficiency. In this area, banks have much to learn from retailers. Of course, the two domains differ. Visiting and transactions patterns differ – though this depends on the type of retailing. Buying a new kitchen has some similarities to buying a pension, eg in terms of frequency, outlay, after-sales requirement and need for advice. There are other reasons for bankers to look 'over the fence'. Retailers are selling banking products using techniques that are not so different from those they use to sell their core produce. Banks now also use franchising techniques developed in areas such as fast food.

Bankers and retailers are both affected by the Internet. Although we no longer expect a complete by-pass of branches by the Internet, it has made a big difference to how branches are evolving, not just in changing the economics of distribution, but also in terms of enabling partnerships with other businesses. Combining e-business techniques with other developments in marketing and service technology (such as advanced analysis and profiling techniques) has allowed branches to focus on the needs of different target customer segments (geographical, demographic, needs-based) and individuals. The more successful users of these approaches have increased branch throughput (both sectors need to maximize yield on expensive real-estate) while reducing marketing costs.

However, in banking, current channels (branches, call centres and e-channels) are very expensive and not delivering the growth and profitability banks want. In many countries the majority of customers use physical branches. Even for customers who rarely use them for transactions, they are still the embodiment of the bank, and often the place at which significant changes in the relationship take place (eg account openings, complex financial products bought or at least investigated, serious problems resolved). Despite the prediction of the branch's demise and the forecast of branches being overtaken by Internet, wireless and call centres, some banks plan to increase their branch numbers in new ways, sometimes in joint ventures with eg retailers, or as franchises.

Branch delivery of service has developed through several stages, from the old 'bricks and personal service only', through introduction of self-service branches, to sales branches with transactions handled in other channels. In the future we may see proliferation of the so-called Branch Portal, combining the best of all approaches but still clearly centred on the branch. This approach includes reviving the human touch, empowering staff to give better and different sales and advice, and integrating e and call centre channels with the branch approach. However, some customer types will move fully to e-banking and abandon the branch altogether. Banks will still continue to be challenged by the fact that these tend to be higher value customers. This trend is not so evident in those areas of retailing where the physical nature of the product favours browsing and the 'see-touch-feel' approach.

Banks that have used classic database marketing and retail techniques – cleaning databases, profiling, targeted cross-selling, combined with appropriate staff policies (remuneration based on customer value rather than product, branch scorecards balancing product, customer and cost indicators, motivation and training focused on customer value and customer service) have succeeded in moving away from the situation where 10 per cent of customers produce more than 100 per cent of the profits. In this area most UK banks are behind some Canadian and Australian banks, and this is at least partly confirmed by our CMAT studies. In the US, perhaps surprisingly, many banks are emerging from a period when they dominated their individual state, and are now learning to compete for customers using these classic techniques. Conclusion – CRM with branch banking is not magic, and some companies are doing it quite well.

KNOW YOUR BAD CUSTOMER: A NEW SET OF REQUIREMENTS

Today, many companies are prone to serious forms of attack from customers, not just hacking, though there is a relationship between this and the move to more remote forms of doing business, whether Internet or call centre. These attacks are attempts to commit fraud – money laundering, illegal trading – or to exploit loopholes in credit or insurance products. These attempts are helped by technological advances because companies have fewer face-to-face opportunities of validating identities, credit-worthiness and the like, and also because the perpetrators often work in teams, using Internet and mobile telephony to communicate quickly with each other in ways authorities find hard to track.

The response of government authorities has been to impose upon companies – particularly those in the financial services sector – a series of requirements in terms of 'know your customers' and 'track and if necessary unwind your transactions'. These requirements incidentally sometimes conflict with data protection and industry-specific requirements designed to protect honest customers. For example, money-laundering monitoring requirements include the need to retain and be able to retrieve information, track and report to the national authorities. For this, record keeping and reporting products are designed to track and report information to regulators or other national authorities, where the detailed requirement, such as a threshold value, is specified. So, financial services companies are now investing in a number of areas designed to support their war against the bad customer. These include very advanced software, designed to pick up new patterns of bad behaviour, the data storage required to ensure that everything can be tracked and where necessary is reversible, and the systems integration work (often including specialist middleware) to ensure that data from various sources can be brought together for 'detection' work.

What is interesting about these developments is that they are some way in advance of recent developments in database marketing in companies with very large customer bases and/or very high volumes of transactions. Rules-based products are used to monitor transactions to identify and filter out potentially suspicious transactions that are outside the norms for an account and customer (or other group). These 'outside limit' or 'out-of-character' transactions are flagged and routed for manual review by bank compliance, audit, or risk management staff. Transactions that appear, after review, to be inconsistent with a customer's business are reported to the appropriate government entity. To achieve this, expert and/or intelligent systems identify non-linear trends and relationships within transaction activity, including associative patterns among accounts, customers, relative to peer or other groupings. These systems examine all possible combinations among transactions, rather than looking at the individual transaction record itself, and apply risk scorings to suspect transactions. There can be significant differences between systems and results depending on the architectural approach and the intelligence technologies used. The most advanced types of software can be programmed to warn about virtually any kind of risk – including imminent system failure due to lack of capacity.

In the financial services industry, value and risk are not far apart. In call centres and Web sites, where the customer is invisible to the supplier, systems have assumed the role of detecting bad customers. The pay-off to good risk management has always been much larger than that to value management, at least in the short run, simply because the costs of failure are so large. However, with increasing volumes of business being done remotely, the need for smarter systems to help companies extract much higher value from customers is increasing. For this reason, banks are starting to investigate how the software and processes they use for detecting bad customers more quickly and accurately can be used for detecting value more quickly. One reason for this is that these products are not cheap, so banks want to extend their use. The products are very advanced, and the very latest products have shown dramatic levels of success, in terms of reducing the incidence of false positives and successful detection of negatives. They do this by creating 'sentinels' which take on much of the role of the data analyst, freeing analysts to work on strategies. For the data analysis industry, these products represent both a threat and an opportunity – an opportunity if used to liberate analysts to focus not on implementing models but on understanding why they work, but a threat if analysts try to compete with them.

RETAILING: TO R OR NOT TO R

There's no doubt that one of the main determinants of success in retailing is good customer management – or CM. But when that little R for relationship creeps into the middle, to create CRM, confusion reigns. The confusion is as much amongst consultants and retail analysts as amongst the retailers themselves. Some retailers have – after a learning period that extended through most of the 1990s – understood both the theory and practice of CRM as applied to retailing, and in particular whether the investment in developing in-depth relationships with named customers, based on a combination of loyalty cards, targeted direct mail and/or point of sales offers, and added services such as financial services, produces a positive return. That learning period resulted in some companies confirming their commitment to fully fledged loyalty-card based CRM. Others discovered the awful truth that whether these things work is not primarily a question of principle, but more a question of the particular relative circumstances of the retailer, in particular its competitive position in terms of market share (overall, by category and by region), the relative strength of its brand, the strength of its portfolio of stores relative to its competitors, the quality and appeal of its merchandise range, and so on. However, even those that believe that their fully fledged scheme works are hard-pressed to answer the really difficult question – is the scheme overall paying its way? They can nearly always show that any individual activity (typically a promotion) within the scheme pays, but as the scheme becomes embedded in their overall marketing approach, they can no more determine the effect of withdrawing it than an airline can quantify the impact of withdrawing a frequent flyer scheme. In some cases, it is clear that the main benefit of the scheme is just a promotional or membership list, which provides an excellent but high cost basis for launching a range of additional services, particularly financial services, utilities etc. If the scheme is popular, it may also have very strong branding benefits. Still, the suspicion lurks that the scheme is an expensive way of rewarding customers for doing what they would have done anyway – confirmed in some cases by the positive results of withdrawing schemes.

In both retail and other market sectors, companies have shown that a strong customer proposition can attract a large membership, with CRM-based incentives focusing on encouraging customers to give more value. Right at the other extreme, some retailers have 'home-grown' their CRM, basing it on several pillars, such as a good customer complaints/feedback management process, a store card, home delivery, Internet, call centre enquiries, guarantees, 'specials' or any other situation in which the customer MUST be managed as an individual, using this to build a basic permission-based mailing list. So, we are left with the feeling that the range of options in CRM, from the basic 'grow-your-own' approach to fully fledged loyalty-card based CRM has not been well understood (especially in the context of the competitive factors mentioned above) and evaluated by many retailers.

THE MAGIC OF CUSTOMER KNOWLEDGE: DARE WE OUTSOURCE IT?

The theory is wonderful. Take a data warehouse, add smart analysis tools, a structured approach to managing inbound and outbound customer contacts, including self-managed Web contacts, and give the cauldron an almighty stir and – Hey Presto – we develop magical insights into customer characteristics and behaviour which give us a strong advantage over our competitors. While increasing numbers of large companies claim to have reached magical levels of insights, we must never forget that when we say 'a company knows', we may be committing the ultimate sin of 'personification' – treating a 'thing' (the company) as an individual.

In fact, when we say 'a company understands or knows its customers', what we mean is that this knowledge of customers resides in a combination of databases (often several), analyses, reports documenting the analyses, and even the minds of certain staff. As customers themselves are constantly changing (the individuals may be different, the behaviour of given individuals changing), this knowledge needs to be refreshed, and whether this happens depends upon the frequency and accuracy of update of the information sources, the re-application of whatever techniques were used to distil knowledge from the information, and the re-communication of results to whoever is deemed to hold the knowledge. This applies whether the source is at the batch end (eg who responds to a direct mail campaign, nature of response) or online (eg site exploration behaviour of particular types of customer).

So, the ingredients of the cauldron are ever changing. What we put in, how we stir it, and how long we let it cook all influence the quality of what we take out. Who determines these? The answer – the custodian of the cauldron. Who is the custodian? Is it the company itself, the data exploitation agency, the direct marketing agency, or the outsourced database bureau? In practice, the answer is usually some combination of these. In very few cases do larger companies do everything themselves. Interestingly, when they do, the result seems to be that customer knowledge is less sophisticated (fewer segments defined, data perhaps less up to date, less accurate), but the knowledge is better used (more consistently, across different channels, as part of well-defined general marketing processes rather than tactically). This is usually for one of two very different reasons. Either the marketing users are themselves more closely involved in the process of specifying and then interpreting analyses, or the internal department charged with developing a customer view becomes an advocate for its good use, and works very closely with marketing users to make sure it is used. In the more advanced examples, they will also provide metrics to show when it is used and what the results have been, to encourage use and to expose misuse.

However, there are also some examples of excellent practice in outsourcing to analysis or database hosting agencies. This works really well when there is a long-term strategic agreement between supplier and client and when the focus of the agreement is not solely or primarily on the input (who holds and analyses the data, or communicates the findings) but on the outputs, ie what business results are expected from the gathering and holding of data, analysis to obtain knowledge, and exploitation of the resulting knowledge. These required outputs may be expressed in tactical terms, eg uplifts to campaign response or conversion rates, or strategic terms, eg increased value of the customer base. Increasingly e-sourcing, e-business on demand (EBOD) and other modern variants of outsourcing are reflecting and including these requirements.

Unfortunately, in most cases, whether customer understanding is in-sourced or out-sourced, the custodianship is poorly allocated – sometimes dropping between the planks, sometimes simply non-existent. This failure is evidenced in many ways. There may be many overlapping segmentation projects with no interface with each other. Segmentation and analysis may be conducted using variables that are not available on the database, so analysis can rarely be acted upon. There may be great lack of awareness amongst users about what is available, what the results of data use have been, or even how to use the knowledge practically. Where these basic problems do not exist, there may be more advanced problems, eg the customer understanding only being used in one channel (perhaps the channel in which the understanding was generated) and not in others. In many cases, failures are due to not understanding that managing customer knowledge is a skilled operation, and whether the skills are in-house or out-house, they must be maintained and improved – to keep up to date with what it is possible to do, and also with the customer knowledge itself.

In most cases, these failures can be traced to a single cause – that no one has asked (let alone answered) the question: 'Who is fully accountable for managing customer knowledge?' In cases where it is badly in-sourced, marketing managers have often taken the view that 'customer knowledge is a strategic asset, and therefore our company will not out-source its management!' Every time I hear such a brave phrase, I know I'm likely to find that the company manages it very badly, because it has not asked the accountability question except by a negative 'not an outsider'.

UNDERSTANDING THE CUSTOMER – INSTANTLY!

In the 1980s, database marketers had a dream. It involved receiving calls or visits from customers and being able to profile them precisely, using information given previously plus new information gathered during the contact. The idea was that this would allow suppliers to tailor their offers to customers so well that response and sales rates would rise dramatically. Twenty years on, the first waves of CRM enthusiasm have passed and we are a bit wiser about using customer data profitably and ethically, but not much wiser. We are wiser in that we know that when we assemble the relevant data and batch-analyse it, we can devise profiles that enable us to customize our customer management at point of contact, producing higher response and sales levels. We can also improve performance by using information given during the contact. However, we are less wise when it comes to understanding the possible invasiveness of this approach. Invasiveness? Why is that an issue? Because in our rush to instant exploitation of data, we may be forgetting some central rules of customer-oriented marketing, as well as risking a rap over the knuckles from data protection or privacy authorities.

Let's start with the central rules of marketing, such as 'the customer always has the choice not to buy from us, enter into a relationship with us, etc'. So, rather than trying to sell more to customers each time they are in contact with us, we might try to discover whether, when and for which products and services they might welcome the approach, and of course whether some customers always refuse the approach. We might also consider whether before using the information, we should seek permission to use data, perhaps after trying to sell the benefits of our using it. Making some kind of declaration is common – 'if you give us this data and the permission to use it, we'll be able to offer you relevant products and services'. However, often the promise is not followed through – relevance is tenuous, and the benefit to the customer is unclear, particularly when the customer is assailed with similar offers on the same or better terms from other suppliers.

You might ask, 'Does it matter, so long as I increase sale and response rates?' It does, because though it may work well in the short term with some customers, if it becomes invasive (the constant cross-sell in the call centre, the banner advertisement for one product when the customer is carrying out an operational or service action for another), it can damage the brand and turn customers off.

The data protection angle is not so clear. If when your relationship with the customer begins, you tell them that all data that they may give you at any time in the relationship, for any purpose, may be used for marketing any of your products and services to them, and you do so in such a way that they have the choice to opt out, you are on the right side of the law – provided that you can show that the customer has a fair chance of understanding the implications of not opting out. However, as you move the margin of data exploitation forward, customers who freely gave consent to the use of their data for marketing purposes when used in the 'old-fashioned batch way' might be surprised at how it is being used in the 'modern online way', for instant profiling and offer proposition.

The test here, as with most data protection law (at least in the UK) is the classic British test of reasonableness, though in some European countries this test is too lenient. Whether on the grounds of good marketing practice or data protection law, if you make a substantial change to the way in which you use customer data, eg from batch, modular use to online highly individualized use, it makes sense to ask the customer again. This may even involve a very explicit script, explaining how you plan to use the data. The rule of 'don't surprise the customer' applies here. Marketing professionals may be surprised and 'delighted' (an over-used word) when they experience proper online or real-time targeting as consumers, but they should not forget that many customers may be surprised and suspicious, wondering how the company got the information (even if it is a clever inference from what they have just told the company). Some customers know that the origin of individual profiling is credit rating, and that what they are not offered may be as interesting as what they are offered. In the rush to CRM, many companies have taken their eye off the ball when it comes to 'reasonable use of customer data' and related privacy issues. This applies particularly when the profiling takes place at a counter or in a call centre, where it is hard to control the individual member of staff and where the energy and motivation of some staff may lead to abuse of data in selling.

However, companies must also be careful about not making offers. The best reminder of the risk here is this old joke. A young man presents his basket at a supermarket checkout – a pack of toilet rolls, a six-pack of beer, a four-pack of baked beans, some frying oil, some bread. The checkout girl asks 'Are you single?' He responds 'How did you know?' 'Because you're ugly,' she replies. We must be careful we're not making similar inferences, as customers do talk to each other. Not making 'relevant, beneficial, personalized' offers to a customer while making the same offer to a neighbour is a bit like calling the former ugly.

THE NEW CALL CENTRE CHALLENGE

It seems just a few years since the idea of the call centre was introduced – even though it is more than twenty. Back then, call centres were the marketer's dream. They allowed companies to handle large numbers of customers making very large numbers of enquiries or transactions, at much lower cost than existing channels. Today, that rosy view has a definite black tinge. As Chapter 31 shows, many people do not really like dealing with call centres. It also showed that quite a few people understood the pressures that call centre staff were under, because they had either worked in one or had friends or family who did. This meant that they understood the imperfections of call centres and the data and systems that support them, and hence the possibility that these centres might not be able to meet their needs.

Many of the industries, such as utilities and simple financial services, in which call centres were installed early on, to handle customer service, have come under such strong margin pressure that their owners are now under pressure to find ways to make them profitable. Banks that have centralized their call handling, away from branches, have discovered that many customers really do want to talk to, and perhaps still need, someone in the branch. Even retailers, using their call centres to support their loyalty cards, Web operations or classic customer service, have their concerns. Of course, many call centres are still performing admirably, delivering a steady stream of profit and satisfied customers. However, the seeds of doubt have been sown.

In retrospect, all we are seeing is a classic product life cycle. The new medium emerges, goes through a long period of gaining acceptance by the customer and companies (much delayed in the UK by the high cost of calling until the deregulation of the telecommunications industry). This period includes much experimentation to establish how the medium should be used in combination with existing media. Then the new medium takes off to sweep all before it, before maturing into a life as just one of the many media available, good for some applications, less good for others, and with established protocols for co-operation with older media such as television, radio and mail.

New media emerge – e-mail, the Web, text messaging, and jostle for their place on the media scene. They too begin their experimentation with existing media. In the case of call centres, this is taking the form of integrated contact centres and IP telephony, typically allowing the different stages of contact with individuals each to be handled by the medium which does it best and/or cheapest. Browse the Web, explore product or service options, buy directly if it's simple, press the call-me button if it's not. Go to the Web, request the service visit, return to the Web to track service call progress/changes, and only press the call-me button if you have a problem with what's displayed.

From the point of view of companies thinking of moving to this next stage, there are two main reasons for doing it. The first is to improve service, the second to reduce cost. In the long run, those who don't use it to do the first are likely to be forced to do the second. However, they need to understand that in either case, for most companies, the step is a much bigger one than previous media decisions. In fact, it is no longer just a media-optimization decision. If the Web side of the contact centre is to do its job, it needs to be connected much more smartly with the operational side of the business – the back office, the service engineer scheduling system, the stock control system, the factory and possibly even with suppliers. This is because the 'straight-through processing' that takes the cost out of the call centres by allowing customers to view inventory, order and track progress means that a lot of systems and process work needs to be done behind the scenes to connect operations with the customer. Many companies simply have not done the work required, and employ labour-intense methods of fulfilling customer requirements, often with process breaks that are only mended through intermittent quality initiatives, and then often break again.

When the work is done to provide excellence in self-service response to the customer there is evidence that some cultures respond to this very readily. For example a major bank centred in Australia has a much larger proportion of voice response systems (IVR) self-service usage by customers rather than assisted service contact via call centres. This can simultaneously enable cost reduction and customer satisfaction improvement.

So, when in competition with companies that have done this work, companies that have not done it must find some way of funding the relatively high cost of handling in the call centre things that could be handled through self-service IVR systems or on the Web. Some take a very dangerous (but sometimes successful) approach – cross-sell on service. Done sensitively, it can work. It requires tough quality control and clever call guides or call scripting; to make sure being sold to when all they want is service does not alienate customers. Done badly, it results not only in longer calls with weak outcomes, but eventually customer dissatisfaction and loss.

The lesson of all this is not surprisingly that companies need to think ahead, and not assume that the relative cost-effectiveness of different media is static. It moves with the advance of technology, it moves as companies and customers learn to use new technology, and it moves as companies connect customer contact technology with their operations. How you manage customers is not just a media decision today, but a strategic decision that has enterprise-wide implications

E-MARKETING AND MULTI-CHANNEL MARKETING: SEAMLESS OR SEAMY?

In Chapter 00, we considered whether opening up an e-channel for customers used to dealing with a company through branches, mail or call centres meant that the same experience should be offered through different channels, or that the experience should be in some way consistent (eg based on the same set of customer data).

As with all marketing questions, the answer is found through a combination of analysis of customer value, behaviour and needs (for example, how much value do customers have available, what products and services do customers need, how much are they prepared to pay for them, how does the availability of an additional channel change the picture?) with decisions about objectives, strategies and implementation (for example, which customers do you want to serve, how does using an additional channel change the picture, what do different channels cost to use, how can the approach of different channels be combined, what systems and data are required to underpin combining their use rather than using them separately, and what are the costs?).

These are serious questions, and you may really need consultants to help you answer them. However, we should heed the lessons of channel management before the e-age or from its early stages. In many industries, customers are already managed through many channels – for example, physical branches, mail order, telephone, field sales and/or service force. Channels can both complement and compete with each other. The 1980s saw the introduction of telemarketing to support and compete with many industrial sales forces. In most large industrial companies, a relatively stable state now exists, in which direct marketing media (mail, telephone) are used as the main channel of distribution for smaller customers, but also a valuable channel of communication for larger customers. There is often a zone of contention with mid-market customers, sometimes resolved by having specialist tele-coverage operations in which field sales people work closely with telemarketers, the former only visiting when the latter identify the need for face-to face calls.

Interestingly, the least integrated experience is usually that of the largest customers, where many decision makers and influencers are exposed to so many different supplier staff and marketing/sales initiatives that consistency is hard to achieve. However, this is not seen as catastrophic by either customer or supplier – customers realize that they have complex needs and that big suppliers can meet them in many ways. Insisting on an over-structured, seamless experience may lead to opportunities being missed on both sides, and also to customers feeling that they are being 'controlled' by the supplier. 'Why can't I just pick up the phone and talk to anyone in your company?' they might ask.

In consumer markets, the same arguments apply. Most major banks are so worried about branch costs that they are diverting all customer calls to call centres (sometimes dressed up as virtual branches). Customer surveys already show how much customers hate this approach. Despite the advent of branch based 'personal advisers', one of the results has been that wiser, higher value customers know that there is often little hope of talking to anybody sensible in the branch. So they take their most profitable business elsewhere, leaving the bank with the rump transaction business, often so managed by these wise customers as to be unprofitable for the bank (free in-credit accounts, any surplus funds whisked off to a high interest deposit account with a direct bank). If they are referred back to the branch by the call centre, it is often because the call centre can't answer a particular query, rather than because it makes sense (to either party) for the customer to be talking to someone in the branch.

Along come e-mail and the Web. Great, says the customer, at last I can e-mail someone in the branch. This means that I don't have to wait for them to answer, and they can answer my query at leisure – next day is usually fine. But what do customers in many (thankfully not all) banks discover? They can't e-mail some or any of the staff in their branch. Branch staff are often not trusted to e-mail, and they may not even have the systems to do it. For the bank, e = Web, so if customers want to talk to the bank electronically, they have to do it via the Web site, where their experience can be controlled. The branch has no Web site – the customer can only talk to the national Web site. The same is true of many other consumer service businesses.

Surely, however, one of the great strengths of e-mail as a channel is that it allows people to correspond in a controlled, non-invasive way. As government is discovering, text messaging and e-mail might be great channels for communicating with most of the population, as older media simply don't get through. Much better, therefore, to get each channel going in ways that suit the customer (of course cost-effectively), and let the customer show the supplier how they want to use each channel. Wise customers also learn to use the channels that give them the best experience. Of course, customers may occasionally complain about different experiences in different channels, but they already complain vociferously about lack of access. Perhaps marketers ought to be arguing for rich, seamy communication between suppliers and customers rather than a controlled, seamless, multi-channel experience?

Of course, marketers have always dreamt of integrated marketing communications. This used to refer just to outbound messages and targeting – marketers controlling the messages received by different customers through different channels – telephone, mail, broadcast media etc. However, customers pop up in many places through different contact media, and often want to control the dialogue, so even if companies managed to achieve this great consistency, it was of doubtful value to us or to our customers. The Internet brought this home to us, although this was not a new requirement – just one that many companies had allowed customers to express. The idea of the customer-managed relationship (CMR) was not just a consultant's play on acronyms, but represented a real customer need.

There are two new forces at work, however – customers' desire for convenience and our desire for effectiveness (whether pure efficiency or achieving more with less). Take convenience first. One reason for declining customer perceptions of service levels is higher expectations. Variety and speed of access is more important to customers than we thought – whether in the context of sales or service. There is a generation difference too – witness the success of text messaging with younger customers and its likely adoption by government as a prime channel for keeping citizens informed about, eg entitlement. In this world of higher expectations, even if customers concentrate their side of the dialogue into one main channel, they expect to be able to use other channels with equal ease, and to be handled as well in each channel that is open to them.

The implication is not necessarily to make everything available in every channel, which could be very expensive, but to make the best level of service available in those channels that most target customers want to use. This is where the second force – effectiveness – comes into play. For example, in banking, customers may want to use branches not for transactions but social and commercial interaction. However, banks cannot afford to make this available all the time through the branch. Could the same customer need be met by combining a branch Web site with telephone support? Technically, there is no barrier to this, as systems and software are available to support it. The issue is one of strategy, organization and processes.

All this requires a change to the campaign management mindset of direct marketers, who tend to influence decisions in this area. More can be achieved with less if customers experience relevant offers in each channel, and can choose or be helped to choose between them. If these offers come from different departments or product units, then rather than allocating a channel slot to each unit, it might be better to treat the whole multi-channel system as a 'client' for each unit, with the unit marketing to the multi-channel system, and the multi-channel system adjusting offers so as to achieve the company's profit objectives, taking into account customers' needs and propensities.

If this approach is to work, profit targeting rather than sales targeting is required, as this gives the multi-channel system a clear basis to prioritizing offers. Sales targeting tends to promote volume, lower profit and a lower quality customer base. For this reason, in the world of multi-channel customer management, measurement is absolutely critical, and this measurement must be based on profit or contribution, rather than just sales. Companies also need pretty sophisticated software to ensure that the right offers are made (in either the CRM or CMR situation) to the right customers at the right time. Interestingly, the measures must also include risk, and need to work not just overall but for individual branches.

SERVICE: THE MOST COMMON CONTACT OF ALL

In most companies customer-side data, such as complaints and comments, or supplier-side data, such as records of service delivery, are rarely matched with customer value and transaction data. If matching is carried out, it is usually on a batch basis, and can only be managed rather crudely. Only a few companies are experimenting with, for example, call records, to match the company's view of how well it dealt with the customer, how the customer perceived they were managed and what they thought about it, and subsequent customer behaviour.

In a project one of the authors is involved in, the aim is real-time integration between customer service, transactions and response data – and this means action, not analysis. The idea is that rather than wait for the customer to contact the company, the company will initiate the contact. So, when a customer gets into contact with the organization, in any channel, for any reason, the organization looks at its purchasing or response data and says, ' I see you bought X from us for the first time last week, did you like it?' Or, 'I see you used to buy Y from us but you've stopped – can you tell us why?' Or, 'I see you're buying less often from us – can you tell us why?' Or, 'You never respond to our direct mail or e-mails – do you actually read them?' Of course, this would be permission-based, so the first question might be, 'Every now and then, when you're in touch with us, we'd like to check that you're happy with us, so would you mind if we….'

Once the programme is going, the company will need to bring customer service, trans-actions and response data together quickly so it does not ask about ancient history (or as the customer might put it '…that was last week, things are different this week'). If the customer is in contact with the company several times a week (for example in a counter-service or Web situation), it will no longer be able to rely on batch analysis, but will need to set up automated processes for bringing together its marketing, sales and service data and actions. This approach is already visible in some companies that use only the Web and e-mail to manage their customers. Doing it in call centres, branch outlets, kiosks, ATMs and the like requires a big step forward.

The technology for doing all this is, as usual, there (though not very often deployed). The business case for doing it (and to whom) needs a long, hard look, of course. Here, it is important to apply classic direct marketing disciplines of measurement and testing, combined with good research. The latter should be used to identify the things that customers say really matter to them – the service that makes them buy more or less, or stop buying entirely, as well as the things they notice (what they say influences their behaviour and what actually does influence it may not be the same).

It is also important to take into account the leads and lags involved. Much academic and business research shows that few customers change their behaviour after one or two good or bad service episodes. For example, loyal and/or previously very satisfied customers tend to forgive bad service, while it may take several episodes of excellent service to make a customer respond really positively to it. However, some customers do respond quickly, so we need to analyse not just averages but distributions. Time must also be taken into account – how long it takes for customers to perceive improved treatment and when they are next likely to buy. In another project in a different sector from the one mentioned above, a slightly improved service treatment that is declared to customers and properly fulfilled has lifted response rates to mailings and subsequent purchase rates.

Most customers are agreeably surprised when they receive better treatment, and are likely to respond by getting into contact more often and buying more, so the business case is unlikely to prove questionable. More questionable will be the company's ability to deliver the required levels of service consistently, thereby reassuring customers that this new, improved company is one they want to give business to over the long term.

THE UNIFYING THEME: KNOW WHERE YOU ARE AND MEASURE WHAT YOU ACHIEVE

In nearly all the issue areas discussed above, there is a common theme – know where you are and measure what you achieve. Many mistakes in CRM are based on using untested assumptions about which customers a company has, what their value is, what they want and what they are prepared to do, what capabilities the company has to meet these needs, or from not measuring the results of improvement actions and learning from the measures.

Index

Rugby

SPORTS SKILLS

Clive Gifford

W
FRANKLIN WATTS
LONDON · SYDNEY

Franklin Watts
First published in Great Britain in 2015 by
The Watts Publishing Group

Copyright © The Watts Publishing Group
2015

Credits

Series Editor: Adrian Cole
Art direction: Peter Scoulding
Series designed and created for
  Franklin Watts by Storeybooks
Designer: Rita Storey
Editor: Nicola Barber
Photography: Tudor Photography,
  Banbury (unless otherwise stated)

Every attempt has been made to clear
copyright. Should there be any inadvertent
omission please apply to the publisher for
rectification.

Dewey number 796.3'33
HB ISBN 978 1 4451 4132 9
Library ebook ISBN 978 1 4451 4342 2

Printed in China

FSC
www.fsc.org

MIX
Paper from
responsible sources
FSC® C104740

Franklin Watts
An imprint of Hachette Children's Group
Part of The Watts Publishing Group
Carmelite House
50 Victoria Embankment
London EC4Y 0DZ

An Hachette UK Company
www.hachette.co.uk

www.franklinwatts.co.uk

Note: At the time of going to press, the
statistics and profiles in this book were up to
date. However, due to some cyclists' active
participation in the sport, it is possible that
some of these may now be out of date.

Picture credits

Shutterstock/ Paolo Bona p.6; Sophia Rugby
/Didier Honoré/Wikimedia Commons;
p.7; Martin Hunter/Getty Images p.21;
Shutterstock/ Maxisport p.22; Bradley Kanaris
/Gettyp.25; Shutterstock/ Max Blain p.26;
Shutterstock/ Neil Balderson p. 27.

Cover images: Tudor Photography, Banbury.

All photos posed by models. Thanks to Joel
Avery, Tim Bennett,

Jamie Bache, Carl Daniels, Josh Deegan, Carl
Taylor, Mark Woodward and Jackson Wray.

The Publisher would like to thank The
Publisher would like to thank Banbury RUFC
for the use of the club's ground.

Previously published by Franklin Watts as
Know Your Sport Rugby.

Taking part in sport is a fun
way to get fit, but like any
form of physical exercise it has
an element of risk, particularly
if you are unfit, overweight
or suffer from any medical
conditions. It is advisable
to consult a healthcare
professional before beginning
any programme of exercise.